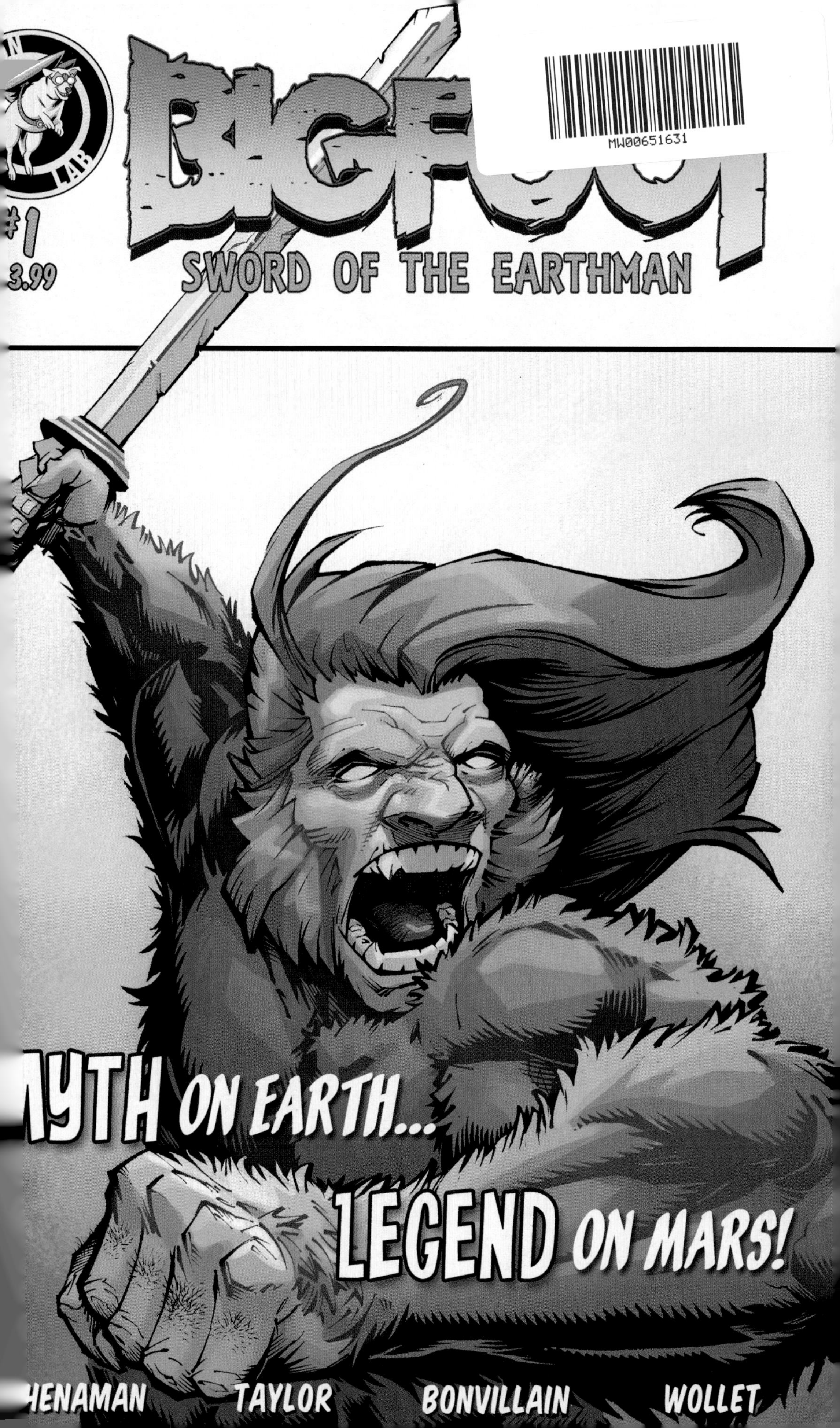
#1
3.99
SWORD OF THE EARTHMAN
ON EARTH...
LEGEND ON MARS!
TAYLOR
BONVILLAIN
WOLLET

THE DYING WORLD NEEDED A HERO.

A LAND OF DINOSAURS, WARRING TRIBES, KINGDOMS AND SORCERY, IT CRIED OUT FOR SOMEONE TO UNITE ITS FRAGMENTED PEOPLE AND DESTROY THOSE WHO WOULD PROFIT FROM DEATH, GREED AND EVIL.

IN DESPERATION, THE MYSTICS OF THE BLUE LOOKED TO THE SKIES AND THE DISTANT PLANET EARTH FOR AID.

WHAT THEY FOUND... WAS A SURVIVOR, A CHAMPION OF OUTRAGEOUS ODDS AND A LONER AMIDST A WORLD THAT FEARED HIM.

WHAT THEY FOUND WAS SOMEONE WHO WOULD NOT BE MISSED... BECAUSE NOBODY BELIEVED HE EXISTED IN THE FIRST PLACE.

SAVAGE, BRUTAL, APE-LIKE AND MUTE.
LOVER OF WOMEN, DESTROYER OF MEN.

THEY FOUND...

BIGFOOT
SWORD OF THE EARTHMAN

Bryan Seaton: Publisher • Kevin Freeman: President • Dave Dwonch: Creative Director • Shawn Gabborin: Editor In
Jamal Igle: Vice-President of Marketing • Vito Delsante: Director of Marketing • Jim Dietz: Social Media Direct
Nicole DAndria: Script Editor • Chad Cicconi: Black Sheep • Colleen Boyd: Submissions Editor

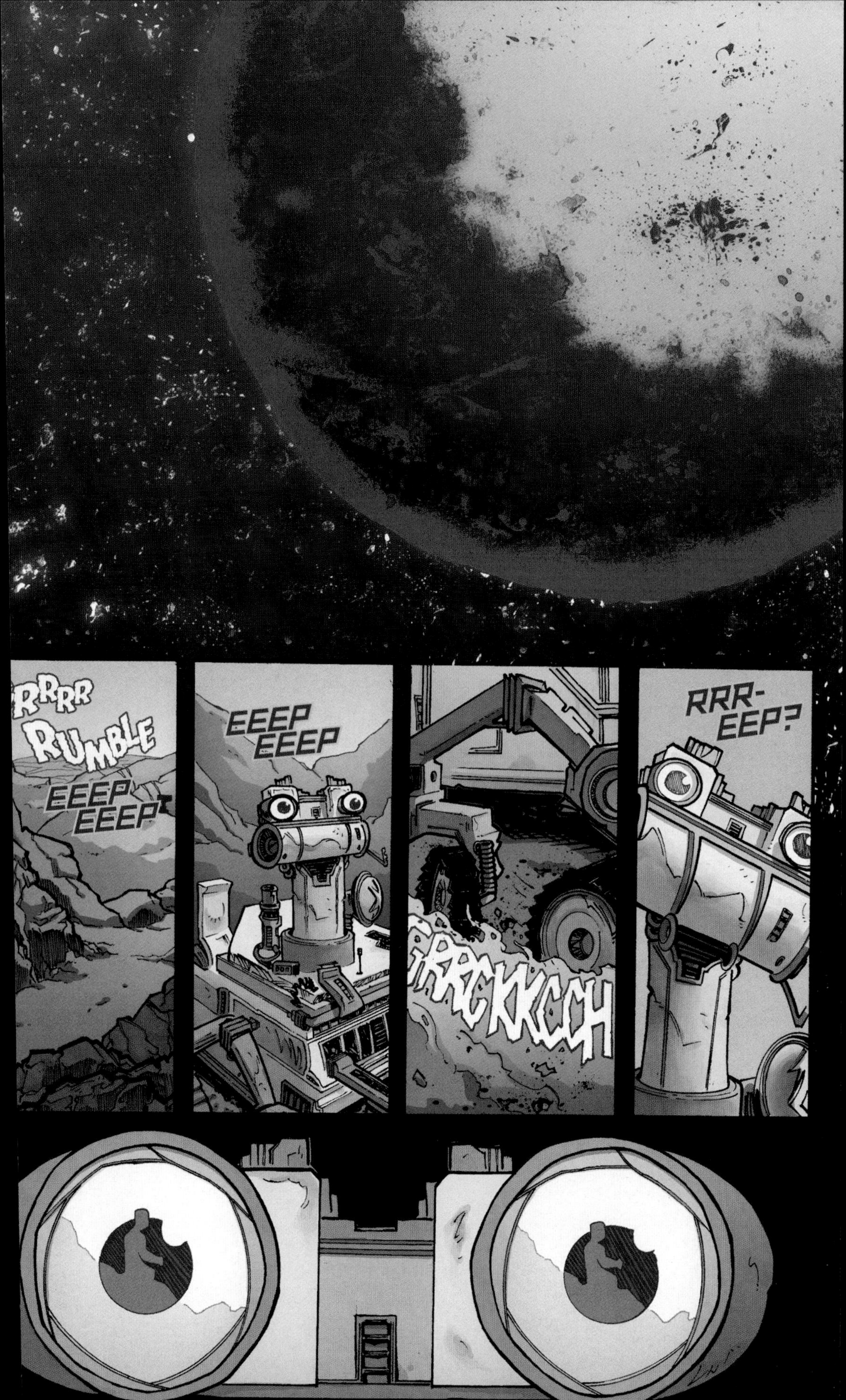
RRRRR
RUMBLE
EEEP
EEEP
EEEP
EEEP
GRRCKKCCH
RRR-
EEP?

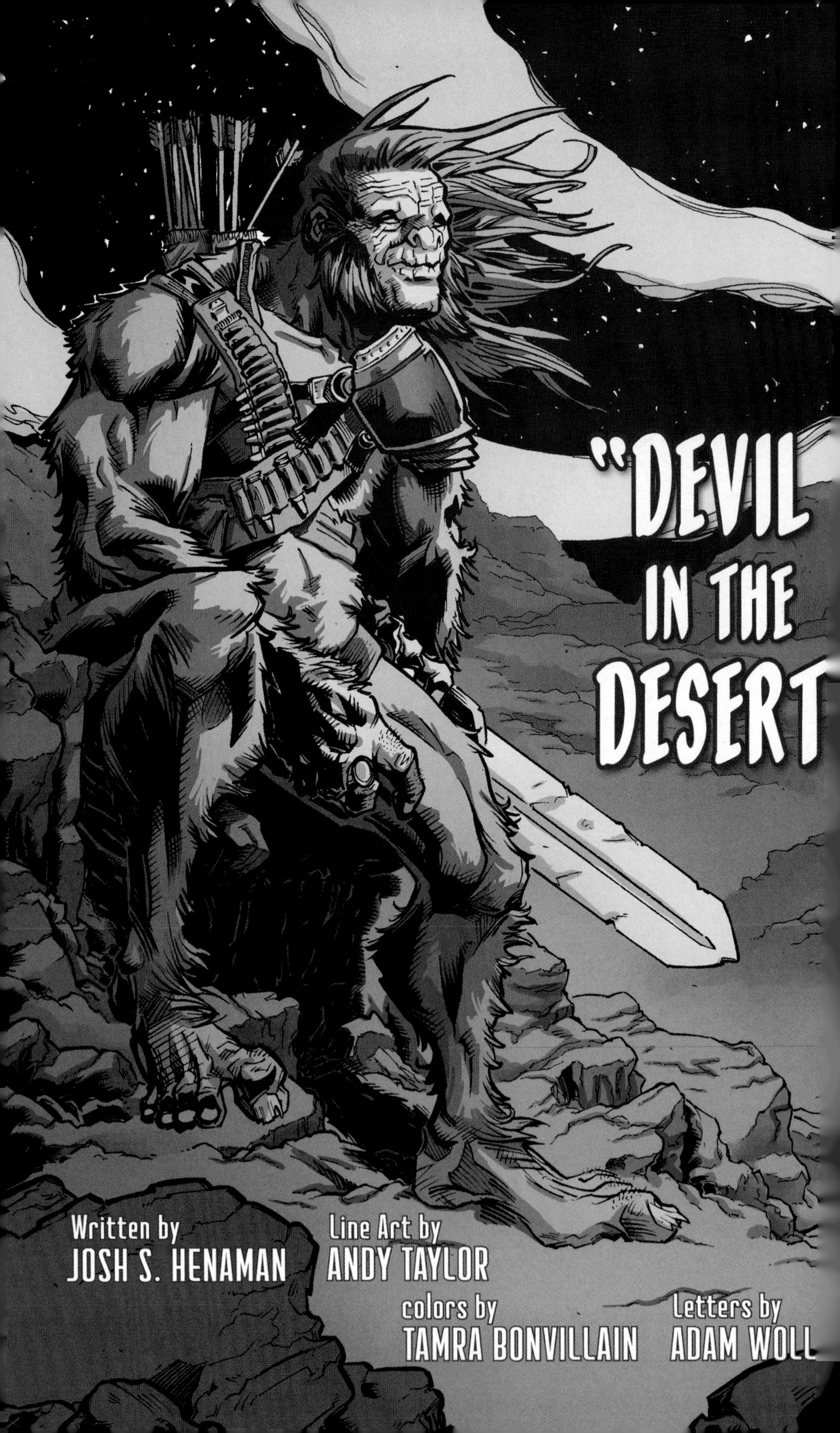
"DEVIL IN THE DESERT
Written by
JOSH S. HENAMAN
Line Art by
ANDY TAYLOR
colors by
TAMRA BONVILLAIN
Letters by
ADAM WOLL

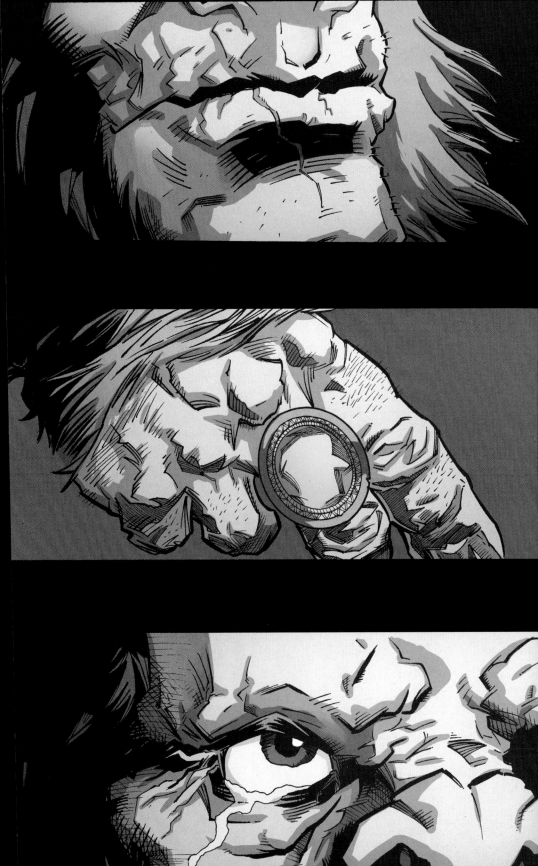

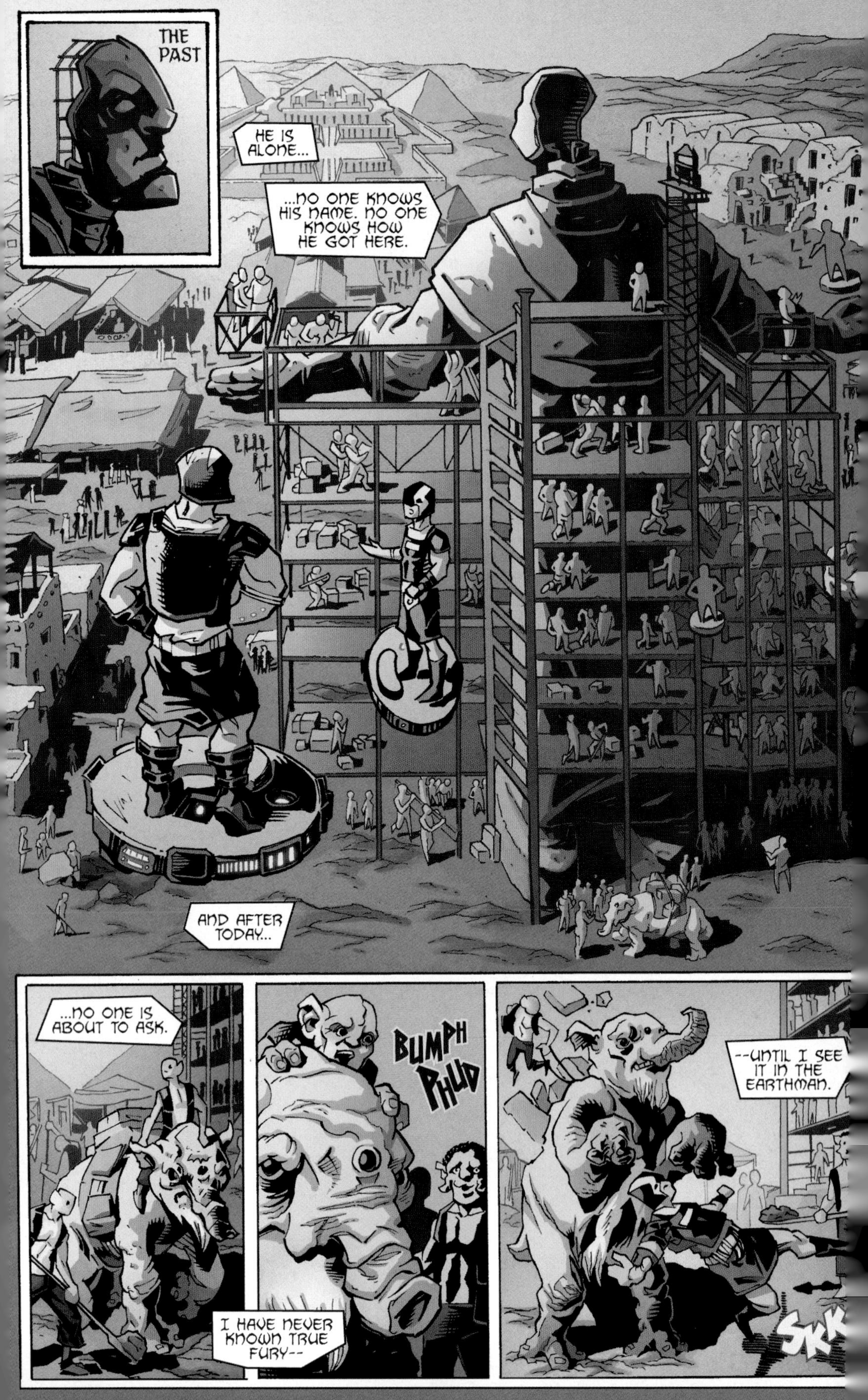
THE PAST
HE IS ALONE...
...NO ONE KNOWS HIS NAME. NO ONE KNOWS HOW HE GOT HERE.
AND AFTER TODAY...
...NO ONE IS ABOUT TO ASK.
BUMPH
PHUD
I HAVE NEVER KNOWN TRUE FURY--
--UNTIL I SEE IT IN THE EARTHMAN.
SKK

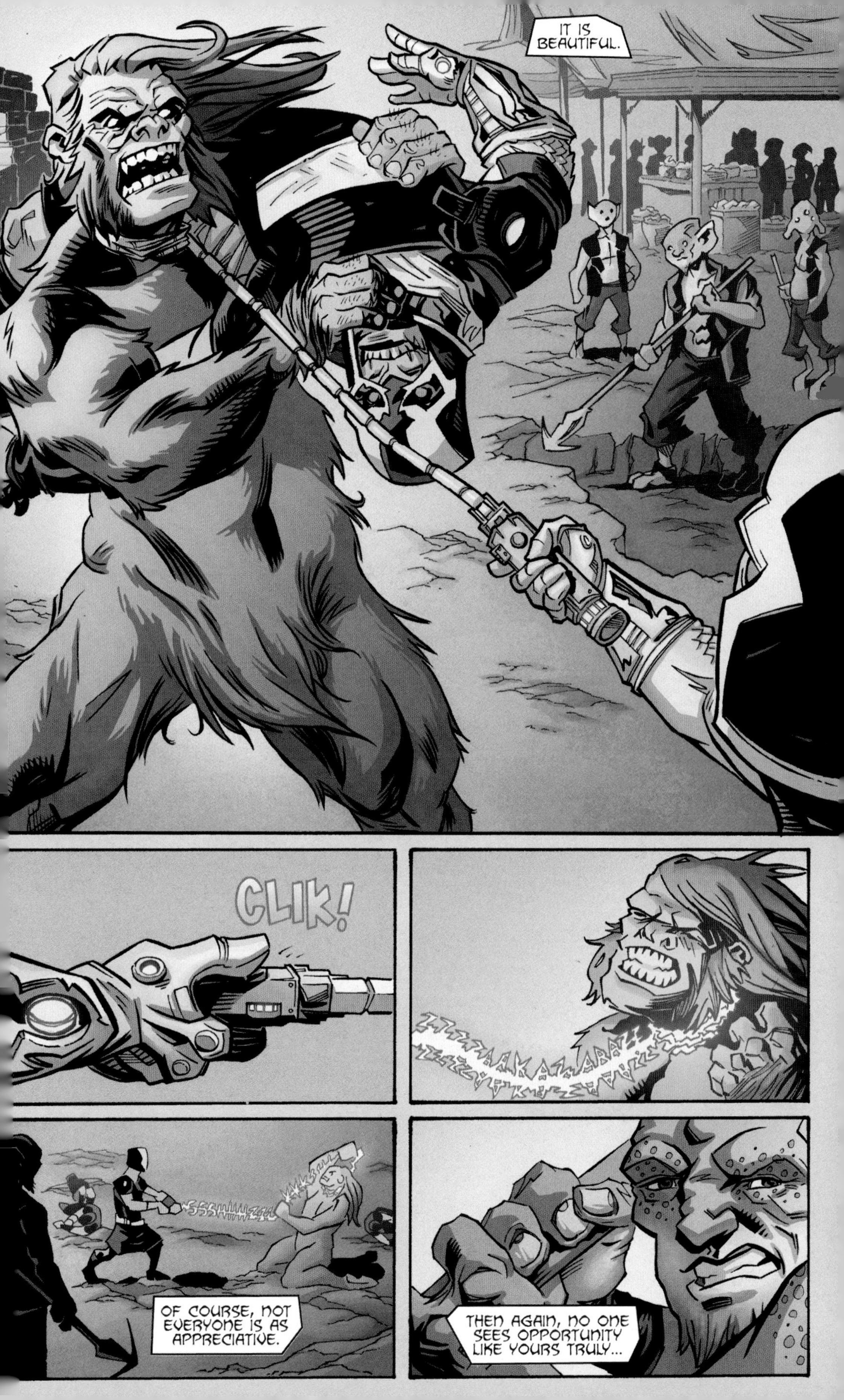
IT IS BEAUTIFUL.
CLIK!
OF COURSE, NOT EVERYONE IS AS APPRECIATIVE.
THEN AGAIN, NO ONE SEES OPPORTUNITY LIKE YOURS TRULY...

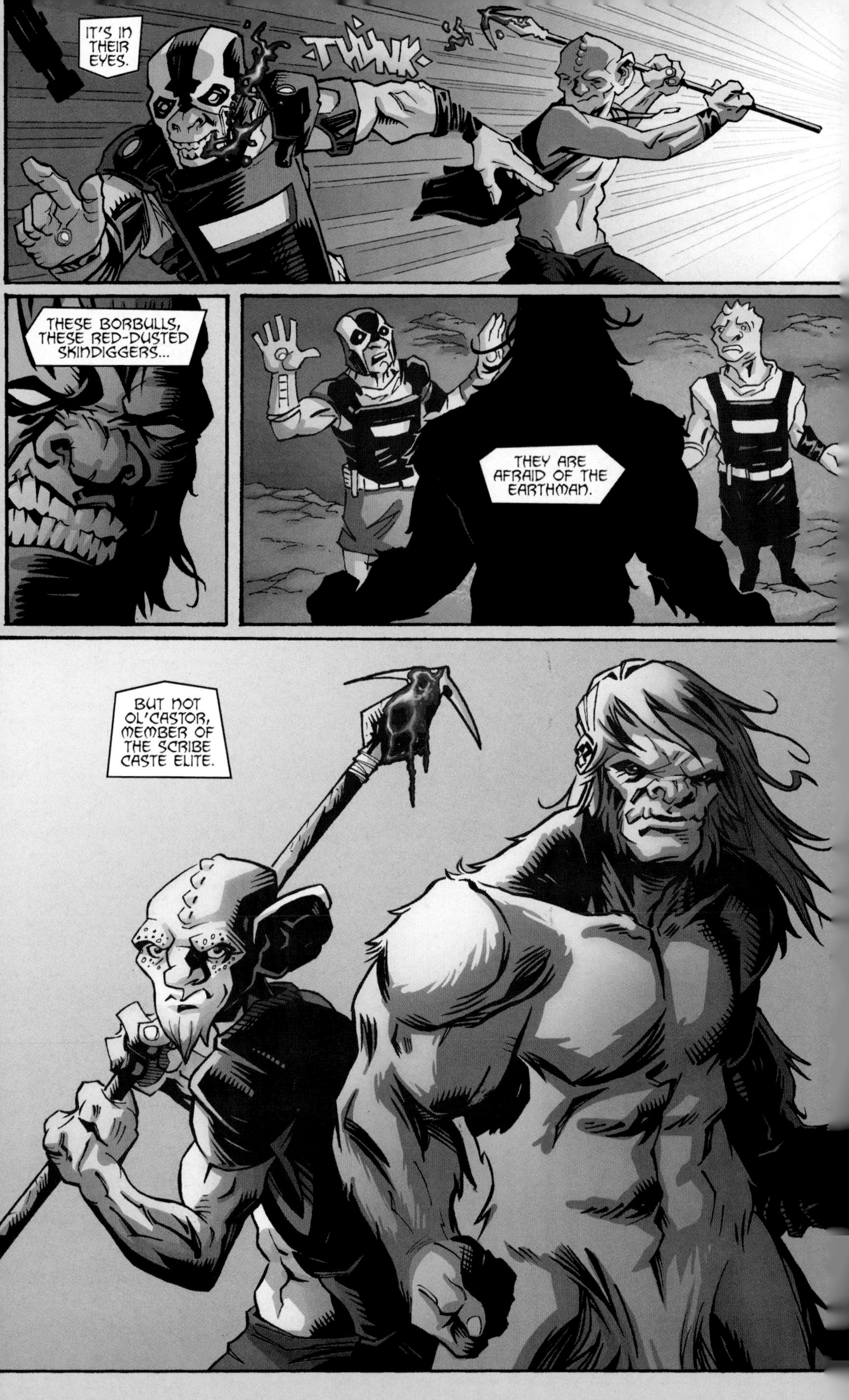
IT'S IN THEIR EYES.
THÜNK
THESE BORBULLS, THESE RED-DUSTED SKINDIGGERS...
THEY ARE AFRAID OF THE EARTHMAN.
BUT NOT OL'CASTOR, MEMBER OF THE SCRIBE CASTE ELITE.

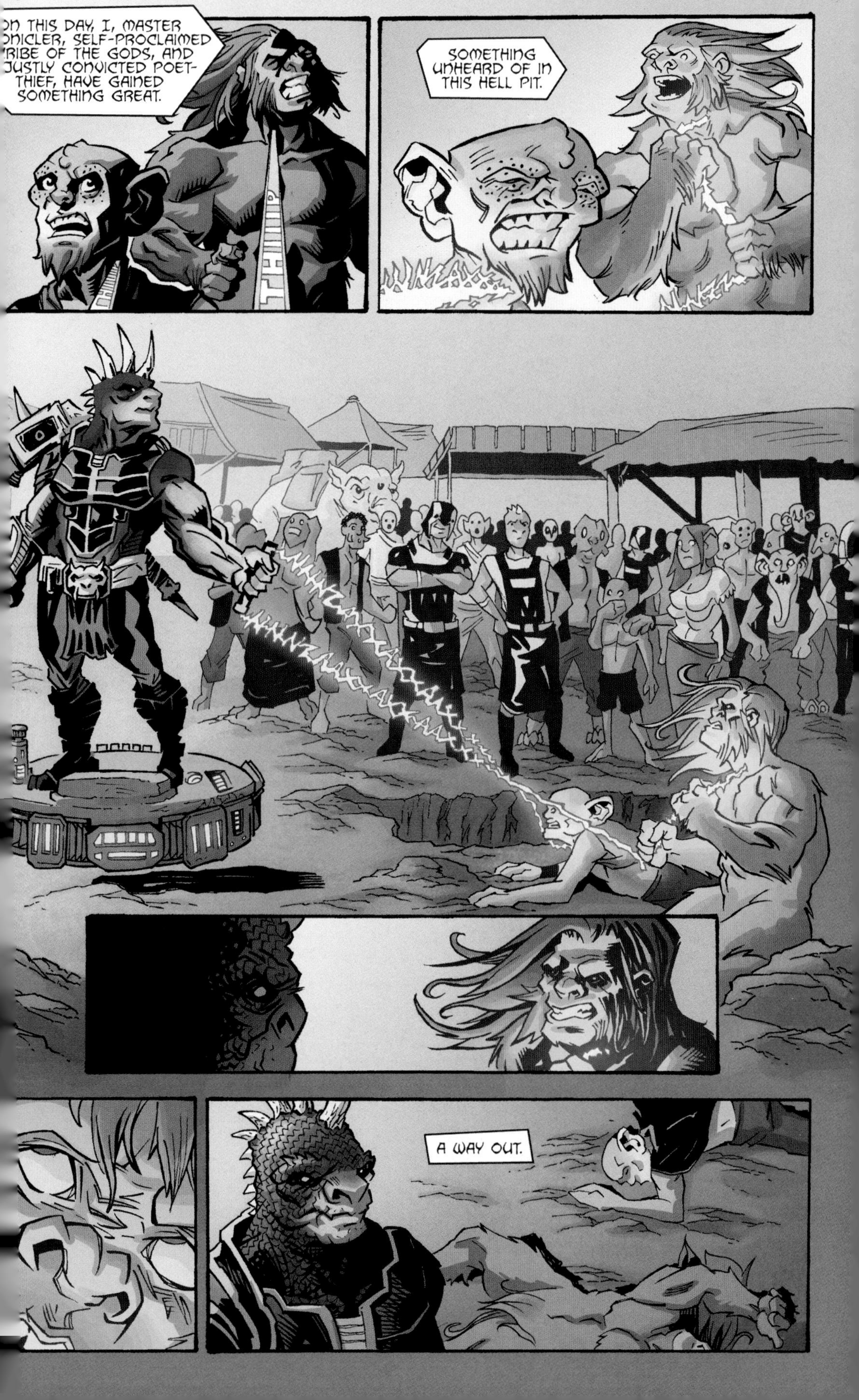
ON THIS DAY, I, MASTER ONICLER, SELF-PROCLAIMED RIBE OF THE GODS, AND JUSTLY CONVICTED POET-THIEF, HAVE GAINED SOMETHING GREAT.
SOMETHING UNHEARD OF IN THIS HELL PIT.
A WAY OUT.

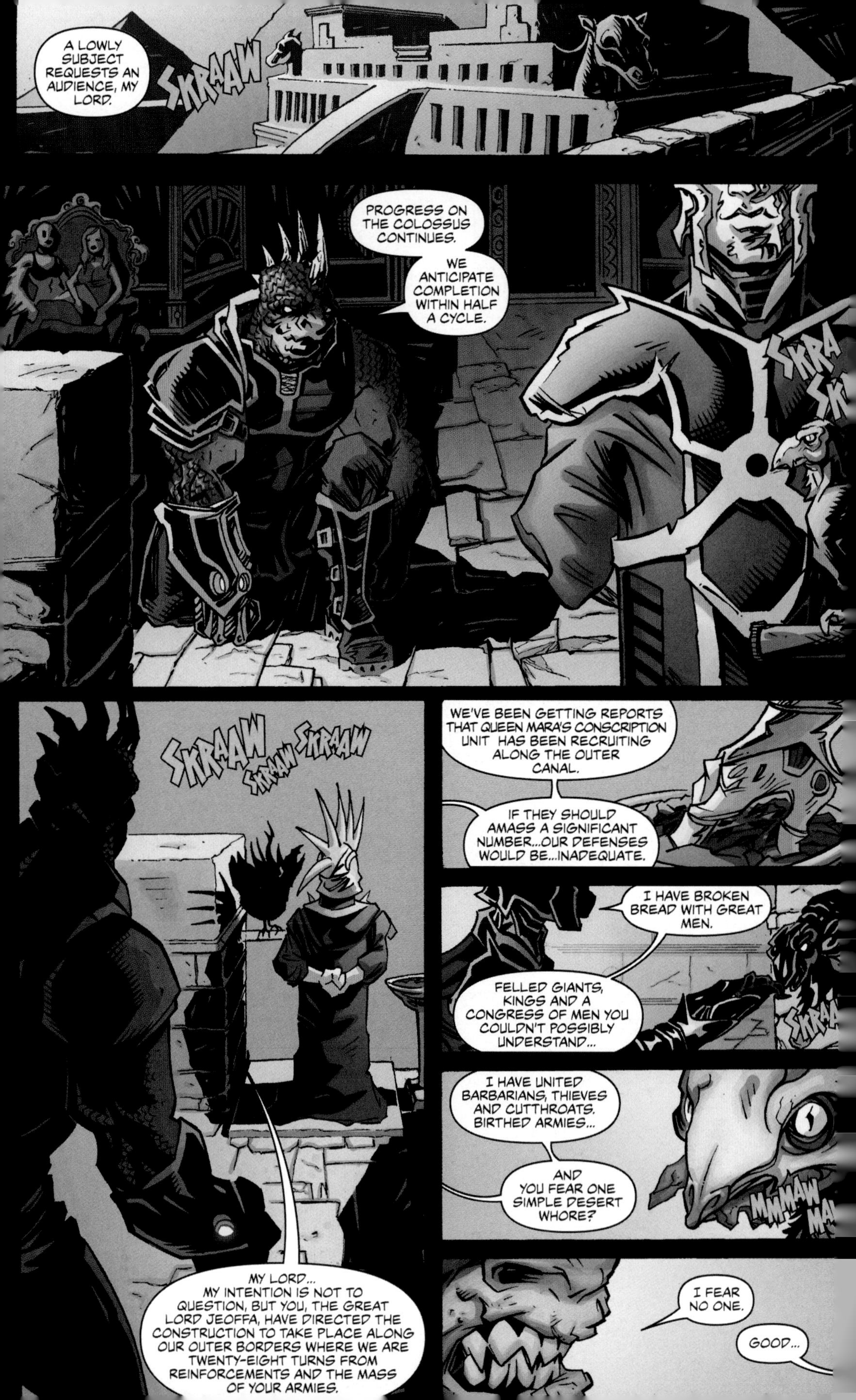

A LOWLY SUBJECT REQUESTS AN AUDIENCE, MY LORD.
SKRAAW
PROGRESS ON THE COLOSSUS CONTINUES.
WE ANTICIPATE COMPLETION WITHIN HALF A CYCLE.
SKRA
SK
SKRAAW
SKRAAW
SKRAAW
MY LORD... MY INTENTION IS NOT TO QUESTION, BUT YOU, THE GREAT LORD JEOFFA, HAVE DIRECTED THE CONSTRUCTION TO TAKE PLACE ALONG OUR OUTER BORDERS WHERE WE ARE TWENTY-EIGHT TURNS FROM REINFORCEMENTS AND THE MASS OF YOUR ARMIES.
WE'VE BEEN GETTING REPORTS THAT QUEEN MARA'S CONSCRIPTION UNIT HAS BEEN RECRUITING ALONG THE OUTER CANAL.
IF THEY SHOULD AMASS A SIGNIFICANT NUMBER...OUR DEFENSES WOULD BE...INADEQUATE.
I HAVE BROKEN BREAD WITH GREAT MEN.
FELLED GIANTS, KINGS AND A CONGRESS OF MEN YOU COULDN'T POSSIBLY UNDERSTAND...
SKRAA
I HAVE UNITED BARBARIANS, THIEVES AND CUTTHROATS. BIRTHED ARMIES...
AND YOU FEAR ONE SIMPLE DESERT WHORE?
MMMAW
I FEAR NO ONE.
GOOD...

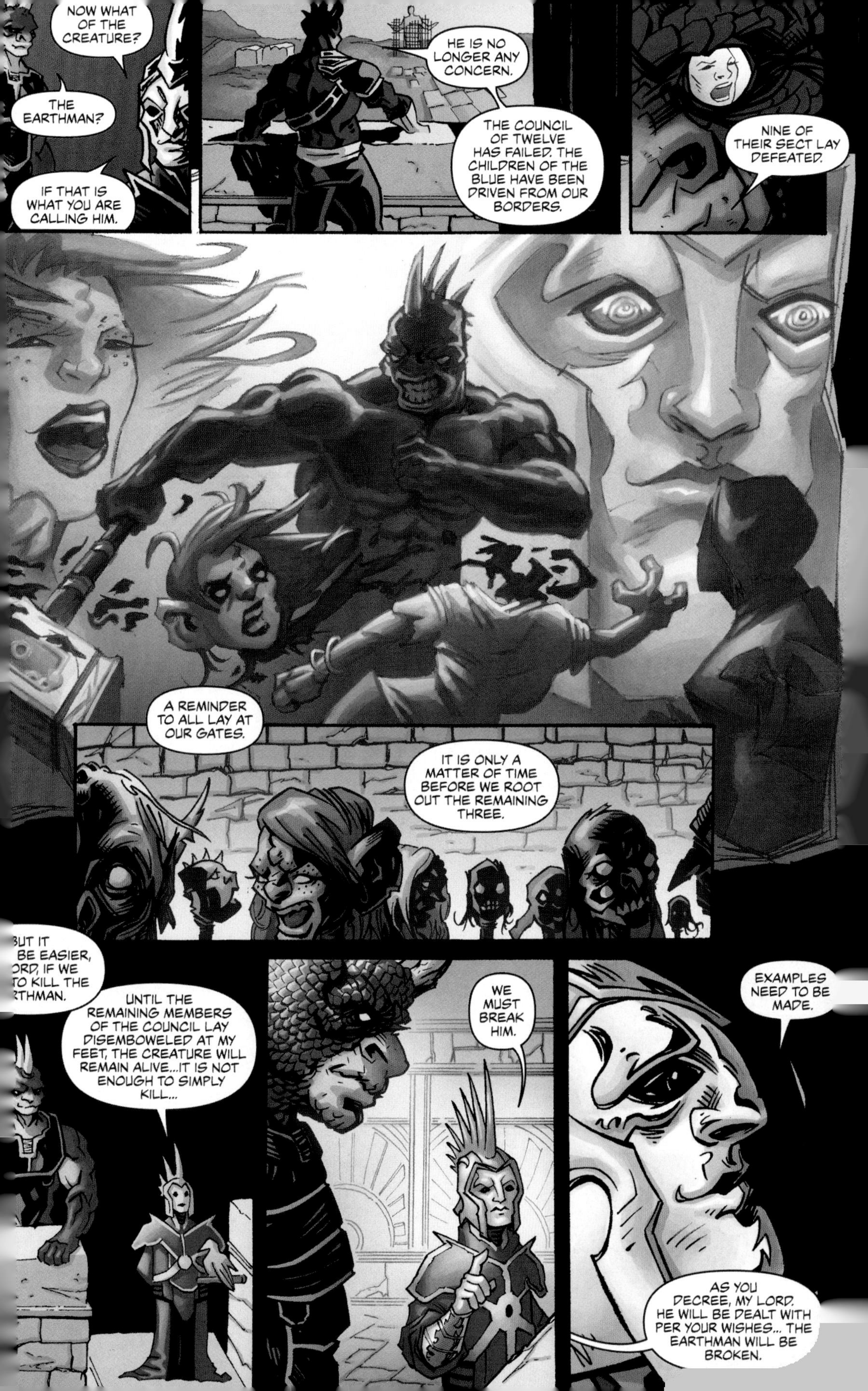
NOW WHAT OF THE CREATURE?
THE EARTHMAN?
IF THAT IS WHAT YOU ARE CALLING HIM.
HE IS NO LONGER ANY CONCERN.
THE COUNCIL OF TWELVE HAS FAILED. THE CHILDREN OF THE BLUE HAVE BEEN DRIVEN FROM OUR BORDERS.
NINE OF THEIR SECT LAY DEFEATED.
A REMINDER TO ALL LAY AT OUR GATES.
IT IS ONLY A MATTER OF TIME BEFORE WE ROOT OUT THE REMAINING THREE.
BUT IT BE EASIER, ORD, IF WE TO KILL THE RTHMAN.
UNTIL THE REMAINING MEMBERS OF THE COUNCIL LAY DISEMBOWELED AT MY FEET, THE CREATURE WILL REMAIN ALIVE...IT IS NOT ENOUGH TO SIMPLY KILL...
WE MUST BREAK HIM.
EXAMPLES NEED TO BE MADE.
AS YOU DECREE, MY LORD. HE WILL BE DEALT WITH PER YOUR WISHES... THE EARTHMAN WILL BE BROKEN.

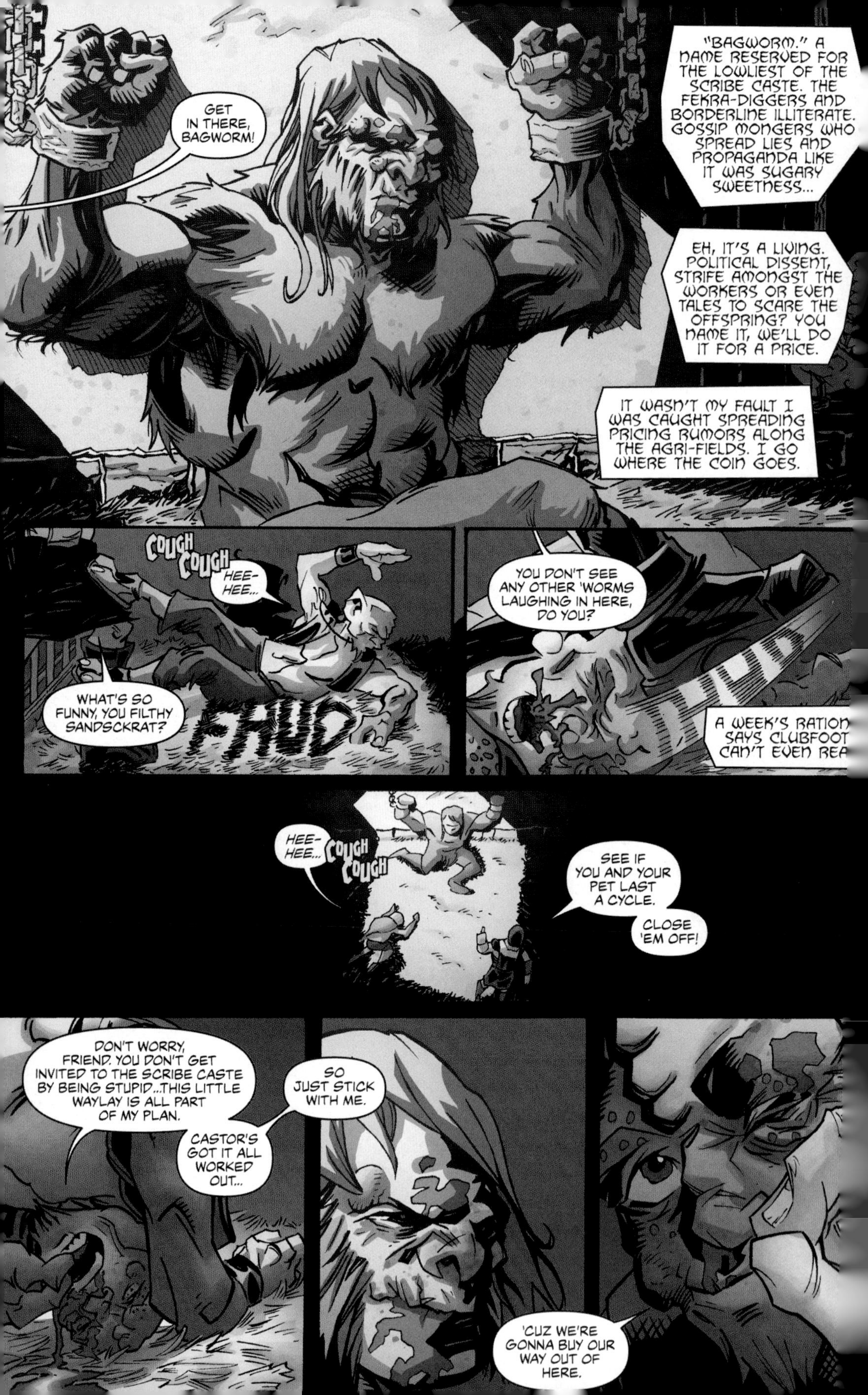

GET IN THERE, BAGWORM!
"BAGWORM." A NAME RESERVED FOR THE LOWLIEST OF THE SCRIBE CASTE. THE FEKRA-DIGGERS AND BORDERLINE ILLITERATE. GOSSIP MONGERS WHO SPREAD LIES AND PROPAGANDA LIKE IT WAS SUGARY SWEETNESS...
EH, IT'S A LIVING. POLITICAL DISSENT, STRIFE AMONGST THE WORKERS OR EVEN TALES TO SCARE THE OFFSPRING? YOU NAME IT, WE'LL DO IT FOR A PRICE.
IT WASN'T MY FAULT I WAS CAUGHT SPREADING PRICING RUMORS ALONG THE AGRI-FIELDS. I GO WHERE THE COIN GOES.
COUGH COUGH
HEE-HEE...
WHAT'S SO FUNNY, YOU FILTHY SANDSCKRAT?
FHUD
YOU DON'T SEE ANY OTHER 'WORMS LAUGHING IN HERE, DO YOU?
THUD
A WEEK'S RATION SAYS CLUBFOOT CAN'T EVEN REA
HEE-HEE... COUGH COUGH
SEE IF YOU AND YOUR PET LAST A CYCLE.
CLOSE 'EM OFF!
DON'T WORRY, FRIEND. YOU DON'T GET INVITED TO THE SCRIBE CASTE BY BEING STUPID...THIS LITTLE WAYLAY IS ALL PART OF MY PLAN.
CASTOR'S GOT IT ALL WORKED OUT...
SO JUST STICK WITH ME.
'CUZ WE'RE GONNA BUY OUR WAY OUT OF HERE.

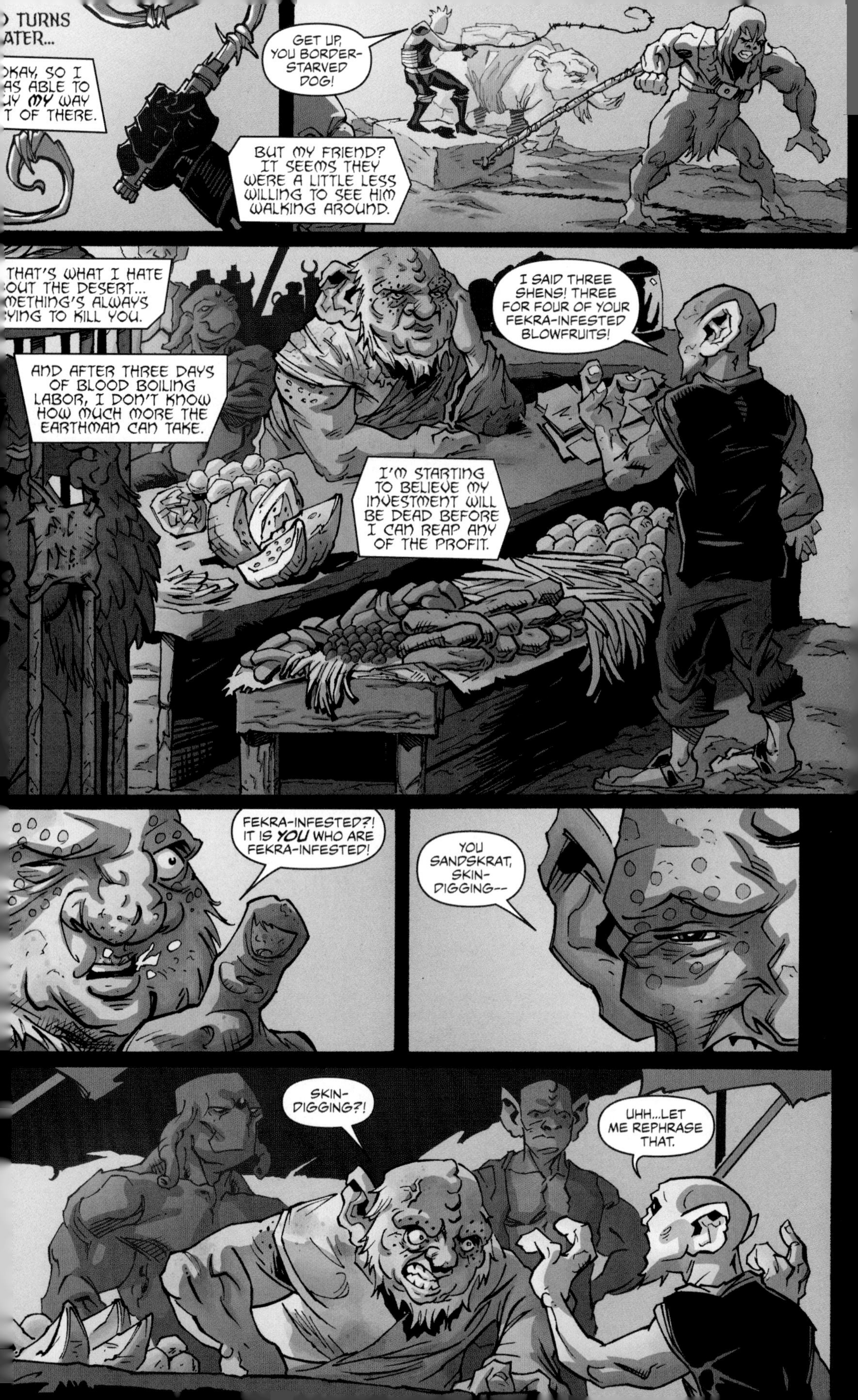

D TURNS
ATER...
OKAY, SO I
AS ABLE TO
UY MY WAY
T OF THERE.
GET UP, YOU BORDER-STARVED DOG!
BUT MY FRIEND? IT SEEMS THEY WERE A LITTLE LESS WILLING TO SEE HIM WALKING AROUND.
THAT'S WHAT I HATE
OUT THE DESERT...
METHING'S ALWAYS
YING TO KILL YOU.
I SAID THREE SHENS! THREE FOR FOUR OF YOUR FEKRA-INFESTED BLOWFRUITS!
AND AFTER THREE DAYS OF BLOOD BOILING LABOR, I DON'T KNOW HOW MUCH MORE THE EARTHMAN CAN TAKE.
I'M STARTING TO BELIEVE MY INVESTMENT WILL BE DEAD BEFORE I CAN REAP ANY OF THE PROFIT.
FEKRA-INFESTED?! IT IS YOU WHO ARE FEKRA-INFESTED!
YOU SANDSKRAT, SKIN-DIGGING--
SKIN-DIGGING?!
UHH...LET ME REPHRASE THAT.

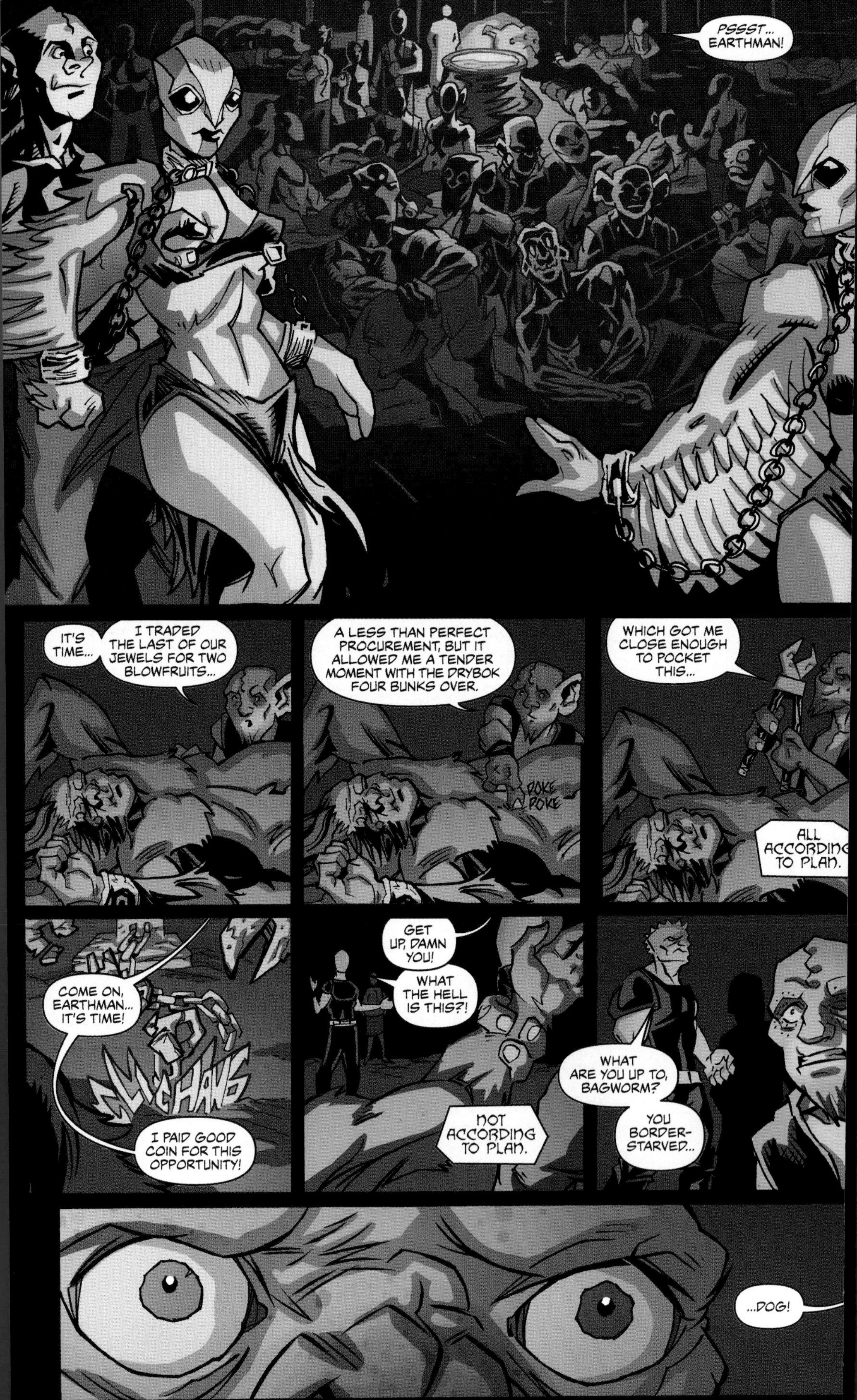
PSSST... EARTHMAN!
IT'S TIME...
I TRADED THE LAST OF OUR JEWELS FOR TWO BLOWFRUITS...
A LESS THAN PERFECT PROCUREMENT, BUT IT ALLOWED ME A TENDER MOMENT WITH THE DRYBOK FOUR BUNKS OVER.
POKE POKE
WHICH GOT ME CLOSE ENOUGH TO POCKET THIS...
ALL ACCORDING TO PLAN.
COME ON, EARTHMAN... IT'S TIME!
CHANG
I PAID GOOD COIN FOR THIS OPPORTUNITY!
GET UP, DAMN YOU!
WHAT THE HELL IS THIS?!
NOT ACCORDING TO PLAN.
WHAT ARE YOU UP TO, BAGWORM?
YOU BORDER-STARVED...
...DOG!

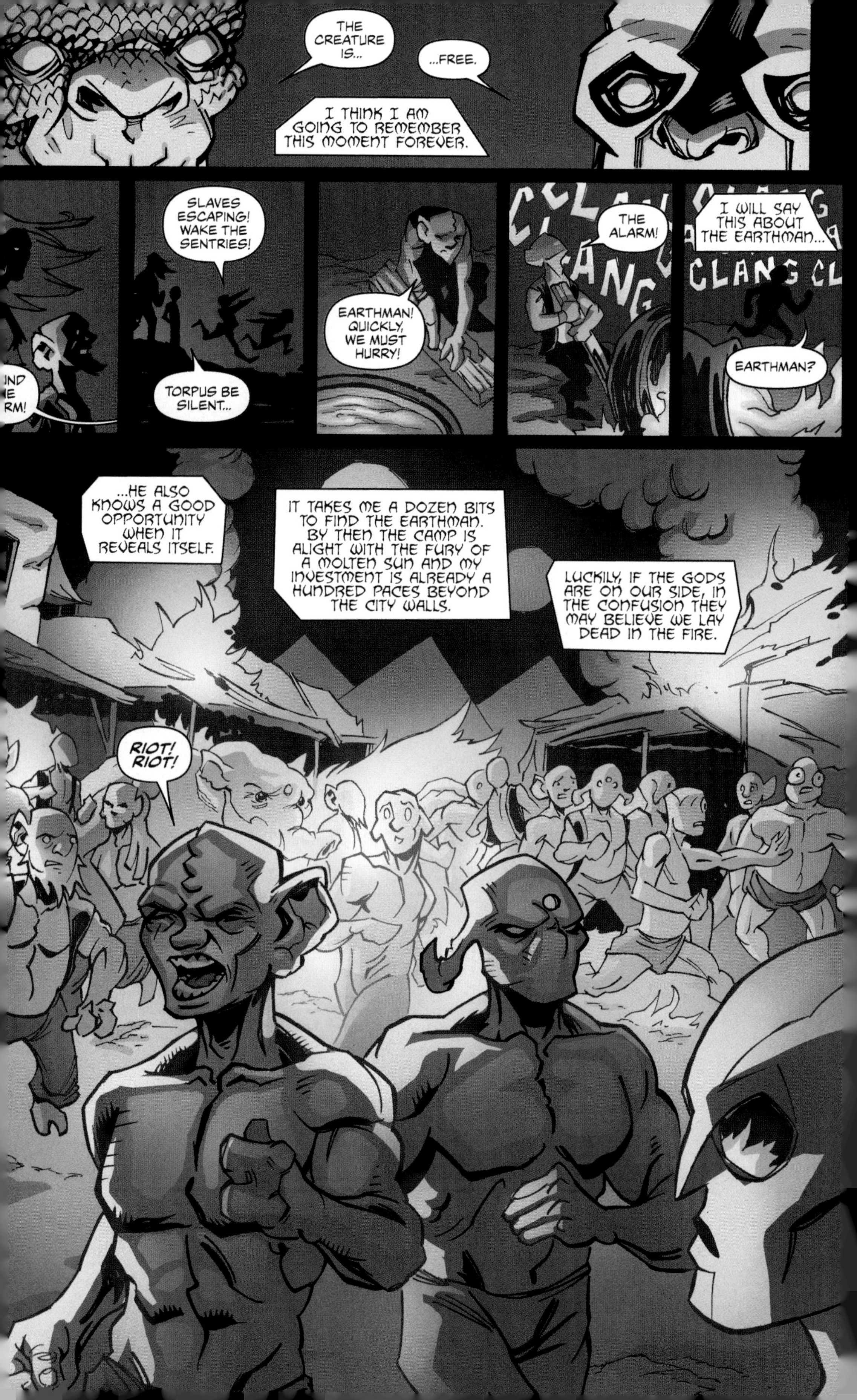
THE CREATURE IS...
...FREE.
I THINK I AM GOING TO REMEMBER THIS MOMENT FOREVER.
SLAVES ESCAPING! WAKE THE SENTRIES!
TORPUS BE SILENT...
EARTHMAN! QUICKLY, WE MUST HURRY!
CLANG
THE ALARM!
I WILL SAY THIS ABOUT THE EARTHMAN...
CLANG
EARTHMAN?
...HE ALSO KNOWS A GOOD OPPORTUNITY WHEN IT REVEALS ITSELF.
IT TAKES ME A DOZEN BITS TO FIND THE EARTHMAN. BY THEN THE CAMP IS ALIGHT WITH THE FURY OF A MOLTEN SUN AND MY INVESTMENT IS ALREADY A HUNDRED PACES BEYOND THE CITY WALLS.
LUCKILY, IF THE GODS ARE ON OUR SIDE, IN THE CONFUSION THEY MAY BELIEVE WE LAY DEAD IN THE FIRE.
RIOT! RIOT!

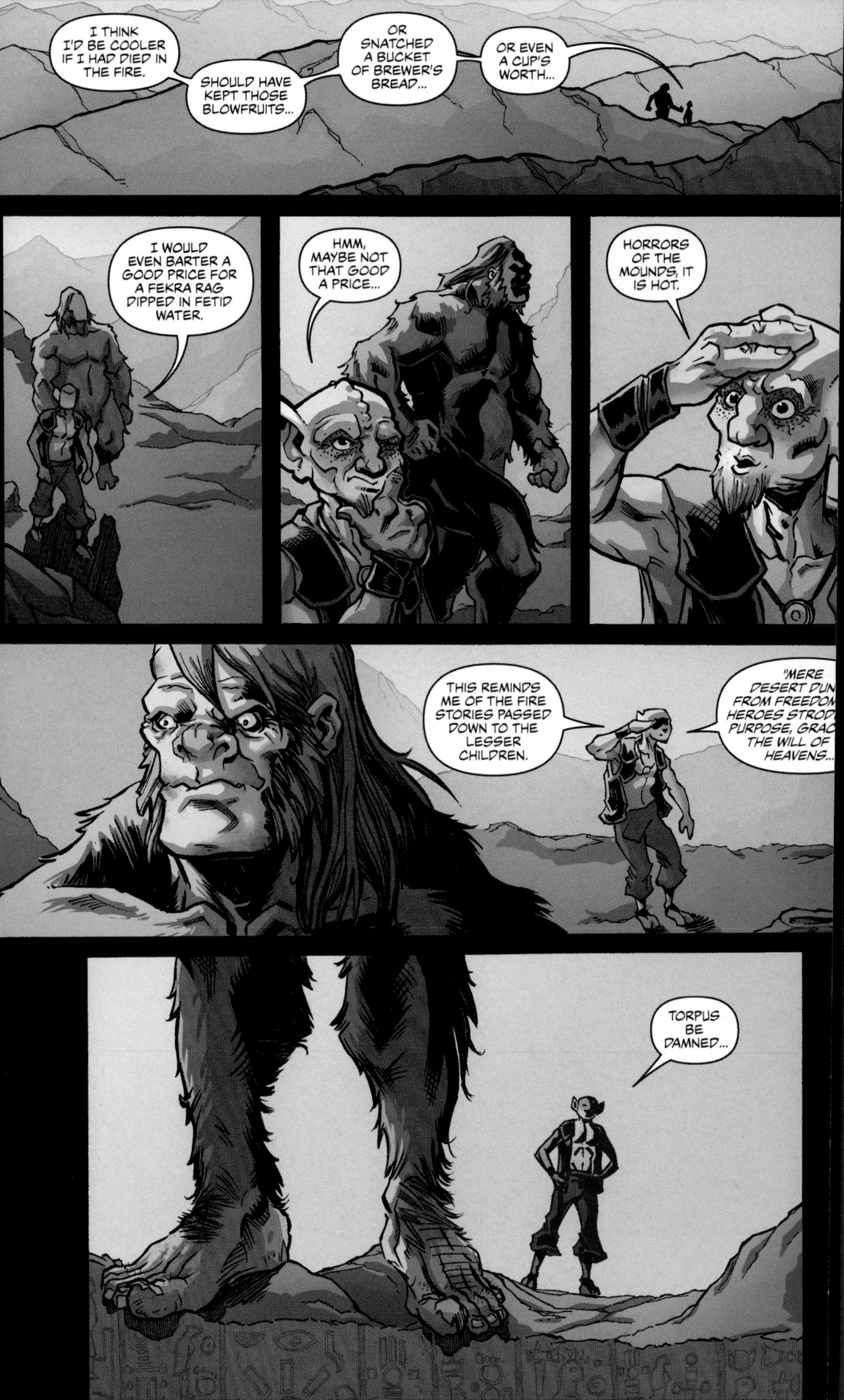
I THINK I'D BE COOLER IF I HAD DIED IN THE FIRE.
SHOULD HAVE KEPT THOSE BLOWFRUITS...
OR SNATCHED A BUCKET OF BREWER'S BREAD...
OR EVEN A CUP'S WORTH...
I WOULD EVEN BARTER A GOOD PRICE FOR A FEKRA RAG DIPPED IN FETID WATER.
HMM, MAYBE NOT THAT GOOD A PRICE...
HORRORS OF THE MOUNDS, IT IS HOT.
THIS REMINDS ME OF THE FIRE STORIES PASSED DOWN TO THE LESSER CHILDREN.
"MERE DESERT DUN FROM FREEDOM HEROES STROD PURPOSE, GRAC THE WILL OF HEAVENS...
TORPUS BE DAMNED...

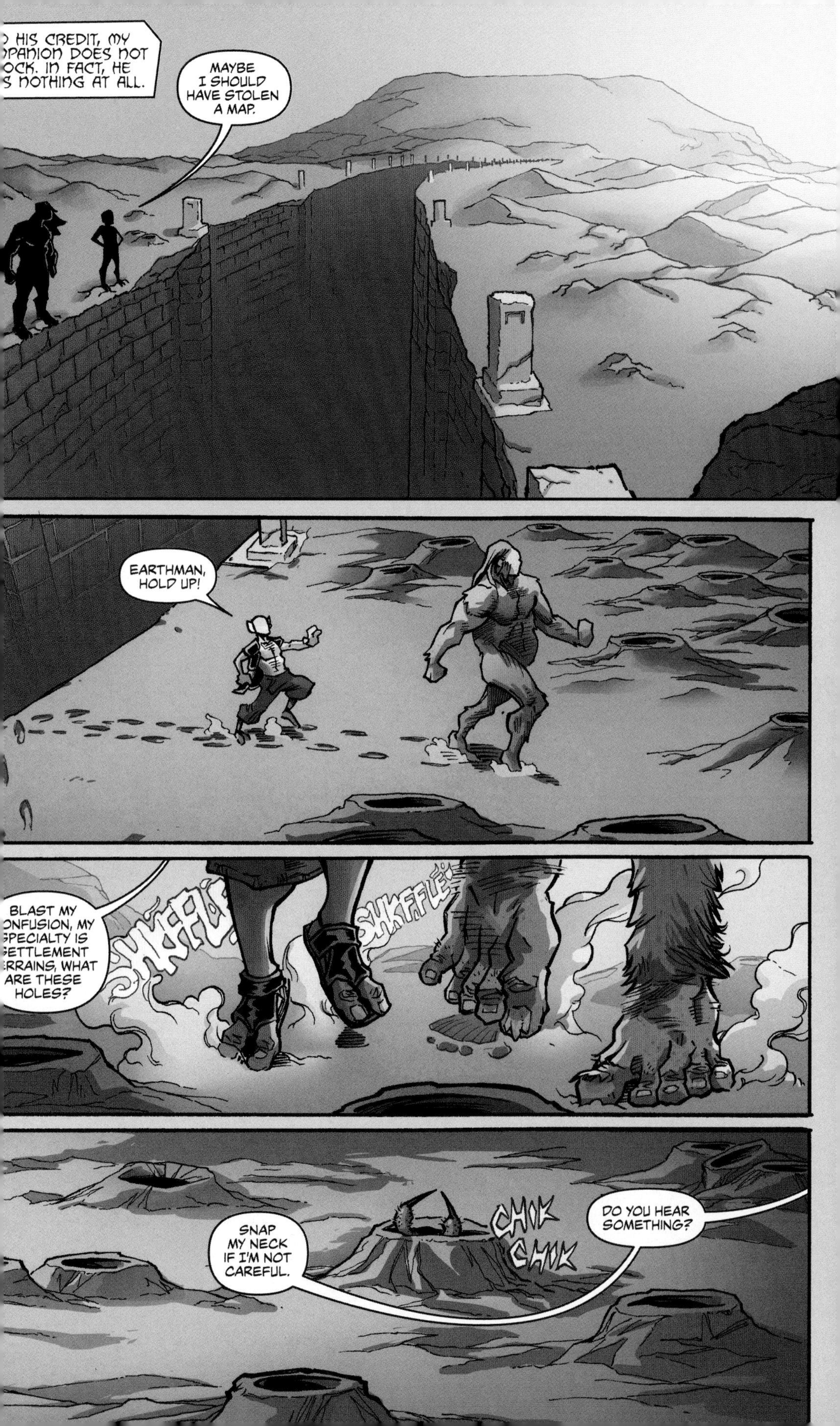
O HIS CREDIT, MY
OPANION DOES NOT
OCK. IN FACT, HE
S NOTHING AT ALL.
MAYBE I SHOULD HAVE STOLEN A MAP.
EARTHMAN, HOLD UP!
BLAST MY
ONFUSION, MY
SPECIALTY IS
SETTLEMENT
ERRAINS, WHAT
ARE THESE
HOLES?
SHKFFLE!
SHKFFLE!
DO YOU HEAR SOMETHING?
CHIK
CHIK
SNAP MY NECK IF I'M NOT CAREFUL.

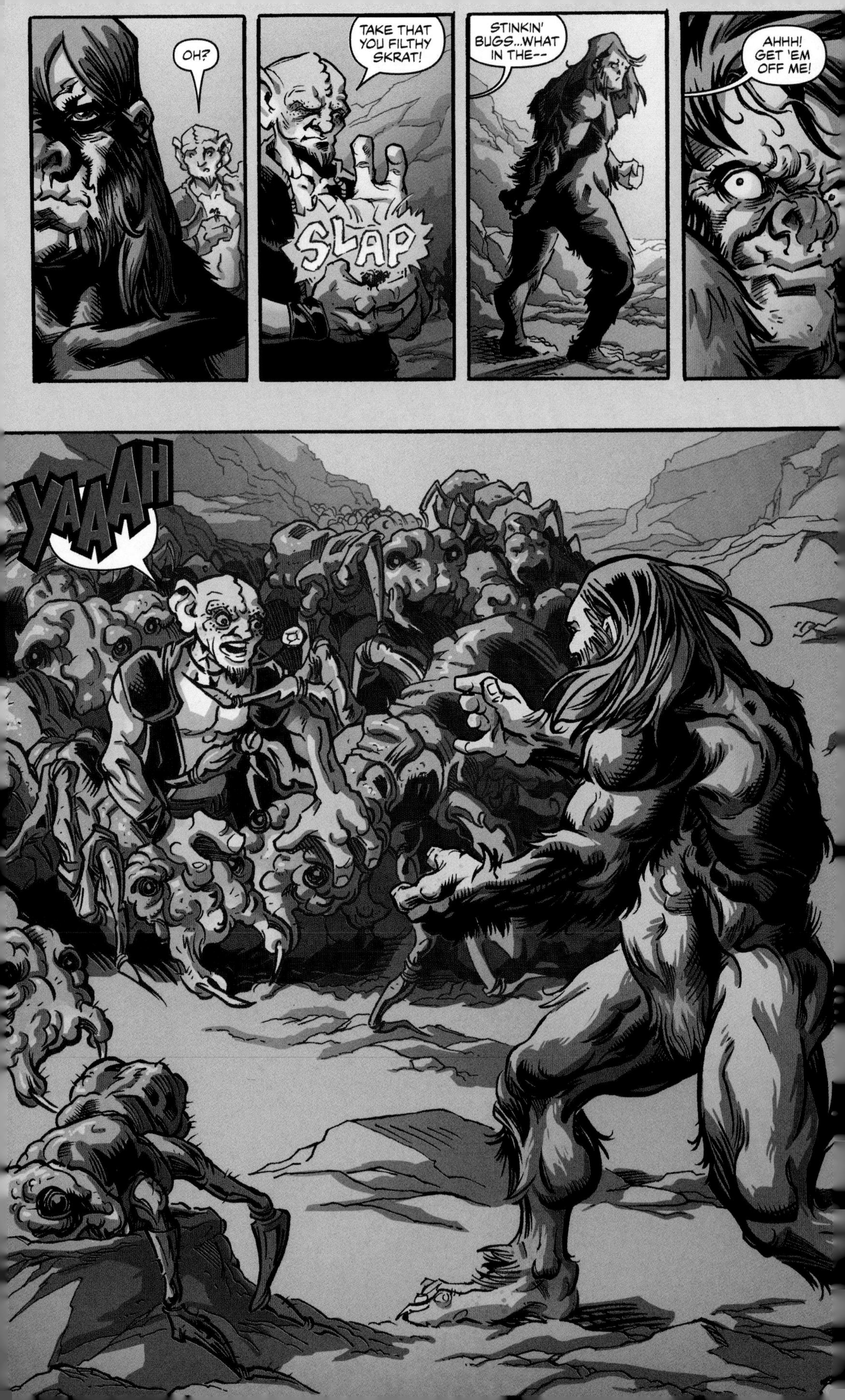
OH?
TAKE THAT YOU FILTHY SKRAT!
SLAP
STINKIN' BUGS...WHAT IN THE--
AHHH! GET 'EM OFF ME!
YAAAAH

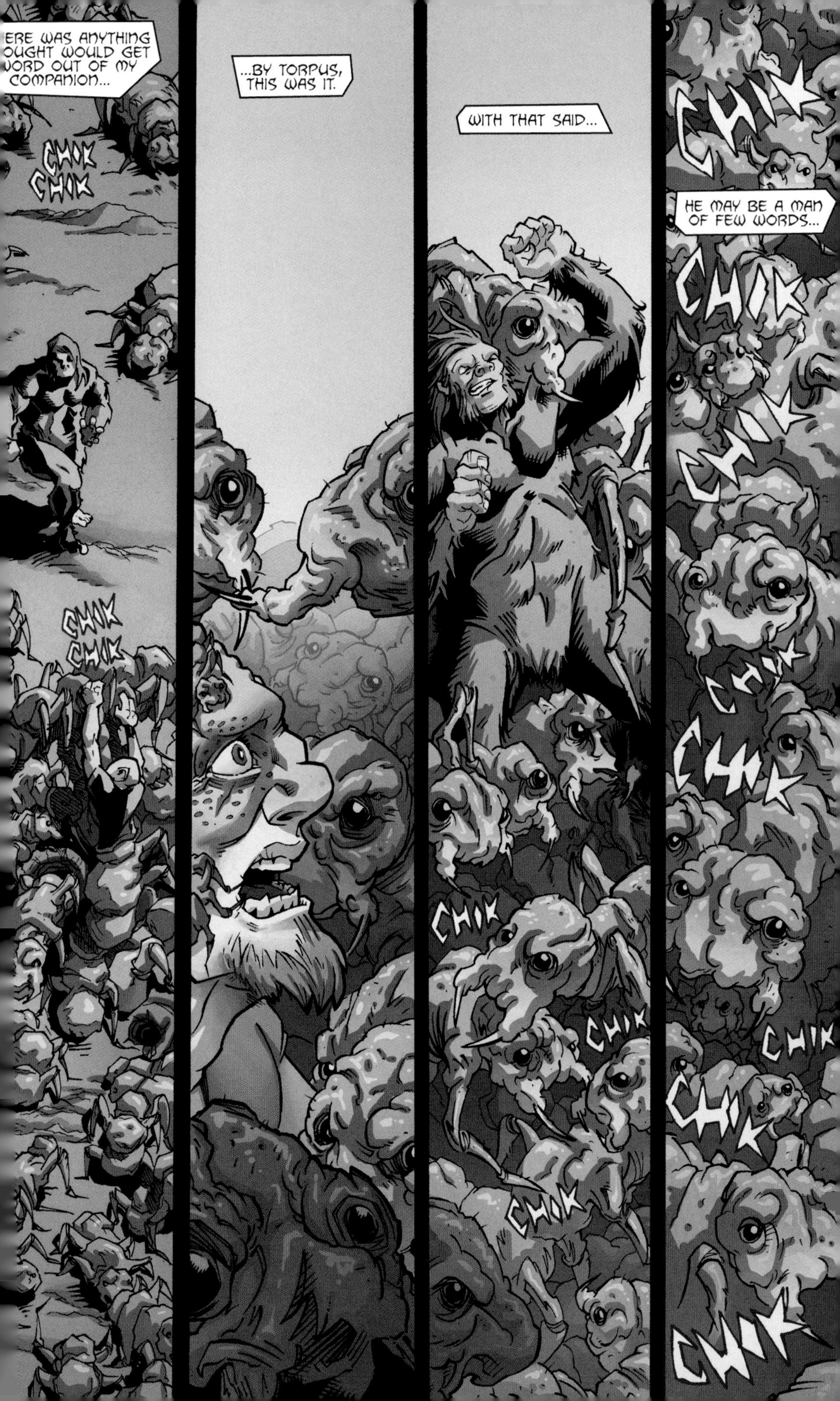
ERE WAS ANYTHING OUGHT WOULD GET ORD OUT OF MY COMPANION...
CHIK CHIK
CHIK CHIK
...BY TORPUS, THIS WAS IT.
WITH THAT SAID...
CHIK
CHIK
CHIK
HE MAY BE A MAN OF FEW WORDS...
CHIK
CHIK
CHIK
CHIK
CHIK
CHIK
CHIK

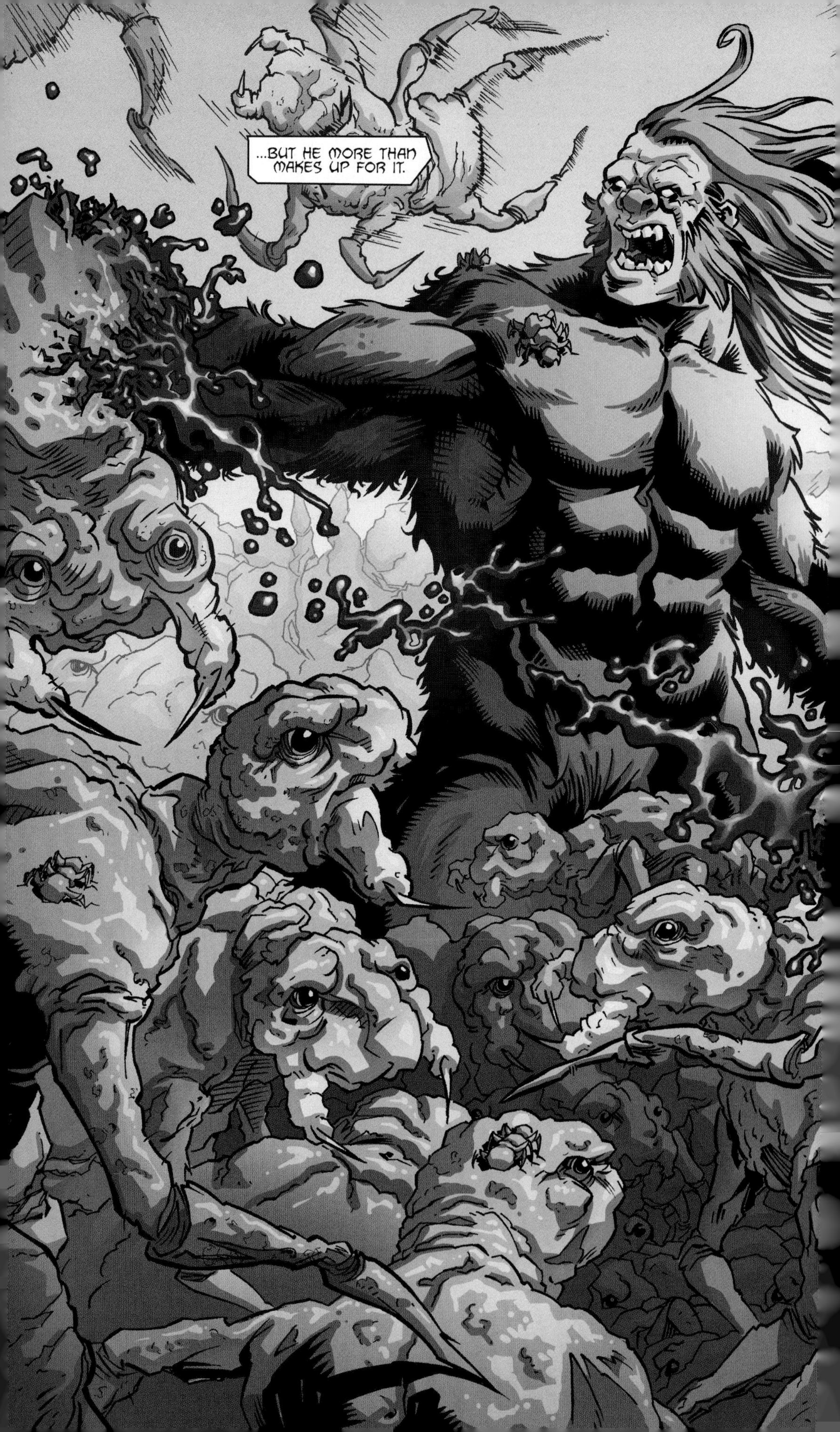
...BUT HE MORE THAN MAKES UP FOR IT.

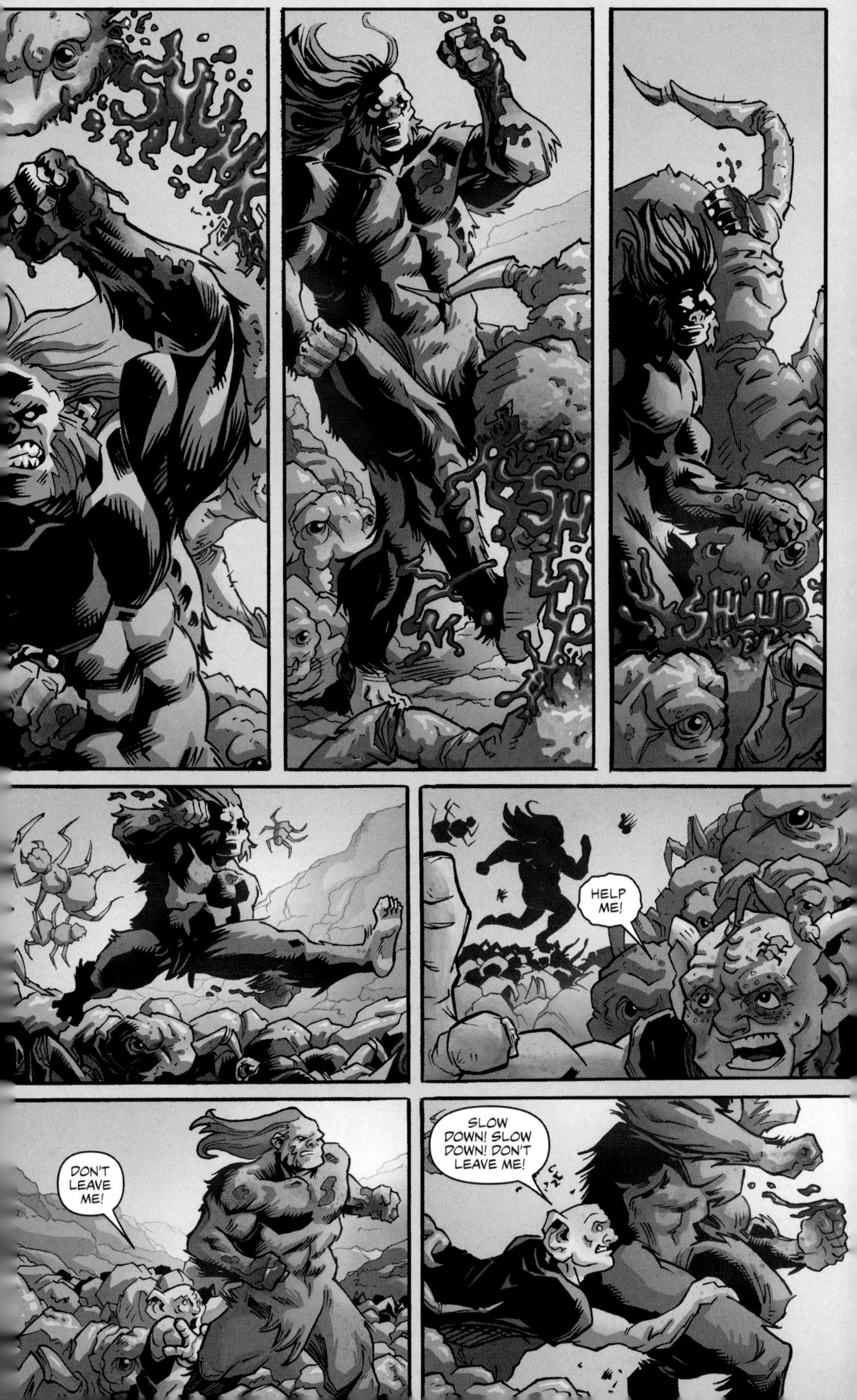
SHUNK
SHLUK
SHLUD
HELP ME!
DON'T LEAVE ME!
SLOW DOWN! SLOW DOWN! DON'T LEAVE ME!

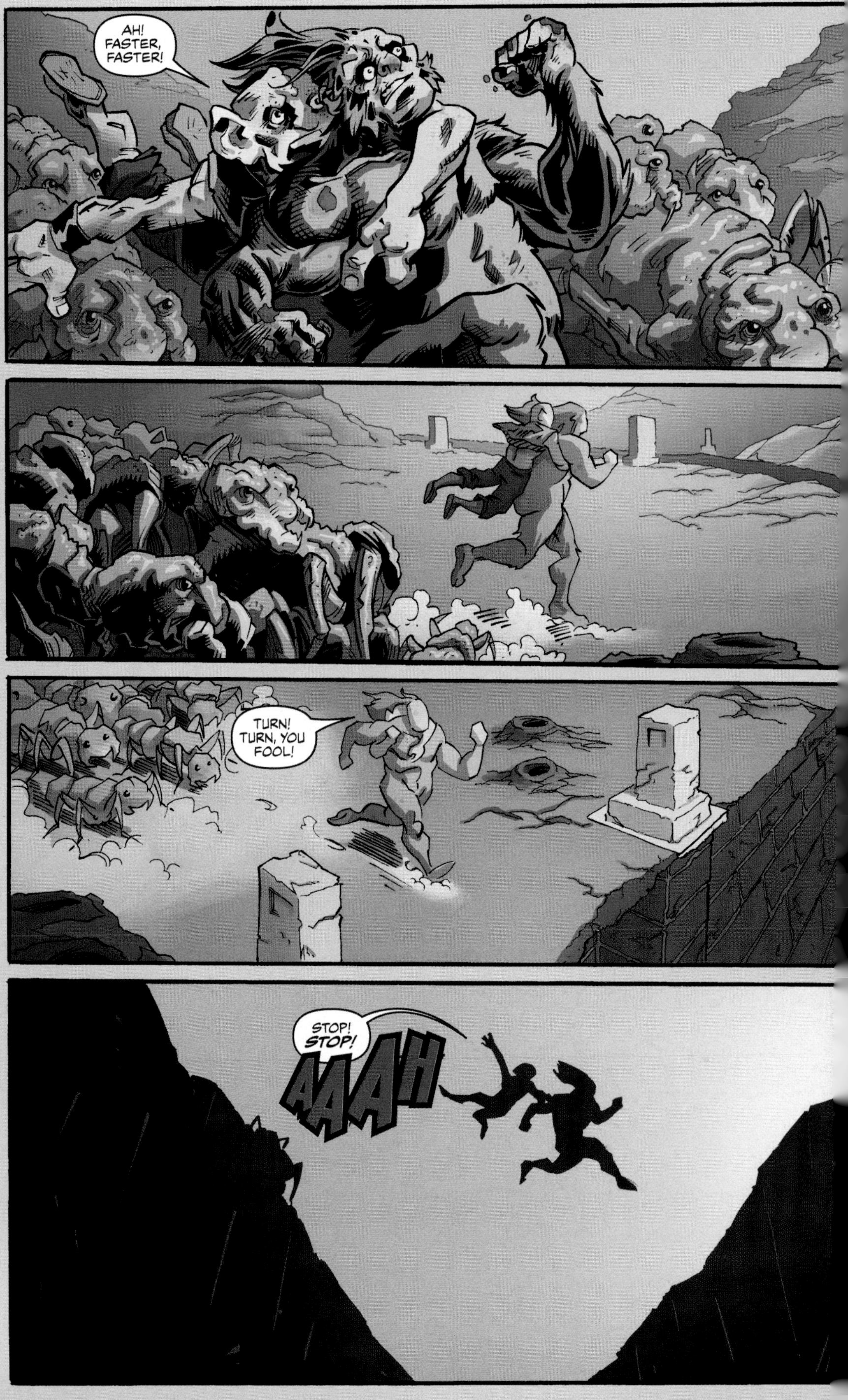
AH! FASTER, FASTER!
TURN! TURN, YOU FOOL!
STOP! STOP!
AAAH

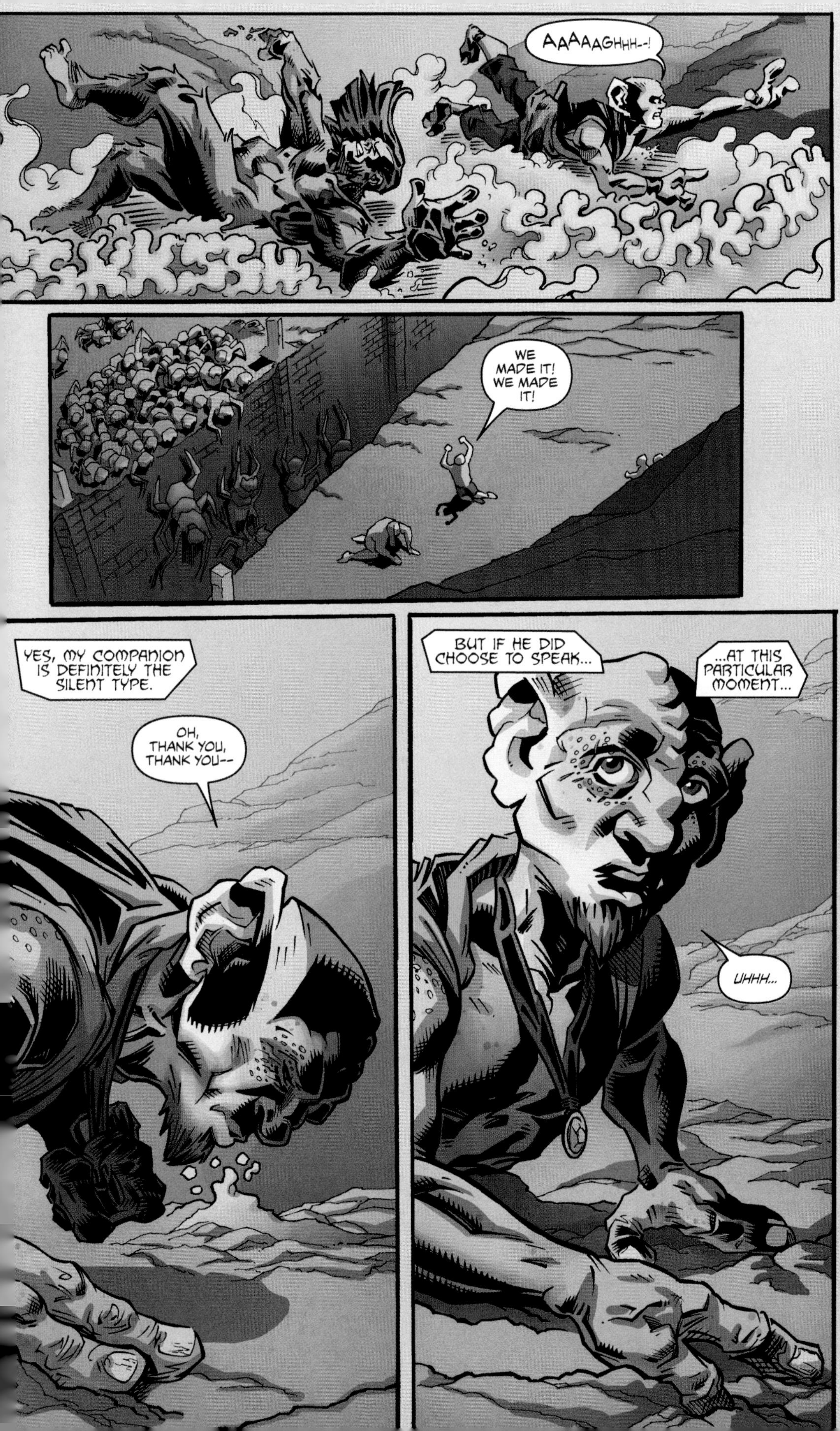
AAAAAGHHH--!
SKKSH SKKSH
WE MADE IT! WE MADE IT!
YES, MY COMPANION IS DEFINITELY THE SILENT TYPE.
OH, THANK YOU, THANK YOU--
BUT IF HE DID CHOOSE TO SPEAK...
...AT THIS PARTICULAR MOMENT...
UHHH...

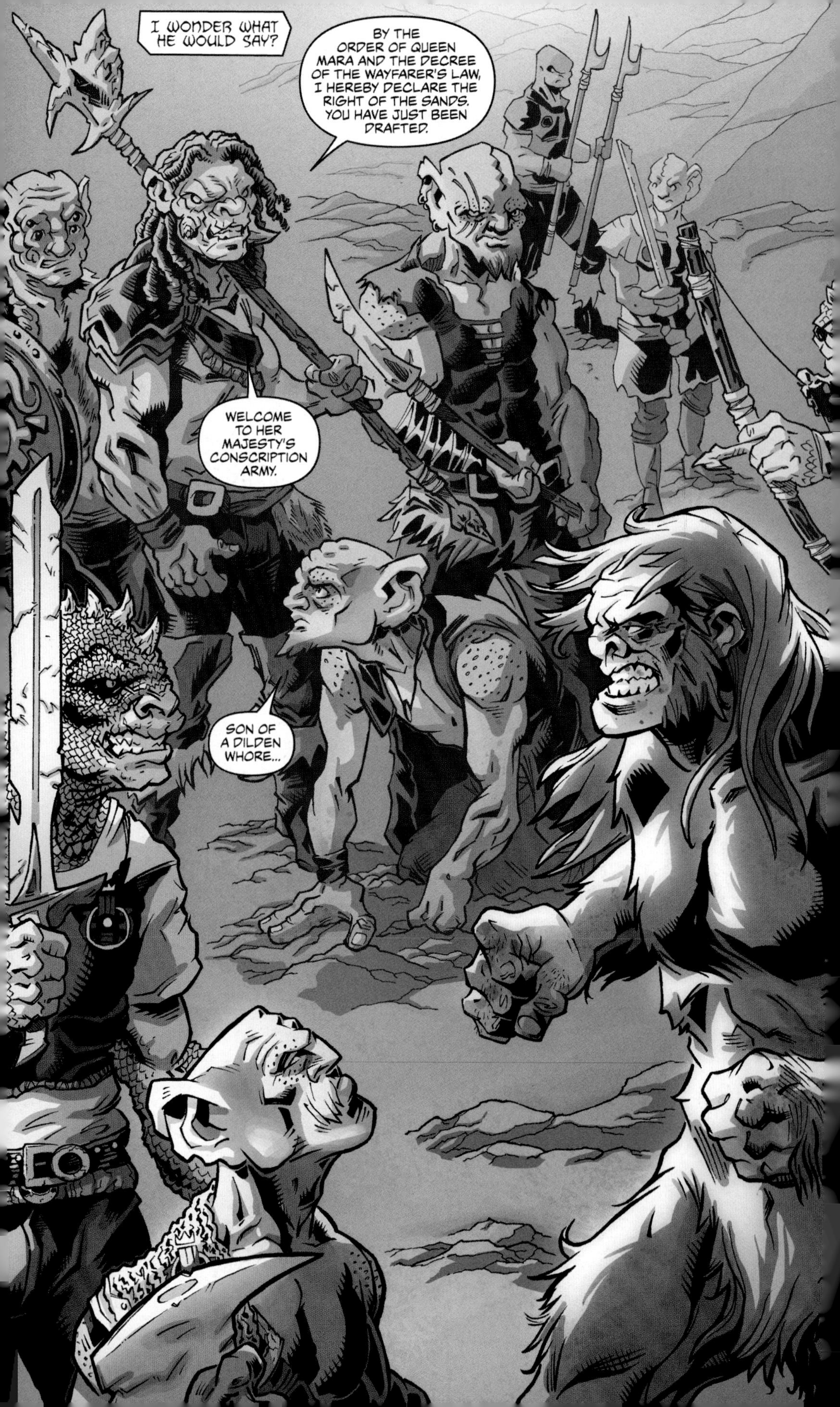
I WONDER WHAT HE WOULD SAY?
BY THE ORDER OF QUEEN MARA AND THE DECREE OF THE WAYFARER'S LAW, I HEREBY DECLARE THE RIGHT OF THE SANDS. YOU HAVE JUST BEEN DRAFTED.
WELCOME TO HER MAJESTY'S CONSCRIPTION ARMY.
SON OF A DILDEN WHORE...

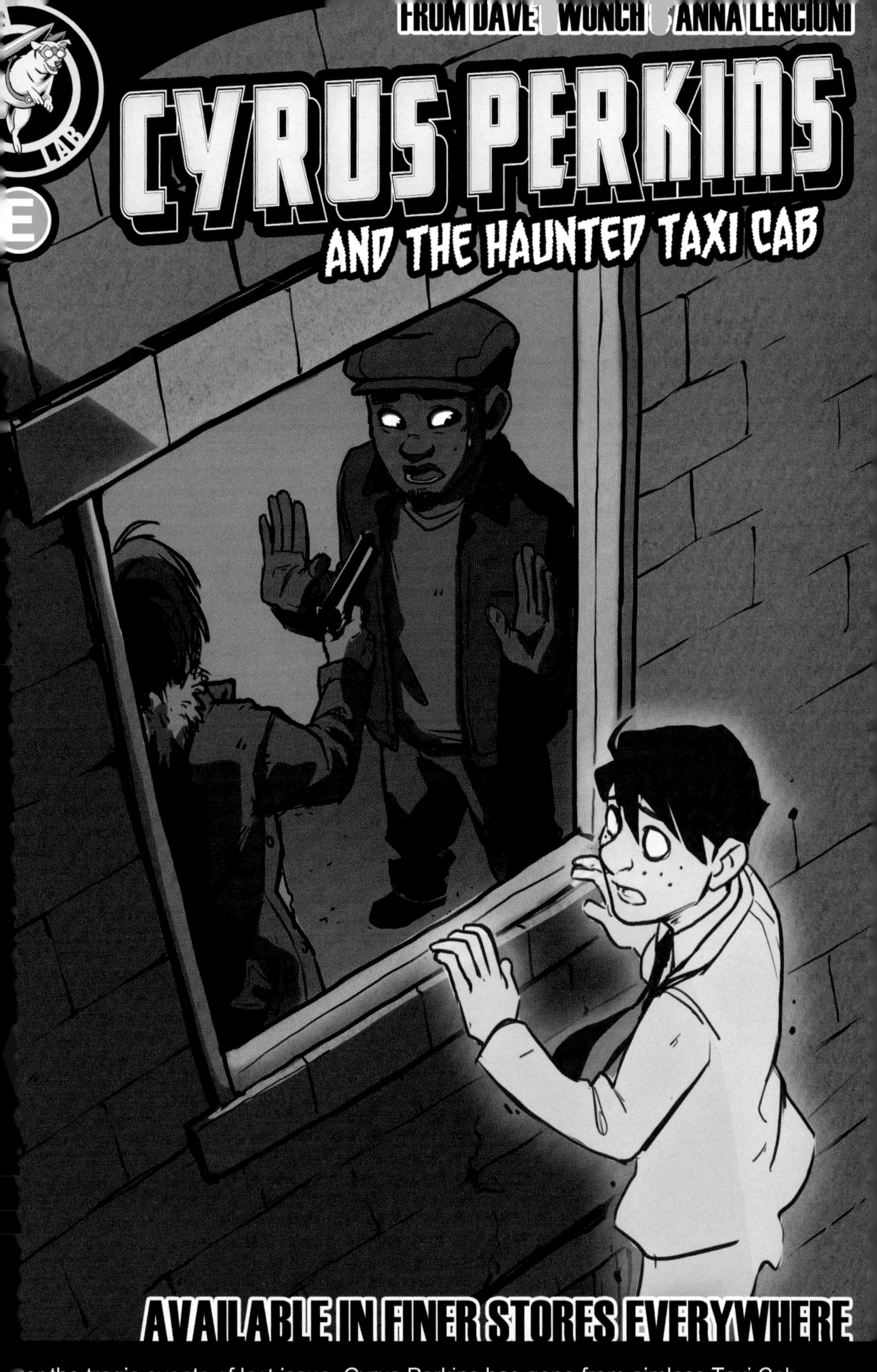
FROM DAVE WONCH & ANNA LENCIONI
CYRUS PERKINS
AND THE HAUNTED TAXI CAB
AVAILABLE IN FINER STORES EVERYWHERE

FROM MAT HEAGERTY & JD F

JUST ANOTHER SHEEP

AVAILABLE IN FINER STORES EVERYWH

In 1969 a timid teen sets out on a road trip. His goal? Find out the origins of his biz super human abilities. Always the follower, his trip is derailed when he befriends a g of extremist war protesters.

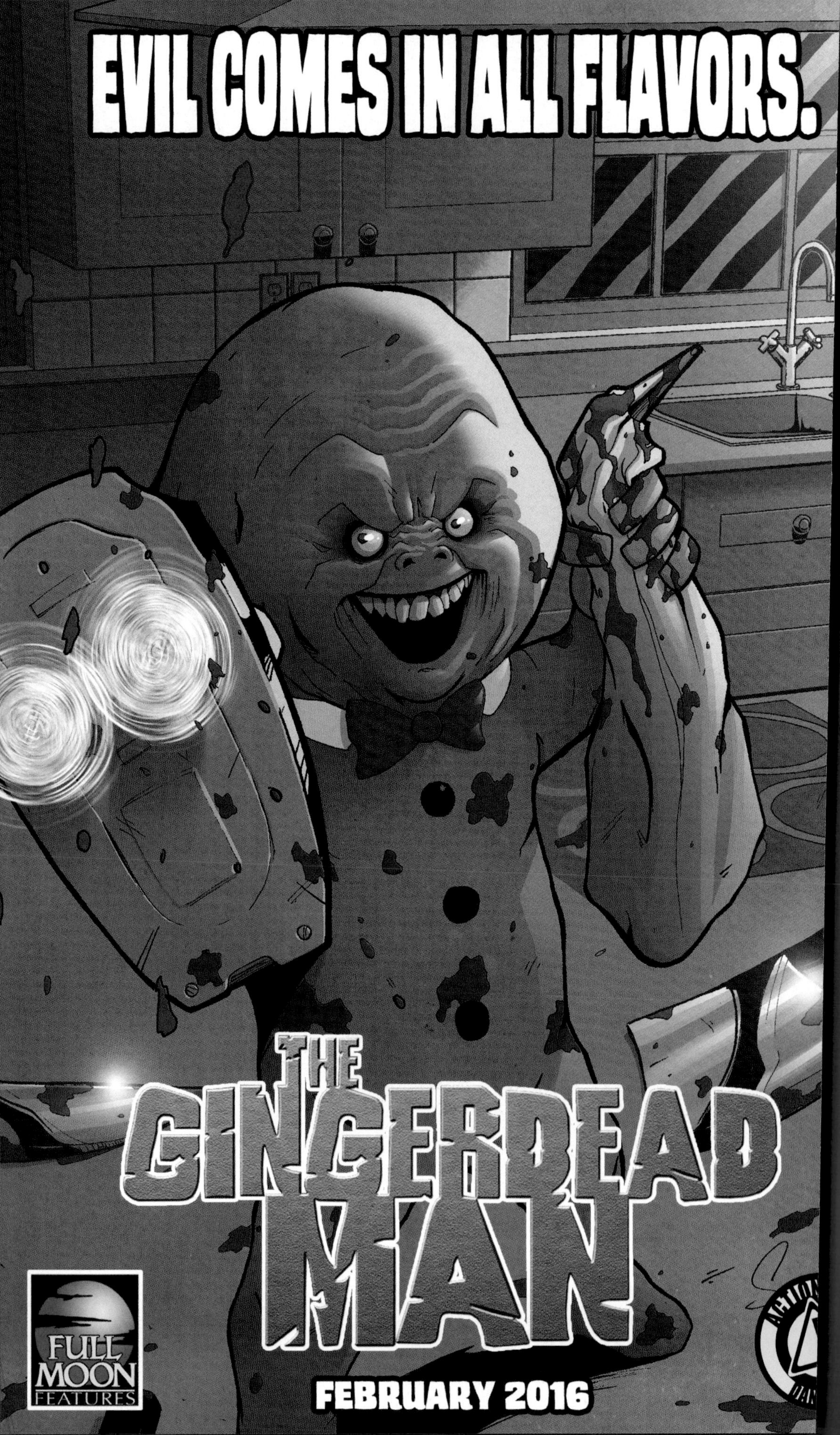
EVIL COMES IN ALL FLAVORS.
THE GINGERDEAD MAN
FULL MOON FEATURES
FEBRUARY 2016

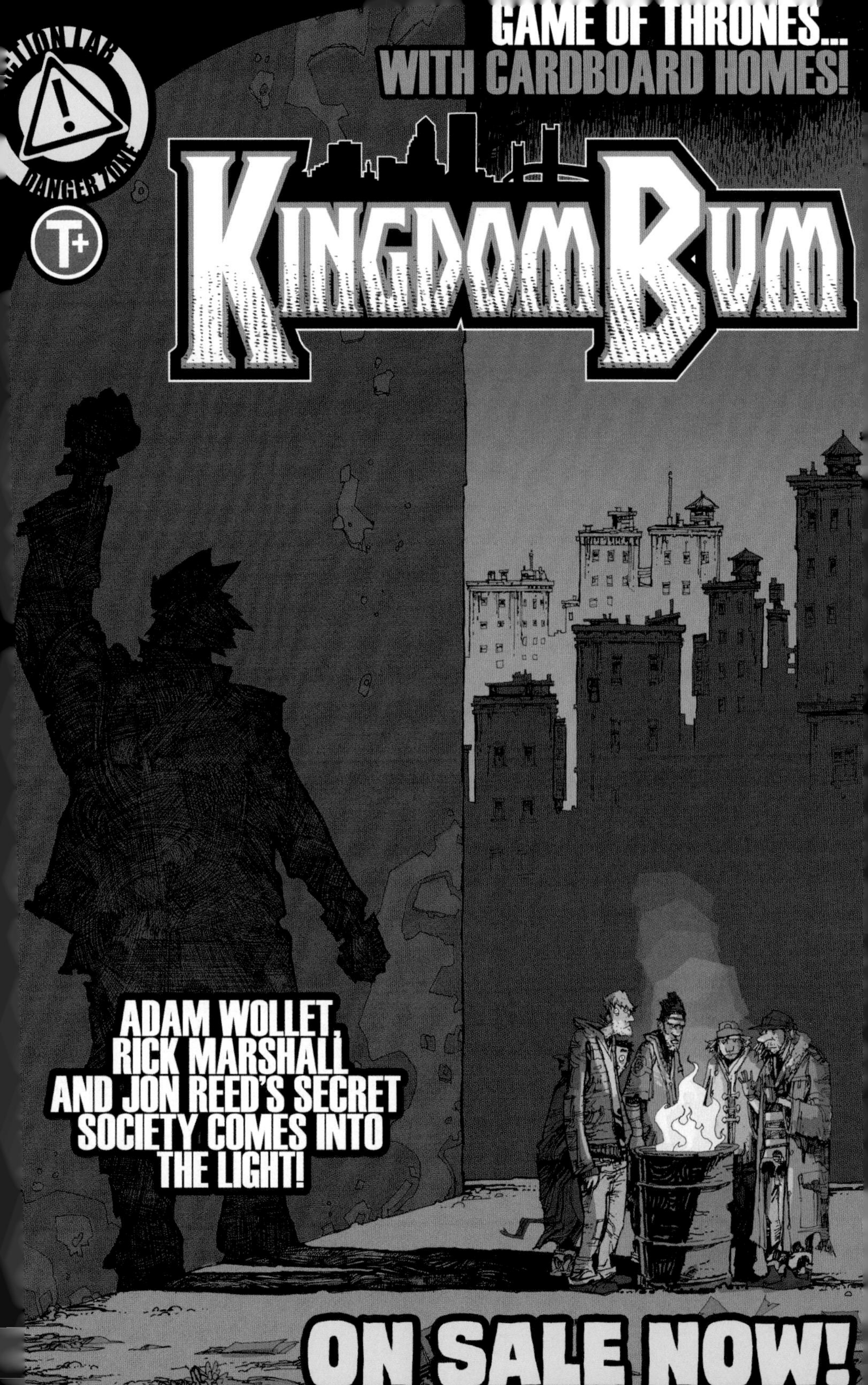
GAME OF THRONES...
WITH CARDBOARD HOMES!
ACTION LAB
DANGER ZONE
T+
KINGDOM BUM
ADAM WOLLET, RICK MARSHALL AND JON REED'S SECRET SOCIETY COMES INTO THE LIGHT!
ON SALE NOW!

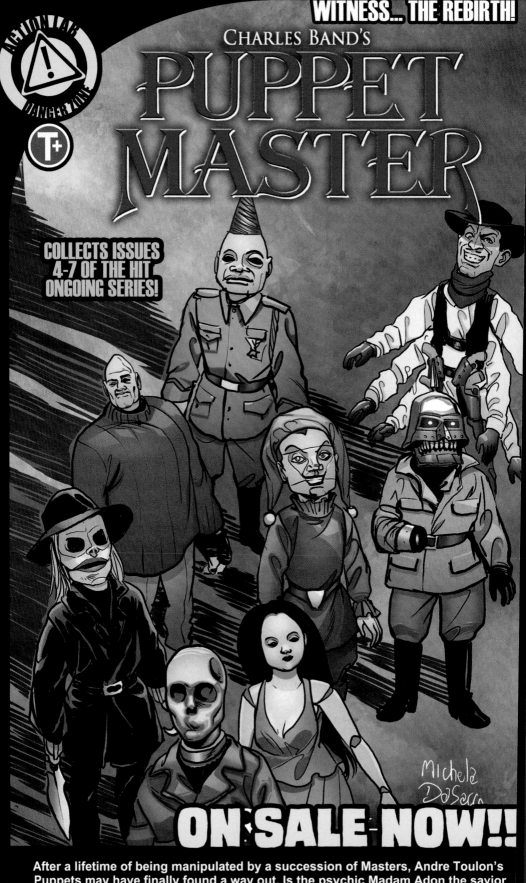

WITNESS... THE REBIRTH!

CHARLES BAND'S

PUPPET MASTER

COLLECTS ISSUES 4-7 OF THE HIT ONGOING SERIES!

Michele DaSecca

ON SALE NOW!!

After a lifetime of being manipulated by a succession of Masters, Andre Toulon's Puppets may have finally found a way out. Is the psychic Madam Adon the savior they have been looking for? And if so, what is the price of freedom? REBIRTH moves the Puppet Master universe in a bold new direction!

FROM ALL-AGES TO MATURE READERS ACTION LAB HAS YOU COVERED.

 **Appropriate for everyone.**

 **Appropriate for age 9 and up. Absent of profanity or adult content.**

 **Suggested for 12 and Up. Comics with this rating are comparable to a PG-13 movie rating. Recommended for our teen and young adult readers.**

 **Appropriate for older teens. Similar to Teen, but featuring more mature themes and/or more graphic imagery.**

 **Contains extreme viloence and some nudity. Basically the Rated-R of comics.**

 FIND YOUR NEW FAVORITE COMICS.

READ MORE NOW

Bigfoot: Sword Of The Earthman - Action Lab
www.actionlabcomics.com

ACTIONLABCOMICS.COM

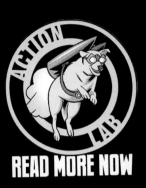

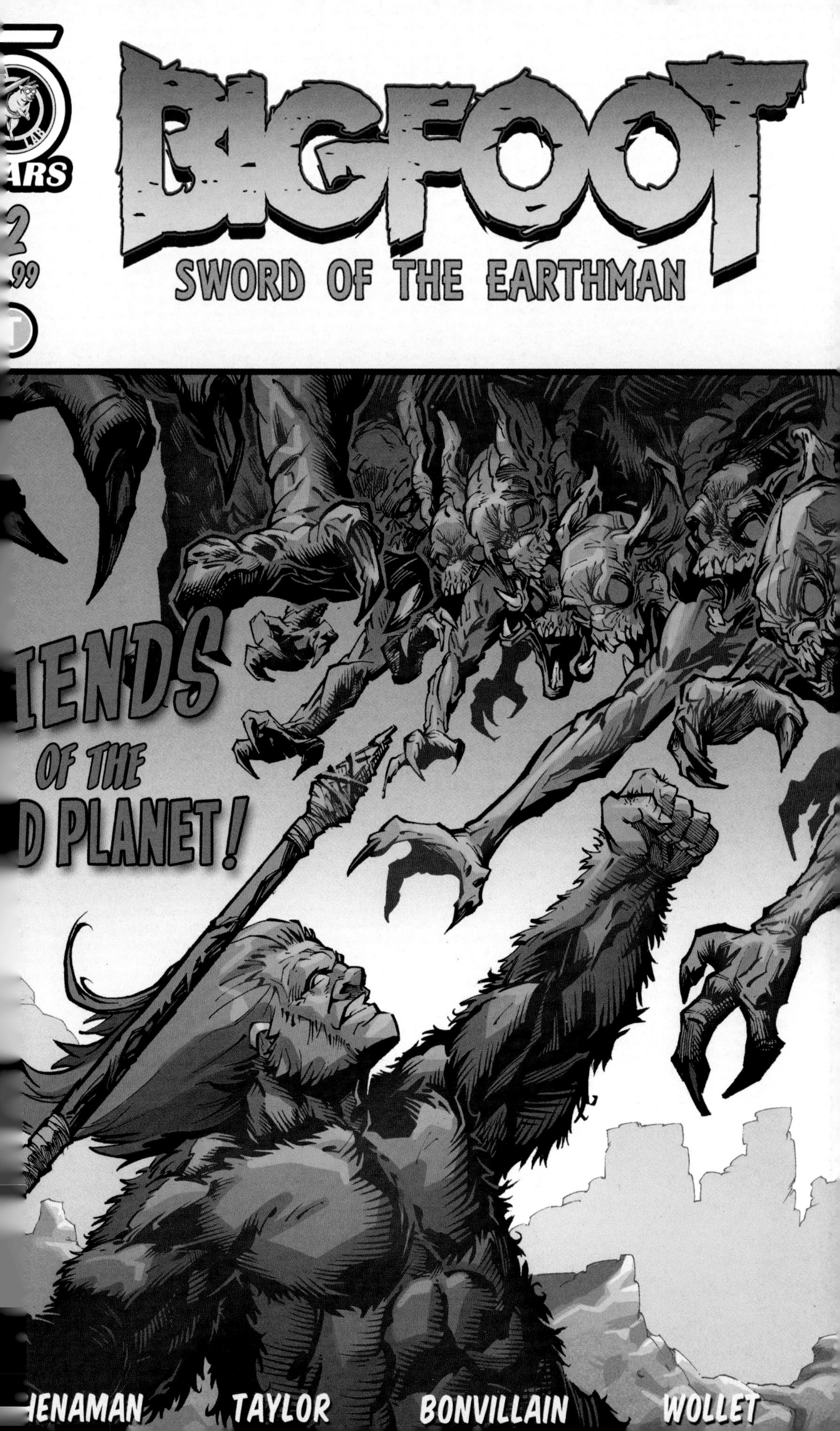
BIGFOOT
SWORD OF THE EARTHMAN
2
.99
IENDS
OF THE
D PLANET!
HENAMAN
TAYLOR
BONVILLAIN
WOLLET

THE PEOPLE LIVED IN FEAR OF THE NIGH

ONCE THE SUN DESCENDED, INSECT-LIKE HORDES OF MOTH-VAMPIRES SWEPT OVER THE LAND. WOMEN AND CHILDREN WERE SLAUGHTERED IN THEIR BEDS. GROWN MEN WERE STOLEN AWAY, NEVER TO RETURN. NOTHING COULD PREVENT THE COMING OF THE DARK. NOTHING COULD PREVENT THE ONSLAUGHT.

SO THE PEOPLE BUILT A BEACON. DESIGNED BY THE GREATEST SCIENTIFIC SCHOLARS, THE BEACON WOULD BECOME THEIR TORCH IN THE NIGHT. A SIREN'S SONG OF DIVINE FIRE BECKONING TO A LEGION OF LOCUST CREATURES THAT KNEW NO MASTER.

AND LIKE MOTHS TO A FLAME, THE HORDE WAS DRAWN INTO THE LIGHT ONLY TO BURN. SO THE GREAT MINDS BUILT ANOTHER... AND ANOTHER.

SOON, THE FEAR OF DARKNESS DIMINISHED AND AS THE YEARS BECAME DECADES AND THE DECADES TURNED INTO CENTURIES, THE PEOPLE FACED A NEW PROBLEM. FAR FROM THE NEAREST SETTLEMENT, SOMEONE WOULD NEED TO KEEP THE GREAT BEACONS ALIGHT. WITH THE GLORY OF THE BEACON SOLDIERS A DISTANT MEMORY, THE PEOPLE TURNED TO THE CRIMINALS TO FILL THE RANKS. THEY TURNED TO THE OUTCASTS THAT WANDER THE BARREN DESERT.

EVENTUALLY, THEY TURNED TO...

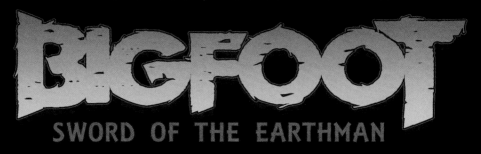

BIGFOOT
SWORD OF THE EARTHMAN

Bryan Seaton: Publisher • Kevin Freeman: President • Dave Dwonch: Creative Director • Shawn Gabborin: Editor I
Jamal Igle: Vice-President of Marketing • Vito Delsante: Director of Marketing • Jim Dietz: Social Media Direc
Nicole DAndria: Script Editor • Chad Cicconi: Black Sheep • Colleen Boyd: Submissions Editor

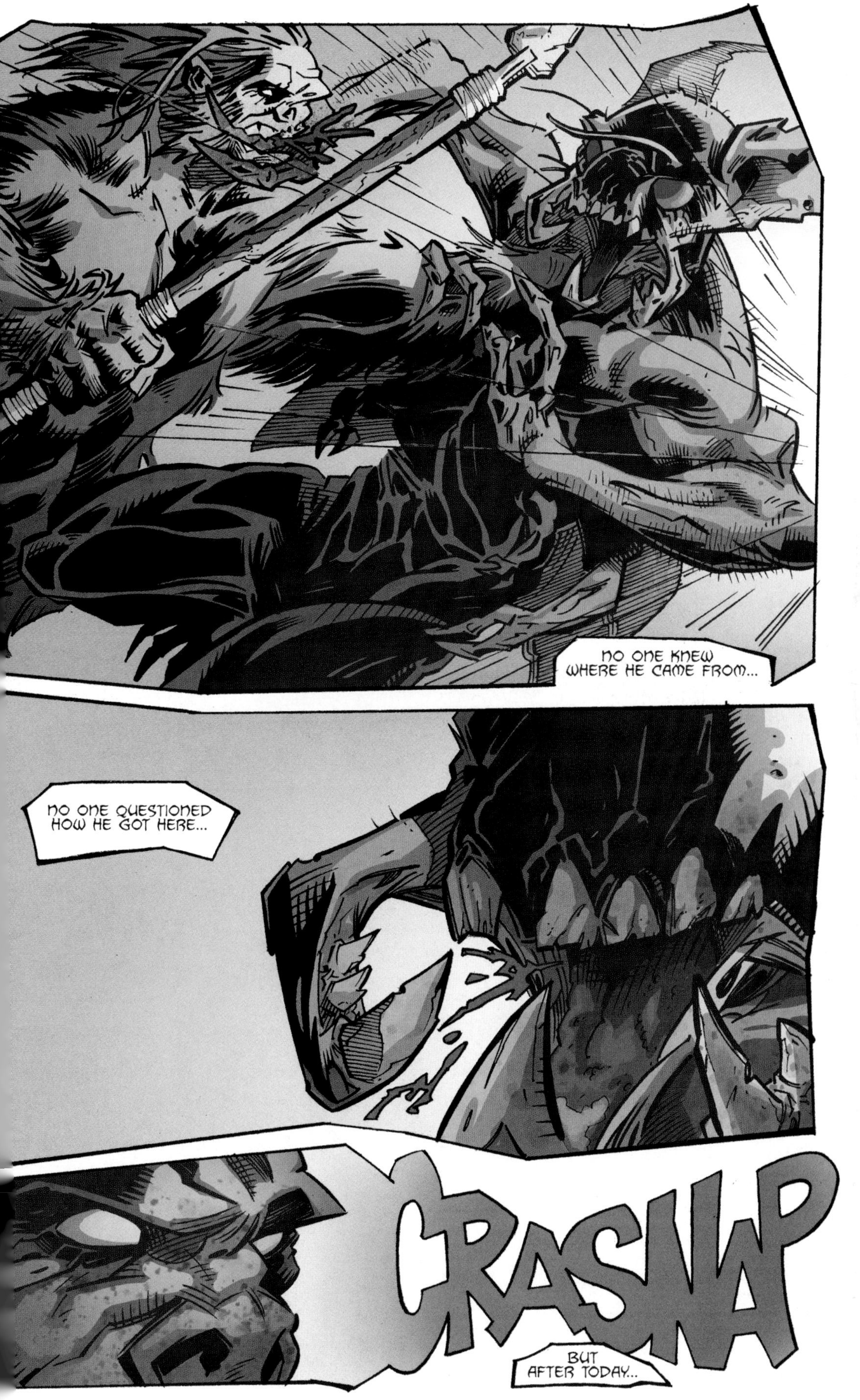
NO ONE KNEW WHERE HE CAME FROM...
NO ONE QUESTIONED HOW HE GOT HERE...
CRASNAP
BUT AFTER TODAY...

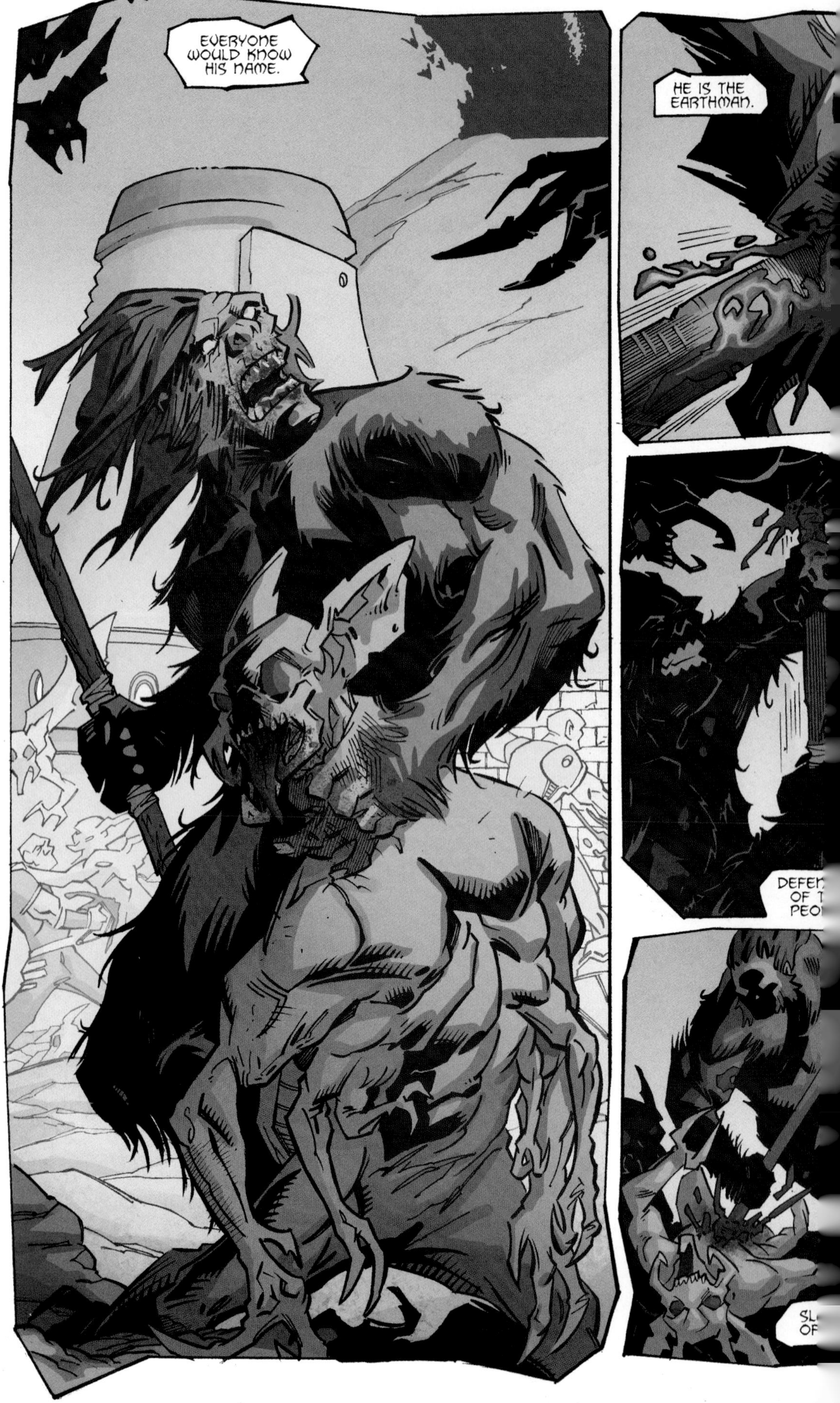
EVERYONE WOULD KNOW HIS NAME.
HE IS THE EARTHMAN.

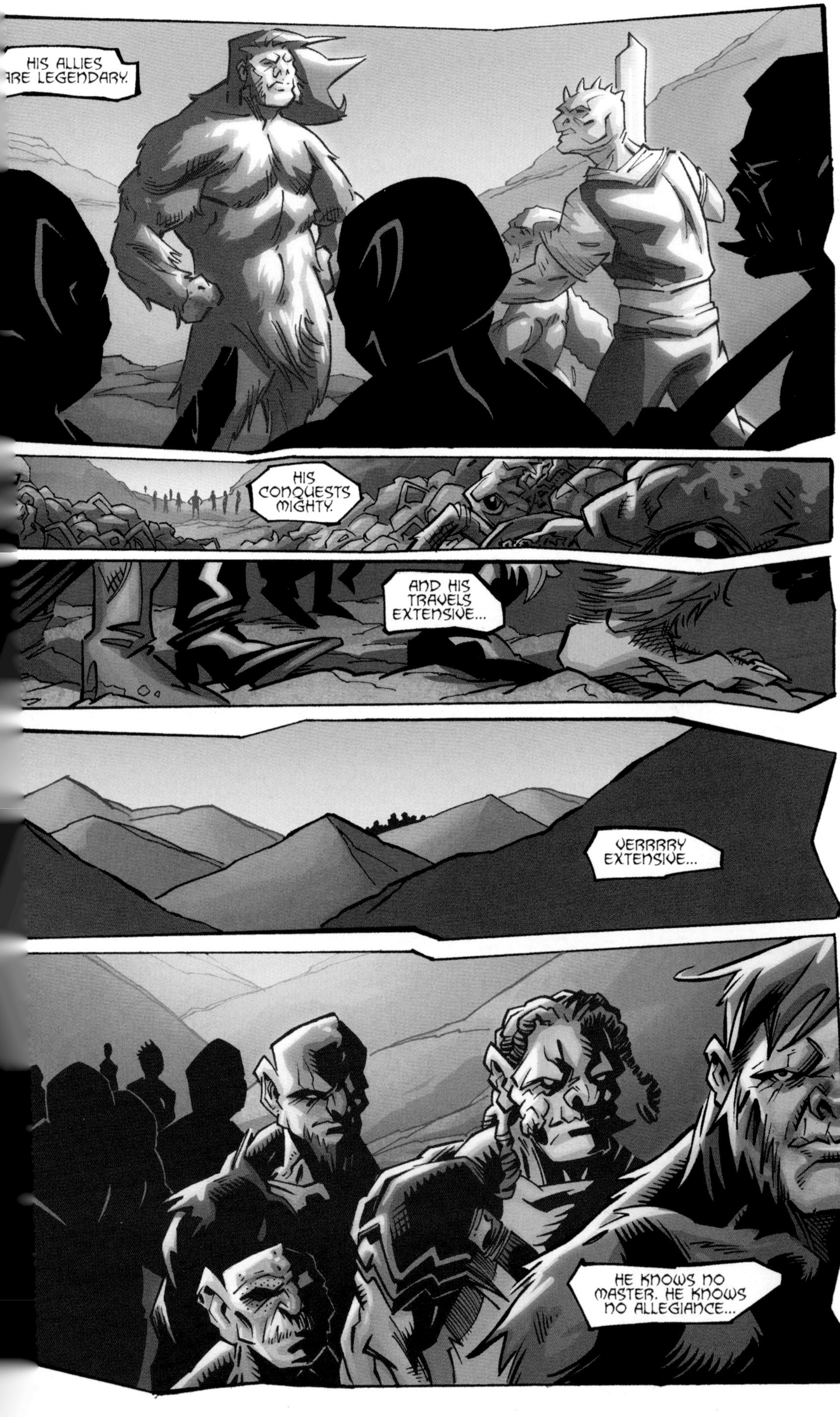
HIS ALLIES ARE LEGENDARY.
HIS CONQUESTS MIGHTY.
AND HIS TRAVELS EXTENSIVE...
VERRRRY EXTENSIVE...
HE KNOWS NO MASTER. HE KNOWS NO ALLEGIANCE...

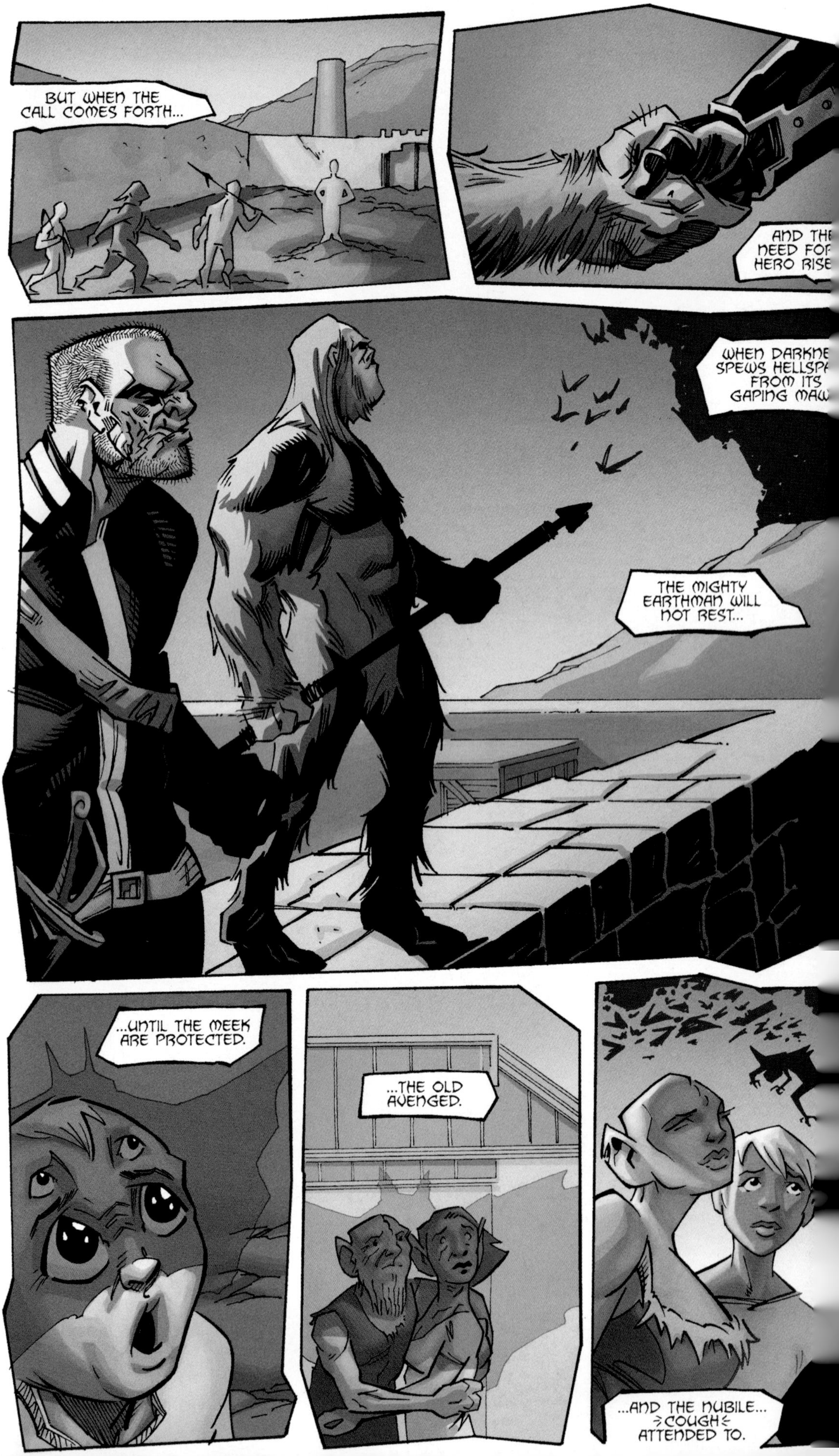
BUT WHEN THE CALL COMES FORTH...
AND THE NEED FOR HERO RISE
WHEN DARKNE SPEWS HELLSPA FROM ITS GAPING MAW
THE MIGHTY EARTHMAN WILL NOT REST...
...UNTIL THE MEEK ARE PROTECTED.
...THE OLD AVENGED.
...AND THE NUBILE... ⇛COUGH⇚ ATTENDED TO.

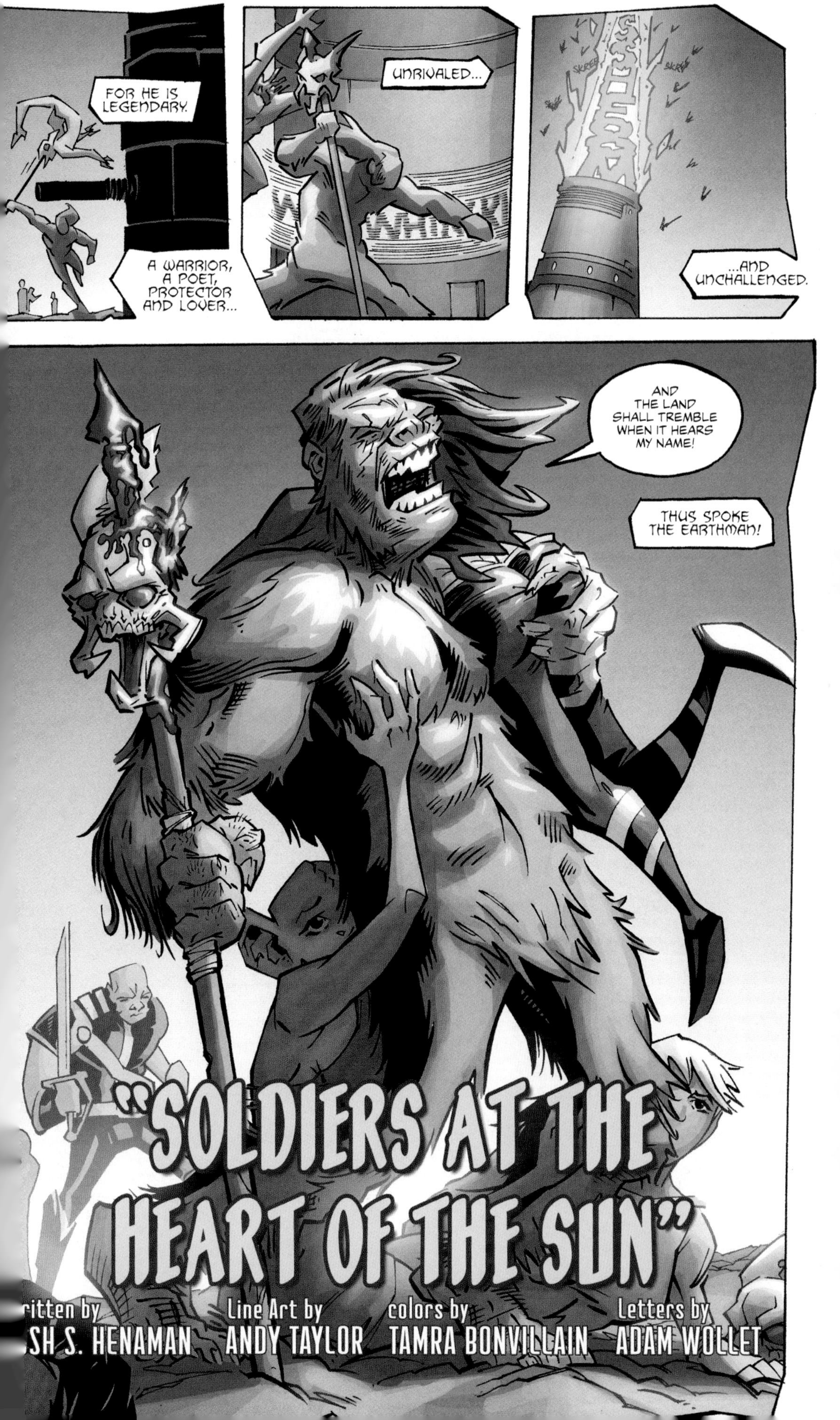
FOR HE IS LEGENDARY.
A WARRIOR, A POET, PROTECTOR AND LOVER...
UNRIVALED...
...AND UNCHALLENGED.
AND THE LAND SHALL TREMBLE WHEN IT HEARS MY NAME!
THUS SPOKE THE EARTHMAN!
"SOLDIERS AT THE HEART OF THE SUN"
ritten by
SH S. HENAMAN
Line Art by
ANDY TAYLOR
colors by
TAMRA BONVILLAIN
Letters by
ADAM WOLLET

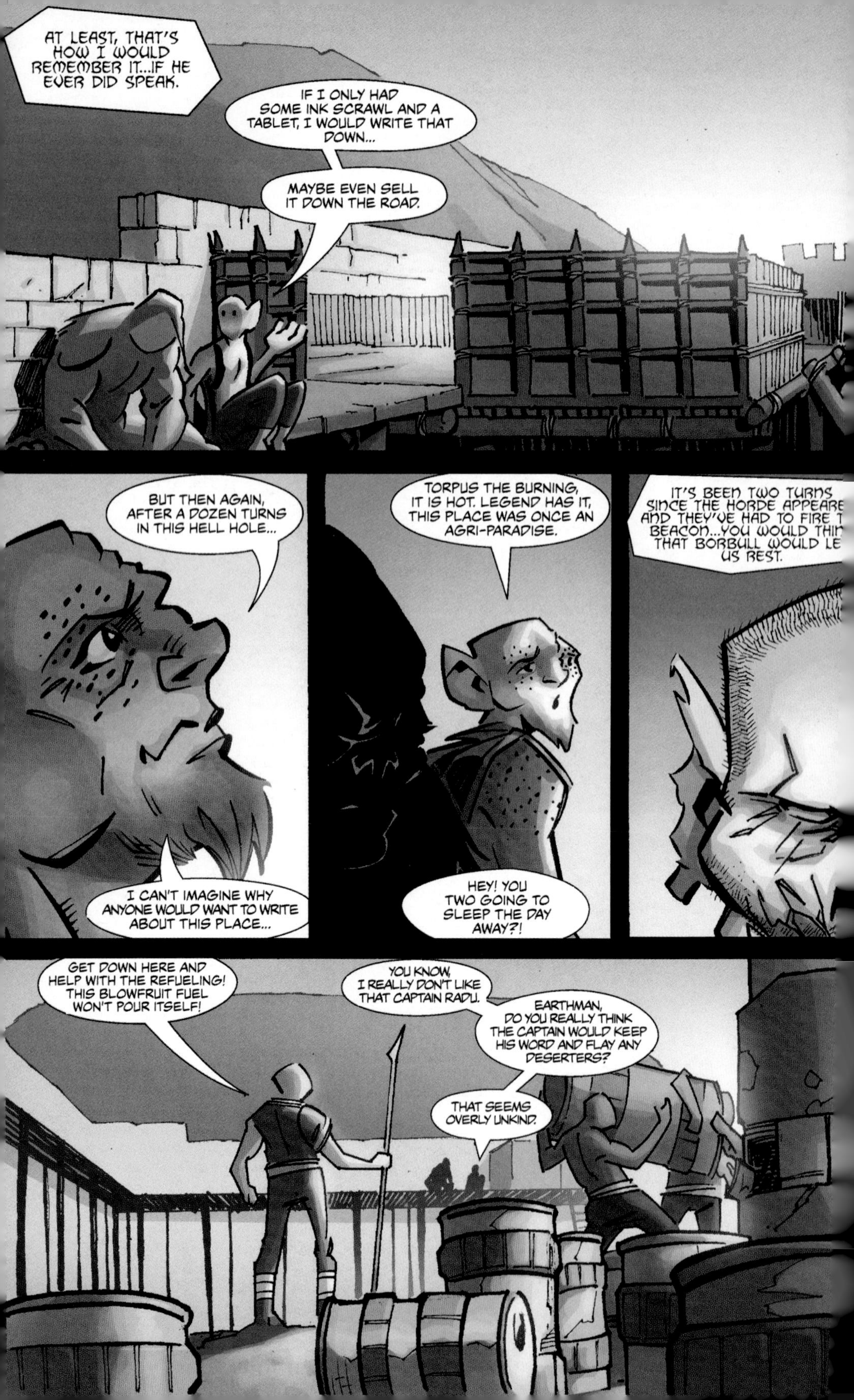
AT LEAST, THAT'S HOW I WOULD REMEMBER IT...IF HE EVER DID SPEAK.
IF I ONLY HAD SOME INK SCRAWL AND A TABLET, I WOULD WRITE THAT DOWN...
MAYBE EVEN SELL IT DOWN THE ROAD.
BUT THEN AGAIN, AFTER A DOZEN TURNS IN THIS HELL HOLE...
I CAN'T IMAGINE WHY ANYONE WOULD WANT TO WRITE ABOUT THIS PLACE...
TORPUS THE BURNING, IT IS HOT. LEGEND HAS IT, THIS PLACE WAS ONCE AN AGRI-PARADISE.
HEY! YOU TWO GOING TO SLEEP THE DAY AWAY?!
IT'S BEEN TWO TURNS SINCE THE HORDE APPEARE AND THEY'VE HAD TO FIRE T BEACON...YOU WOULD THIN THAT BORBULL WOULD LE US REST.
GET DOWN HERE AND HELP WITH THE REFUELING! THIS BLOWFRUIT FUEL WON'T POUR ITSELF!
YOU KNOW, I REALLY DON'T LIKE THAT CAPTAIN RADU.
EARTHMAN, DO YOU REALLY THINK THE CAPTAIN WOULD KEEP HIS WORD AND FLAY ANY DESERTERS?
THAT SEEMS OVERLY UNKIND.

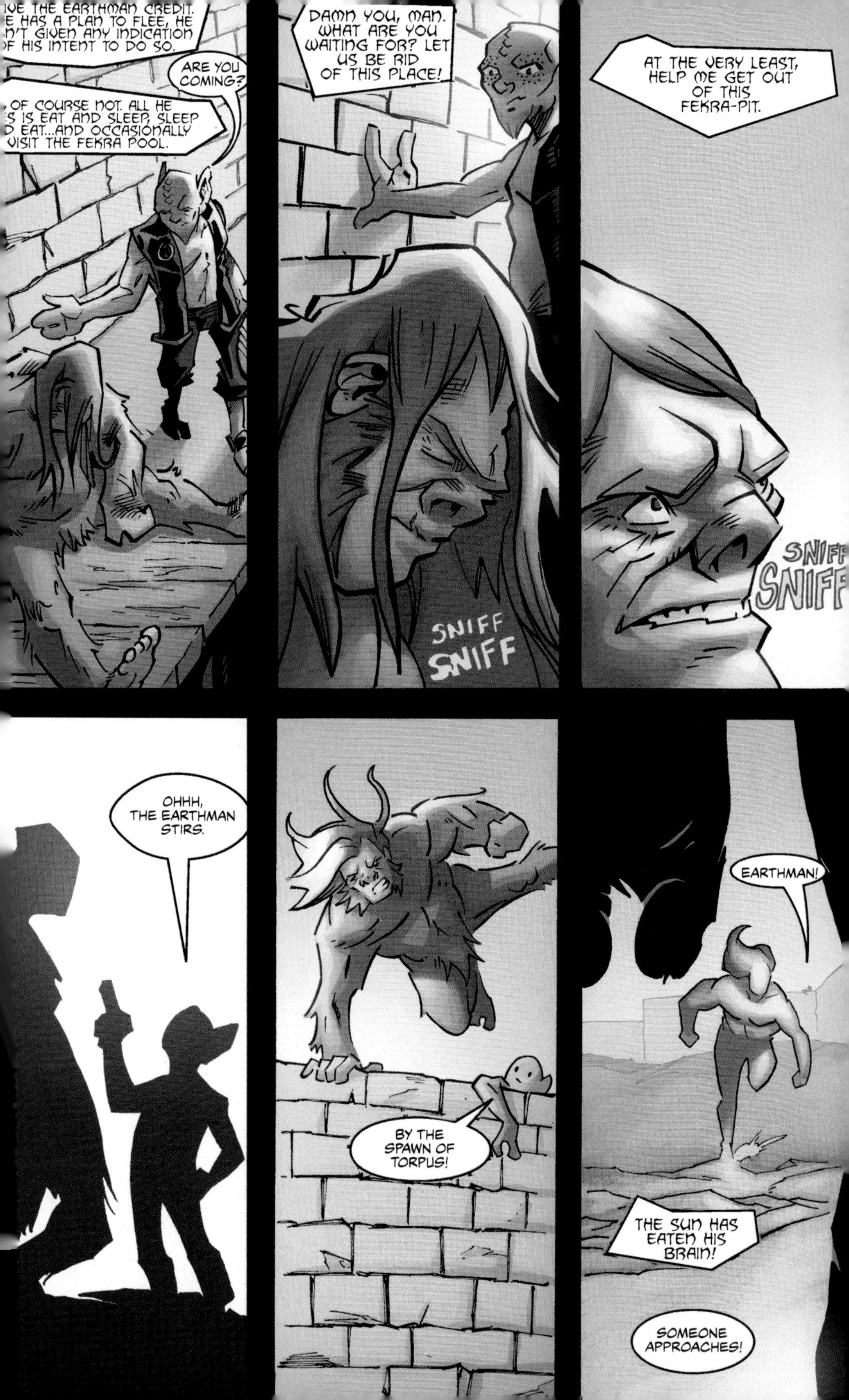

...IVE THE EARTHMAN CREDIT. ...E HAS A PLAN TO FLEE, HE ...N'T GIVEN ANY INDICATION ...F HIS INTENT TO DO SO.
ARE YOU COMING?
..., OF COURSE NOT. ALL HE ...S IS EAT AND SLEEP, SLEEP ...D EAT...AND OCCASIONALLY VISIT THE FEKRA POOL.
DAMN YOU, MAN. WHAT ARE YOU WAITING FOR? LET US BE RID OF THIS PLACE!
SNIFF SNIFF
AT THE VERY LEAST, HELP ME GET OUT OF THIS FEKRA-PIT.
SNIFF SNIFF
OHHH, THE EARTHMAN STIRS.
BY THE SPAWN OF TORPUS!
EARTHMAN!
THE SUN HAS EATEN HIS BRAIN!
SOMEONE APPROACHES!

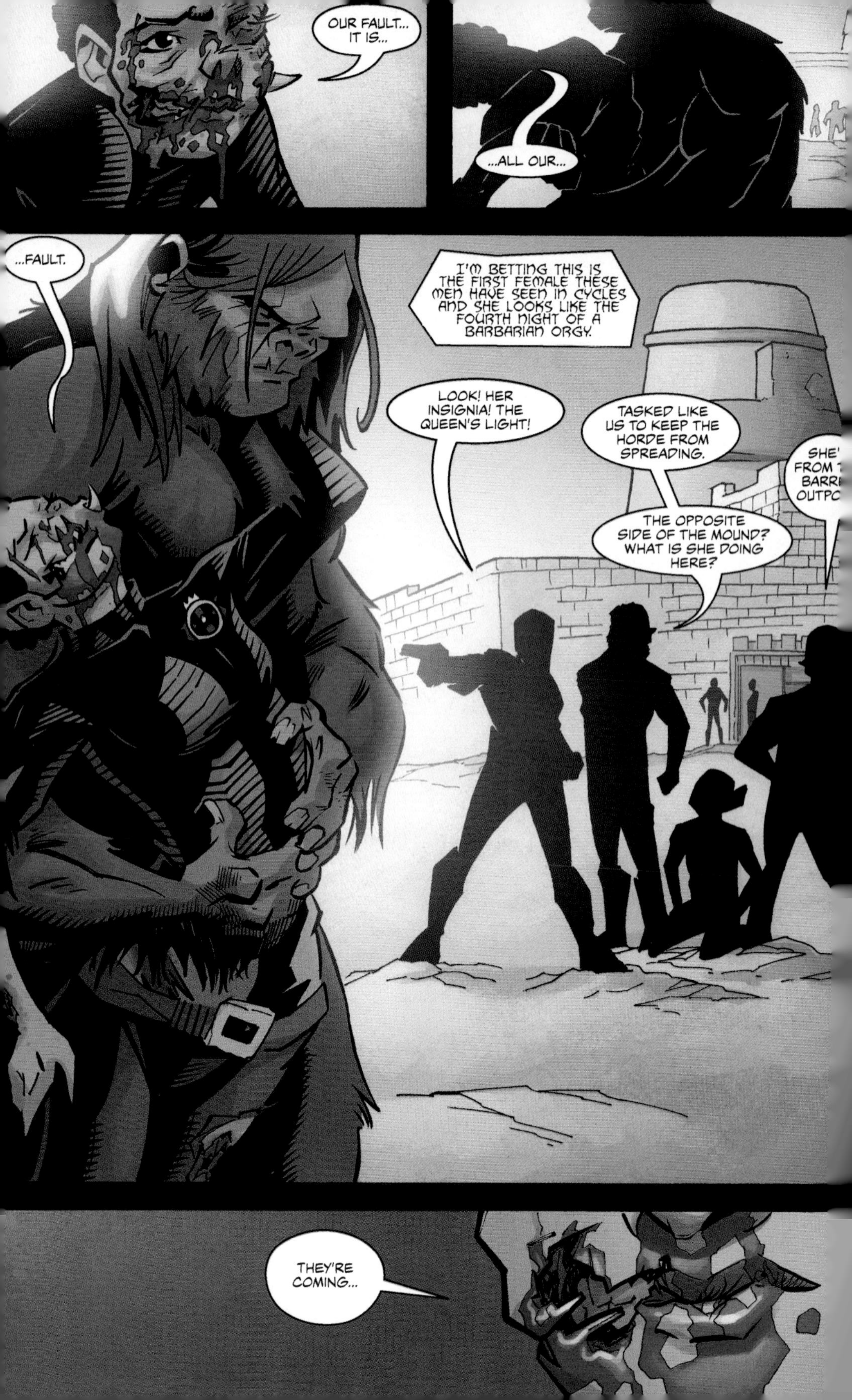
OUR FAULT... IT IS...
...ALL OUR...
...FAULT.
I'M BETTING THIS IS THE FIRST FEMALE THESE MEN HAVE SEEN IN CYCLES AND SHE LOOKS LIKE THE FOURTH NIGHT OF A BARBARIAN ORGY.
LOOK! HER INSIGNIA! THE QUEEN'S LIGHT!
TASKED LIKE US TO KEEP THE HORDE FROM SPREADING.
THE OPPOSITE SIDE OF THE MOUND? WHAT IS SHE DOING HERE?
THEY'RE COMING...

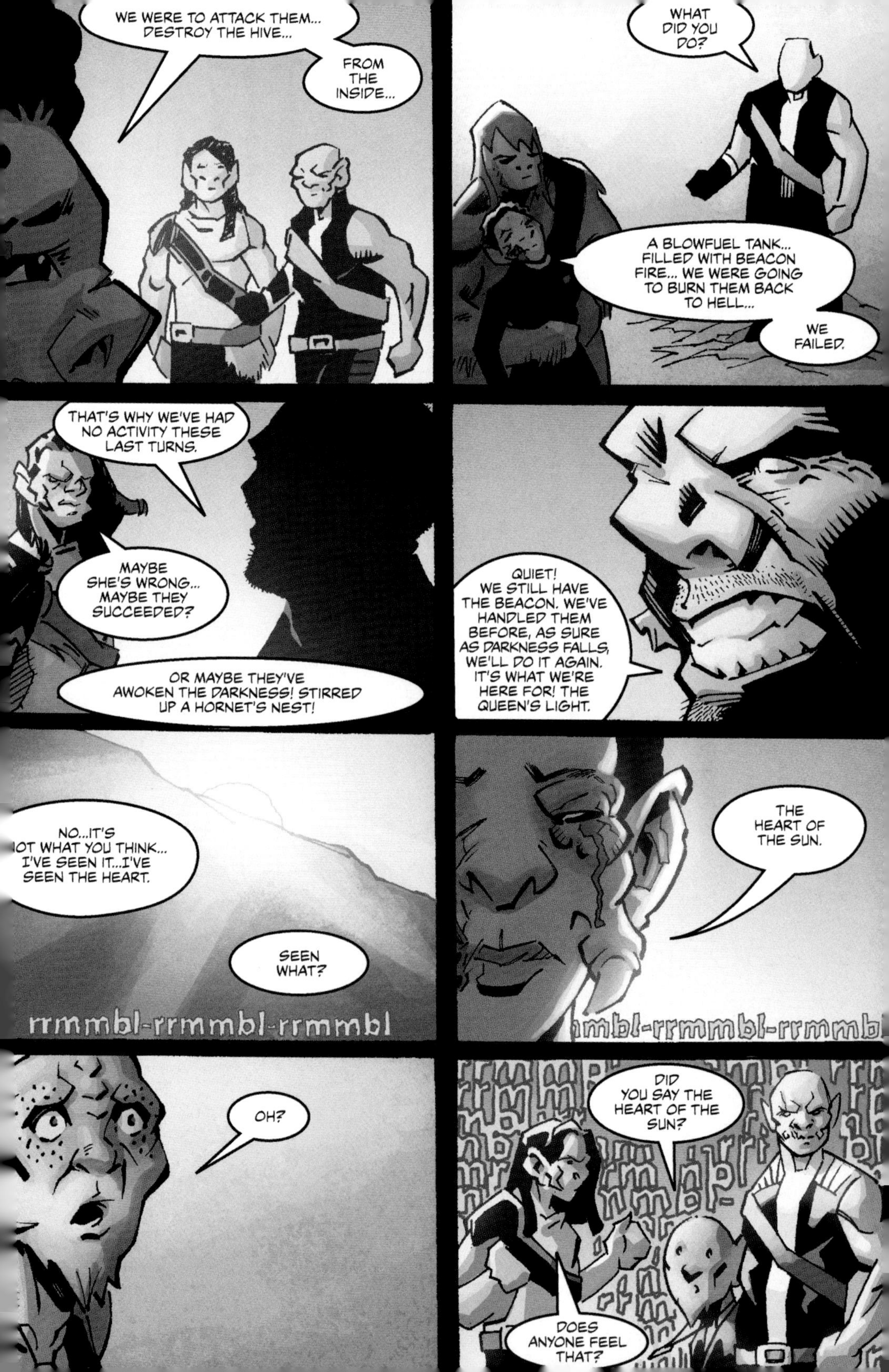
WE WERE TO ATTACK THEM... DESTROY THE HIVE...
FROM THE INSIDE...
WHAT DID YOU DO?
A BLOWFUEL TANK... FILLED WITH BEACON FIRE... WE WERE GOING TO BURN THEM BACK TO HELL...
WE FAILED.
THAT'S WHY WE'VE HAD NO ACTIVITY THESE LAST TURNS.
MAYBE SHE'S WRONG... MAYBE THEY SUCCEEDED?
OR MAYBE THEY'VE AWOKEN THE DARKNESS! STIRRED UP A HORNET'S NEST!
QUIET! WE STILL HAVE THE BEACON. WE'VE HANDLED THEM BEFORE, AS SURE AS DARKNESS FALLS, WE'LL DO IT AGAIN. IT'S WHAT WE'RE HERE FOR! THE QUEEN'S LIGHT.
NO...IT'S IOT WHAT YOU THINK... I'VE SEEN IT...I'VE SEEN THE HEART.
SEEN WHAT?
rrmmbl-rrmmbl-rrmmbl
THE HEART OF THE SUN.
mmbl-rrmmbl-rrmmb
OH?
DID YOU SAY THE HEART OF THE SUN?
DOES ANYONE FEEL THAT?

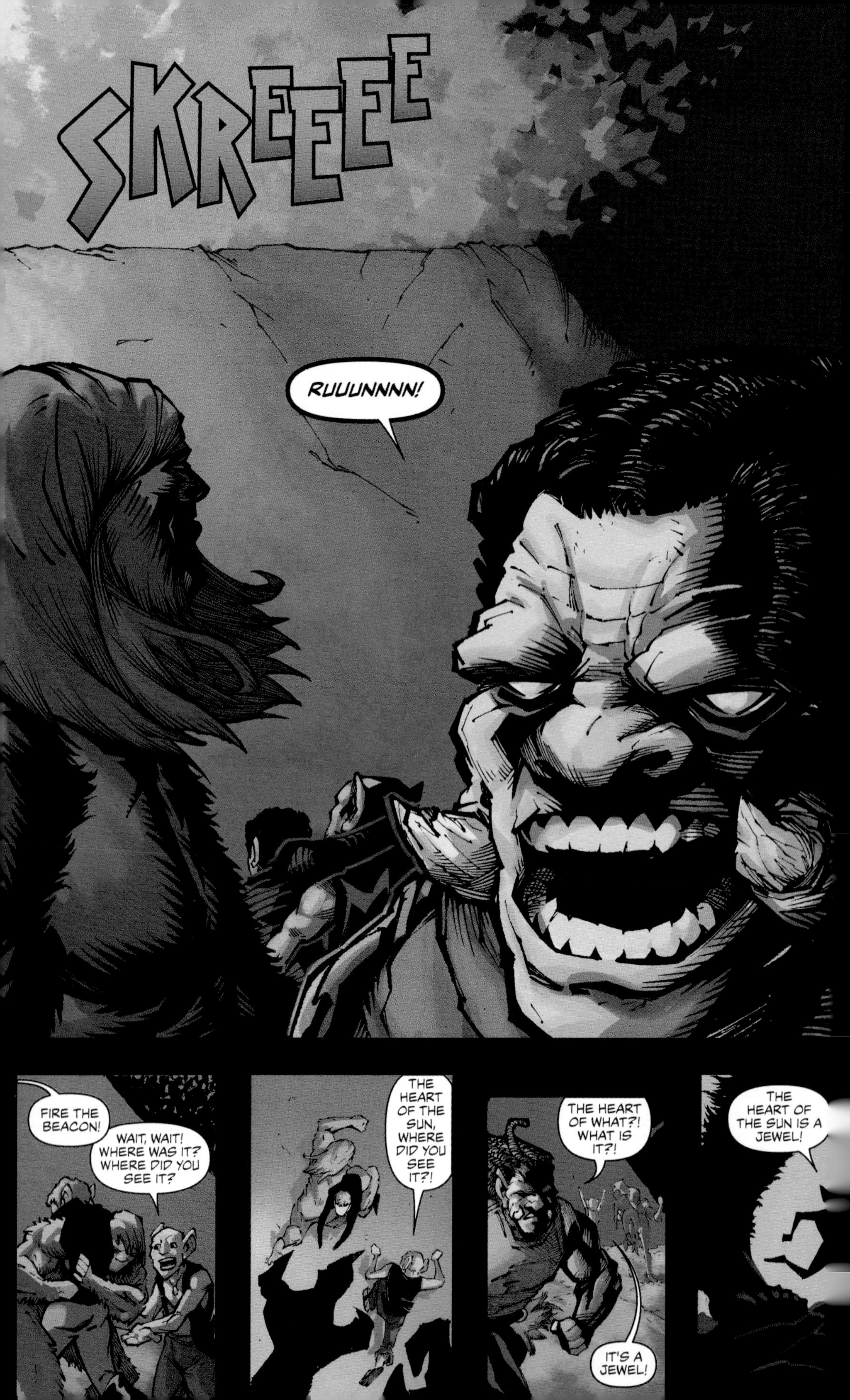
SKREEEE
RUUUNNNN!
FIRE THE BEACON!
WAIT, WAIT! WHERE WAS IT? WHERE DID YOU SEE IT?
THE HEART OF THE SUN, WHERE DID YOU SEE IT?!
THE HEART OF WHAT?! WHAT IS IT?!
IT'S A JEWEL!
THE HEART OF THE SUN IS A JEWEL!

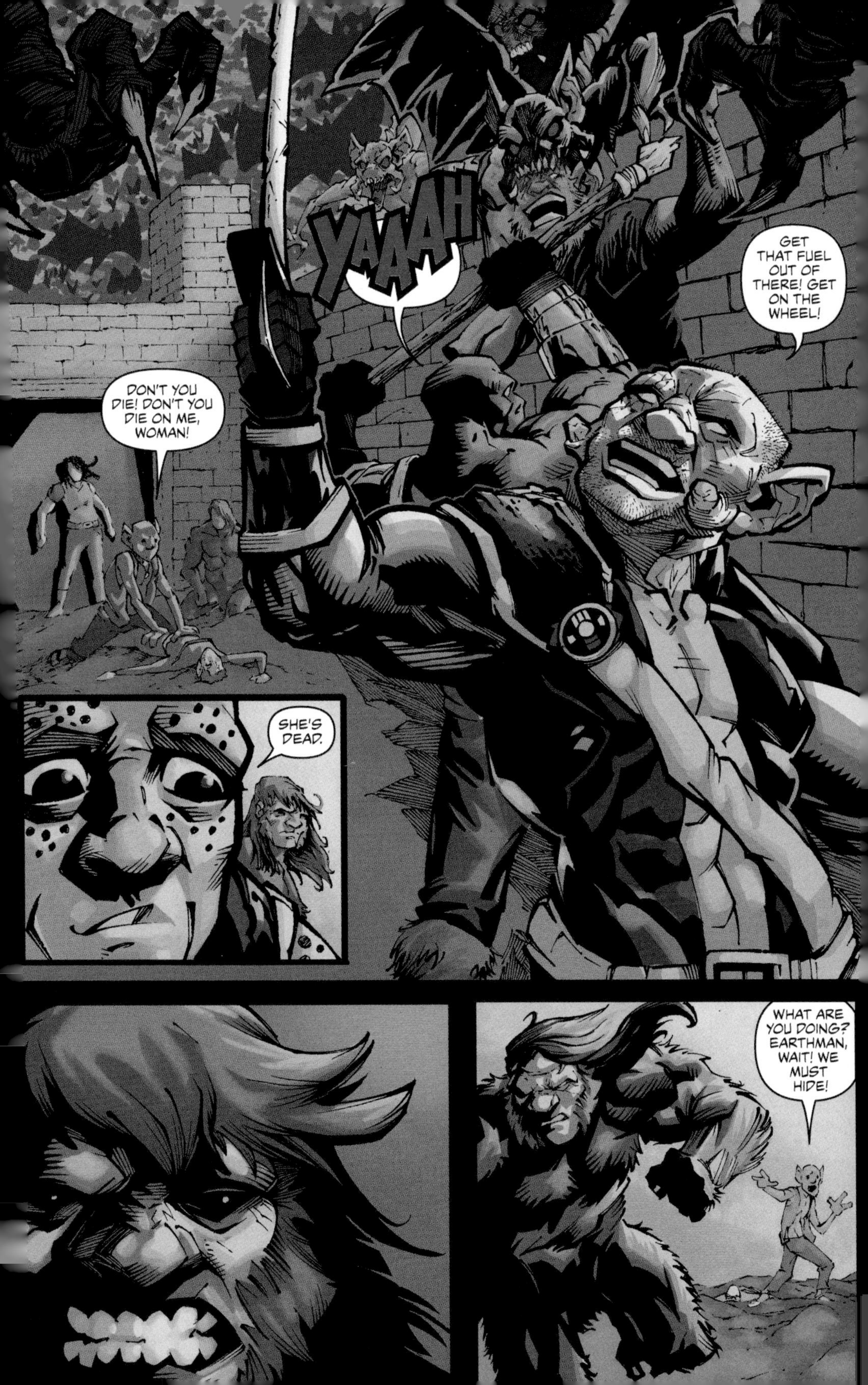
YAAAH
GET THAT FUEL OUT OF THERE! GET ON THE WHEEL!
DON'T YOU DIE! DON'T YOU DIE ON ME, WOMAN!
SHE'S DEAD.
WHAT ARE YOU DOING? EARTHMAN, WAIT! WE MUST HIDE!

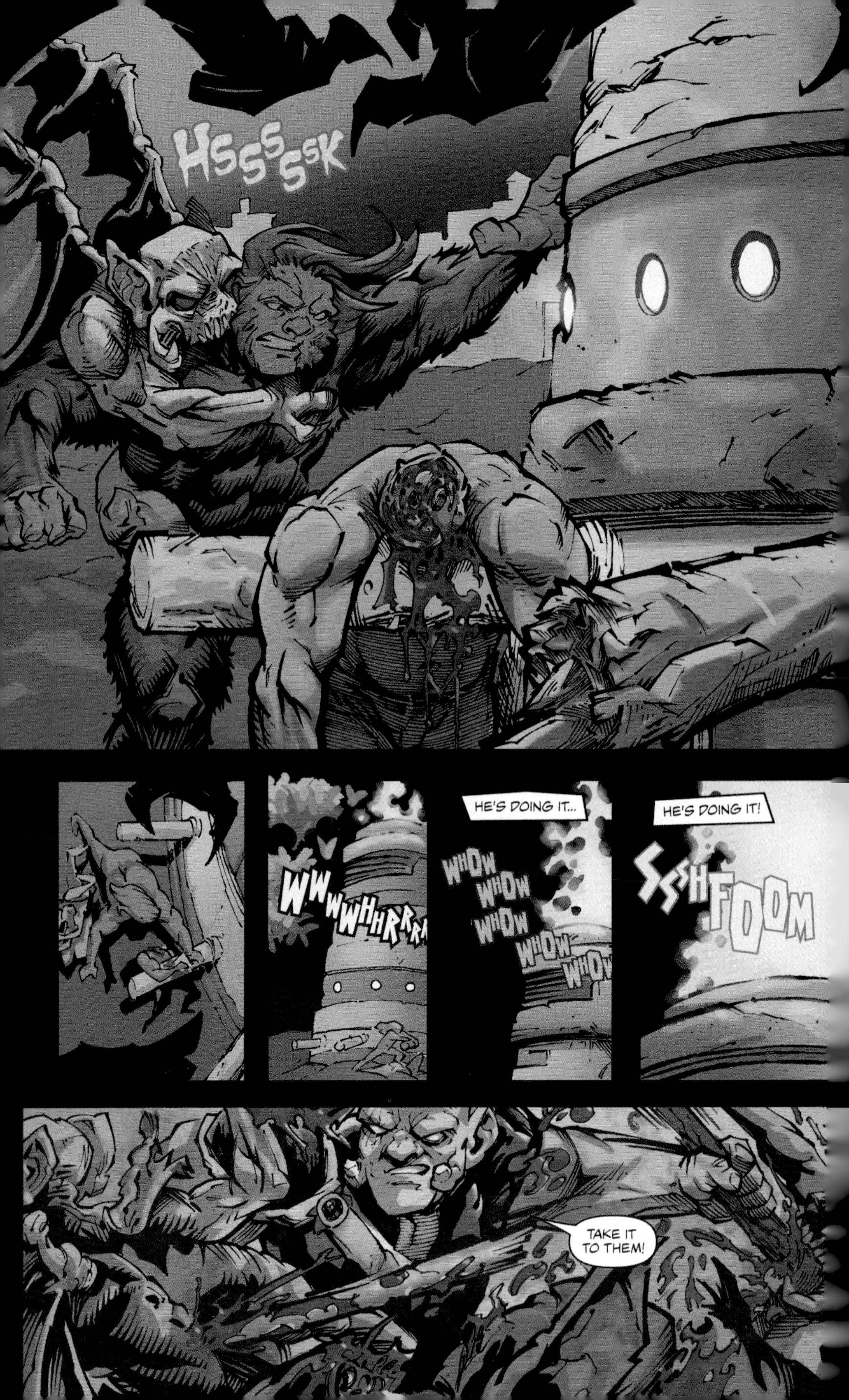
HSSSSSK
WWWWHHRRRR
HE'S DOING IT...
WHOW WHOW WHOW WHOW WHOW
HE'S DOING IT!
SSSHFOOM
TAKE IT TO THEM!

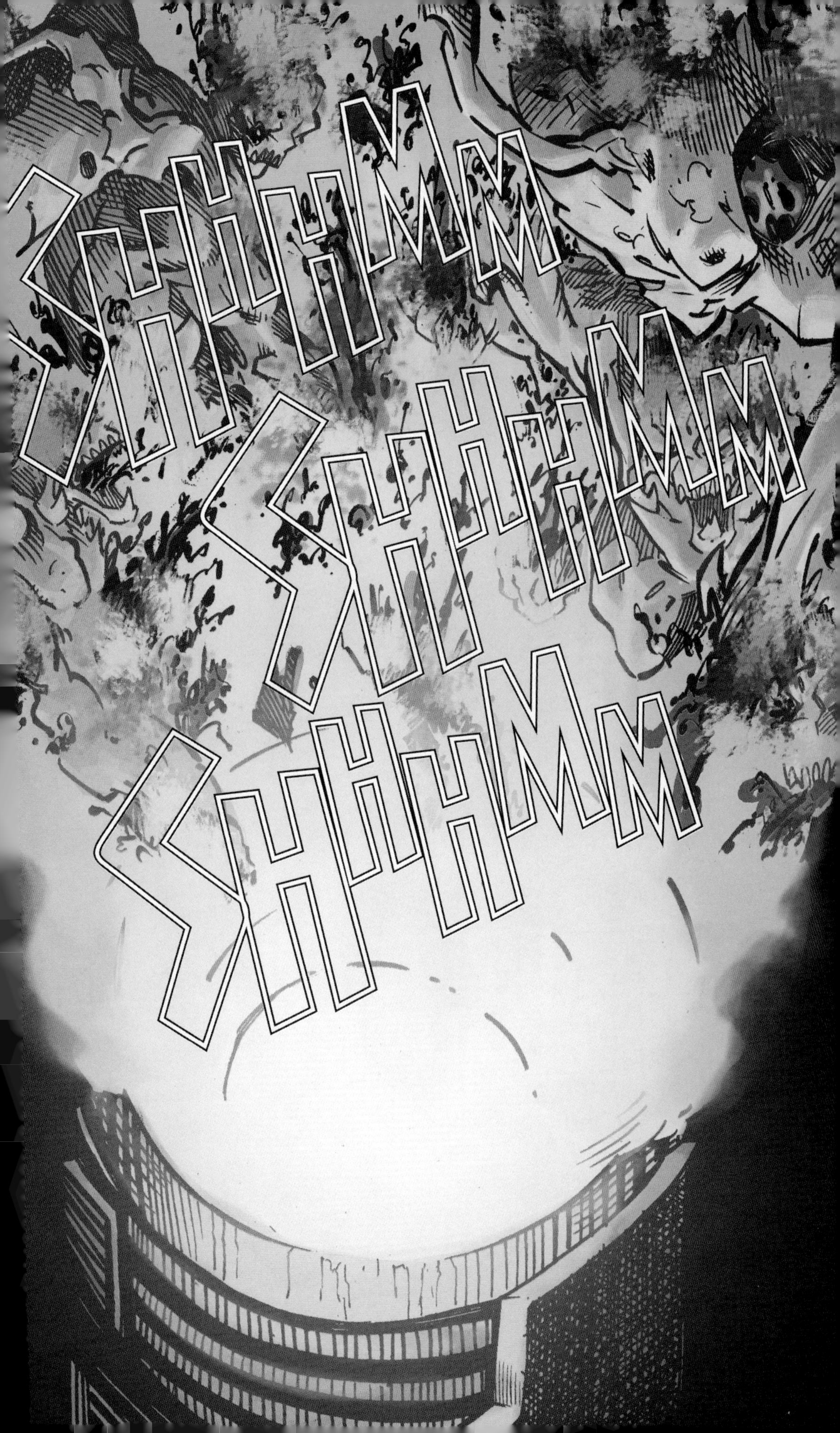
SHHHMMM
SHHHHMMM
SHHHHMMM

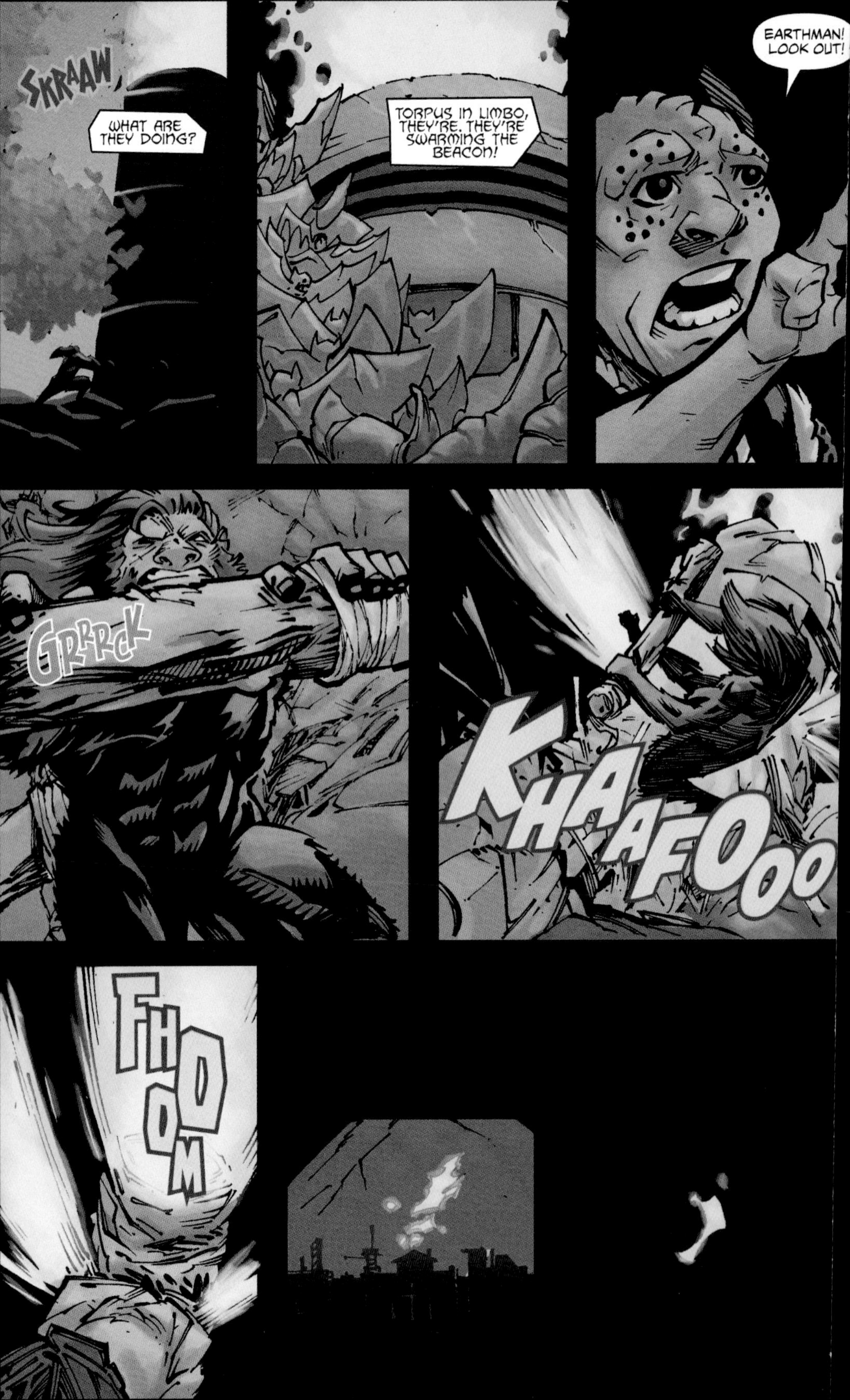

SKRAAW
WHAT ARE THEY DOING?
TORPUS IN LIMBO, THEY'RE. THEY'RE SWARMING THE BEACON!
EARTHMAN! LOOK OUT!
GRRRCK
KHAAFOOO
FHOOM

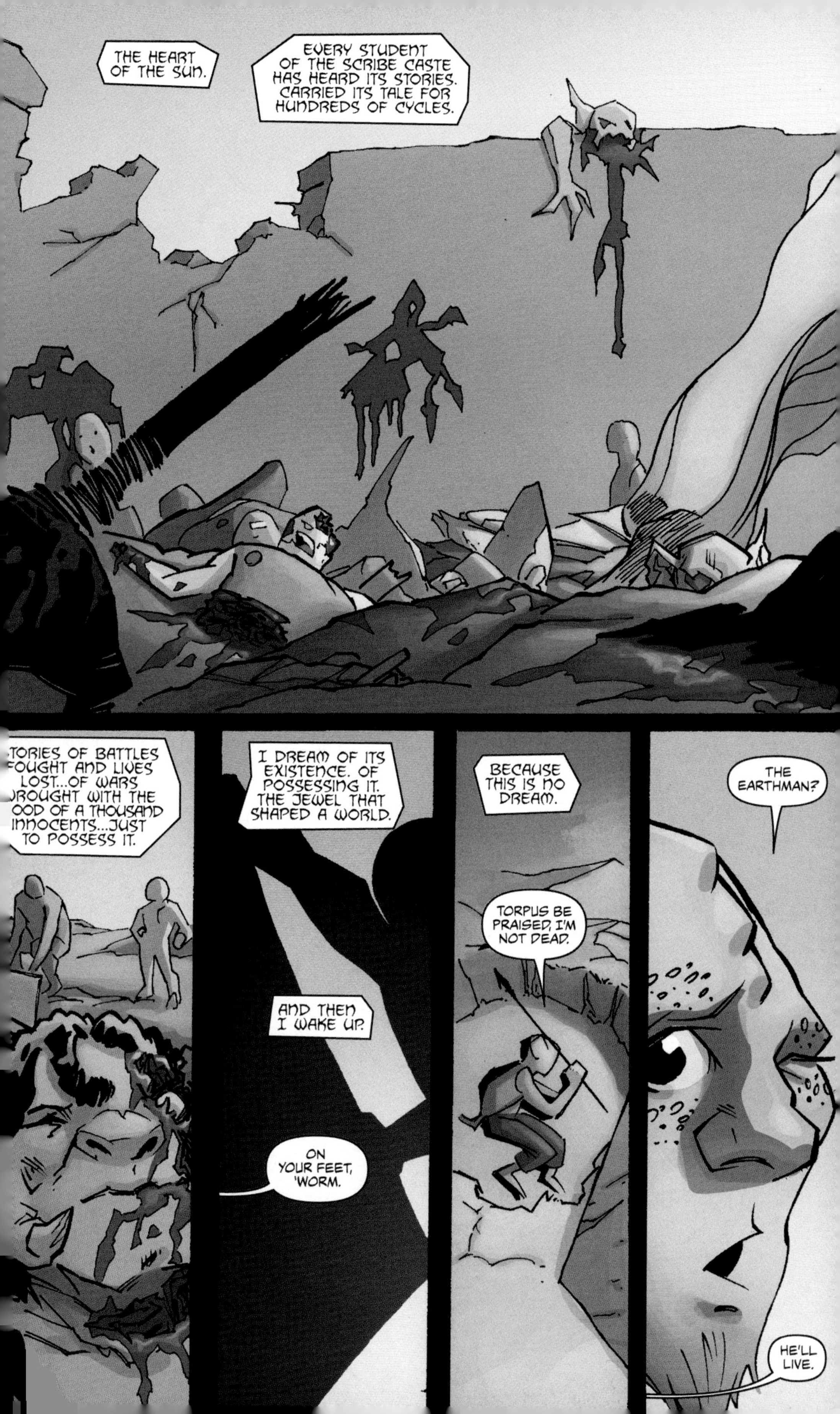
THE HEART OF THE SUN.
EVERY STUDENT OF THE SCRIBE CASTE HAS HEARD ITS STORIES. CARRIED ITS TALE FOR HUNDREDS OF CYCLES.
TORIES OF BATTLES FOUGHT AND LIVES LOST...OF WARS WROUGHT WITH THE OOD OF A THOUSAND INNOCENTS...JUST TO POSSESS IT.
I DREAM OF ITS EXISTENCE. OF POSSESSING IT. THE JEWEL THAT SHAPED A WORLD.
AND THEN I WAKE UP.
ON YOUR FEET, 'WORM.
BECAUSE THIS IS NO DREAM.
TORPUS BE PRAISED, I'M NOT DEAD.
THE EARTHMAN?
HE'LL LIVE.

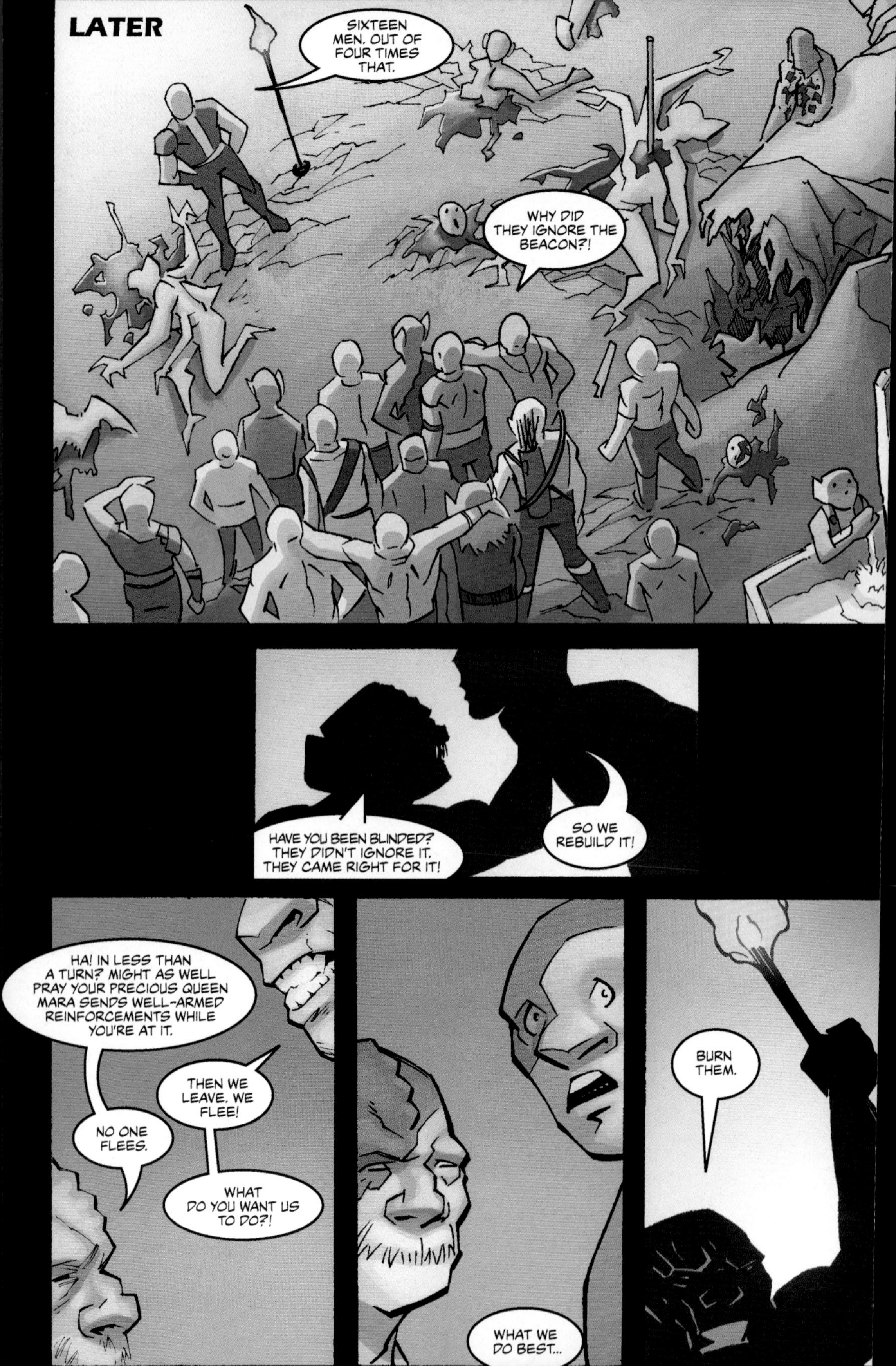
LATER
SIXTEEN MEN. OUT OF FOUR TIMES THAT.
WHY DID THEY IGNORE THE BEACON?!
HAVE YOU BEEN BLINDED? THEY DIDN'T IGNORE IT. THEY CAME RIGHT FOR IT!
SO WE REBUILD IT!
HA! IN LESS THAN A TURN? MIGHT AS WELL PRAY YOUR PRECIOUS QUEEN MARA SENDS WELL-ARMED REINFORCEMENTS WHILE YOU'RE AT IT.
THEN WE LEAVE. WE FLEE!
NO ONE FLEES.
WHAT DO YOU WANT US TO DO?!
WHAT WE DO BEST...
BURN THEM.

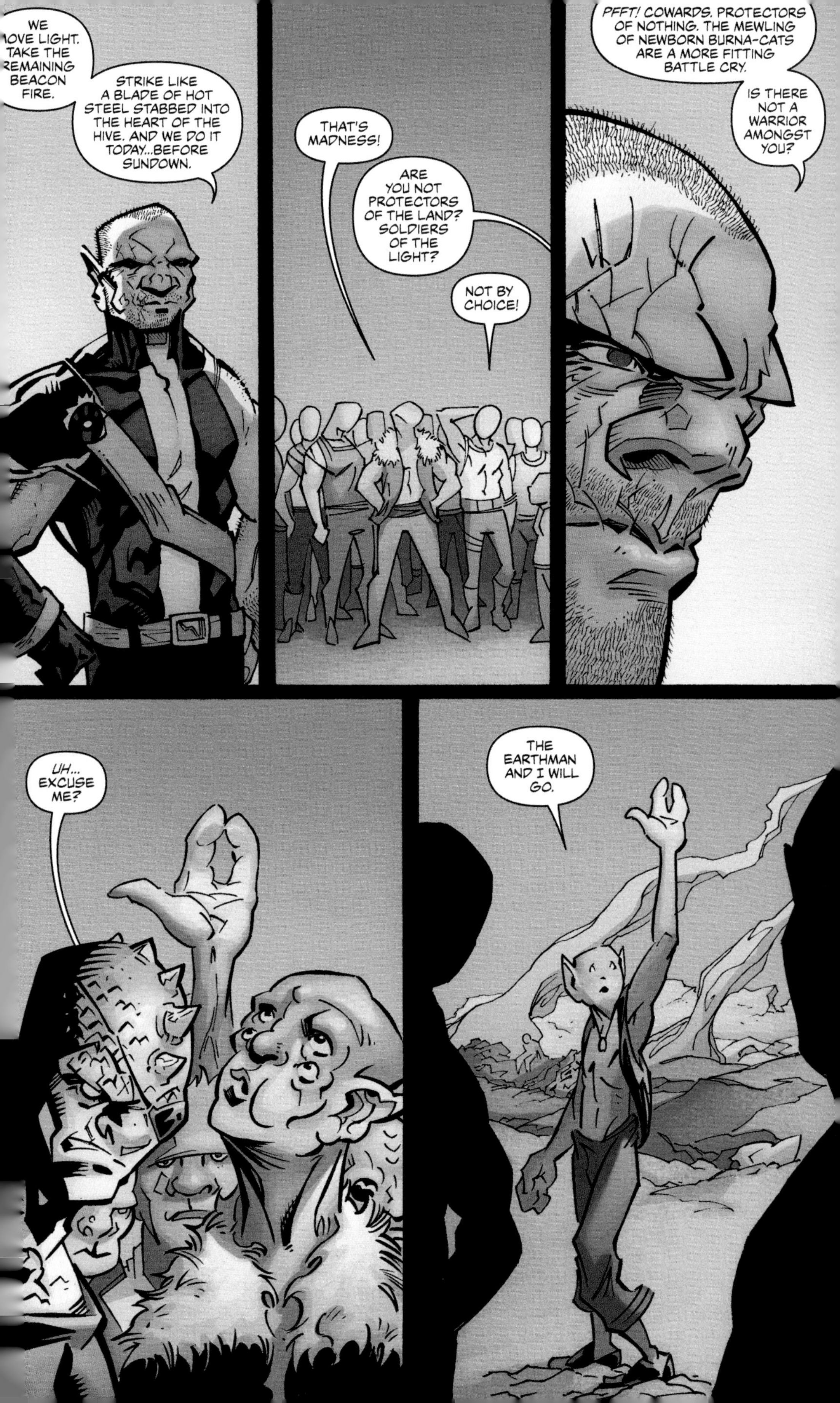
WE OVE LIGHT. TAKE THE REMAINING BEACON FIRE.
STRIKE LIKE A BLADE OF HOT STEEL STABBED INTO THE HEART OF THE HIVE. AND WE DO IT TODAY...BEFORE SUNDOWN.
THAT'S MADNESS!
NOT BY CHOICE!
ARE YOU NOT PROTECTORS OF THE LAND? SOLDIERS OF THE LIGHT?
PFFT! COWARDS. PROTECTORS OF NOTHING. THE MEWLING OF NEWBORN BURNA-CATS ARE A MORE FITTING BATTLE CRY.
IS THERE NOT A WARRIOR AMONGST YOU?
UH... EXCUSE ME?
THE EARTHMAN AND I WILL GO.

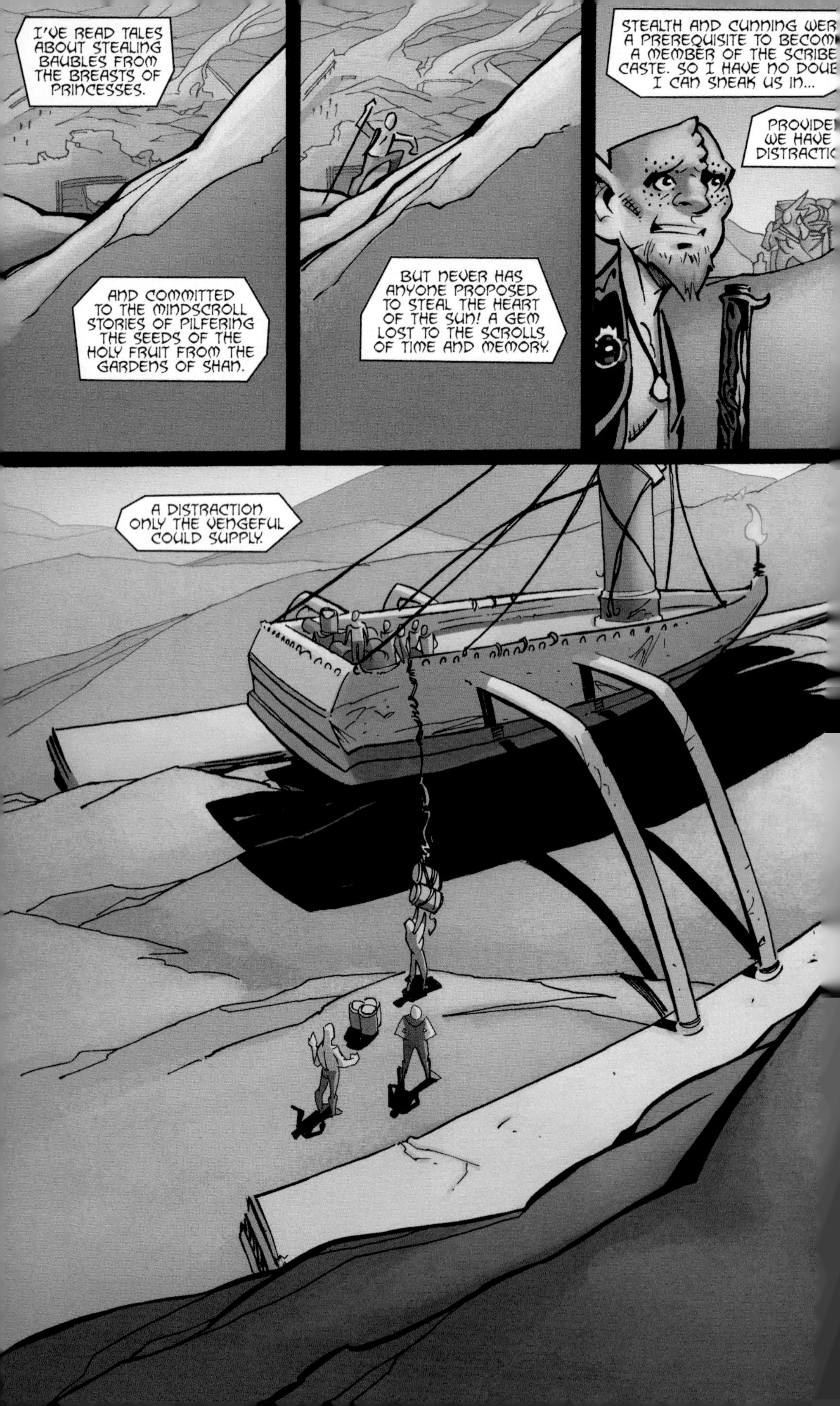
I'VE READ TALES ABOUT STEALING BAUBLES FROM THE BREASTS OF PRINCESSES.
AND COMMITTED TO THE MINDSCROLL STORIES OF PILFERING THE SEEDS OF THE HOLY FRUIT FROM THE GARDENS OF SHAN.
BUT NEVER HAS ANYONE PROPOSED TO STEAL THE HEART OF THE SUN! A GEM LOST TO THE SCROLLS OF TIME AND MEMORY.
STEALTH AND CUNNING WER A PREREQUISITE TO BECOM A MEMBER OF THE SCRIBE CASTE. SO I HAVE NO DOUB I CAN SNEAK US IN...
PROVIDE WE HAVE DISTRACTIO
A DISTRACTION ONLY THE VENGEFUL COULD SUPPLY.

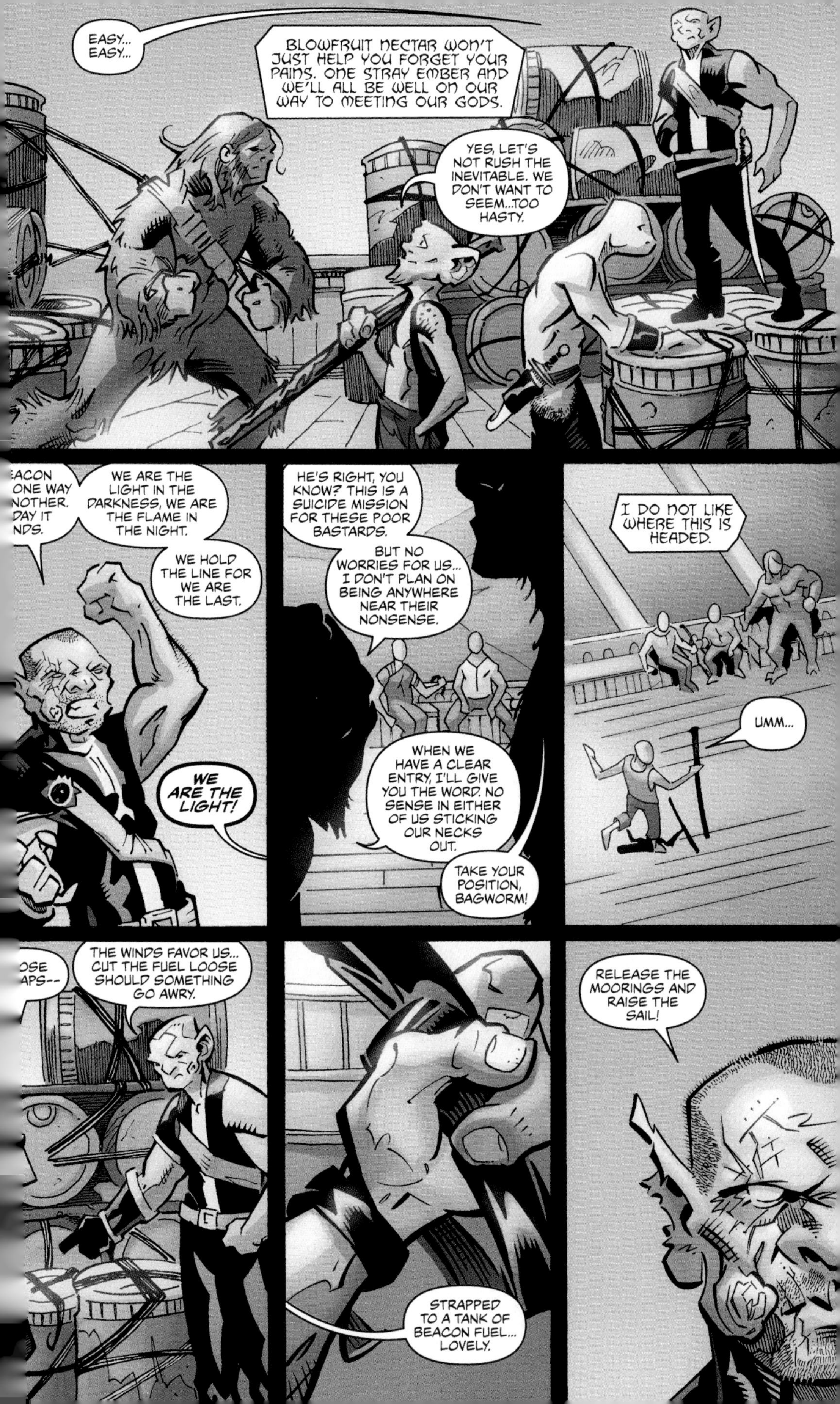
EASY... EASY...
BLOWFRUIT NECTAR WON'T JUST HELP YOU FORGET YOUR PAINS. ONE STRAY EMBER AND WE'LL ALL BE WELL ON OUR WAY TO MEETING OUR GODS.
YES, LET'S NOT RUSH THE INEVITABLE. WE DON'T WANT TO SEEM...TOO HASTY.
WE ARE THE LIGHT IN THE DARKNESS, WE ARE THE FLAME IN THE NIGHT.
WE HOLD THE LINE FOR WE ARE THE LAST.
WE ARE THE LIGHT!
HE'S RIGHT, YOU KNOW? THIS IS A SUICIDE MISSION FOR THESE POOR BASTARDS.
BUT NO WORRIES FOR US... I DON'T PLAN ON BEING ANYWHERE NEAR THEIR NONSENSE.
WHEN WE HAVE A CLEAR ENTRY, I'LL GIVE YOU THE WORD. NO SENSE IN EITHER OF US STICKING OUR NECKS OUT.
TAKE YOUR POSITION, BAGWORM!
I DO NOT LIKE WHERE THIS IS HEADED.
UMM...
THE WINDS FAVOR US... CUT THE FUEL LOOSE SHOULD SOMETHING GO AWRY.
STRAPPED TO A TANK OF BEACON FUEL... LOVELY.
RELEASE THE MOORINGS AND RAISE THE SAIL!

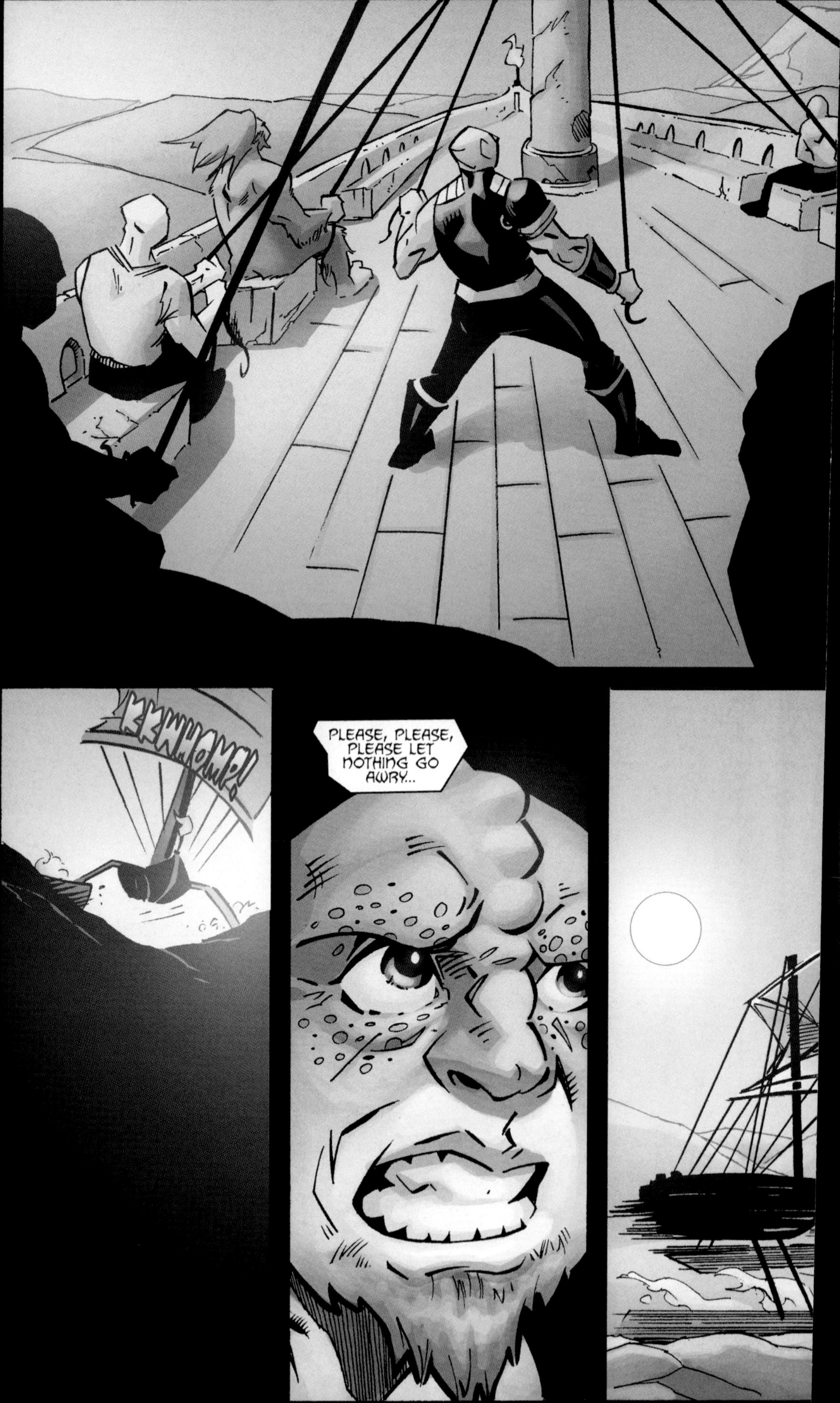
KKWHOMP!
PLEASE, PLEASE, PLEASE LET NOTHING GO AWRY...

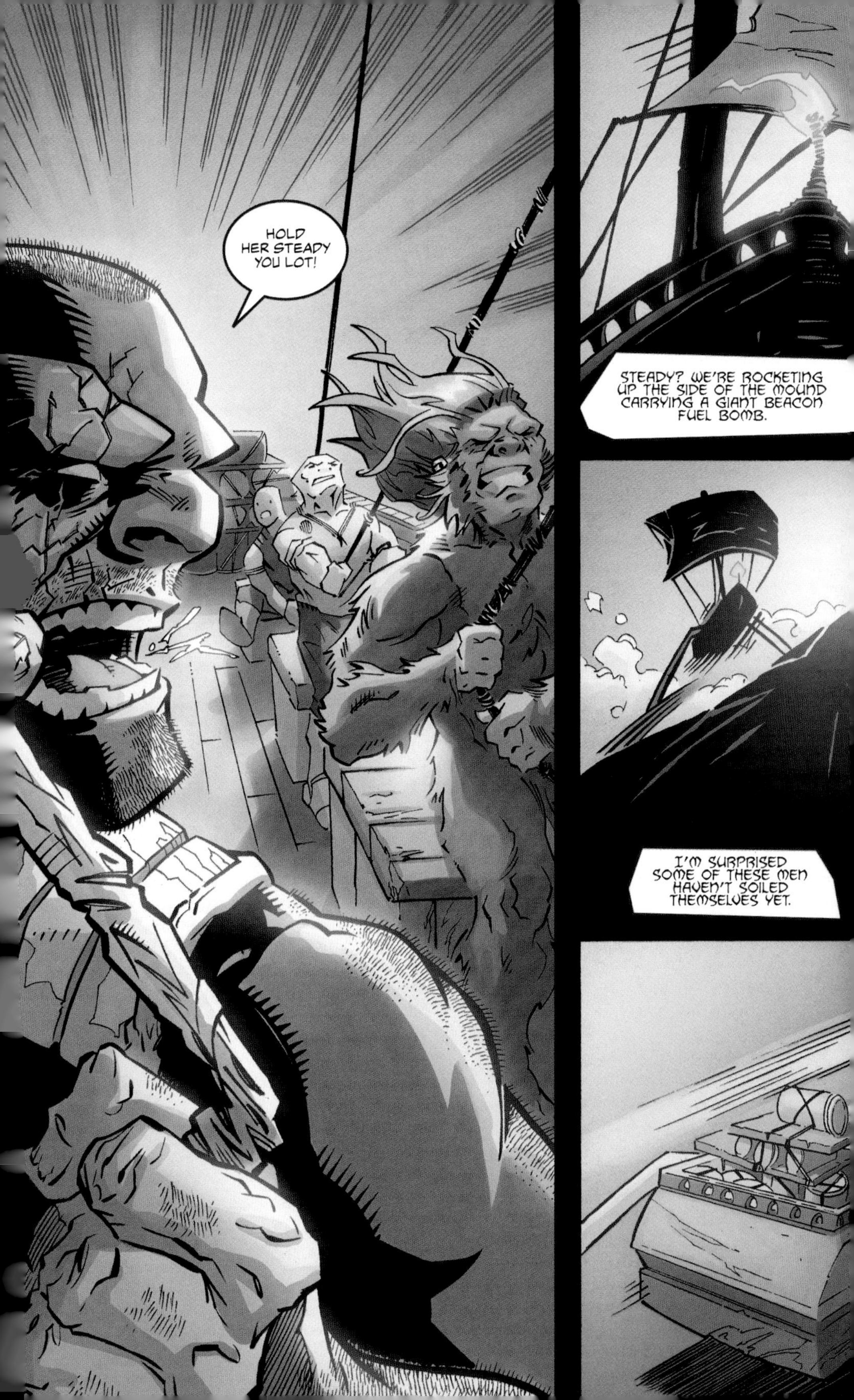
HOLD HER STEADY YOU LOT!
STEADY? WE'RE ROCKETING UP THE SIDE OF THE MOUND CARRYING A GIANT BEACON FUEL BOMB.
I'M SURPRISED SOME OF THESE MEN HAVEN'T SOILED THEMSELVES YET.

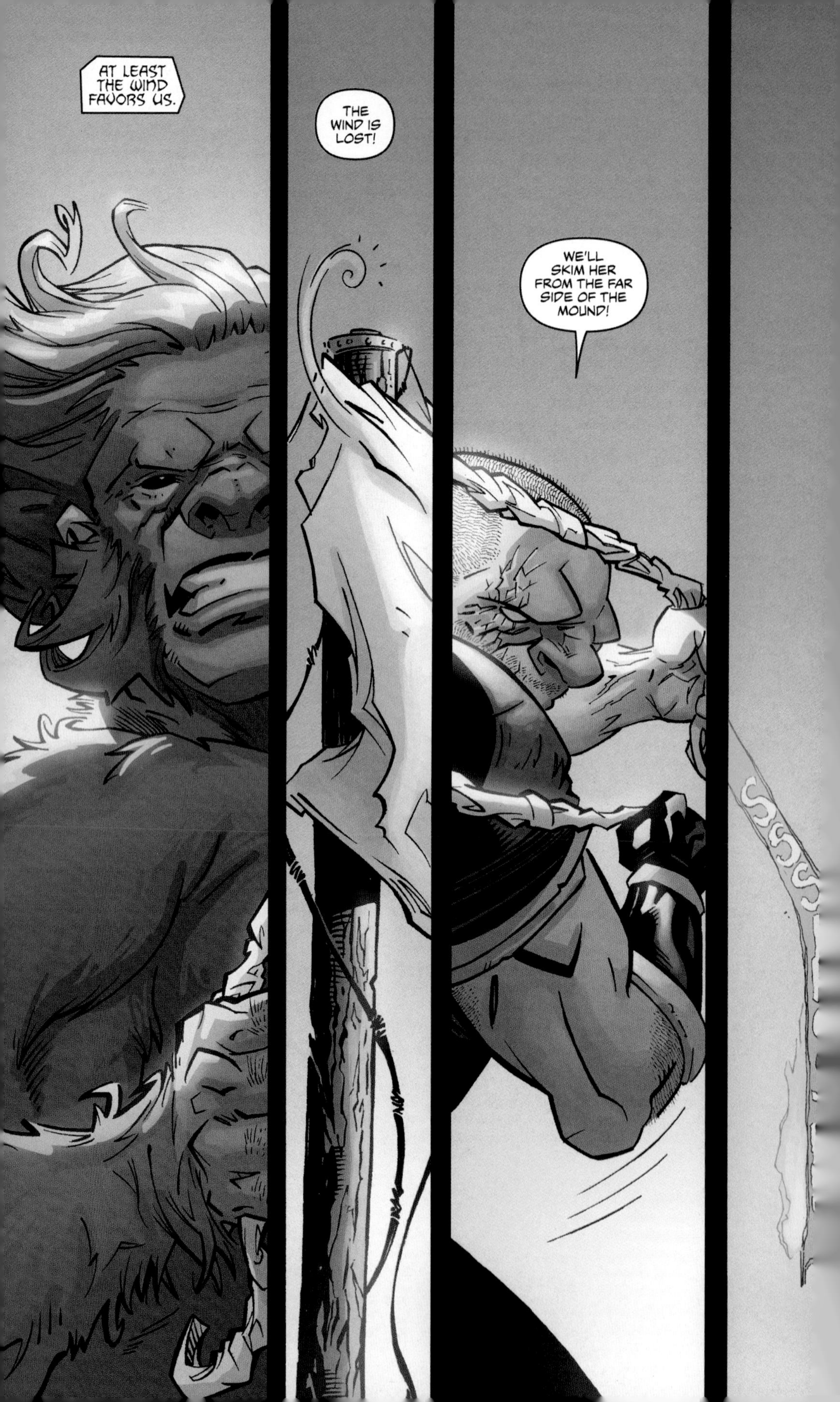
AT LEAST THE WIND FAVORS US.
THE WIND IS LOST!
WE'LL SKIM HER FROM THE FAR SIDE OF THE MOUND!

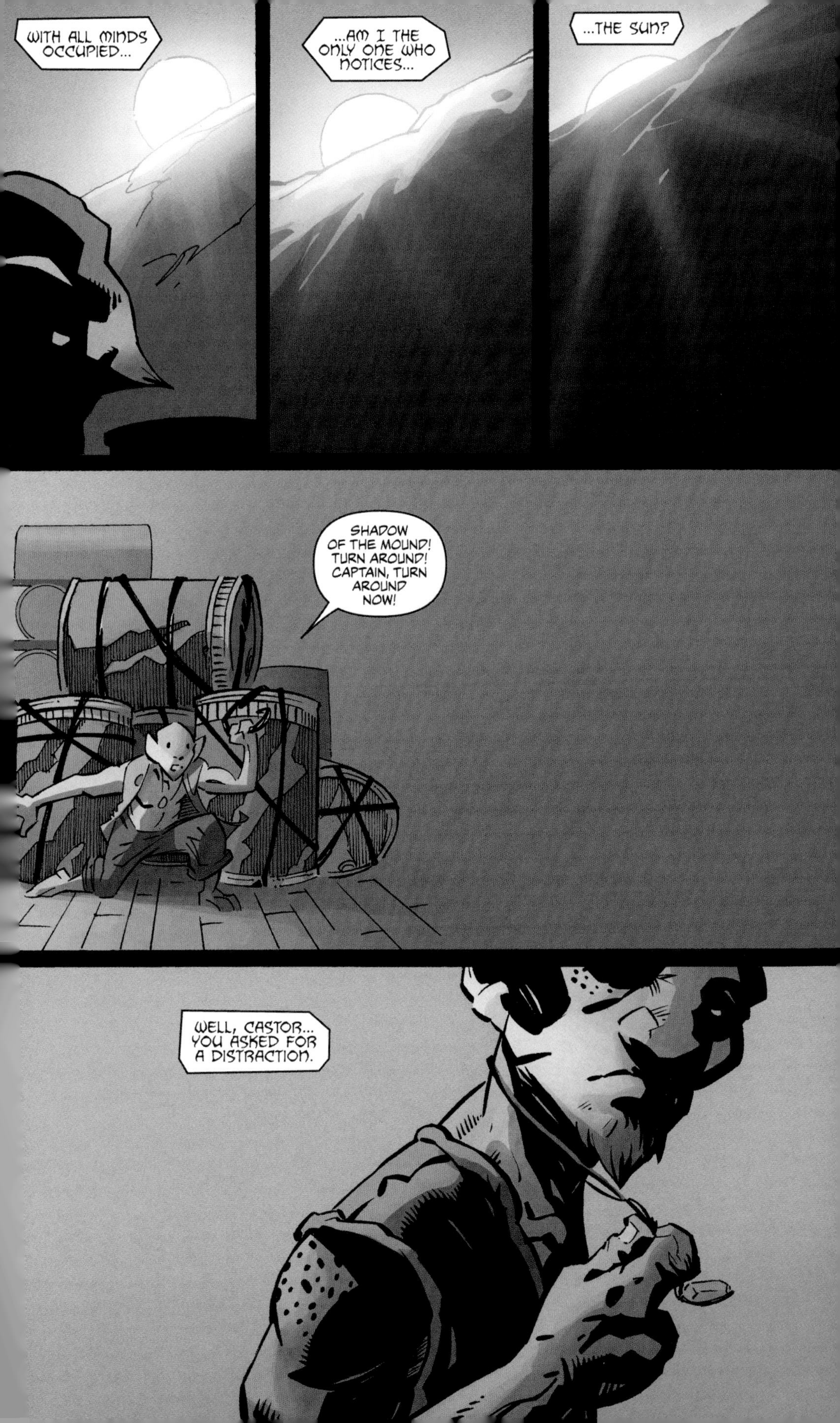
WITH ALL MINDS OCCUPIED...
...AM I THE ONLY ONE WHO NOTICES...
...THE SUN?
SHADOW OF THE MOUND! TURN AROUND! CAPTAIN, TURN AROUND NOW!
WELL, CASTOR... YOU ASKED FOR A DISTRACTION.

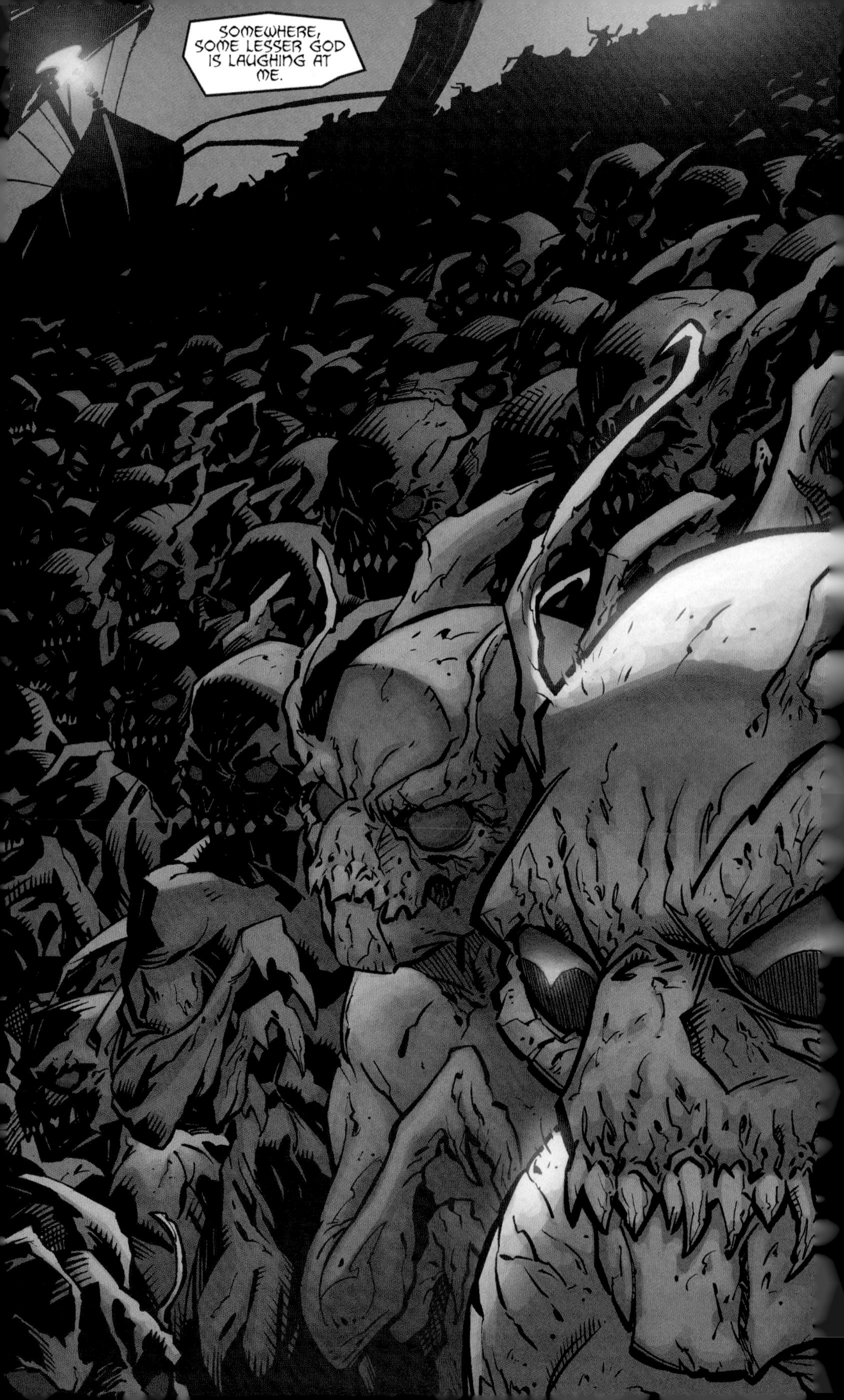
SOMEWHERE, SOME LESSER GOD IS LAUGHING AT ME.

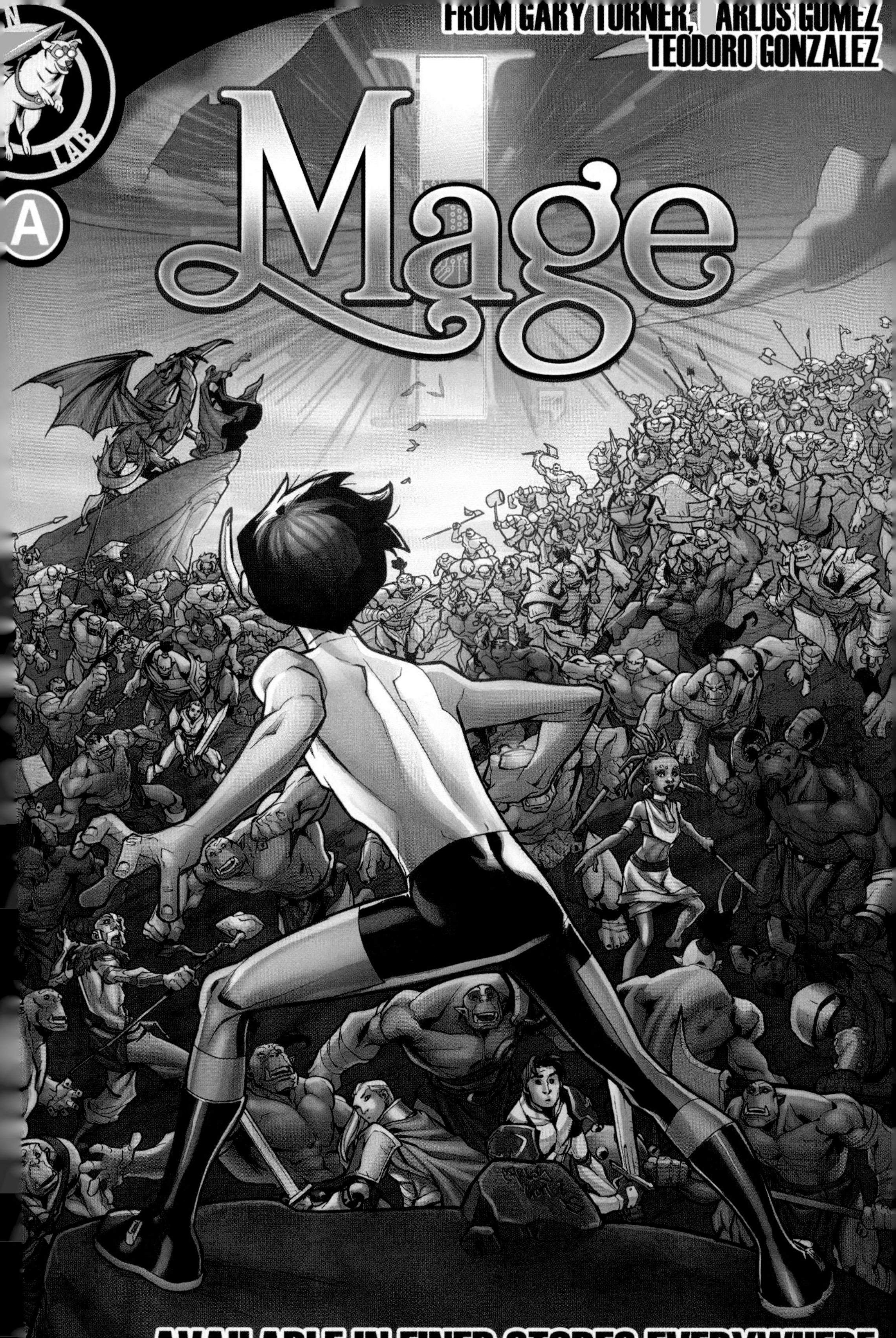
FROM GARY TURNER, ARLOS GOMEZ
TEODORO GONZALEZ
LAB
A
Mage
AVAILABLE IN FINER STORES EVERYWHERE

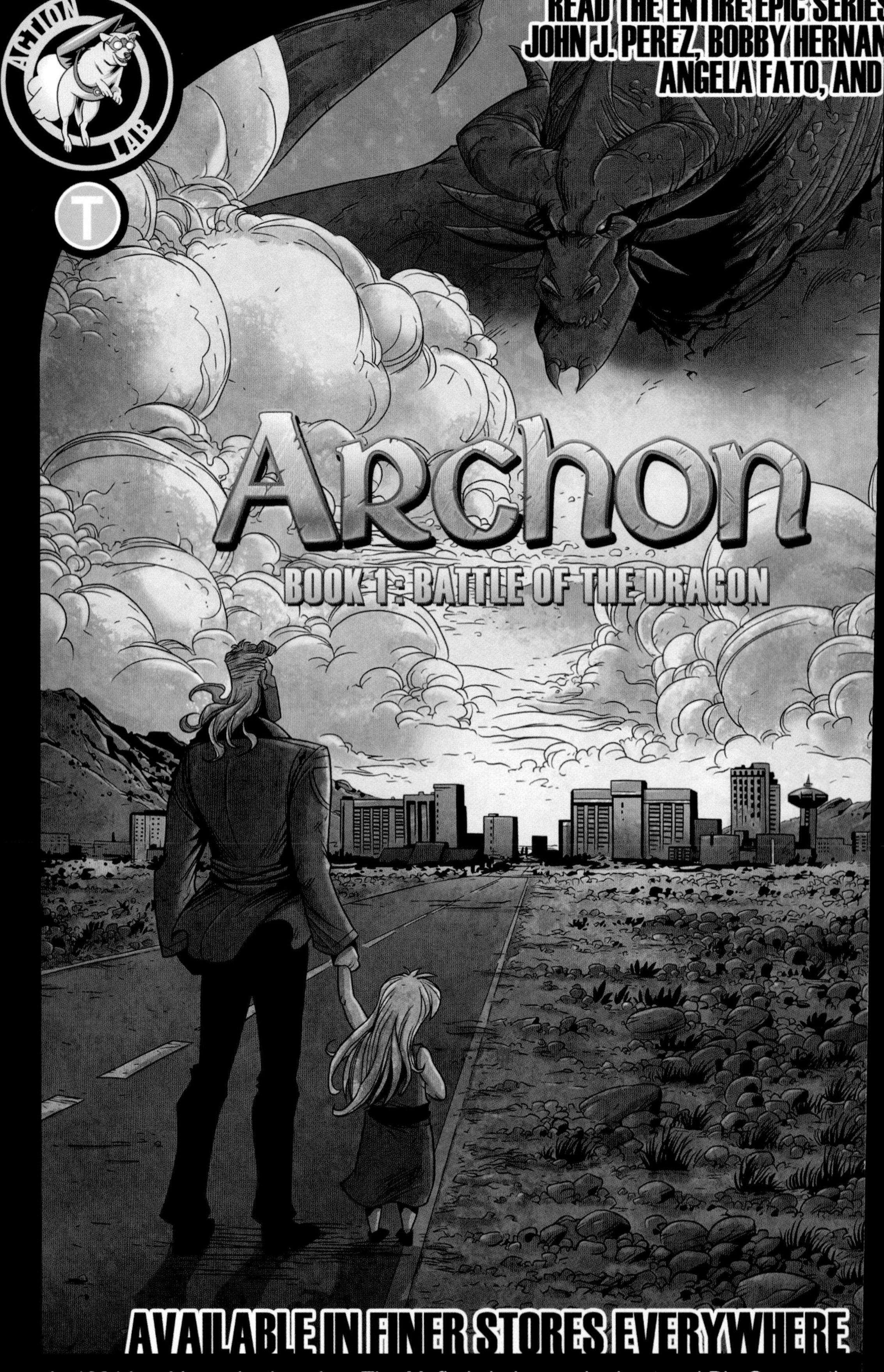
ACTION LAB
T
READ THE ENTIRE EPIC SERIES
JOHN J. PEREZ, BOBBY HERNAN
ANGELA FATO, AND
Archon
BOOK 1: BATTLE OF THE DRAGON
AVAILABLE IN FINER STORES EVERYWHERE

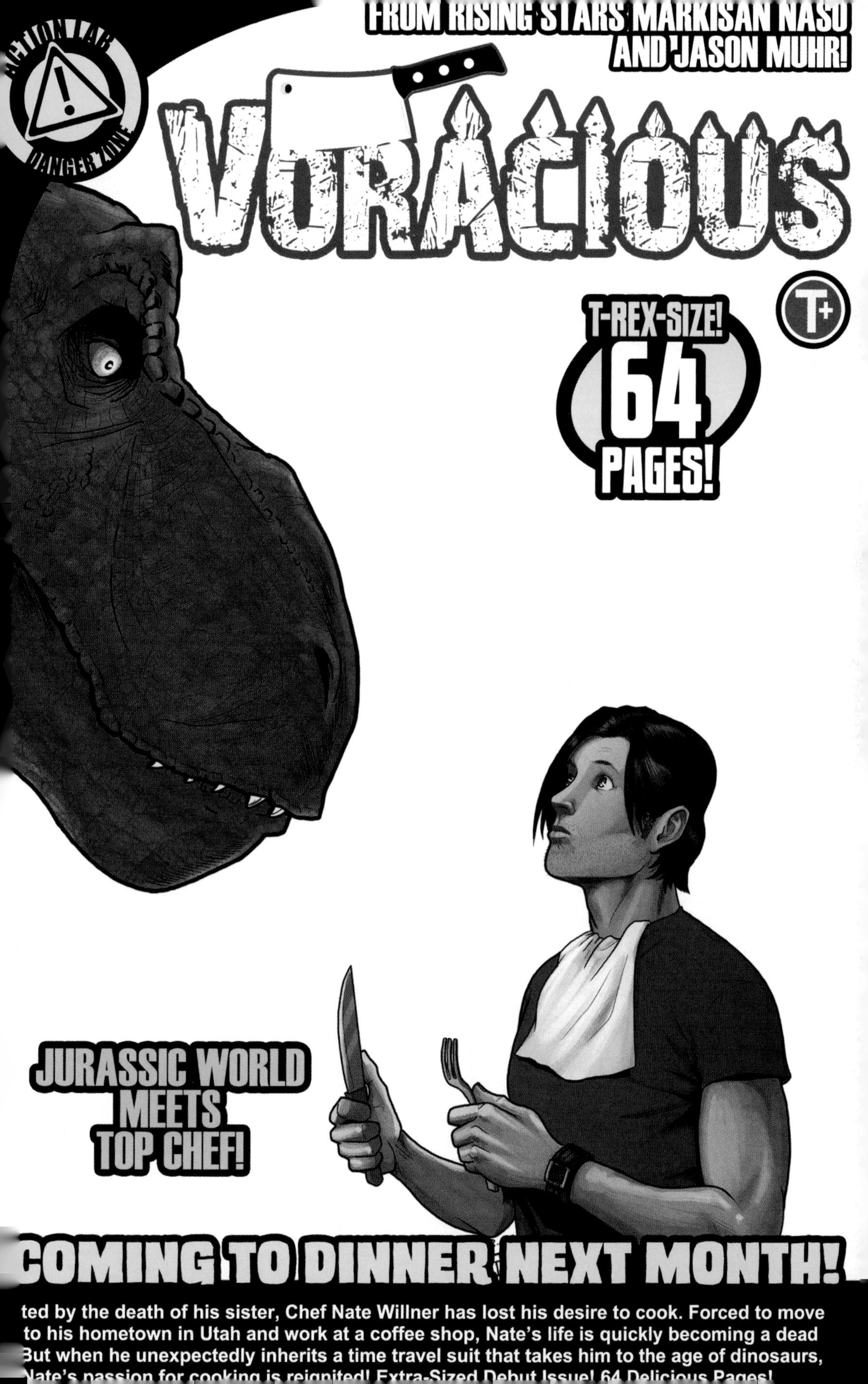
FROM RISING STARS MARKISAN NASO AND JASON MUHR!
ACTION LAB
DANGER ZONE
VORACIOUS
T+
T-REX-SIZE! 64 PAGES!
JURASSIC WORLD MEETS TOP CHEF!
COMING TO DINNER NEXT MONTH!
ted by the death of his sister, Chef Nate Willner has lost his desire to cook. Forced to move
to his hometown in Utah and work at a coffee shop, Nate's life is quickly becoming a dead
But when he unexpectedly inherits a time travel suit that takes him to the age of dinosaurs,
Nate's passion for cooking is reignited! Extra-Sized Debut Issue! 64 Delicious Pages!

THE CASK OF MONTILLECADO

Bigfoot: Sword Of The Earthman - Action Lab
www.actionlabcomics.com

00211

7 02382 69116 5

ACTIONLABCOMICS.COM

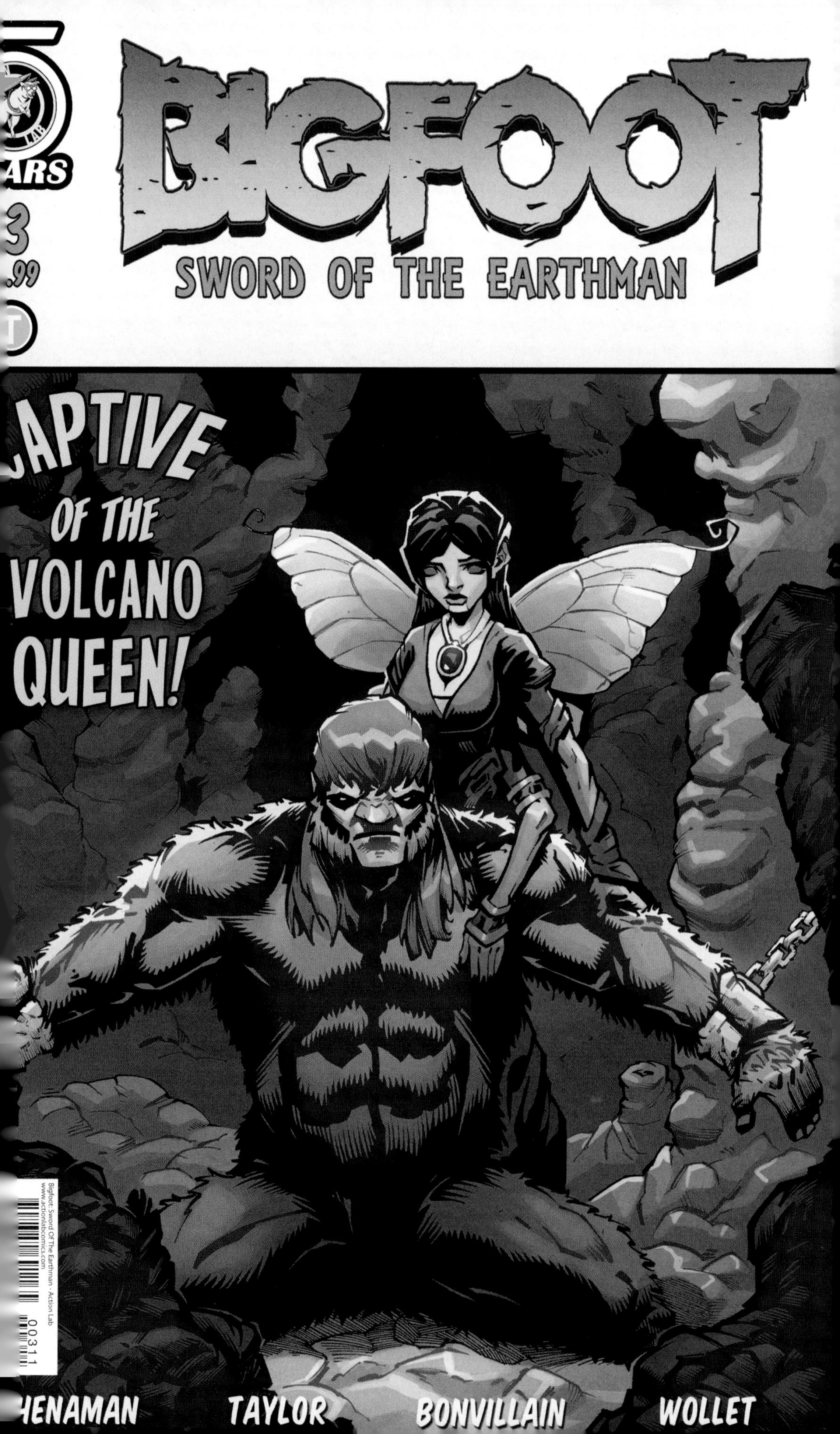
ARS
3
.99
BIGFOOT
SWORD OF THE EARTHMAN
APTIVE OF THE VOLCANO QUEEN!
Bigfoot: Sword Of The Earthman - Action Lab
www.actionlabcomics.com
00311
HENAMAN
TAYLOR
BONVILLAIN
WOLLET

FOR A THOUSAND CYCLES,
IT EXISTED ONLY IN RUMOR.

A CHILD'S BAUBLE...
A CITY'S POWER...
OR A MADMAN'S TREASURE...

IT WAS MANY THINGS IN MANY TALES.
THE SOURCE OF ALL KNOWLEDGE.
AND THE CURSE OF A PRINCESS.

IT WAS THE JEWEL THAT SHAPED THE WORLD

THE HEART OF THE SUN.

THOUSANDS WOULD DIE TO POSSESS IT.
KINGDOMS WERE BURIED TO DESTROY IT

BUT NO ONE HAD EVER TRIED TO STEAL IT

NO ONE, EXCEPT...

BIGFOOT
SWORD OF THE EARTHMAN

Bryan Seaton: Publisher • Kevin Freeman: President • Dave Dwonch: Creative Director • Shawn Gabborin: Editor In
Jamal Igle: Vice-President of Marketing • Vito Delsante: Director of Marketing • Jim Dietz: Social Media Direc
Nicole DAndria: Script Editor • Chad Cicconi: Black Sheep • Colleen Boyd: Submissions Editor

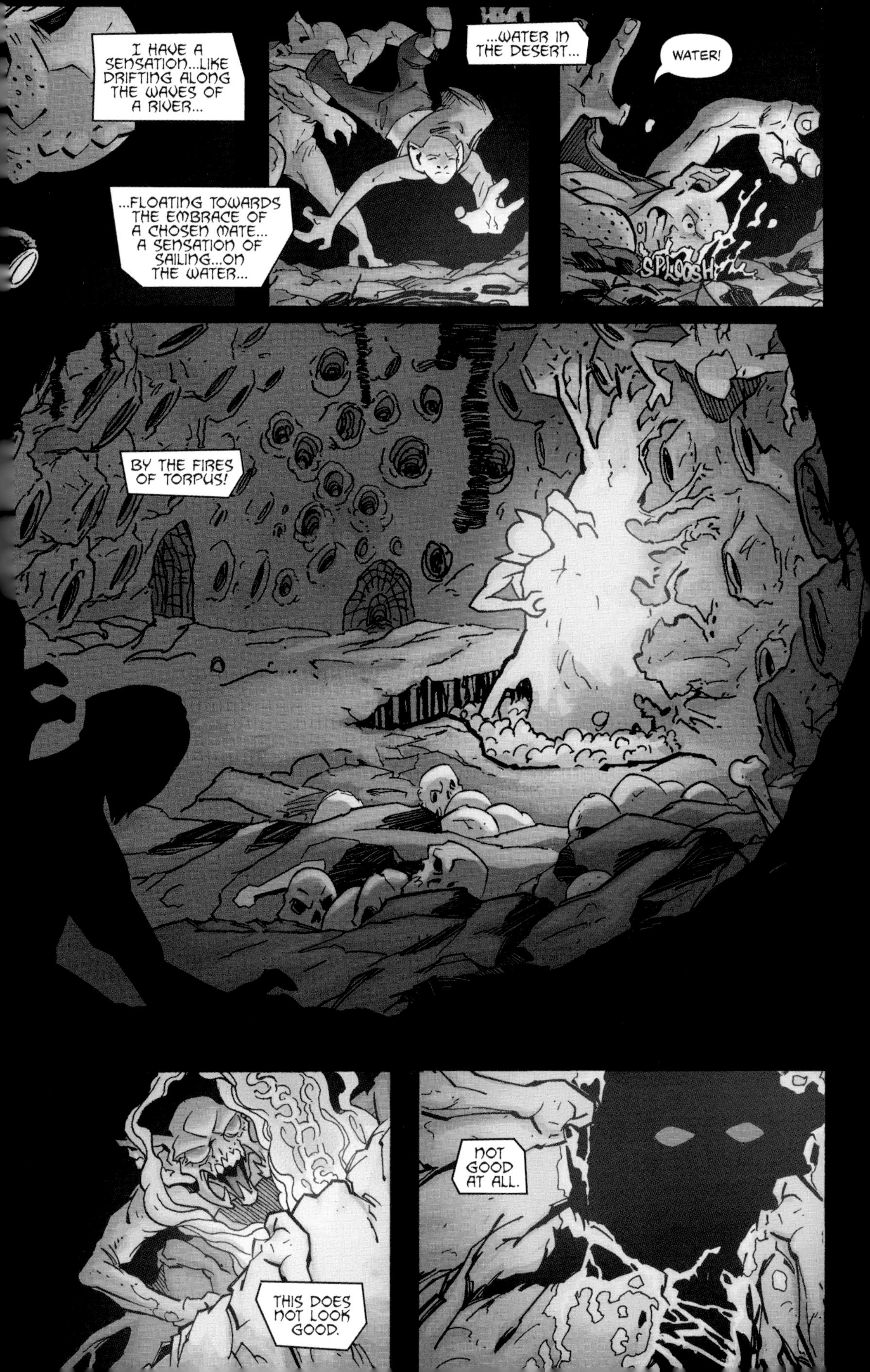
I HAVE A SENSATION...LIKE DRIFTING ALONG THE WAVES OF A RIVER...
...FLOATING TOWARDS THE EMBRACE OF A CHOSEN MATE... A SENSATION OF SAILING...ON THE WATER...
...WATER IN THE DESERT...
WATER!
SPLOOSH
BY THE FIRES OF TORPUS!
THIS DOES NOT LOOK GOOD.
NOT GOOD AT ALL.

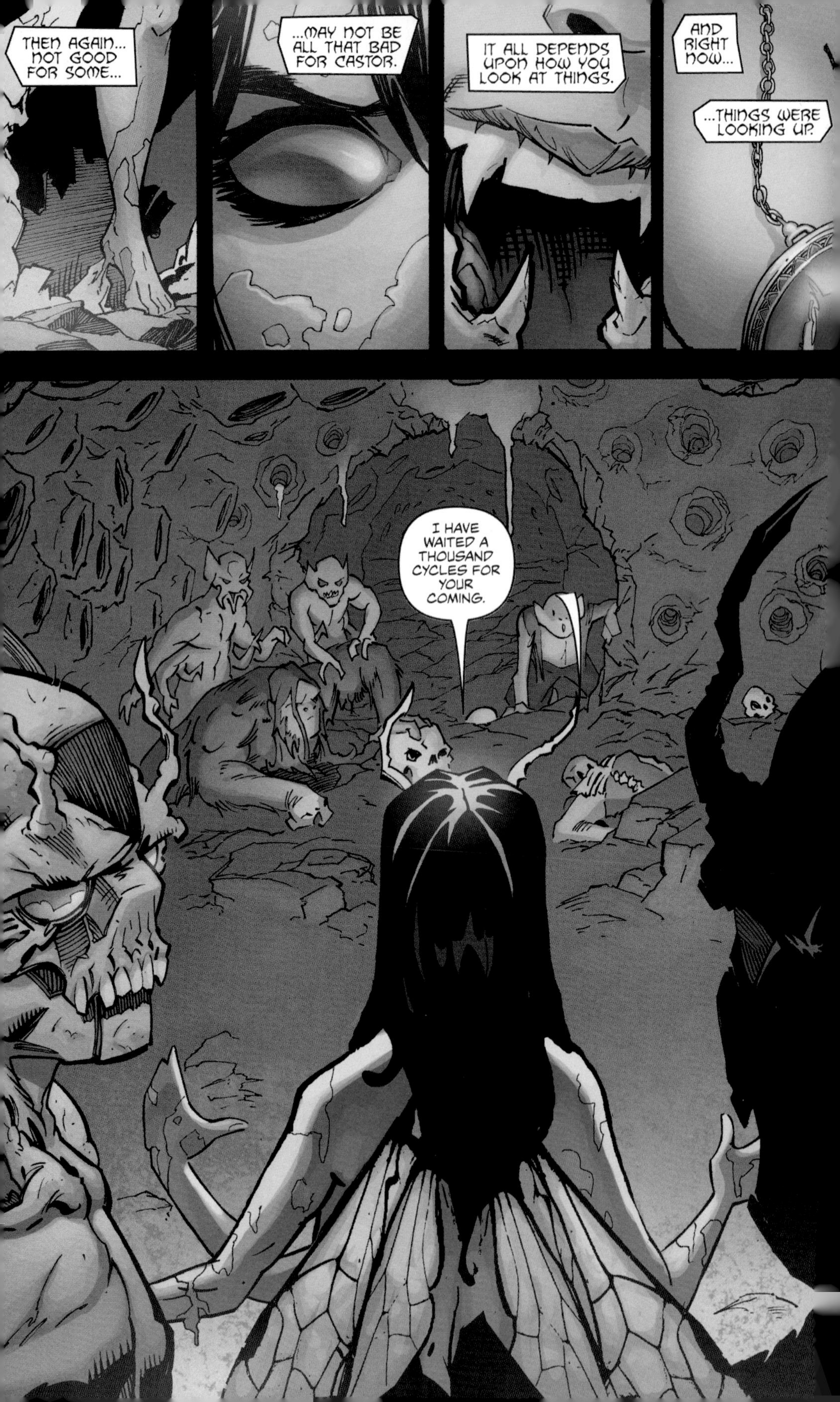
THEN AGAIN... NOT GOOD FOR SOME...
...MAY NOT BE ALL THAT BAD FOR CASTOR.
IT ALL DEPENDS UPON HOW YOU LOOK AT THINGS.
AND RIGHT NOW...
...THINGS WERE LOOKING UP.
I HAVE WAITED A THOUSAND CYCLES FOR YOUR COMING.

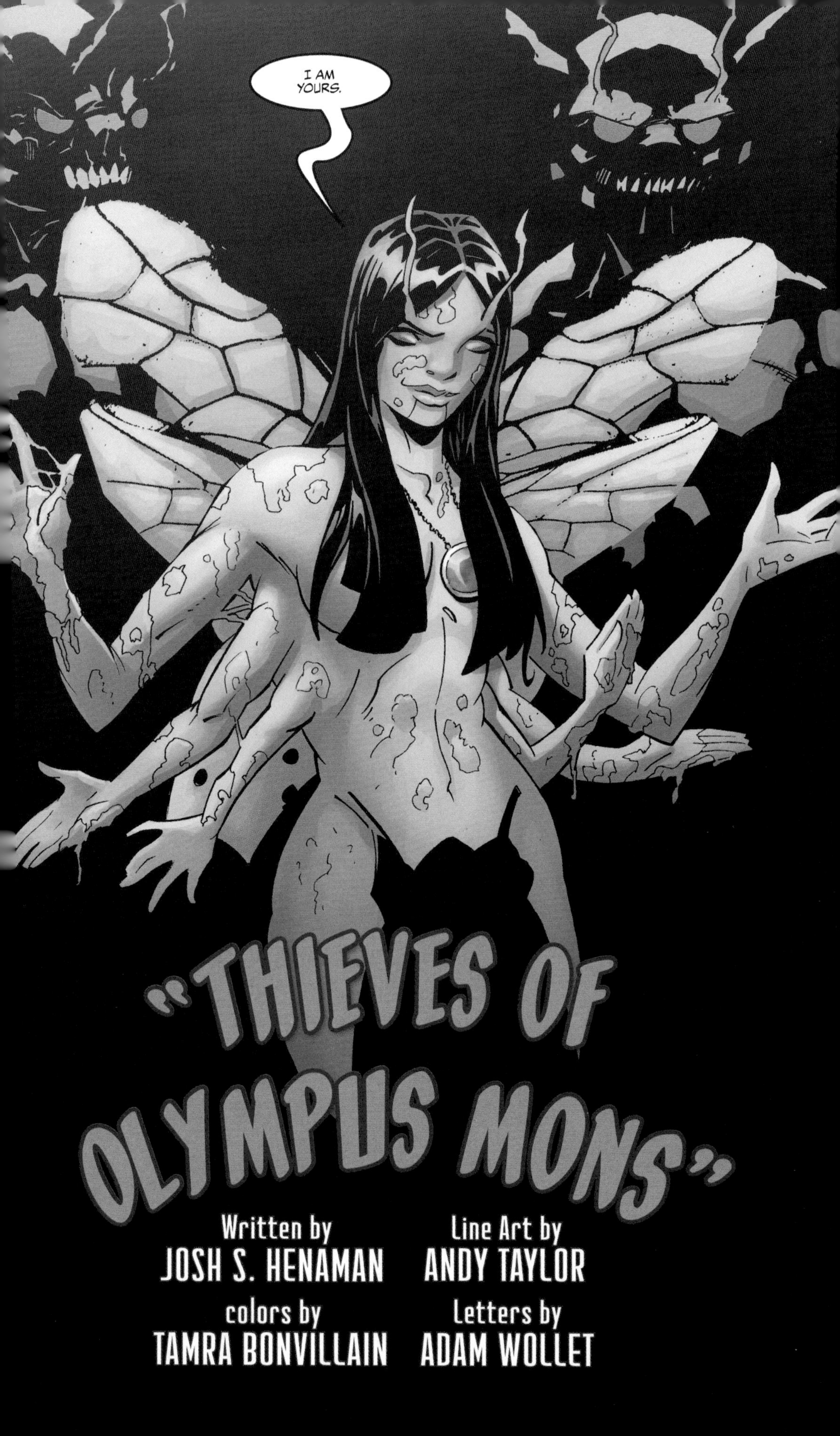
I AM YOURS.
"THIEVES OF OLYMPUS MONS"
Written by JOSH S. HENAMAN
Line Art by ANDY TAYLOR
colors by TAMRA BONVILLAIN
Letters by ADAM WOLLET

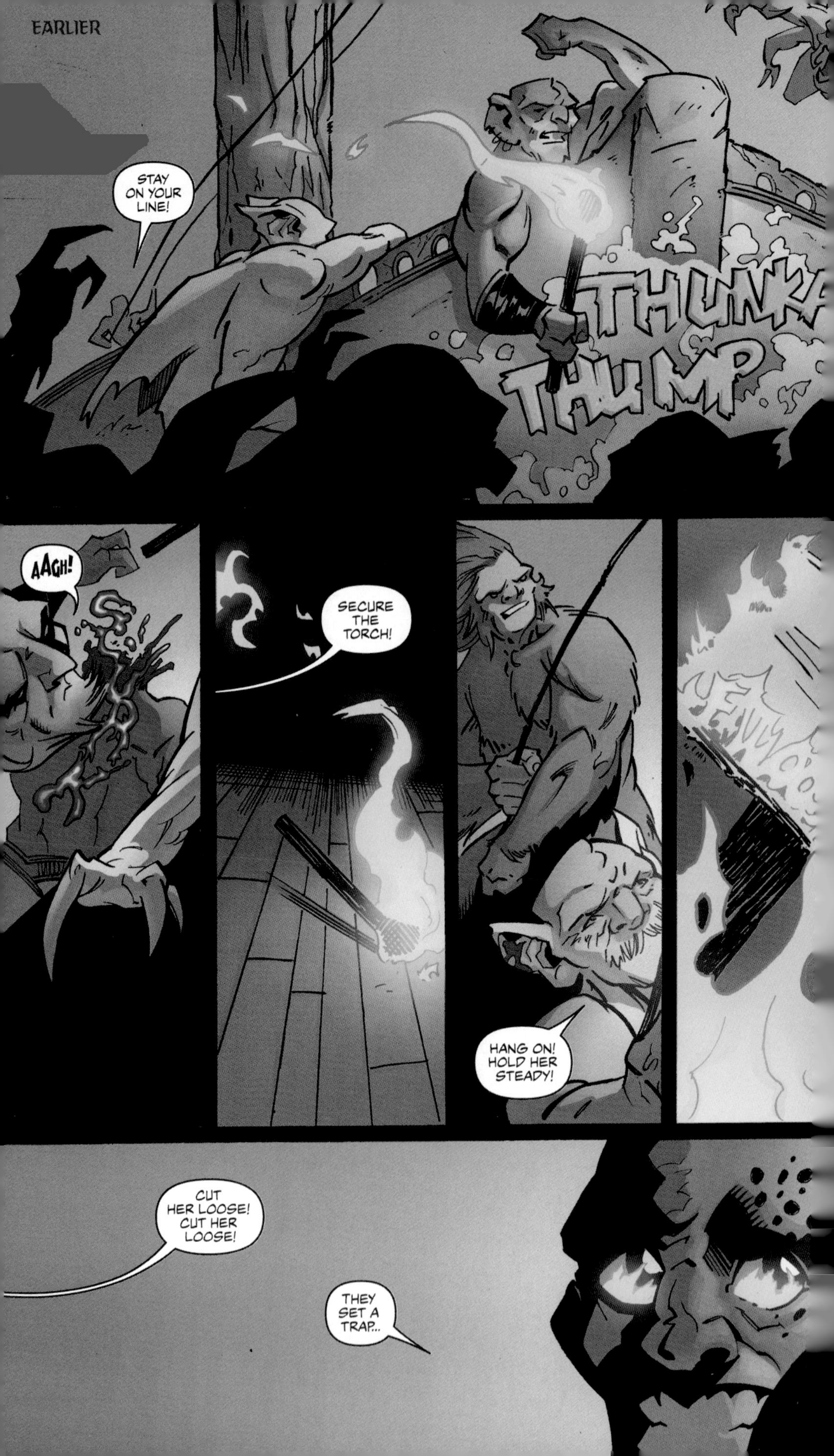
EARLIER
STAY ON YOUR LINE!
THUNK
THUMP
AAGH!
SECURE THE TORCH!
HANG ON! HOLD HER STEADY!
CUT HER LOOSE! CUT HER LOOSE!
THEY SET A TRAP...

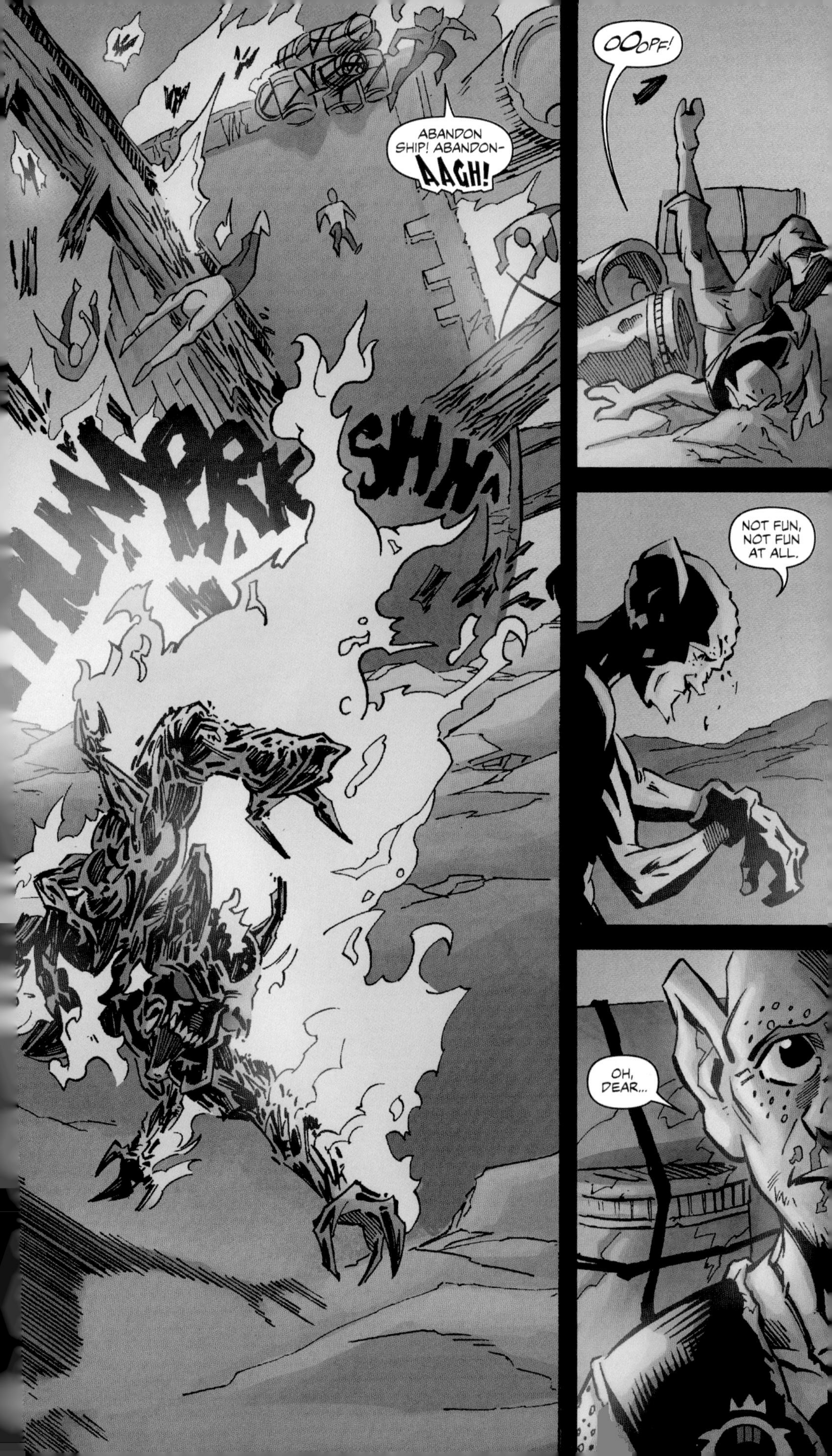
ABANDON SHIP! ABANDON-
AAGH!
OOOPF!
NOT FUN, NOT FUN AT ALL.
OH, DEAR...

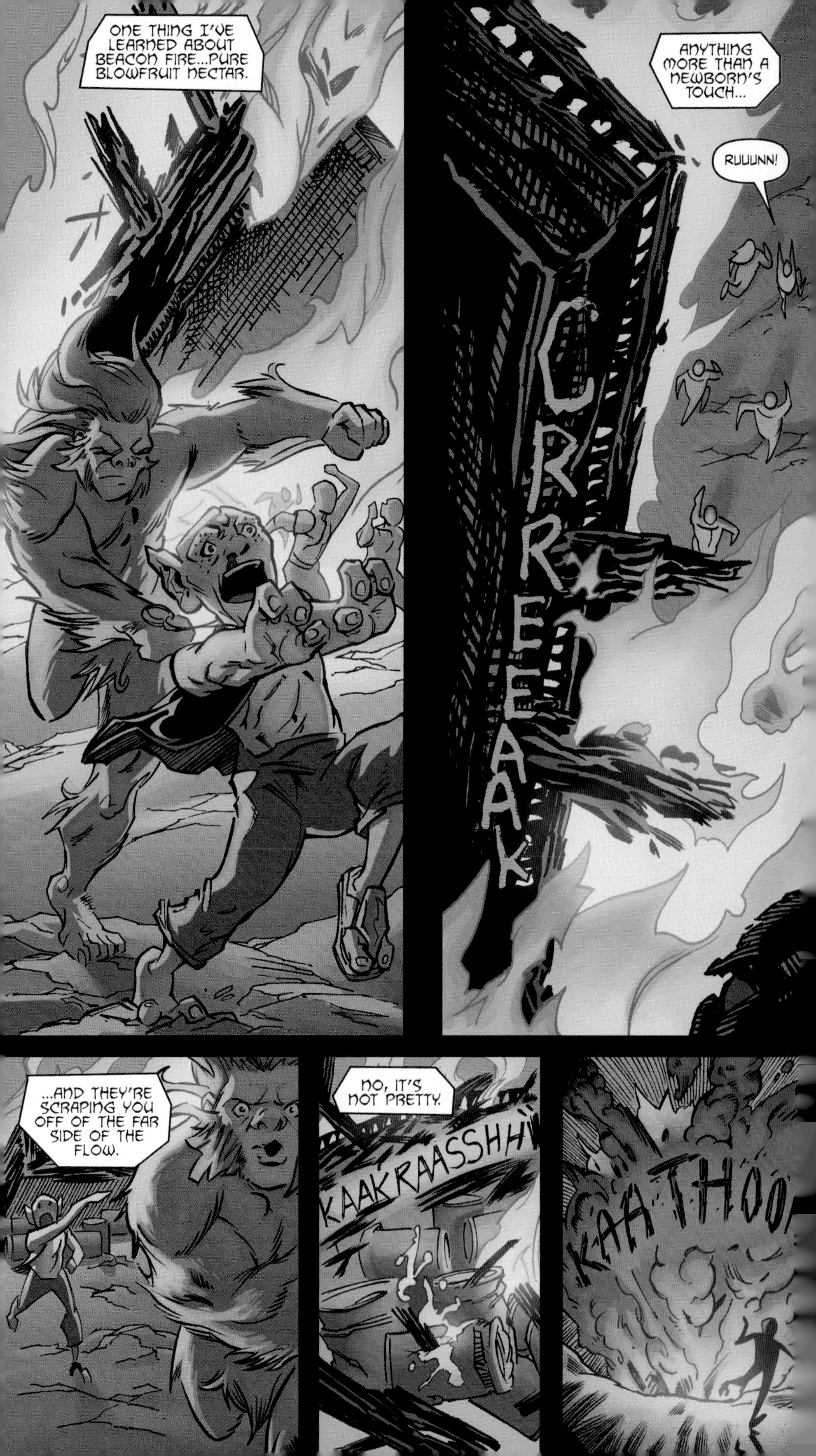
ONE THING I'VE LEARNED ABOUT BEACON FIRE...PURE BLOWFRUIT NECTAR.
ANYTHING MORE THAN A NEWBORN'S TOUCH...
RUUUNN!
CRREEAAK
...AND THEY'RE SCRAPING YOU OFF OF THE FAR SIDE OF THE FLOW.
NO, IT'S NOT PRETTY.
KAAKRAASSHH
KAATHOO

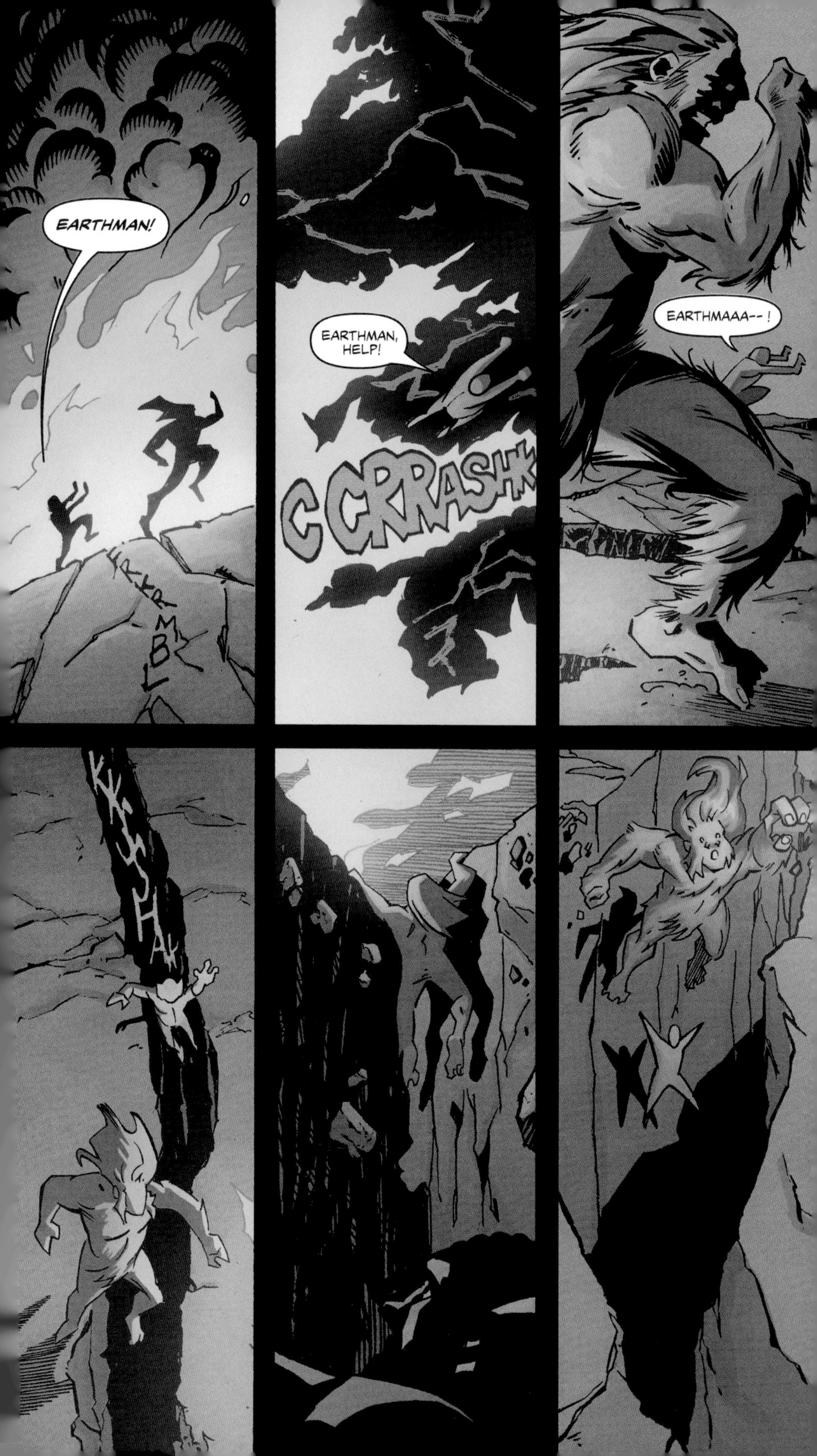
EARTHMAN!
EARTHMAN, HELP!
EARTHMAAA-- !

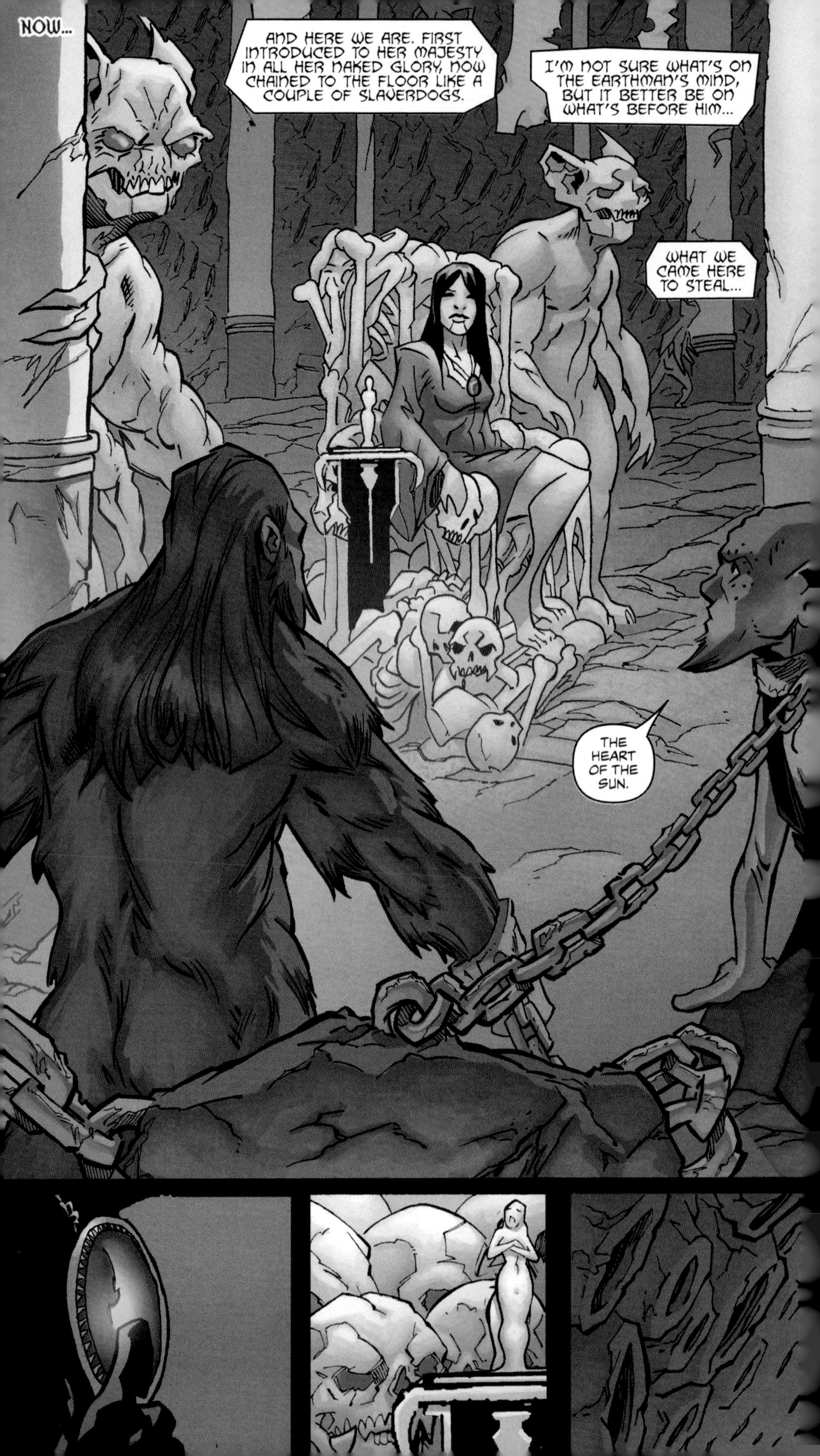
NOW...
AND HERE WE ARE. FIRST INTRODUCED TO HER MAJESTY IN ALL HER NAKED GLORY, NOW CHAINED TO THE FLOOR LIKE A COUPLE OF SLAVERDOGS.
I'M NOT SURE WHAT'S ON THE EARTHMAN'S MIND, BUT IT BETTER BE ON WHAT'S BEFORE HIM...
WHAT WE CAME HERE TO STEAL...
THE HEART OF THE SUN.

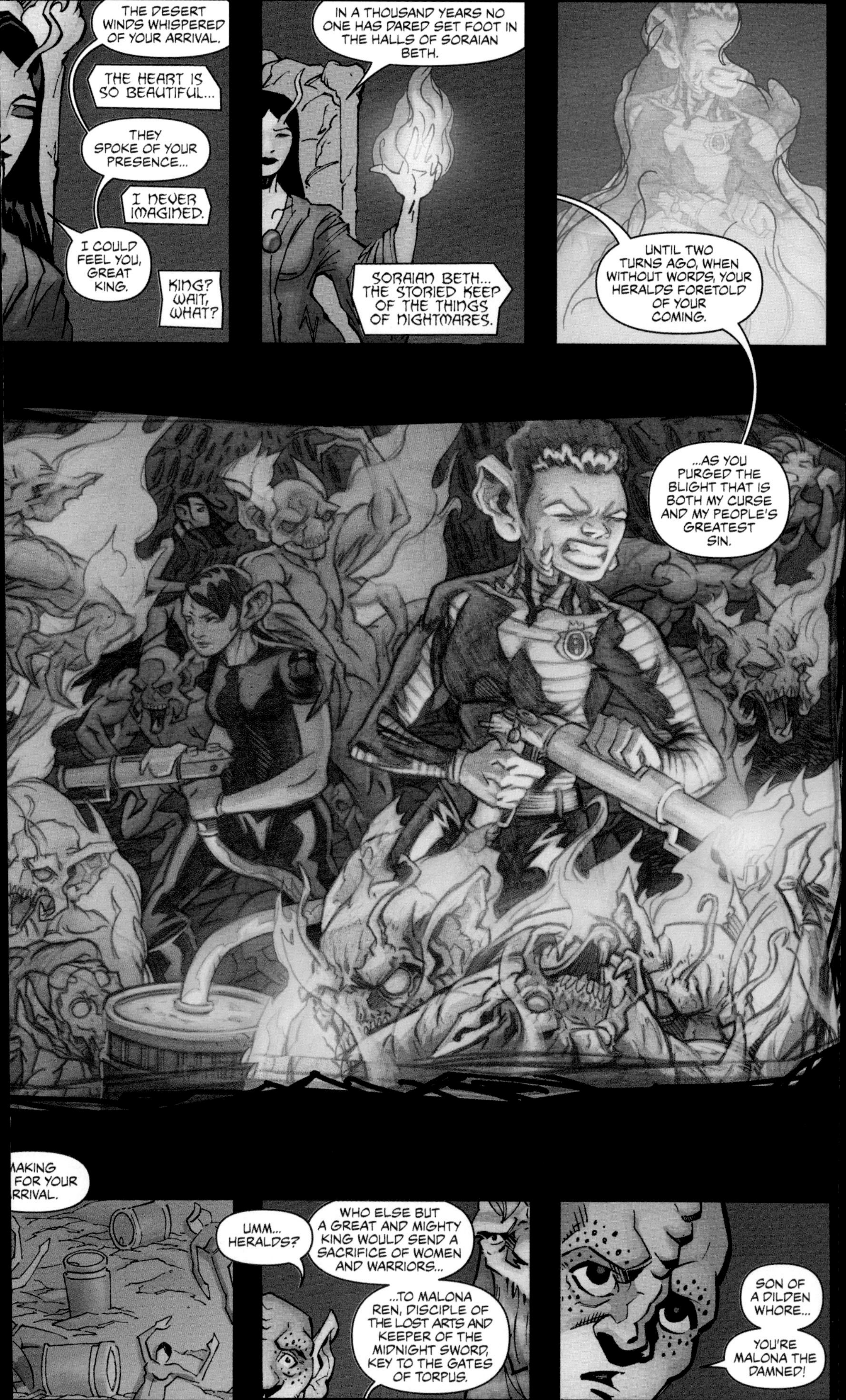
THE DESERT WINDS WHISPERED OF YOUR ARRIVAL.
THE HEART IS SO BEAUTIFUL...
THEY SPOKE OF YOUR PRESENCE...
I NEVER IMAGINED.
I COULD FEEL YOU, GREAT KING.
KING? WAIT, WHAT?
IN A THOUSAND YEARS NO ONE HAS DARED SET FOOT IN THE HALLS OF SORAIAN BETH.
SORAIAN BETH... THE STORIED KEEP OF THE THINGS OF NIGHTMARES.
UNTIL TWO TURNS AGO, WHEN WITHOUT WORDS, YOUR HERALDS FORETOLD OF YOUR COMING.
...AS YOU PURGED THE BLIGHT THAT IS BOTH MY CURSE AND MY PEOPLE'S GREATEST SIN.
AKING FOR YOUR RRIVAL.
UMM... HERALDS?
WHO ELSE BUT A GREAT AND MIGHTY KING WOULD SEND A SACRIFICE OF WOMEN AND WARRIORS...
...TO MALONA REN, DISCIPLE OF THE LOST ARTS AND KEEPER OF THE MIDNIGHT SWORD, KEY TO THE GATES OF TORPUS.
SON OF A DILDEN WHORE...
YOU'RE MALONA THE DAMNED!

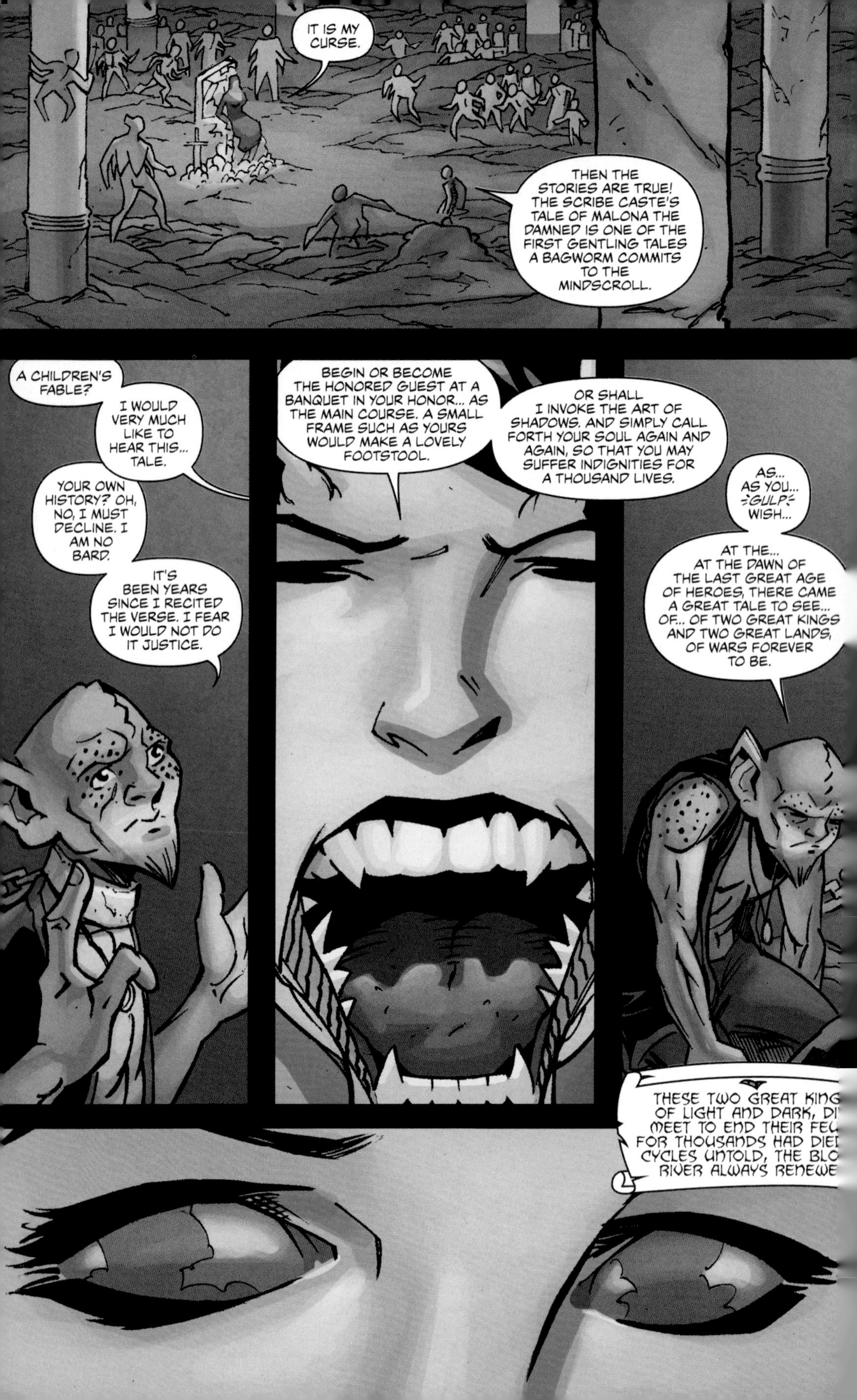
IT IS MY CURSE.
THEN THE STORIES ARE TRUE! THE SCRIBE CASTE'S TALE OF MALONA THE DAMNED IS ONE OF THE FIRST GENTLING TALES A BAGWORM COMMITS TO THE MINDSCROLL.
A CHILDREN'S FABLE?
I WOULD VERY MUCH LIKE TO HEAR THIS... TALE.
YOUR OWN HISTORY? OH, NO, I MUST DECLINE. I AM NO BARD.
IT'S BEEN YEARS SINCE I RECITED THE VERSE. I FEAR I WOULD NOT DO IT JUSTICE.
BEGIN OR BECOME THE HONORED GUEST AT A BANQUET IN YOUR HONOR... AS THE MAIN COURSE. A SMALL FRAME SUCH AS YOURS WOULD MAKE A LOVELY FOOTSTOOL.
OR SHALL I INVOKE THE ART OF SHADOWS. AND SIMPLY CALL FORTH YOUR SOUL AGAIN AND AGAIN, SO THAT YOU MAY SUFFER INDIGNITIES FOR A THOUSAND LIVES.
AS... AS YOU... GULP WISH...
AT THE... AT THE DAWN OF THE LAST GREAT AGE OF HEROES, THERE CAME A GREAT TALE TO SEE... OF... OF TWO GREAT KINGS AND TWO GREAT LANDS, OF WARS FOREVER TO BE.
THESE TWO GREAT KING OF LIGHT AND DARK, DI MEET TO END THEIR FEU FOR THOUSANDS HAD DIED CYCLES UNTOLD, THE BLO RIVER ALWAYS RENEWE

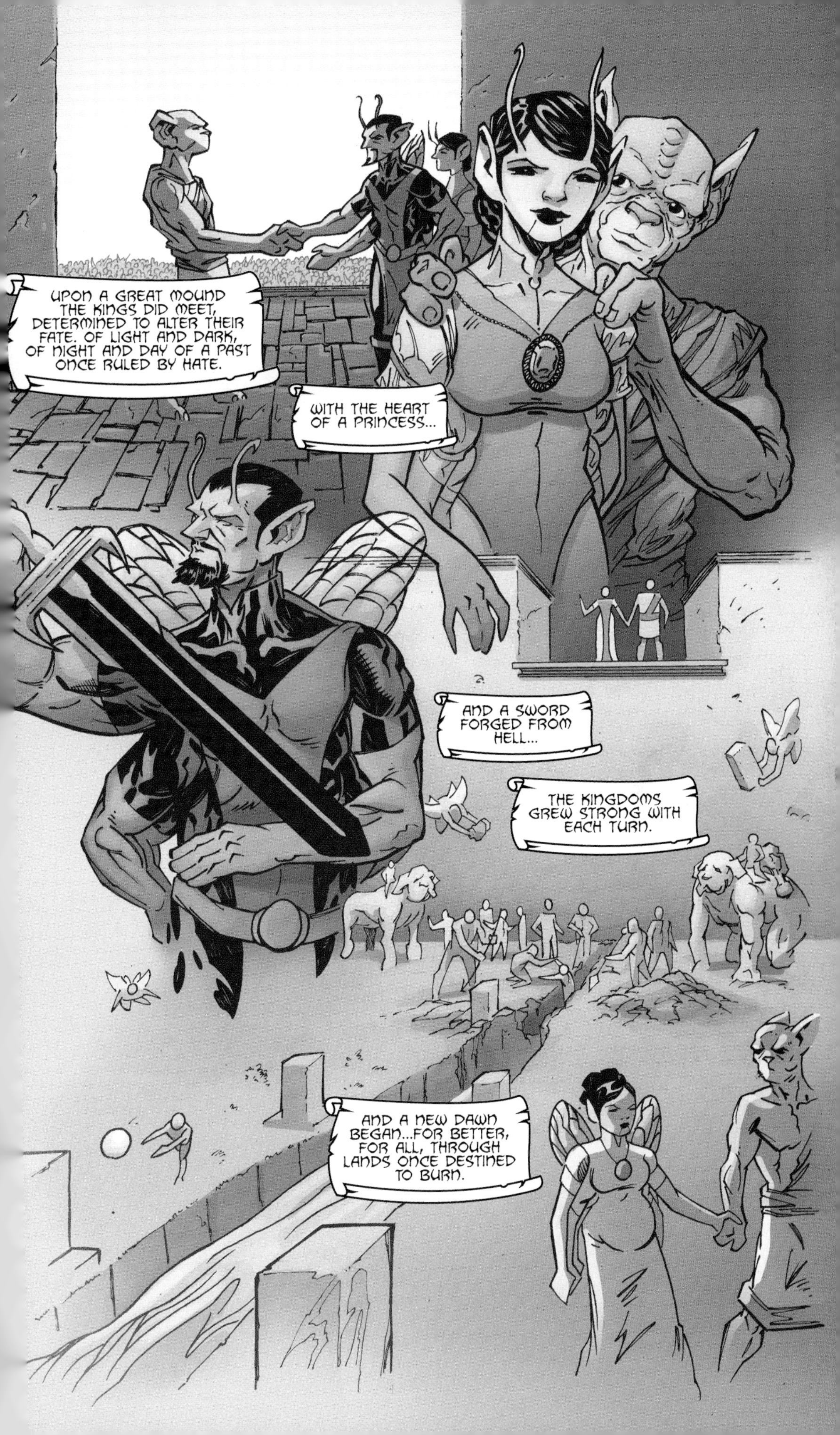
UPON A GREAT MOUND THE KINGS DID MEET, DETERMINED TO ALTER THEIR FATE. OF LIGHT AND DARK, OF NIGHT AND DAY OF A PAST ONCE RULED BY HATE.
WITH THE HEART OF A PRINCESS...
AND A SWORD FORGED FROM HELL...
THE KINGDOMS GREW STRONG WITH EACH TURN.
AND A NEW DAWN BEGAN...FOR BETTER, FOR ALL, THROUGH LANDS ONCE DESTINED TO BURN.

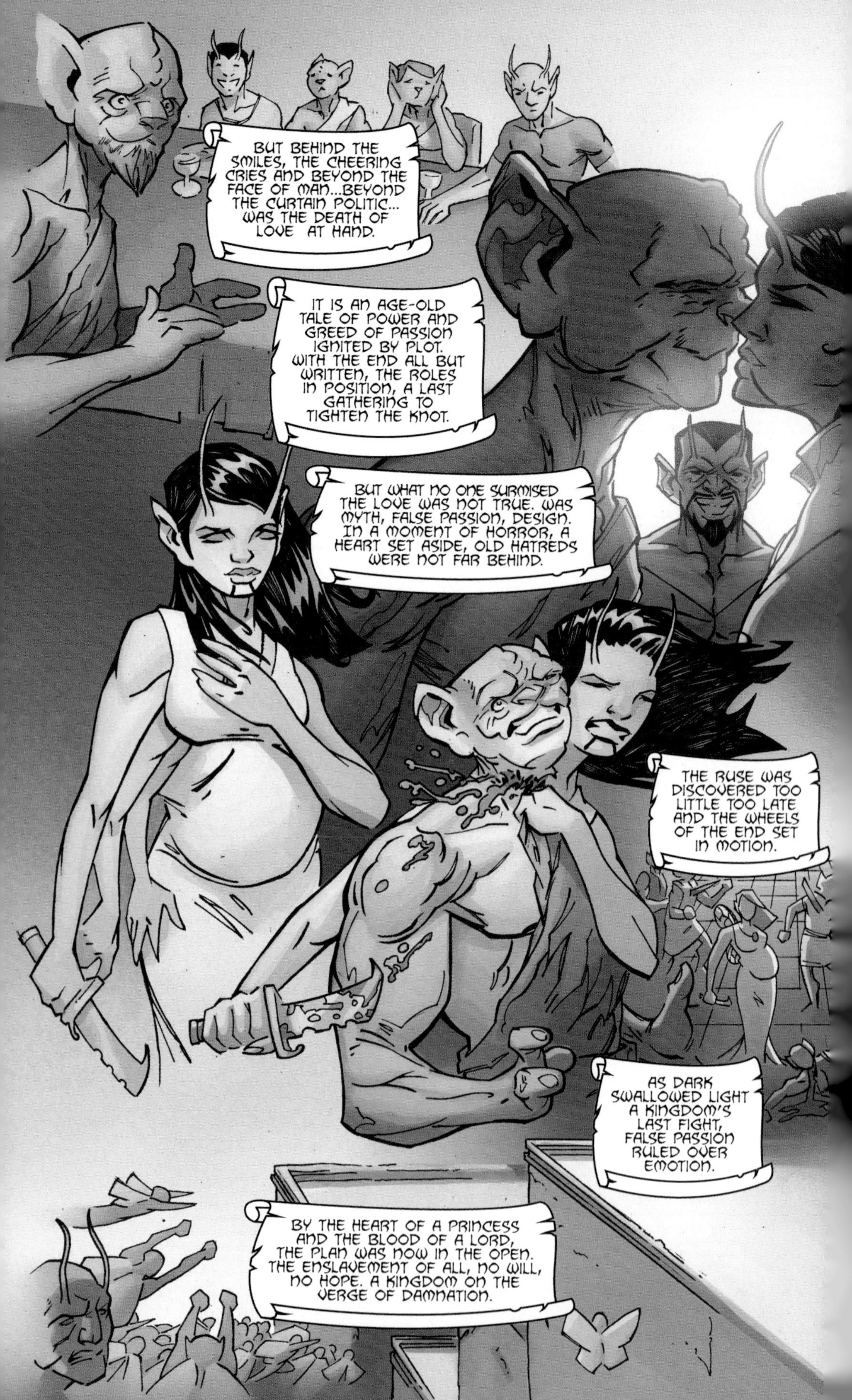
BUT BEHIND THE SMILES, THE CHEERING CRIES AND BEYOND THE FACE OF MAN...BEYOND THE CURTAIN POLITIC... WAS THE DEATH OF LOVE AT HAND.
IT IS AN AGE-OLD TALE OF POWER AND GREED OF PASSION IGNITED BY PLOT. WITH THE END ALL BUT WRITTEN, THE ROLES IN POSITION, A LAST GATHERING TO TIGHTEN THE KNOT.
BUT WHAT NO ONE SURMISED THE LOVE WAS NOT TRUE. WAS MYTH, FALSE PASSION, DESIGN. IN A MOMENT OF HORROR, A HEART SET ASIDE, OLD HATREDS WERE NOT FAR BEHIND.
THE RUSE WAS DISCOVERED TOO LITTLE TOO LATE AND THE WHEELS OF THE END SET IN MOTION.
AS DARK SWALLOWED LIGHT A KINGDOM'S LAST FIGHT, FALSE PASSION RULED OVER EMOTION.
BY THE HEART OF A PRINCESS AND THE BLOOD OF A LORD, THE PLAN WAS NOW IN THE OPEN. THE ENSLAVEMENT OF ALL, NO WILL, NO HOPE. A KINGDOM ON THE VERGE OF DAMNATION.

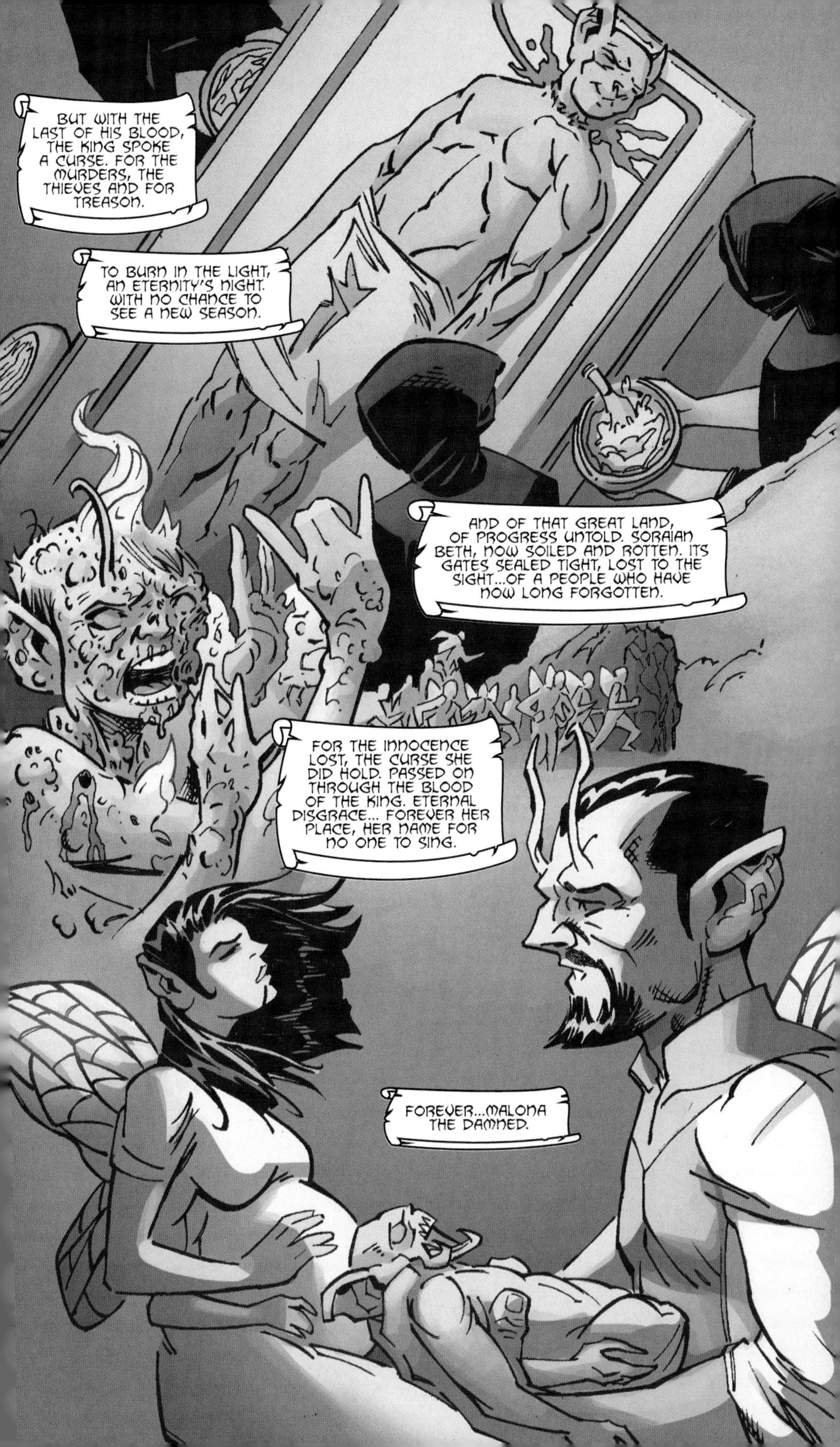
BUT WITH THE LAST OF HIS BLOOD, THE KING SPOKE A CURSE. FOR THE MURDERS, THE THIEVES AND FOR TREASON.
TO BURN IN THE LIGHT, AN ETERNITY'S NIGHT. WITH NO CHANCE TO SEE A NEW SEASON.
AND OF THAT GREAT LAND, OF PROGRESS UNTOLD. SORAIAN BETH, NOW SOILED AND ROTTEN. ITS GATES SEALED TIGHT, LOST TO THE SIGHT...OF A PEOPLE WHO HAVE NOW LONG FORGOTTEN.
FOR THE INNOCENCE LOST, THE CURSE SHE DID HOLD. PASSED ON THROUGH THE BLOOD OF THE KING. ETERNAL DISGRACE... FOREVER HER PLACE, HER NAME FOR NO ONE TO SING.
FOREVER...MALONA THE DAMNED.

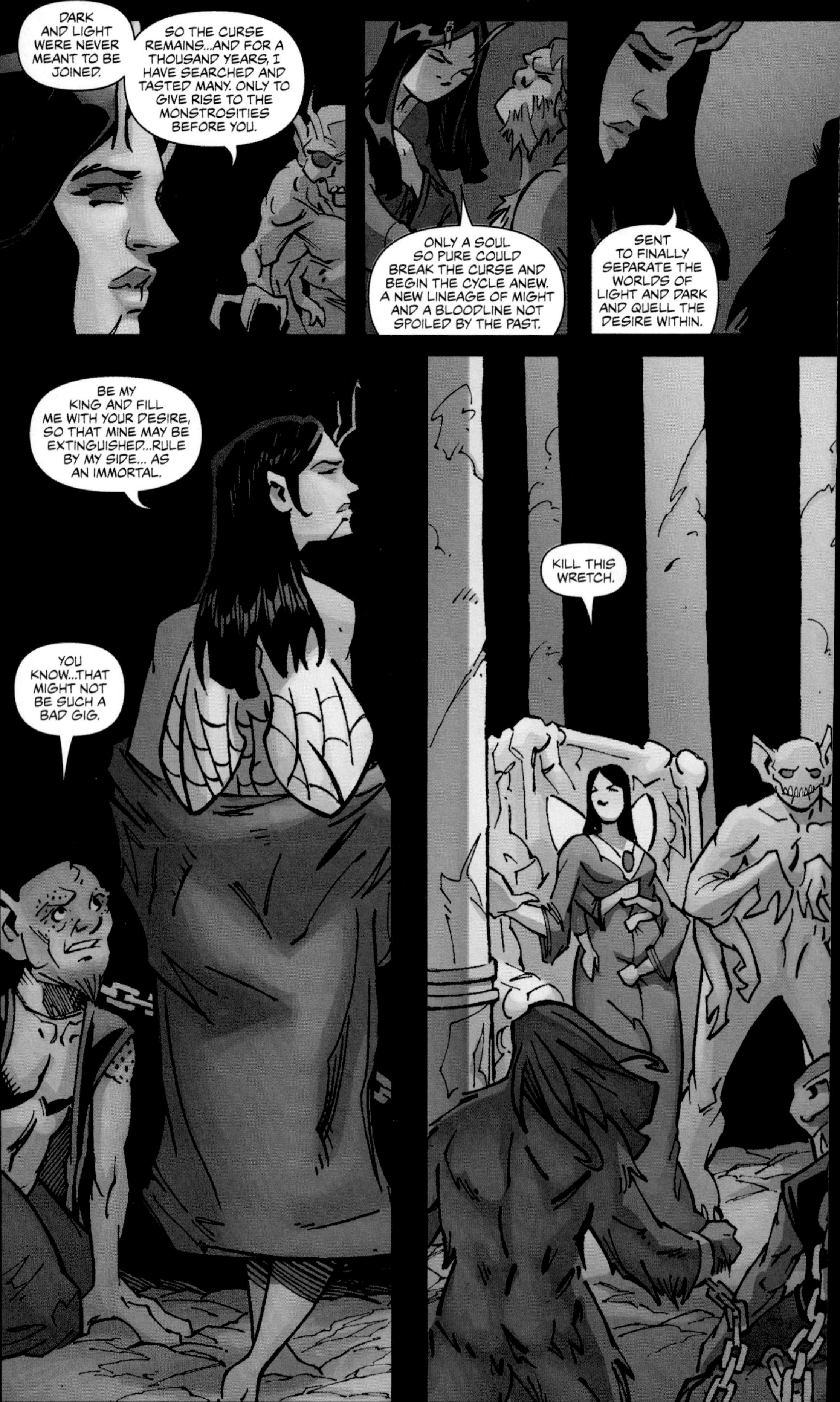
DARK AND LIGHT WERE NEVER MEANT TO BE JOINED.
SO THE CURSE REMAINS...AND FOR A THOUSAND YEARS, I HAVE SEARCHED AND TASTED MANY. ONLY TO GIVE RISE TO THE MONSTROSITIES BEFORE YOU.
ONLY A SOUL SO PURE COULD BREAK THE CURSE AND BEGIN THE CYCLE ANEW. A NEW LINEAGE OF MIGHT AND A BLOODLINE NOT SPOILED BY THE PAST.
SENT TO FINALLY SEPARATE THE WORLDS OF LIGHT AND DARK AND QUELL THE DESIRE WITHIN.
BE MY KING AND FILL ME WITH YOUR DESIRE, SO THAT MINE MAY BE EXTINGUISHED...RULE BY MY SIDE... AS AN IMMORTAL.
YOU KNOW...THAT MIGHT NOT BE SUCH A BAD GIG.
KILL THIS WRETCH.

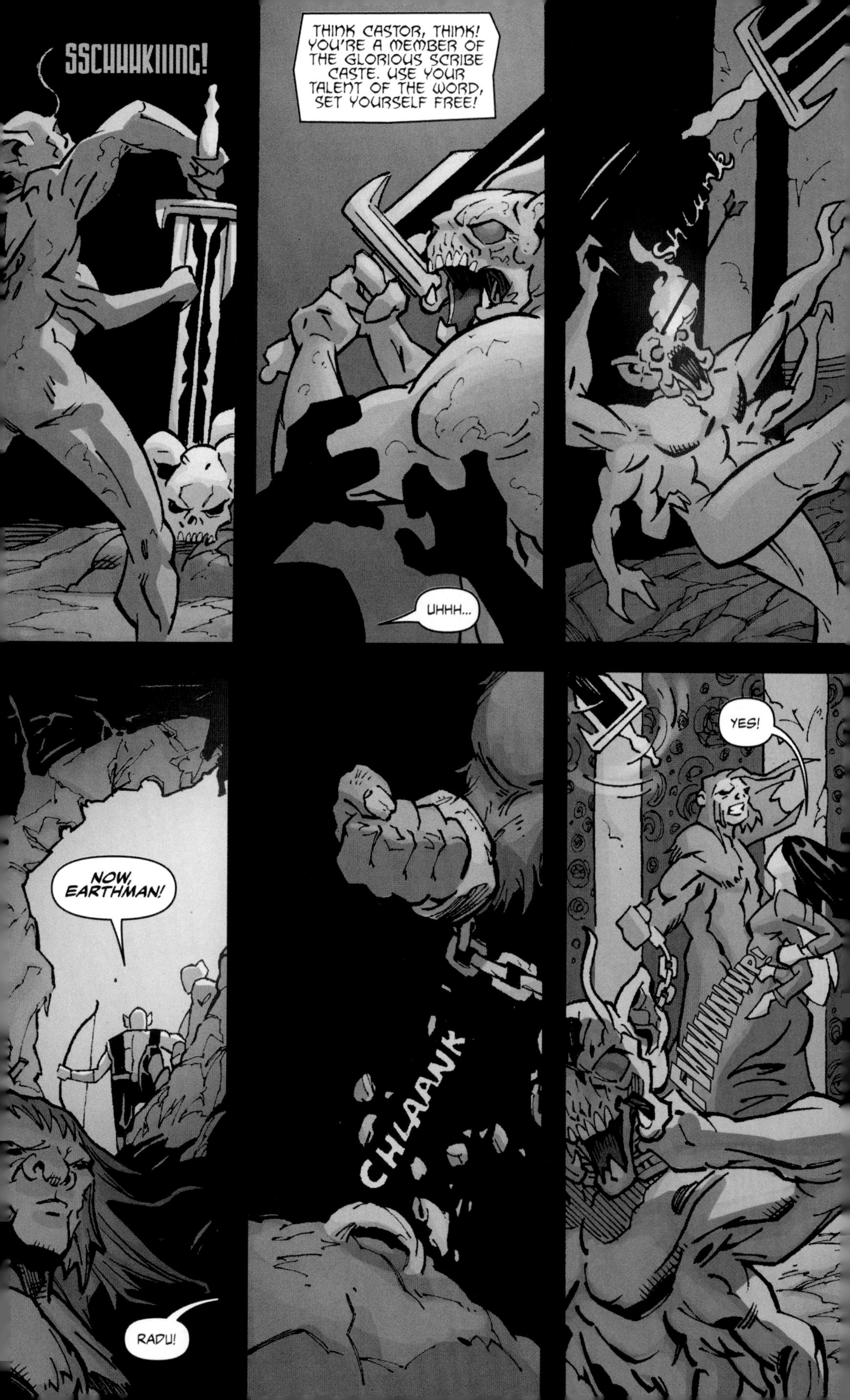
SSCHHHKIIING!
THINK CASTOR, THINK! YOU'RE A MEMBER OF THE GLORIOUS SCRIBE CASTE. USE YOUR TALENT OF THE WORD, SET YOURSELF FREE!
UHHH...
shunk
NOW, EARTHMAN!
RADU!
CHLAANK
YES!

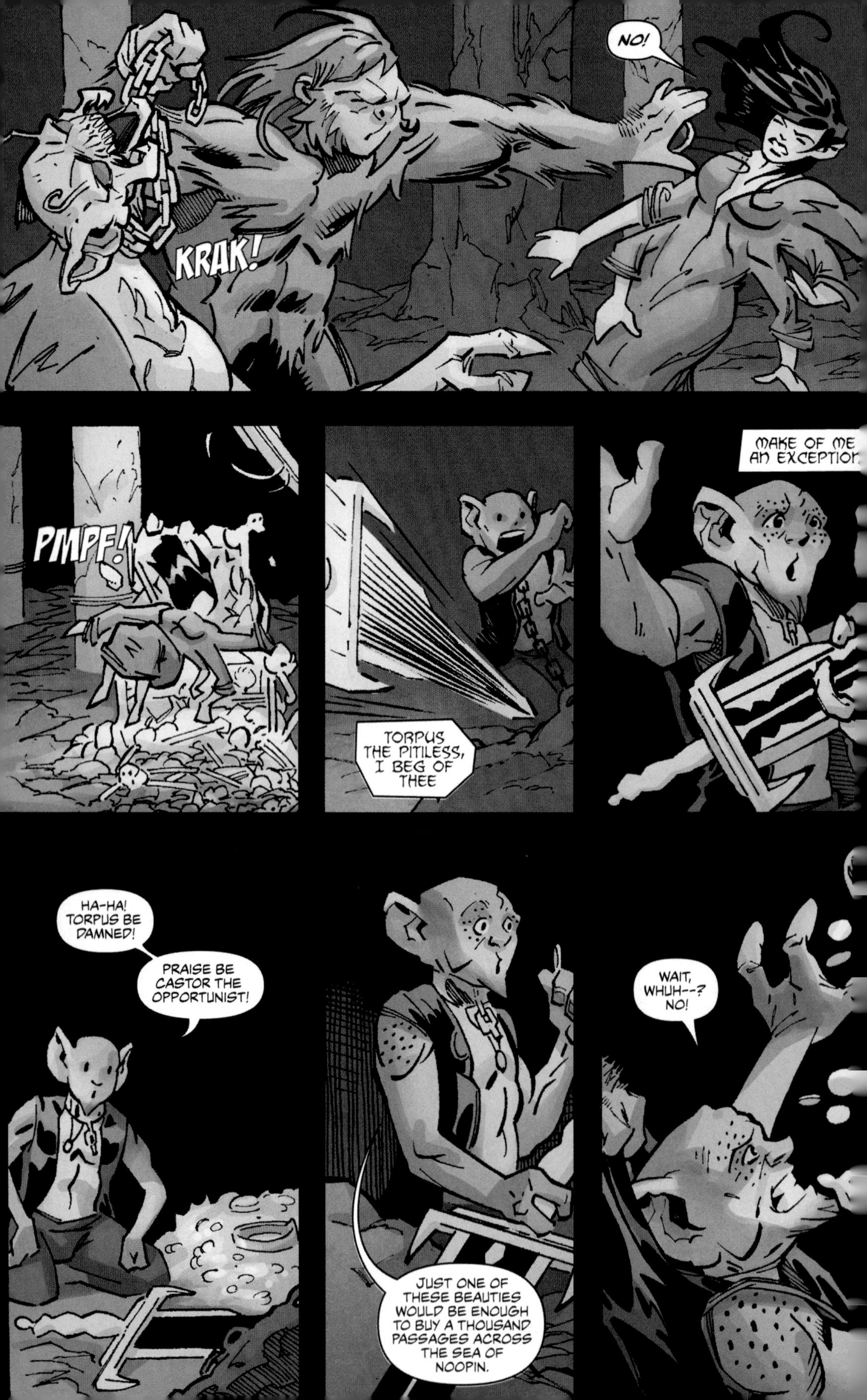
NO!
KRAK!
PMPF!
TORPUS THE PITILESS, I BEG OF THEE
MAKE OF ME AN EXCEPTION
HA-HA! TORPUS BE DAMNED!
PRAISE BE CASTOR THE OPPORTUNIST!
JUST ONE OF THESE BEAUTIES WOULD BE ENOUGH TO BUY A THOUSAND PASSAGES ACROSS THE SEA OF NOOPIN.
WAIT, WHUH--? NO!

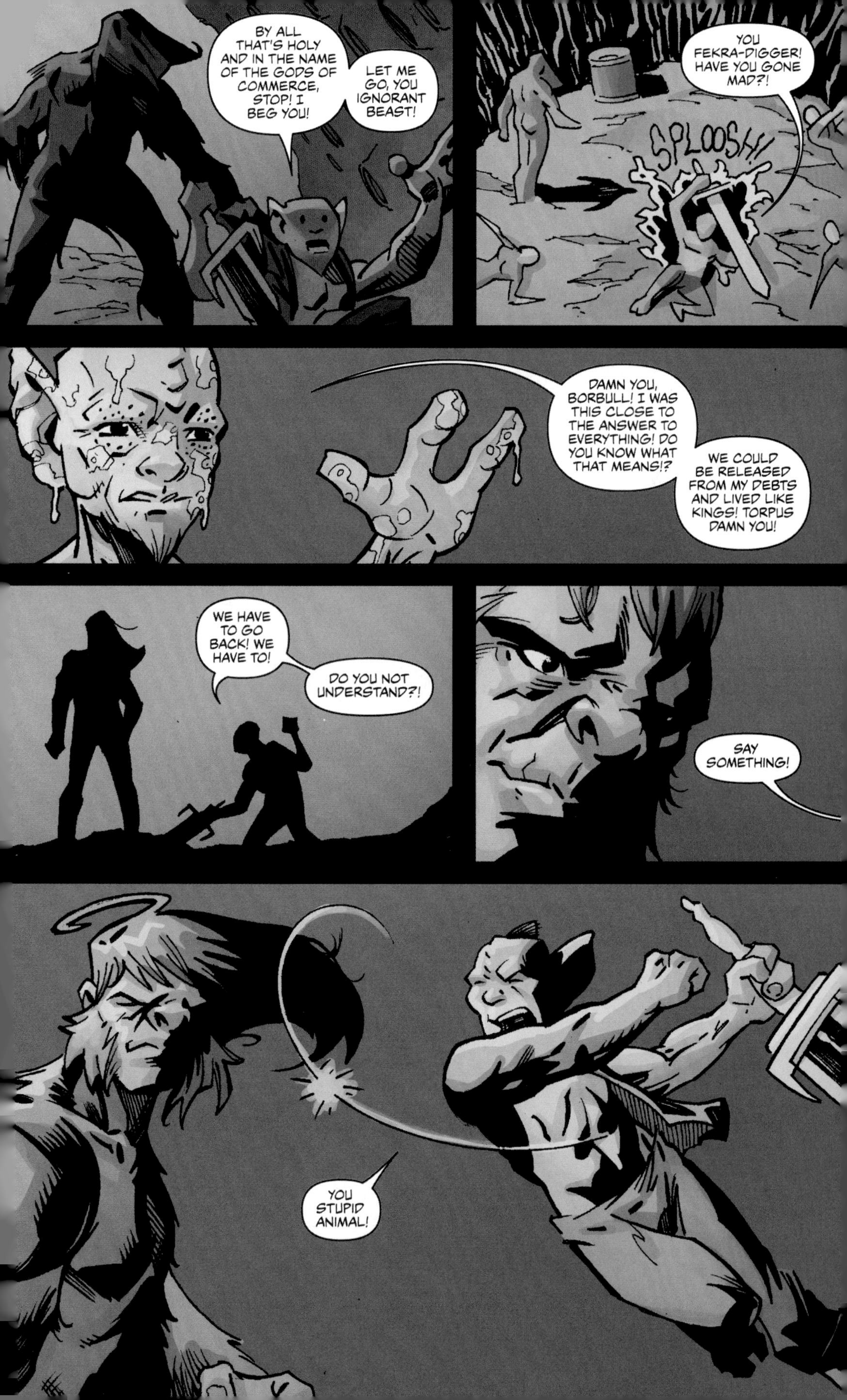
BY ALL THAT'S HOLY AND IN THE NAME OF THE GODS OF COMMERCE, STOP! I BEG YOU!
LET ME GO, YOU IGNORANT BEAST!
YOU FEKRA-DIGGER! HAVE YOU GONE MAD?!
SPLOOSH!
DAMN YOU, BORBULL! I WAS THIS CLOSE TO THE ANSWER TO EVERYTHING! DO YOU KNOW WHAT THAT MEANS!?
WE COULD BE RELEASED FROM MY DEBTS AND LIVED LIKE KINGS! TORPUS DAMN YOU!
WE HAVE TO GO BACK! WE HAVE TO!
DO YOU NOT UNDERSTAND?!
SAY SOMETHING!
YOU STUPID ANIMAL!

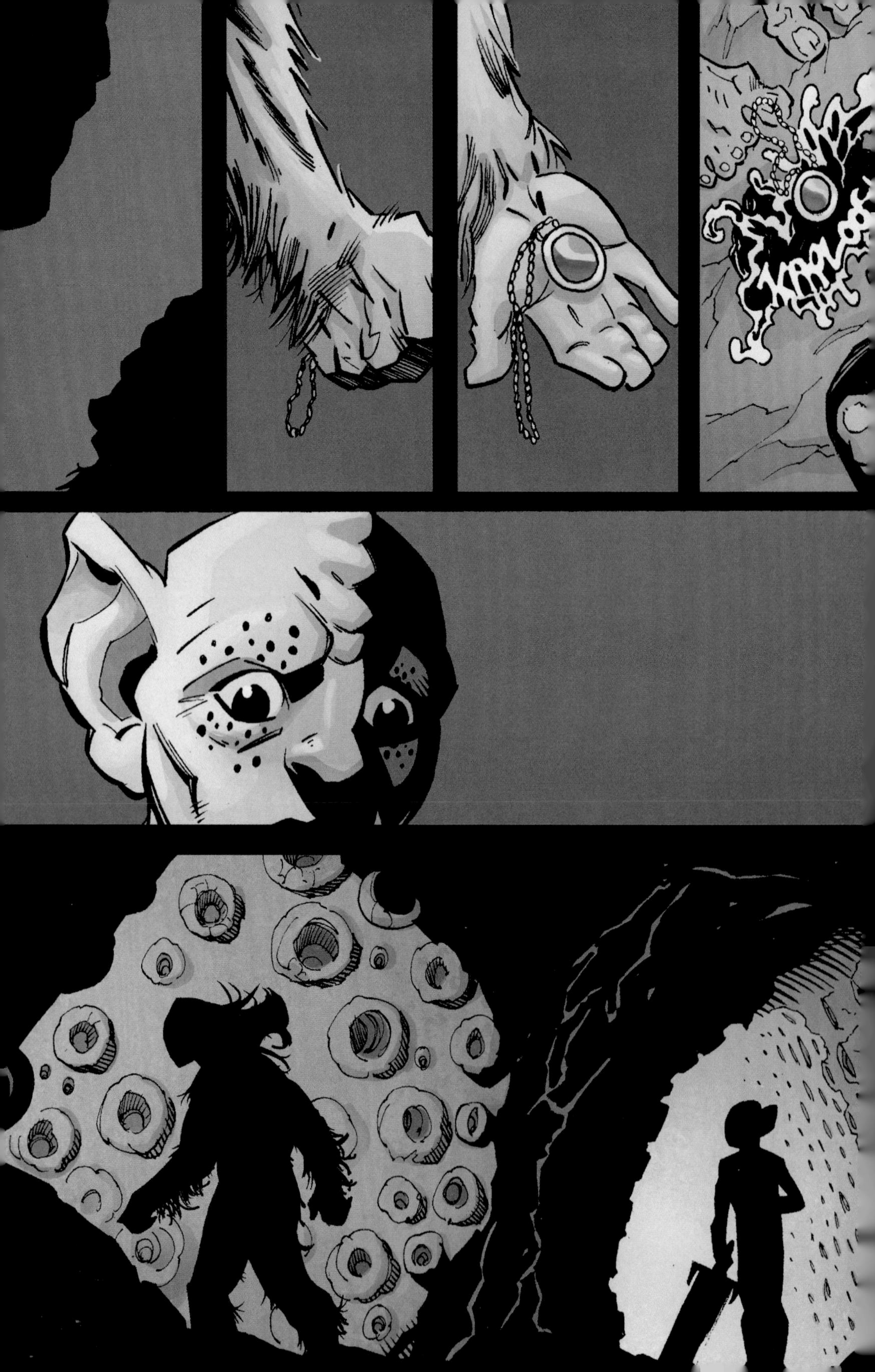

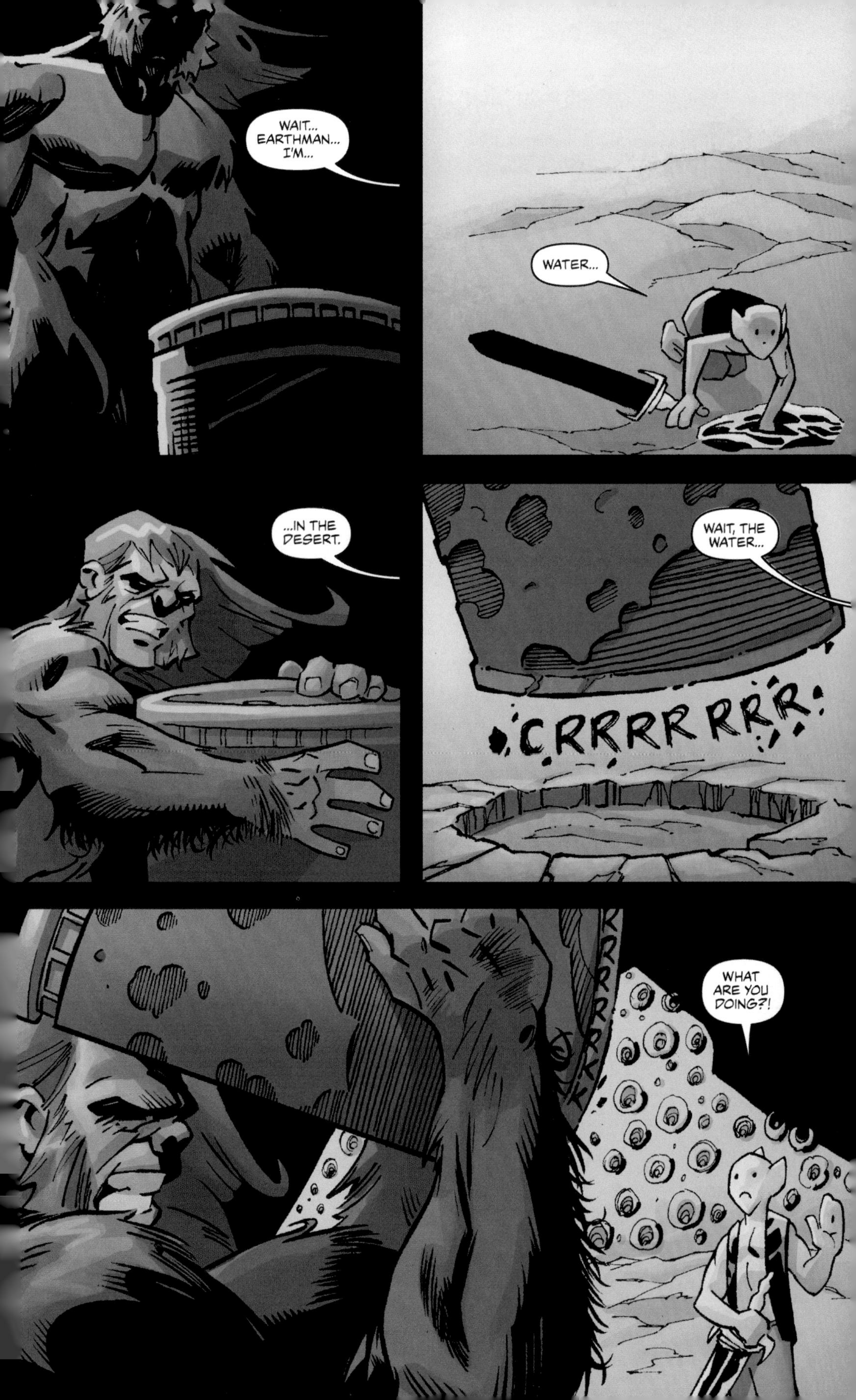
WAIT... EARTHMAN... I'M...
WATER...
...IN THE DESERT.
WAIT, THE WATER...
CRRRRRRR
WHAT ARE YOU DOING?!

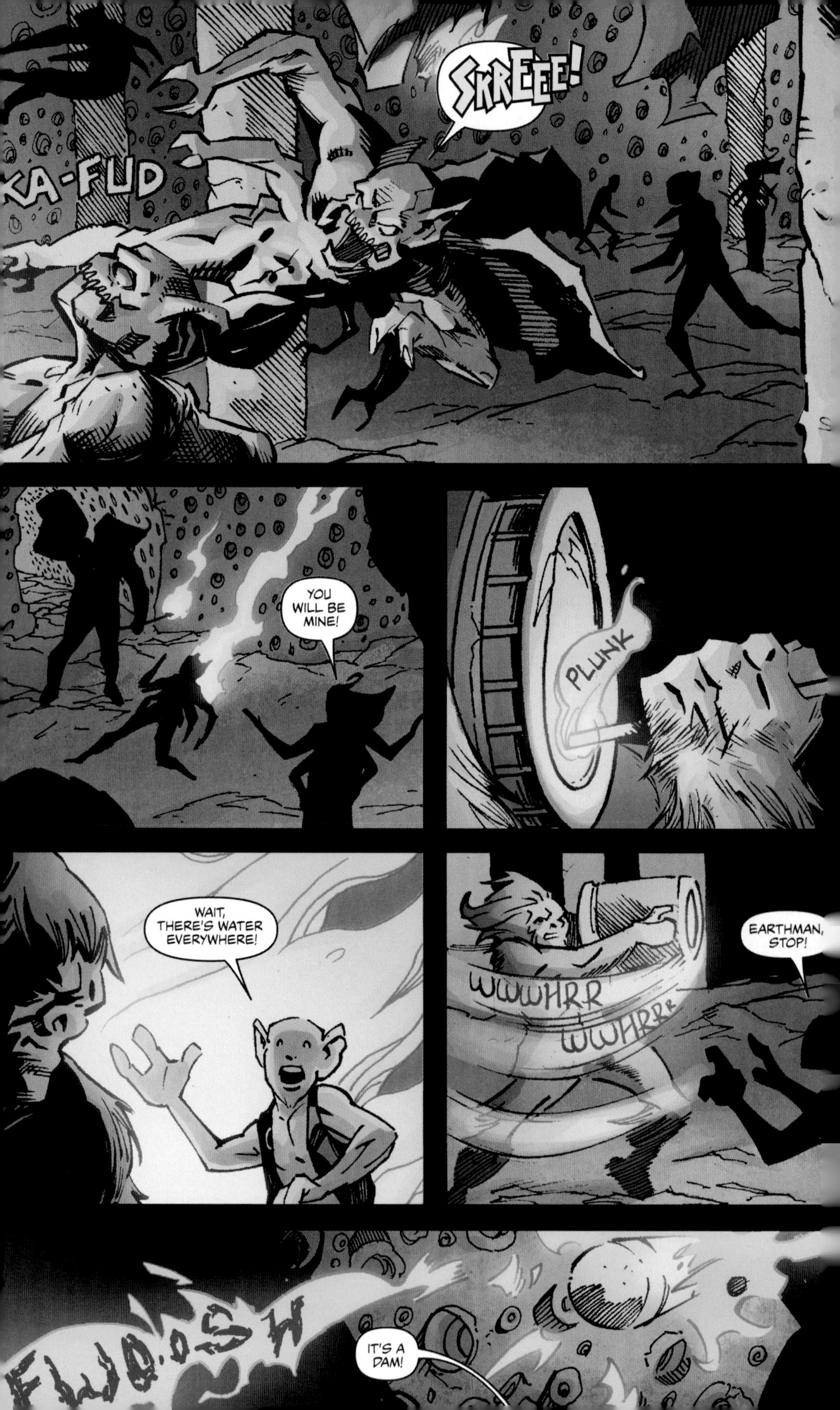
KA-FUD
SKREEE!
YOU WILL BE MINE!
PLUNK
WAIT, THERE'S WATER EVERYWHERE!
WWWHRR
WWHRRR
EARTHMAN, STOP!
FWOOSH
IT'S A DAM!

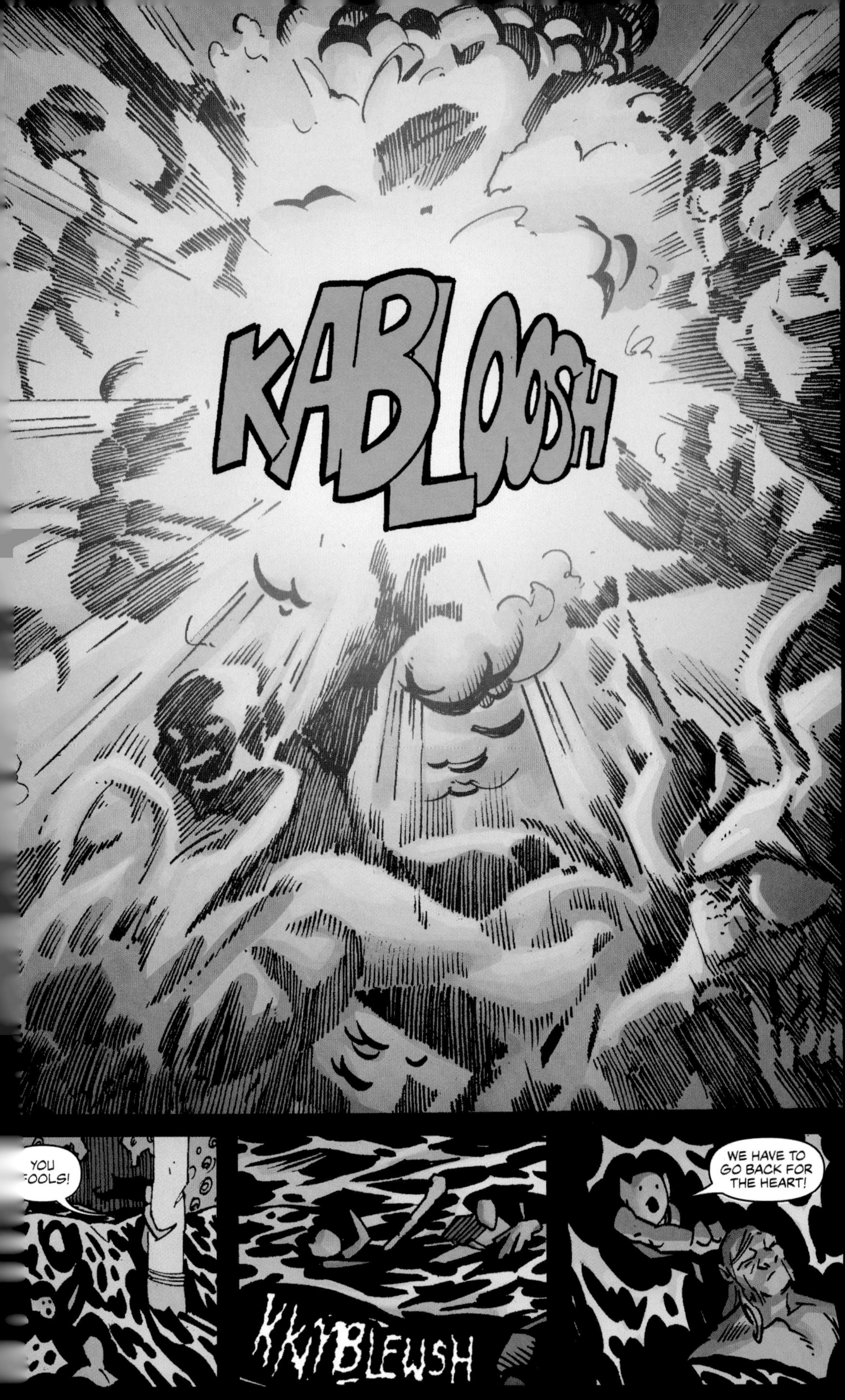
KABLOOSH
YOU FOOLS!
KKABLEWSH
WE HAVE TO GO BACK FOR THE HEART!

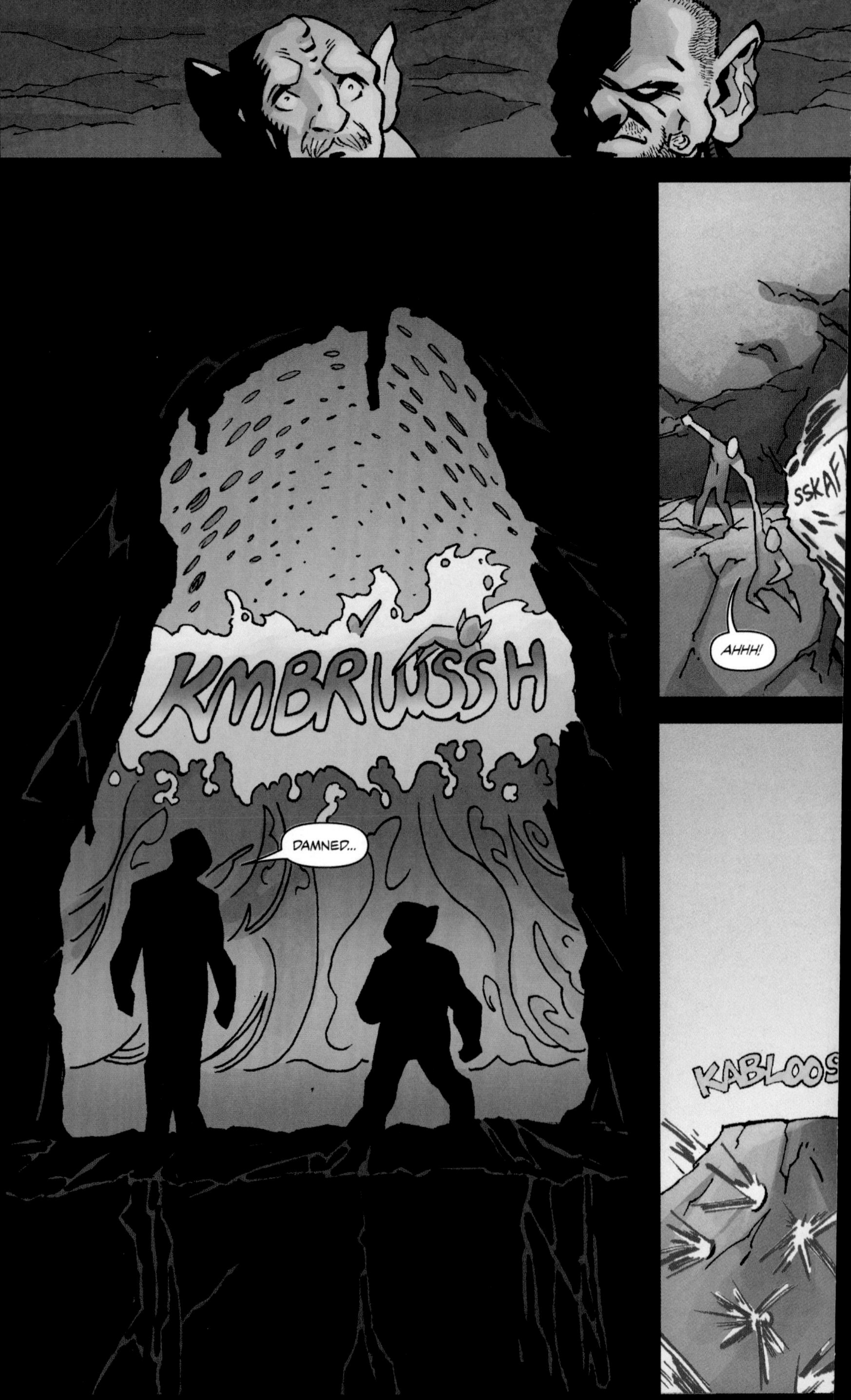
KMBRUSSH
DAMNED...
SSKAF
AHHH!
KABLOOS

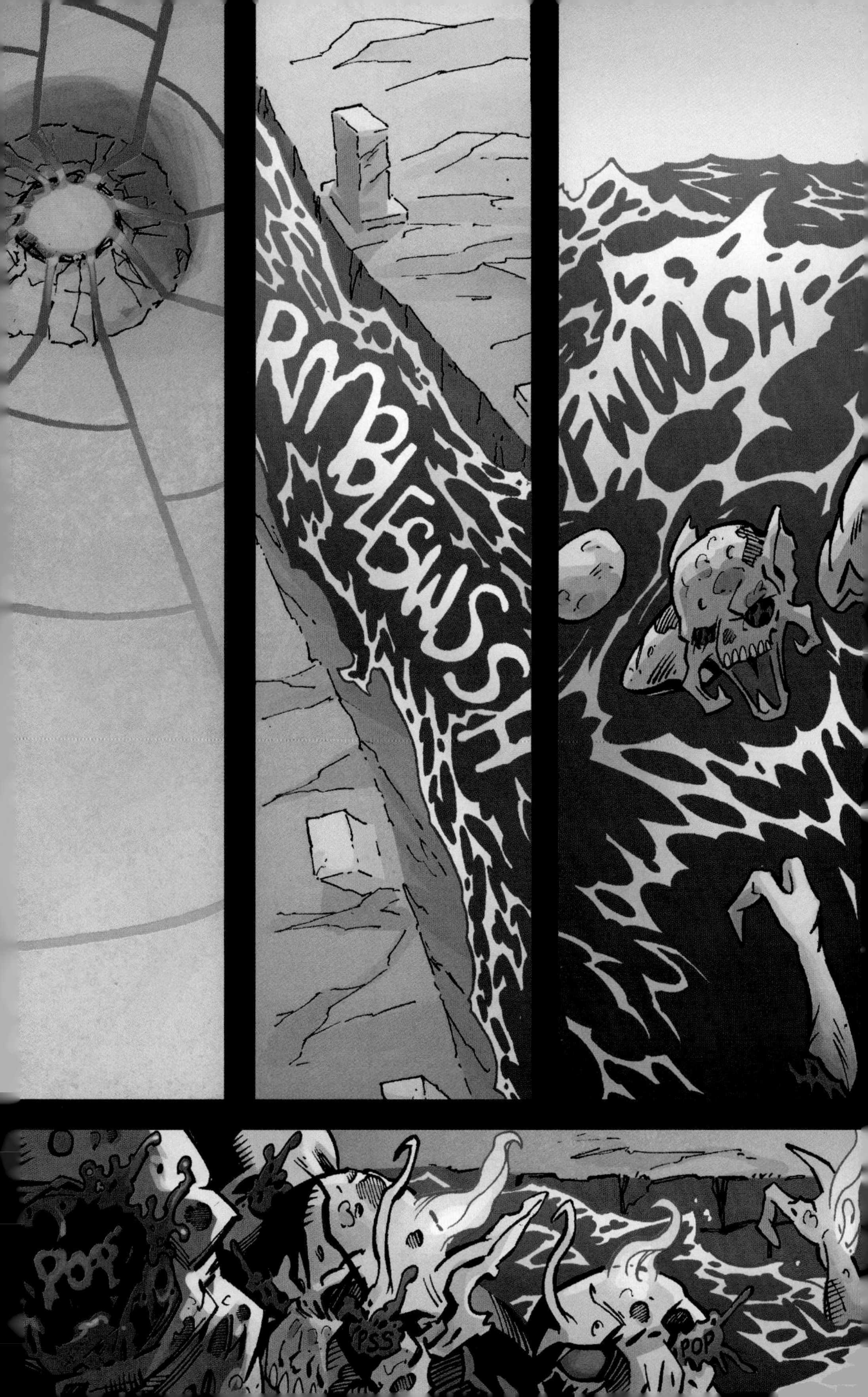
RMBLESWUSSH
FWOOSH
POP
PSS
POP

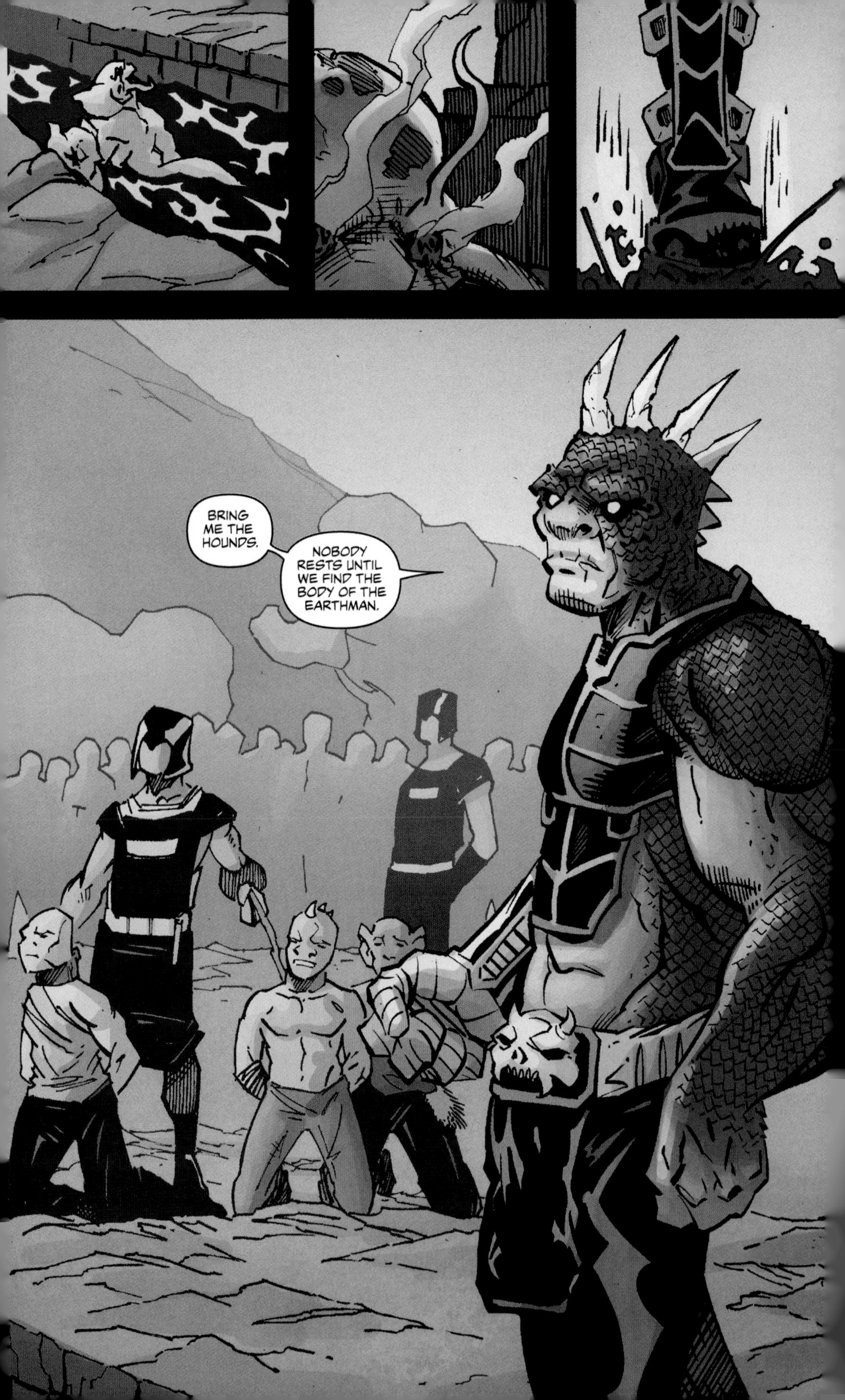
BRING ME THE HOUNDS.
NOBODY RESTS UNTIL WE FIND THE BODY OF THE EARTHMAN.

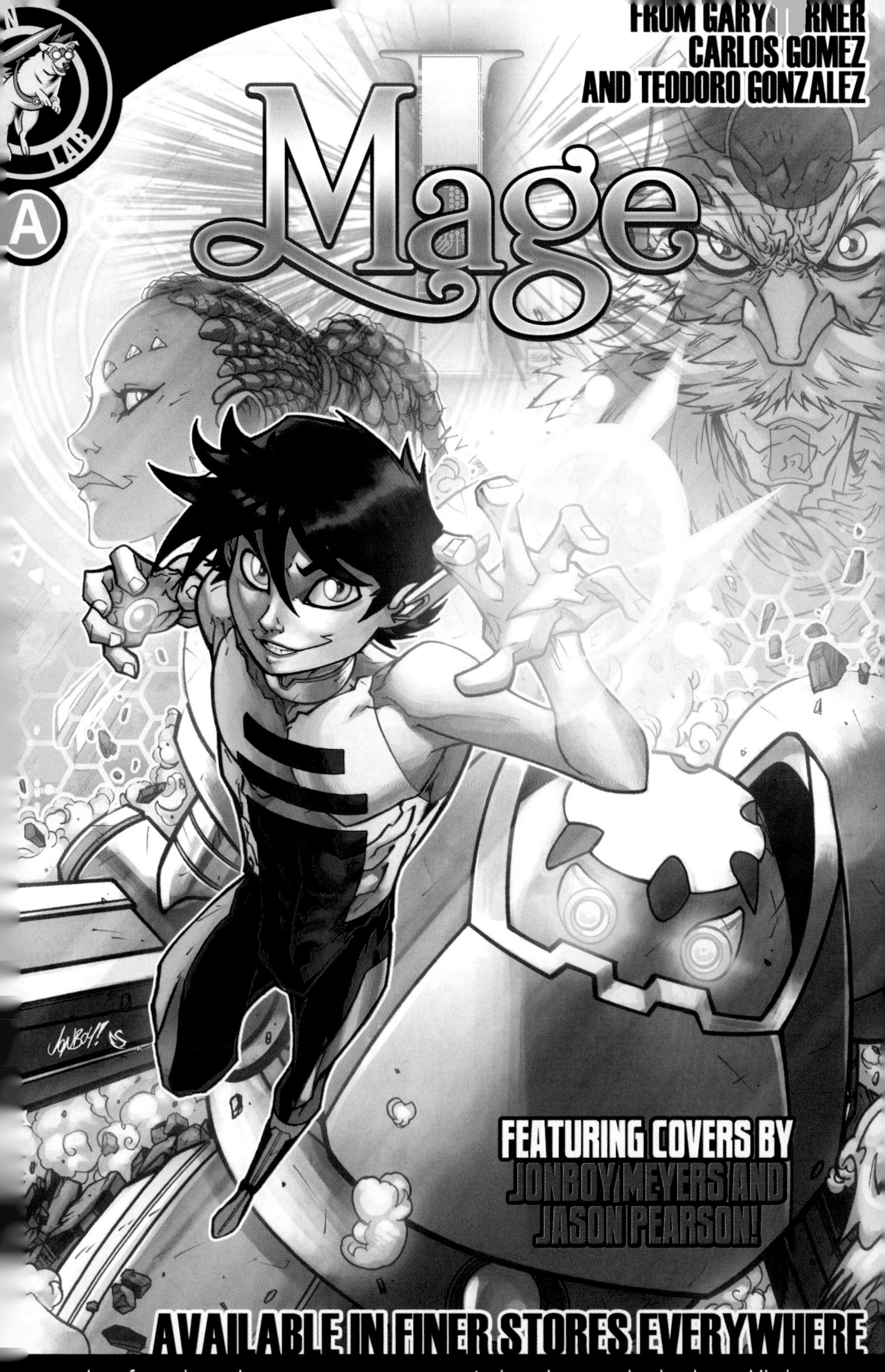

FROM GARY RNER
CARLOS GOMEZ
AND TEODORO GONZALEZ
Mage
FEATURING COVERS BY
JONBOY MEYERS AND
JASON PEARSON!
AVAILABLE IN FINER STORES EVERYWHERE

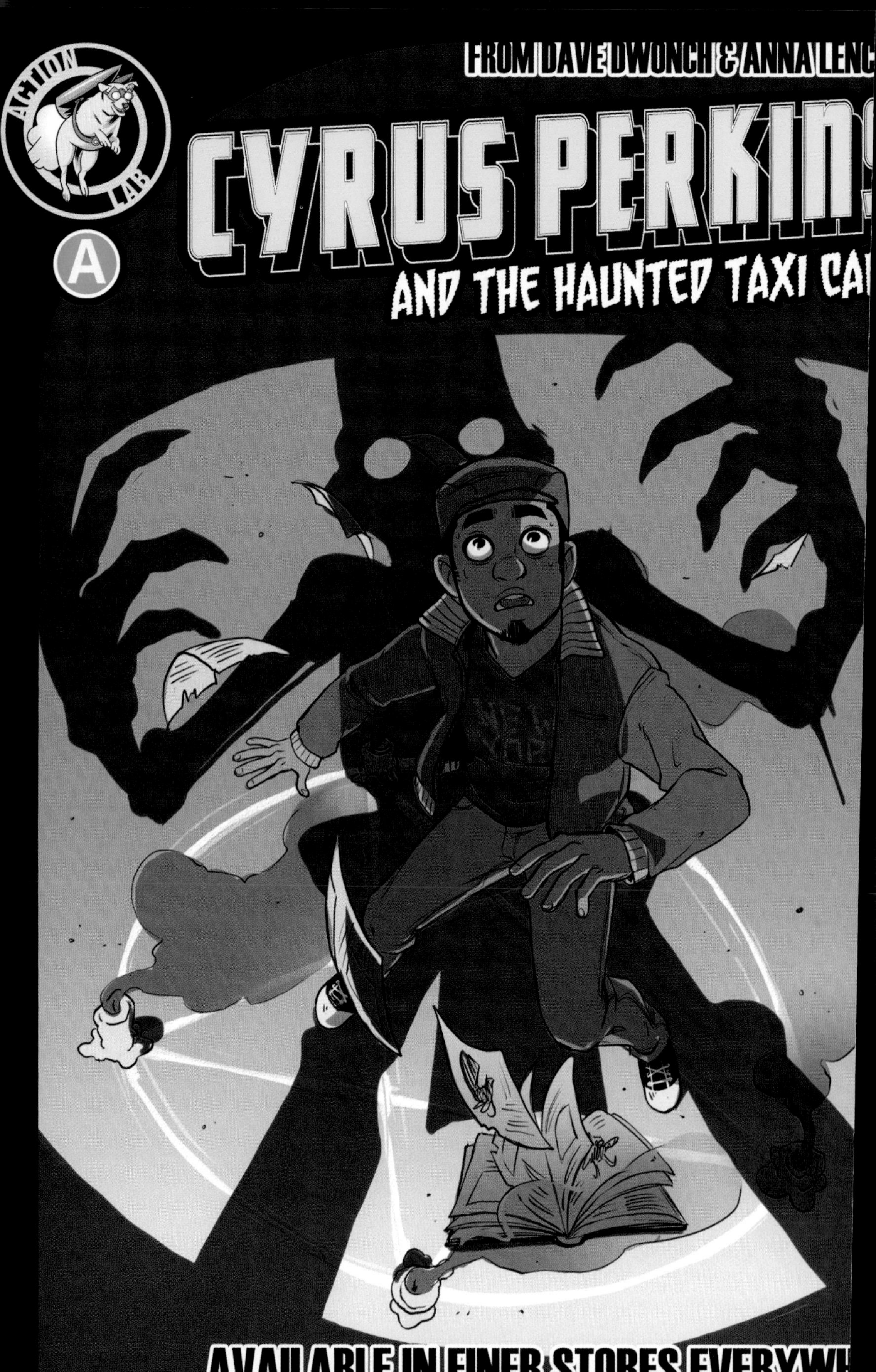
ACTION LAB
FROM DAVE DWONCH & ANNA LENC
CYRUS PERKIN
AND THE HAUNTED TAXI CA
AVAILABLE IN FINER STORES EVERYWH

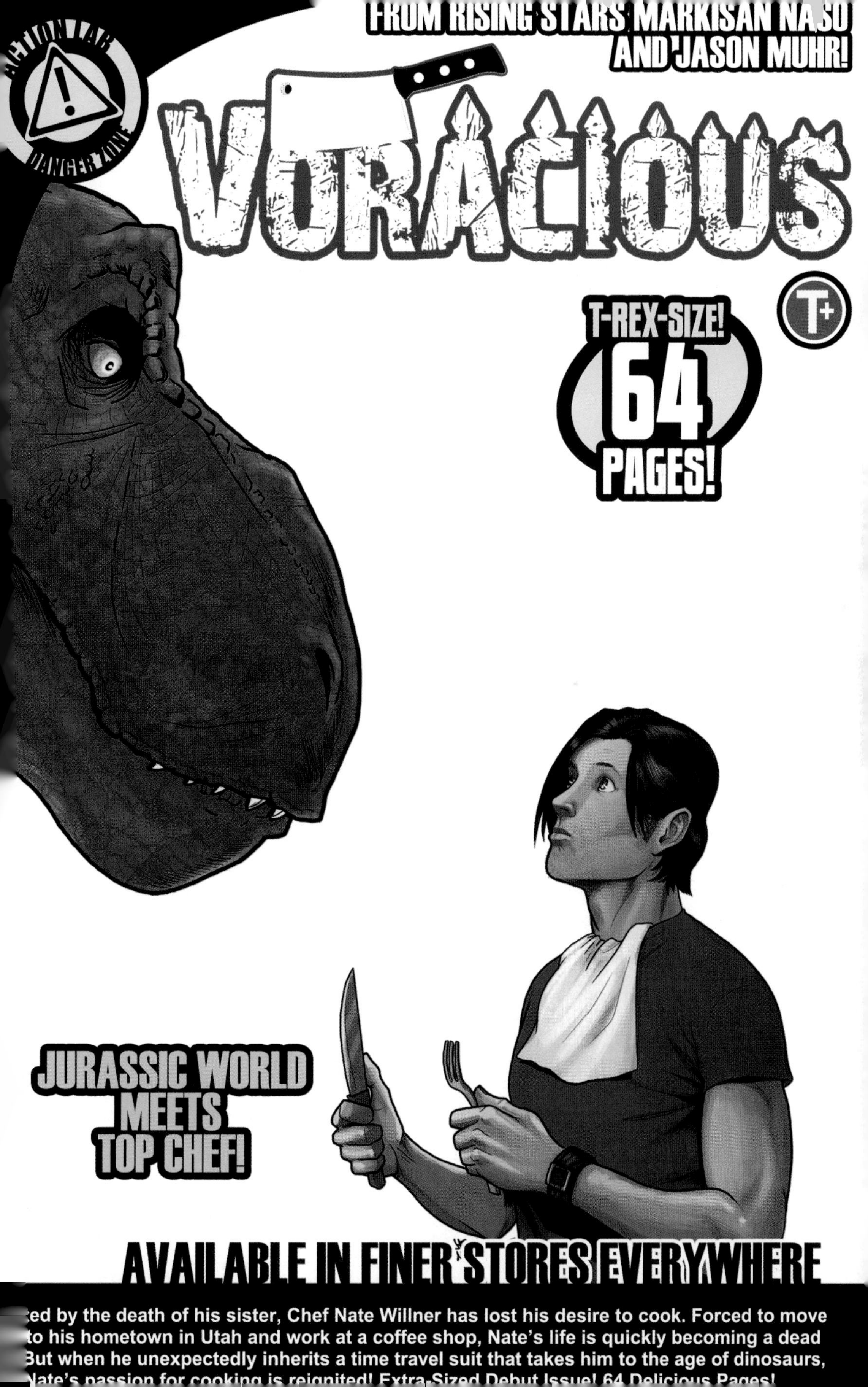
ACTION LAB DANGER ZONE
FROM RISING STARS MARKISAN NASO AND JASON MUHR!
VORACIOUS
T-REX-SIZE! 64 PAGES!
T+
JURASSIC WORLD MEETS TOP CHEF!
AVAILABLE IN FINER STORES EVERYWHERE
ed by the death of his sister, Chef Nate Willner has lost his desire to cook. Forced to move
to his hometown in Utah and work at a coffee shop, Nate's life is quickly becoming a dead
But when he unexpectedly inherits a time travel suit that takes him to the age of dinosaurs,
Nate's passion for cooking is reignited! Extra-Sized Debut Issue! 64 Delicious Pages!

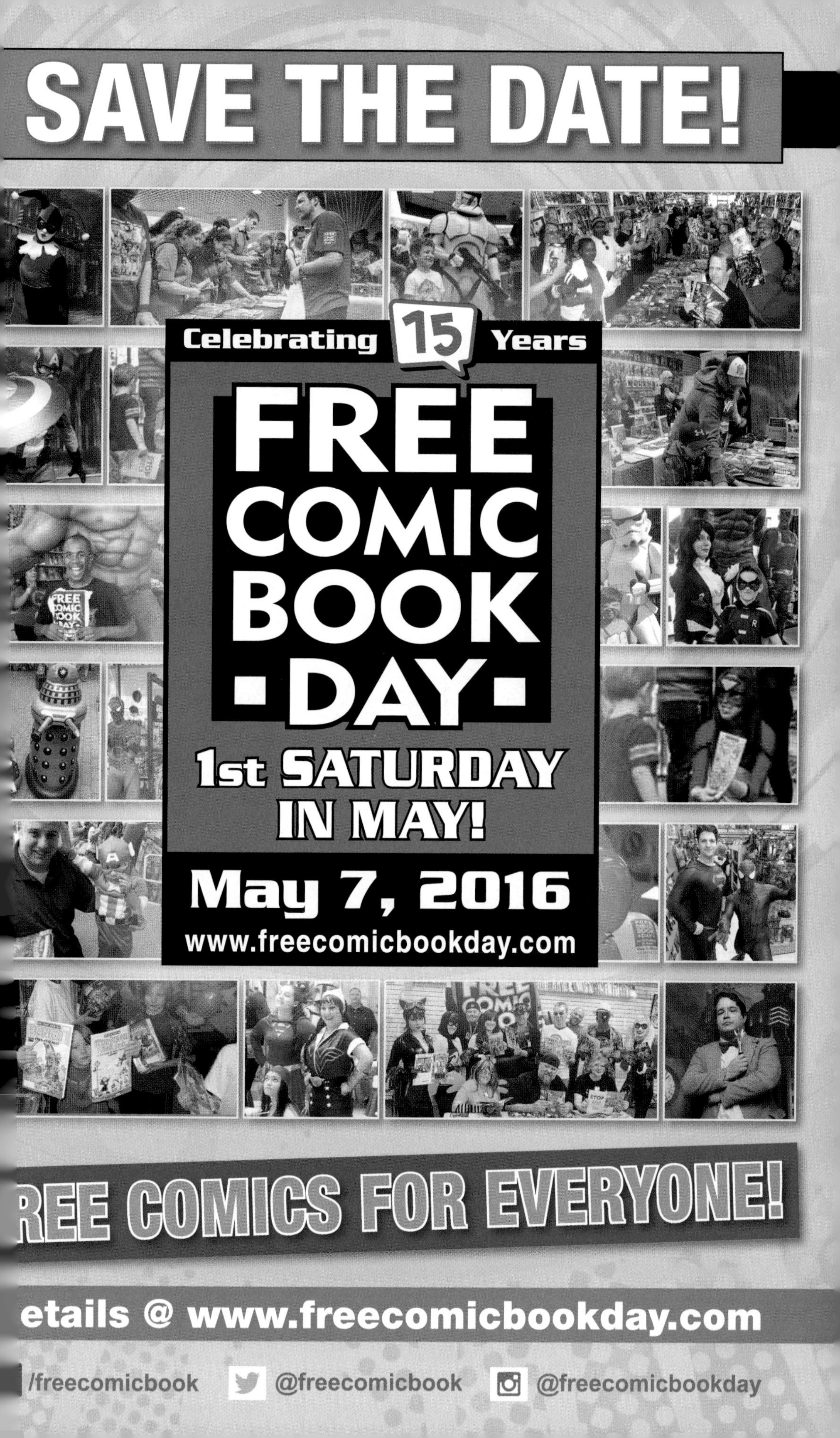
SAVE THE DATE!
Celebrating 15 Years
FREE COMIC BOOK DAY
1st SATURDAY IN MAY!
May 7, 2016
www.freecomicbookday.com
REE COMICS FOR EVERYONE!
etails @ www.freecomicbookday.com
/freecomicbook
@freecomicbook
@freecomicbookday

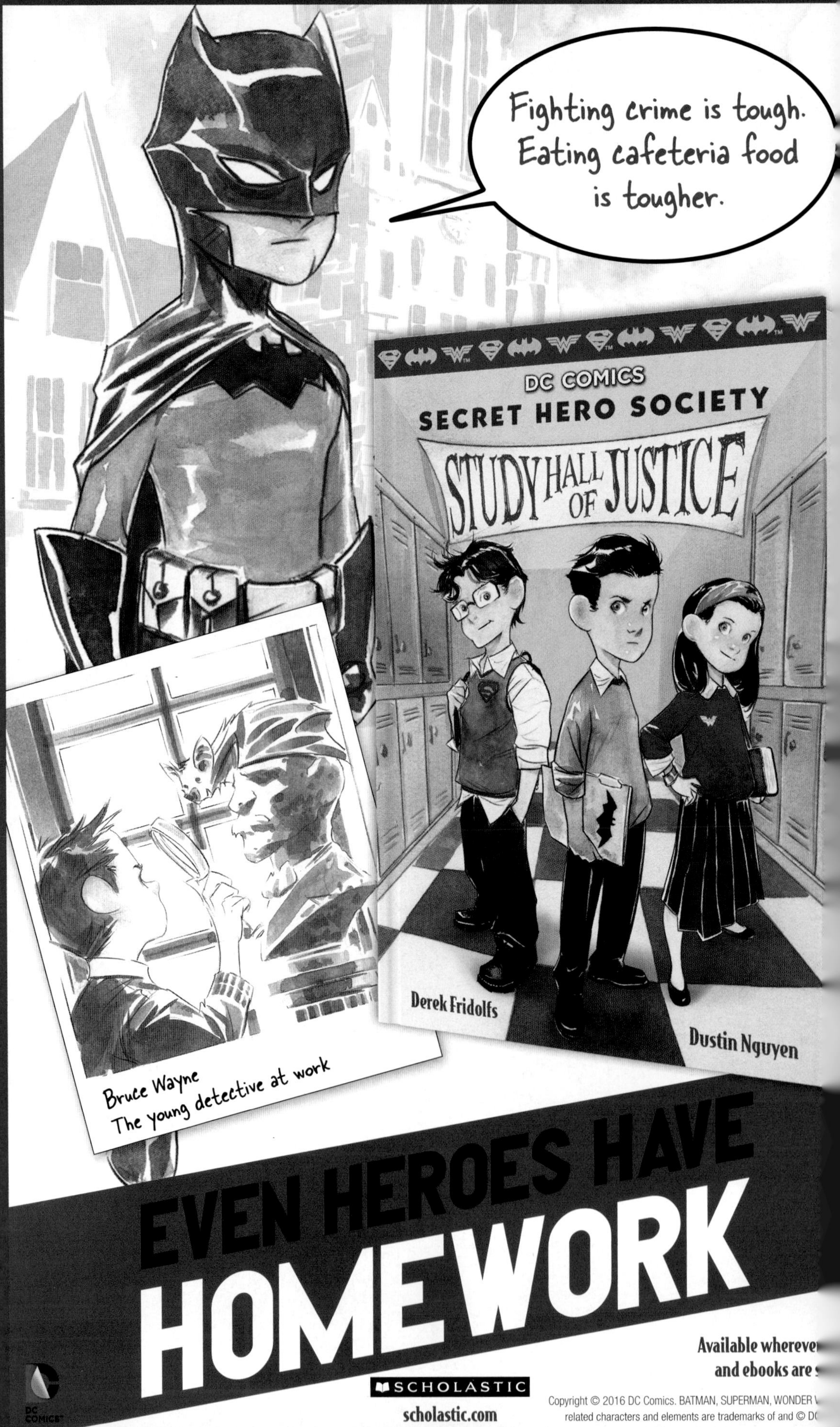
Fighting crime is tough. Eating cafeteria food is tougher.
DC COMICS
SECRET HERO SOCIETY
STUDY HALL OF JUSTICE
Derek Fridolfs
Dustin Nguyen
Bruce Wayne
The young detective at work
EVEN HEROES HAVE
HOMEWORK
Available wherever
and ebooks are
SCHOLASTIC
scholastic.com
Copyright © 2016 DC Comics. BATMAN, SUPERMAN, WONDER
related characters and elements are trademarks of and © DC
DC COMICS

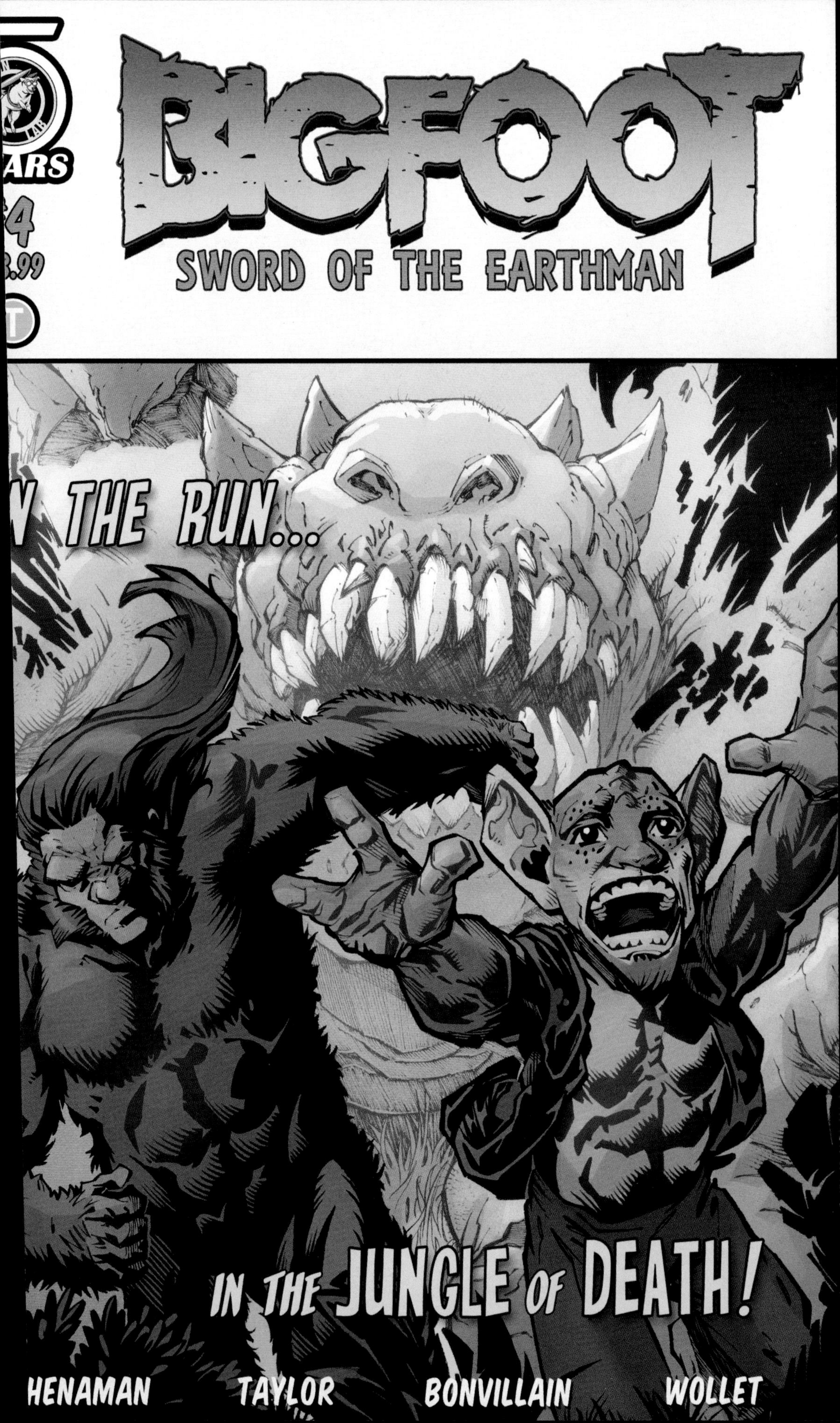
BIGFOOT
SWORD OF THE EARTHMAN
N THE RUN...
IN THE JUNGLE OF DEATH!
HENAMAN
TAYLOR
BONVILLAIN
WOLLET

DEATH STALKS THE JUNGLES
OF TURONIA.

IN YEARS PAST, POETS WROTE THAT THE JUNGLES OF
TURONIA STRETCHED AS FAR AS THE EYE COULD SEE.
A BOUNTIFUL LAND OF PLEASURES UNTOLD,
TREASURES UNDISCOVERED AND BEAUTY UNBRIDLED.

IT WAS PARADISE...

BUT THAT WAS THE PAST.

NOW IT IS WRITTEN, "THE WINDS OF HELL
BREATHE HEAVY AT HER GATES".

LOCATED AT THE EDGE OF THE BARREN DESERT, THE
TURONIAN JUNGLE IS A FRACTION OF ITS FORMER
SIZE. A DWINDLING HABITAT OF PREDATORS,
PROTECTORS, AND POISONOUS PLANTS, IT IS
SAID THAT EVEN THE HARDY DIE IN TURONIA.

NOW A HAVEN FOR POACHERS, FUGITIVES, PIRATES
AND THIEVES, ONLY THE FOOLHARDY VENTURE INTO
THE JUNGLE'S EMBRACE, ONLY THE MURDERERS SEEK
ITS ASYLUM AND ONLY THE PSYCHOTIC WELCOME ITS
SHADOW.

DEATH STALKS THE JUNGLES OF TURONIA.

DEATH AWAITS...

BIGFOOT

SWORD OF THE EARTHMAN

Bryan Seaton: Publisher • Kevin Freeman: President • Dave Dwonch: Creative Director • Shawn Gabborin: Editor In
Jamal Igle: Vice-President of Marketing • Vito Delsante: Director of Marketing • Jim Dietz: Social Media Direct
Nicole DAndria: Script Editor • Chad Cicconi: Black Sheep • Colleen Boyd: Submissions Editor

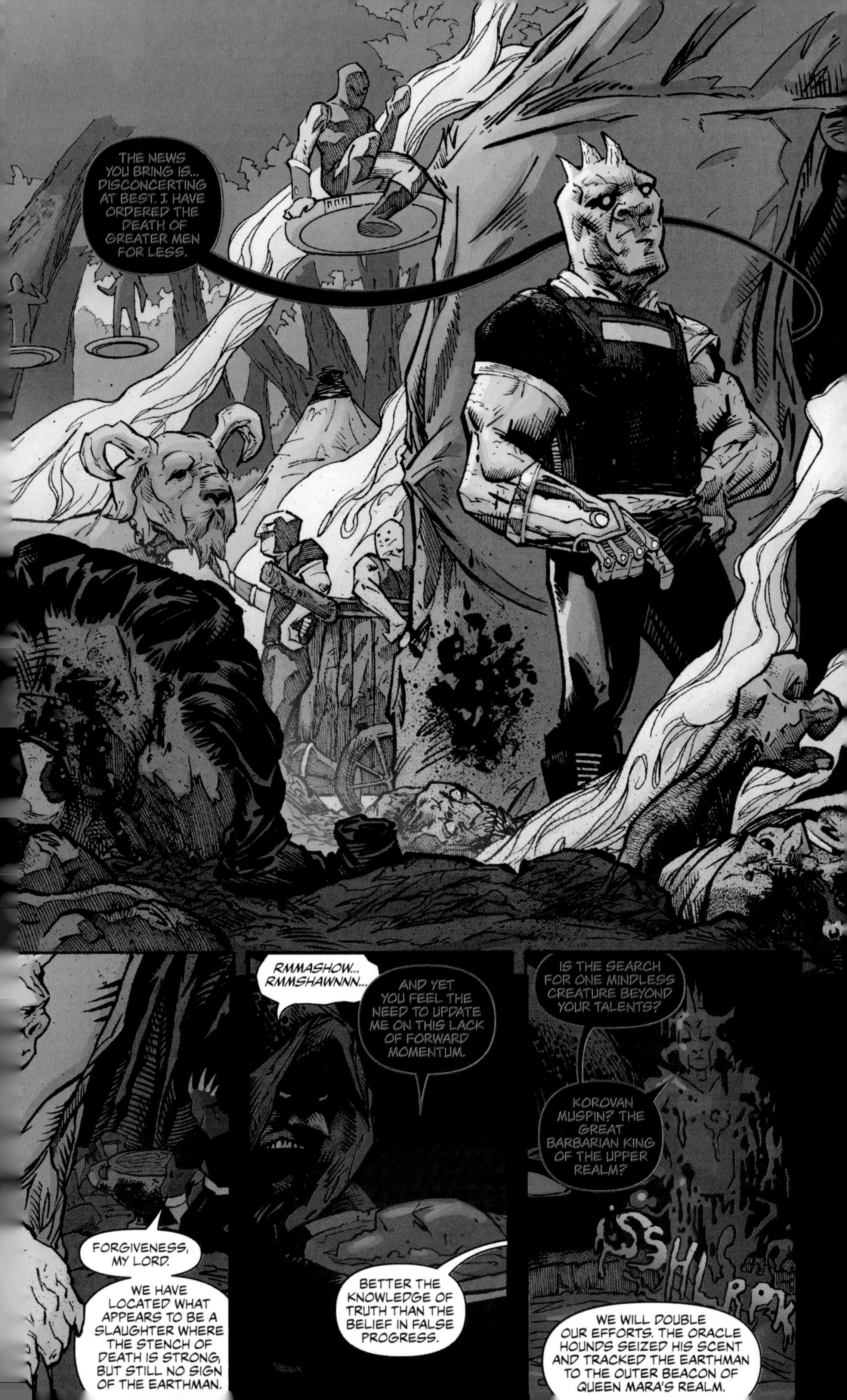
THE NEWS YOU BRING IS... DISCONCERTING AT BEST. I HAVE ORDERED THE DEATH OF GREATER MEN FOR LESS.
FORGIVENESS, MY LORD.
WE HAVE LOCATED WHAT APPEARS TO BE A SLAUGHTER WHERE THE STENCH OF DEATH IS STRONG, BUT STILL NO SIGN OF THE EARTHMAN.
RMMASHOW... RMMSHAWNNN...
AND YET YOU FEEL THE NEED TO UPDATE ME ON THIS LACK OF FORWARD MOMENTUM.
BETTER THE KNOWLEDGE OF TRUTH THAN THE BELIEF IN FALSE PROGRESS.
IS THE SEARCH FOR ONE MINDLESS CREATURE BEYOND YOUR TALENTS?
KOROVAN MUSPIN? THE GREAT BARBARIAN KING OF THE UPPER REALM?
SSHLRPK
WE WILL DOUBLE OUR EFFORTS. THE ORACLE HOUNDS SEIZED HIS SCENT AND TRACKED THE EARTHMAN TO THE OUTER BEACON OF QUEEN MARA'S REALM.

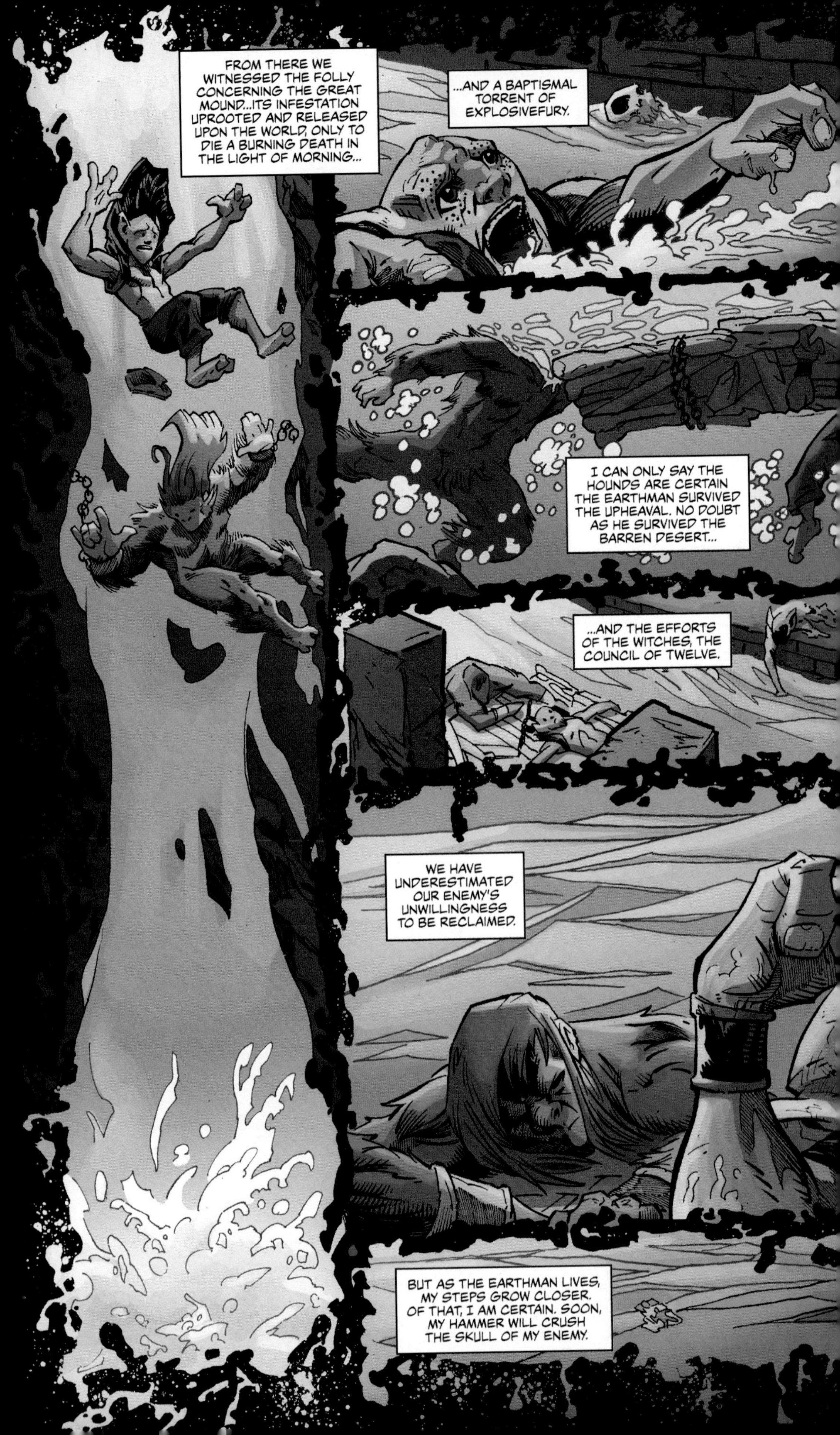
FROM THERE WE WITNESSED THE FOLLY CONCERNING THE GREAT MOUND...ITS INFESTATION UPROOTED AND RELEASED UPON THE WORLD, ONLY TO DIE A BURNING DEATH IN THE LIGHT OF MORNING...
...AND A BAPTISMAL TORRENT OF EXPLOSIVEFURY.
I CAN ONLY SAY THE HOUNDS ARE CERTAIN THE EARTHMAN SURVIVED THE UPHEAVAL. NO DOUBT AS HE SURVIVED THE BARREN DESERT...
...AND THE EFFORTS OF THE WITCHES, THE COUNCIL OF TWELVE.
WE HAVE UNDERESTIMATED OUR ENEMY'S UNWILLINGNESS TO BE RECLAIMED.
BUT AS THE EARTHMAN LIVES, MY STEPS GROW CLOSER. OF THAT, I AM CERTAIN. SOON, MY HAMMER WILL CRUSH THE SKULL OF MY ENEMY.

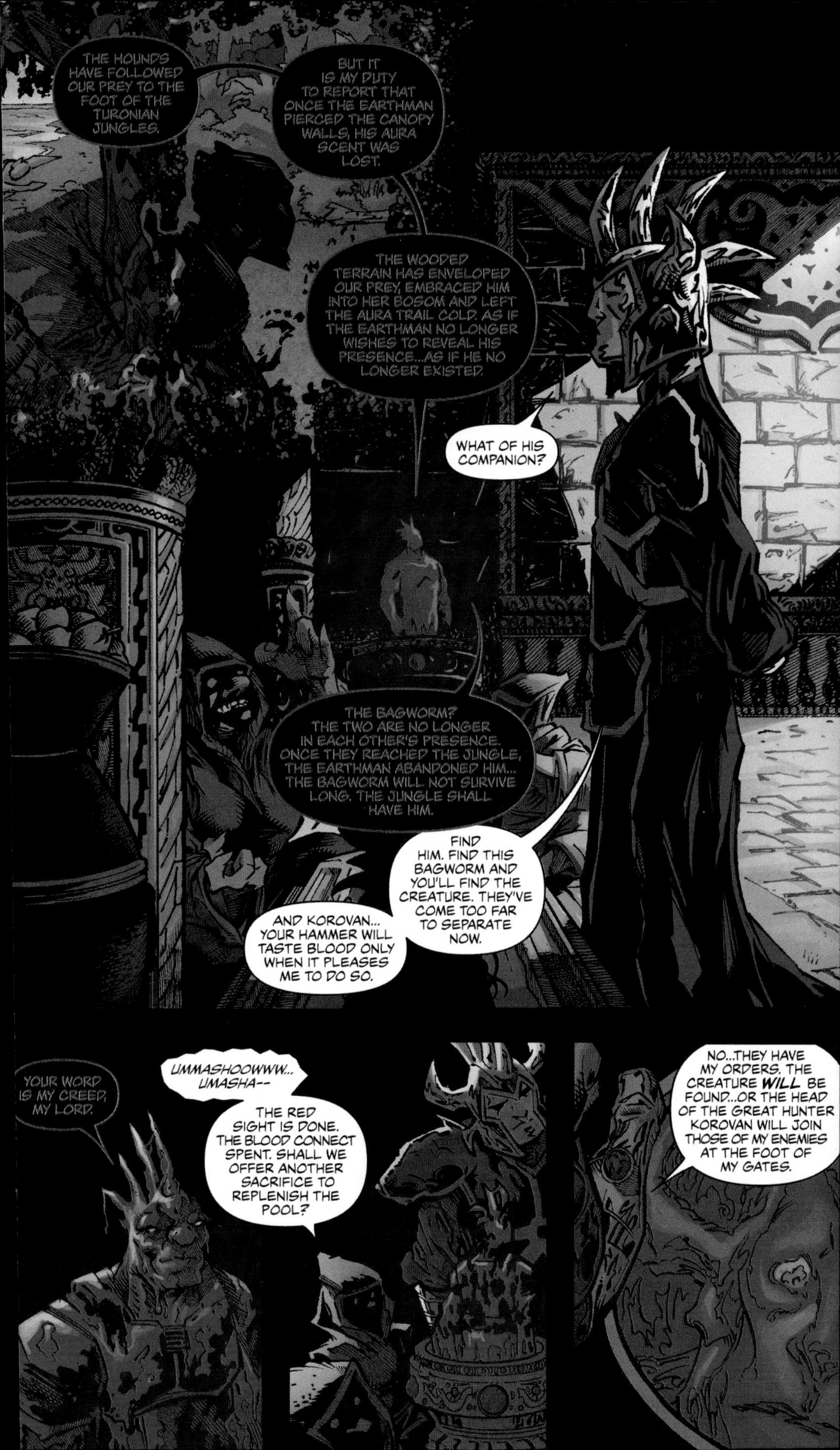
THE HOUNDS HAVE FOLLOWED OUR PREY TO THE FOOT OF THE TURONIAN JUNGLES.
BUT IT IS MY DUTY TO REPORT THAT ONCE THE EARTHMAN PIERCED THE CANOPY WALLS, HIS AURA SCENT WAS LOST.
THE WOODED TERRAIN HAS ENVELOPED OUR PREY, EMBRACED HIM INTO HER BOSOM AND LEFT THE AURA TRAIL COLD. AS IF THE EARTHMAN NO LONGER WISHES TO REVEAL HIS PRESENCE...AS IF HE NO LONGER EXISTED.
WHAT OF HIS COMPANION?
THE BAGWORM? THE TWO ARE NO LONGER IN EACH OTHER'S PRESENCE. ONCE THEY REACHED THE JUNGLE, THE EARTHMAN ABANDONED HIM... THE BAGWORM WILL NOT SURVIVE LONG. THE JUNGLE SHALL HAVE HIM.
FIND HIM. FIND THIS BAGWORM AND YOU'LL FIND THE CREATURE. THEY'VE COME TOO FAR TO SEPARATE NOW.
AND KOROVAN... YOUR HAMMER WILL TASTE BLOOD ONLY WHEN IT PLEASES ME TO DO SO.
YOUR WORD IS MY CREED, MY LORD.
UMMASHOOWWW... UMASHA--
THE RED SIGHT IS DONE. THE BLOOD CONNECT SPENT. SHALL WE OFFER ANOTHER SACRIFICE TO REPLENISH THE POOL?
NO...THEY HAVE MY ORDERS. THE CREATURE WILL BE FOUND...OR THE HEAD OF THE GREAT HUNTER KOROVAN WILL JOIN THOSE OF MY ENEMIES AT THE FOOT OF MY GATES.

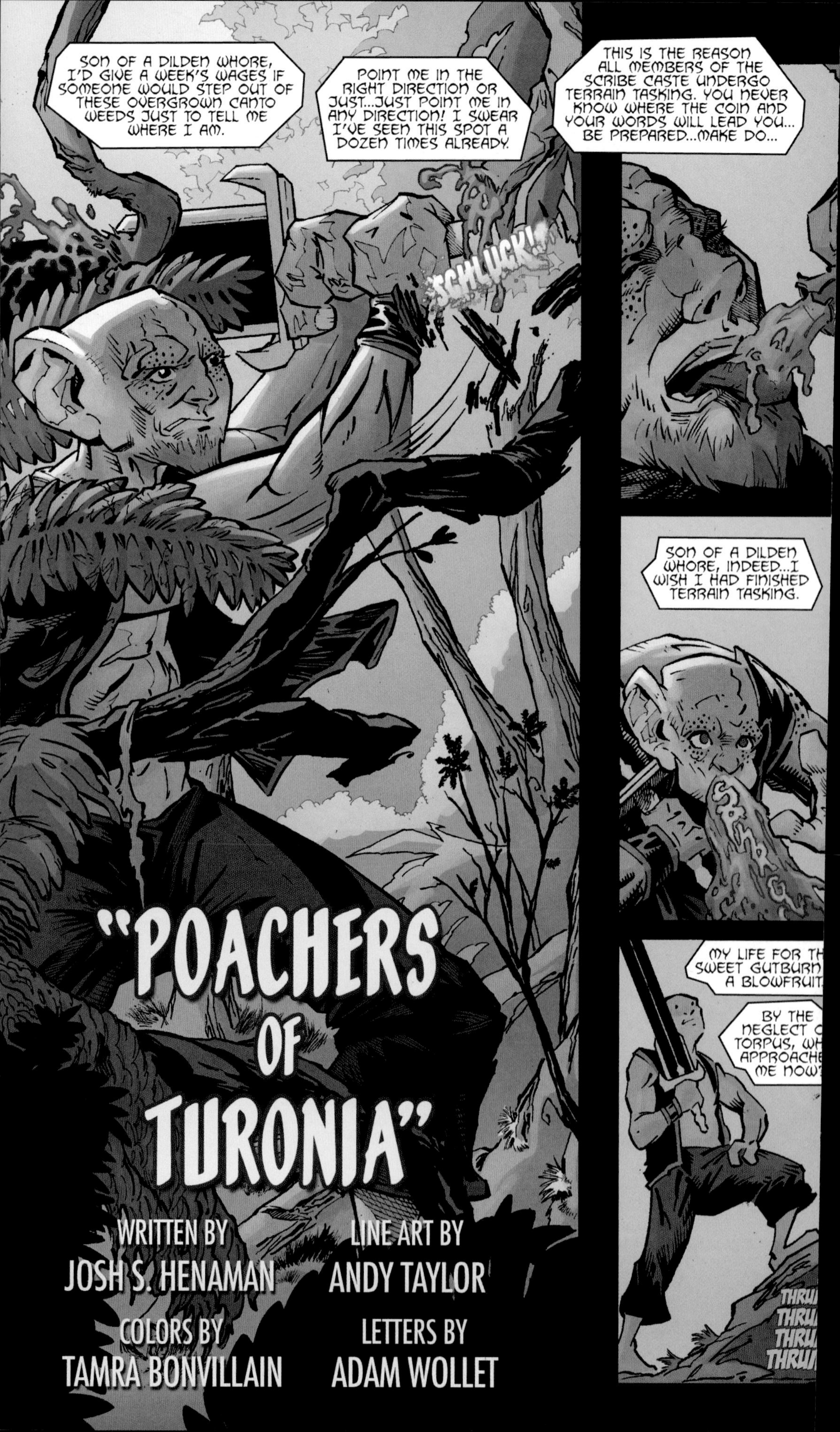
SON OF A DILDEN WHORE, I'D GIVE A WEEK'S WAGES IF SOMEONE WOULD STEP OUT OF THESE OVERGROWN CANTO WEEDS JUST TO TELL ME WHERE I AM.
POINT ME IN THE RIGHT DIRECTION OR JUST...JUST POINT ME IN ANY DIRECTION! I SWEAR I'VE SEEN THIS SPOT A DOZEN TIMES ALREADY.
SCHLUCK!
"POACHERS OF TURONIA"
WRITTEN BY
JOSH S. HENAMAN
LINE ART BY
ANDY TAYLOR
COLORS BY
TAMRA BONVILLAIN
LETTERS BY
ADAM WOLLET
THIS IS THE REASON ALL MEMBERS OF THE SCRIBE CASTE UNDERGO TERRAIN TASKING. YOU NEVER KNOW WHERE THE COIN AND YOUR WORDS WILL LEAD YOU... BE PREPARED...MAKE DO...
SON OF A DILDEN WHORE, INDEED...I WISH I HAD FINISHED TERRAIN TASKING.
MY LIFE FOR TH
SWEET GUTBURN
A BLOWFRUIT
BY THE NEGLECT O
TORPUS, WH
APPROACHE
ME NOW?
THRU
THRU
THRU
THRU

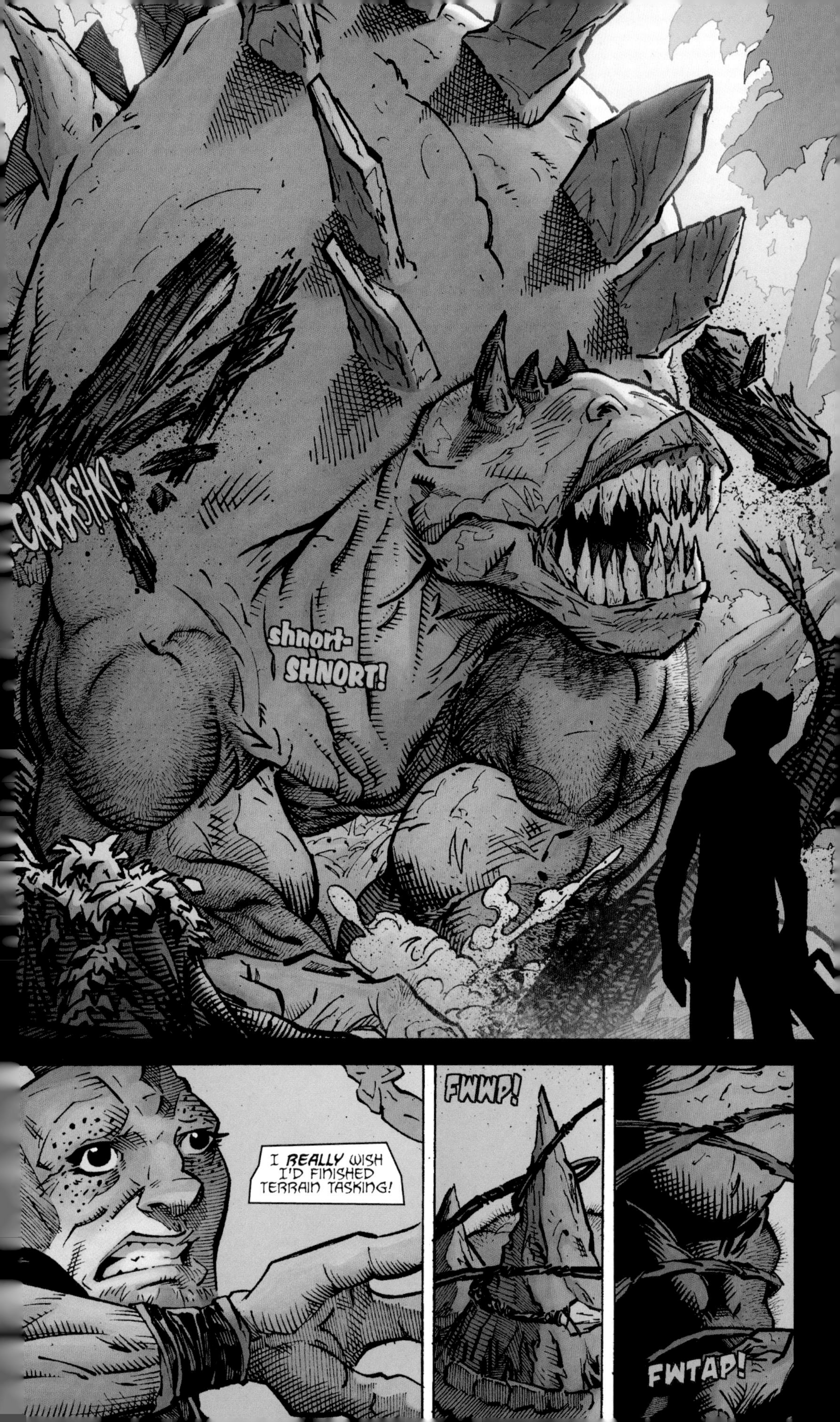
CRAASH!
shnort-
SHNORT!
I REALLY WISH I'D FINISHED TERRAIN TASKING!
FWWP!
FWTAP!

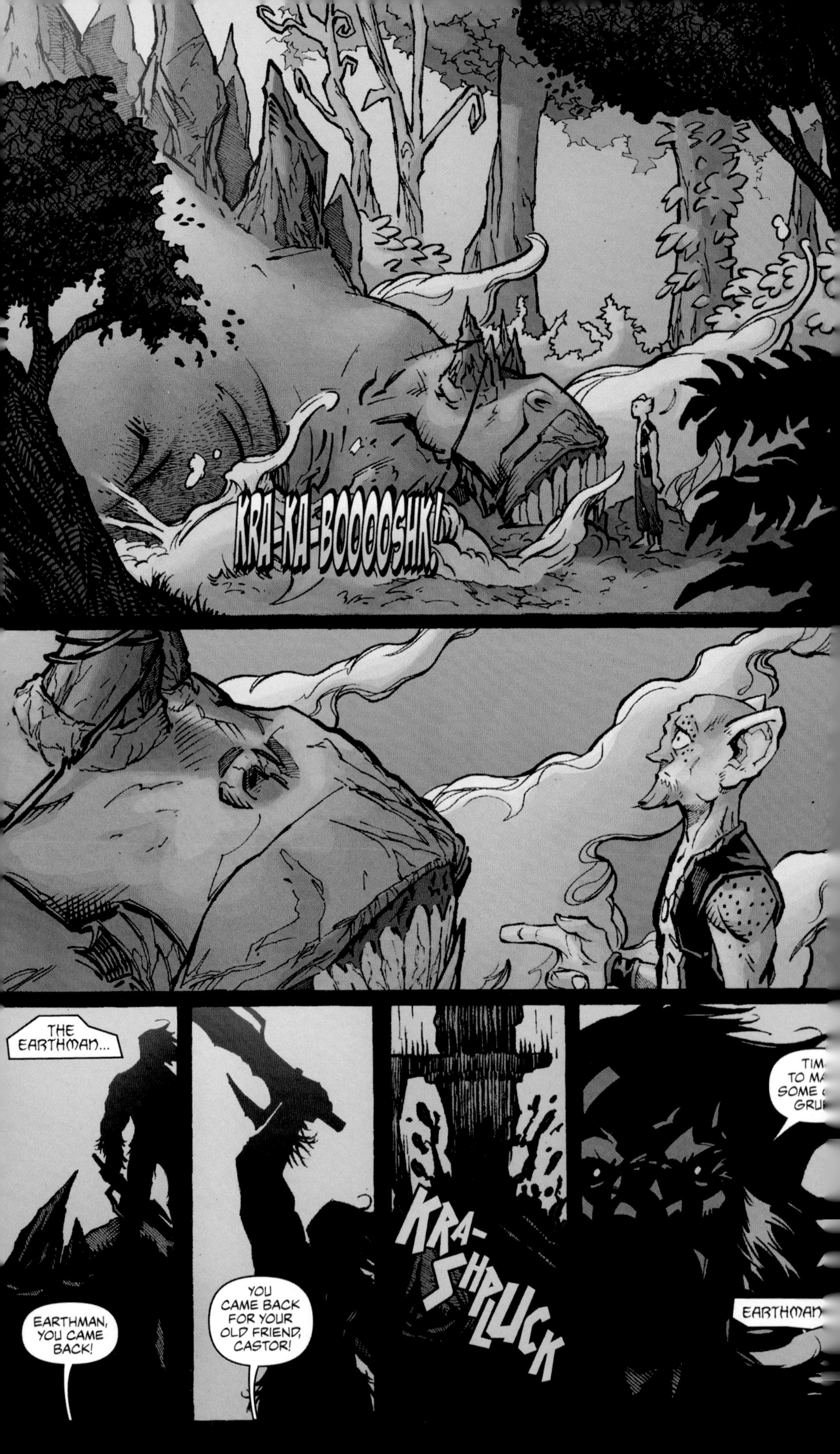
KRA-KA-BOOOOSHK!
THE EARTHMAN...
EARTHMAN, YOU CAME BACK!
YOU CAME BACK FOR YOUR OLD FRIEND, CASTOR!
KRA-SHPLUCK
EARTHMAN

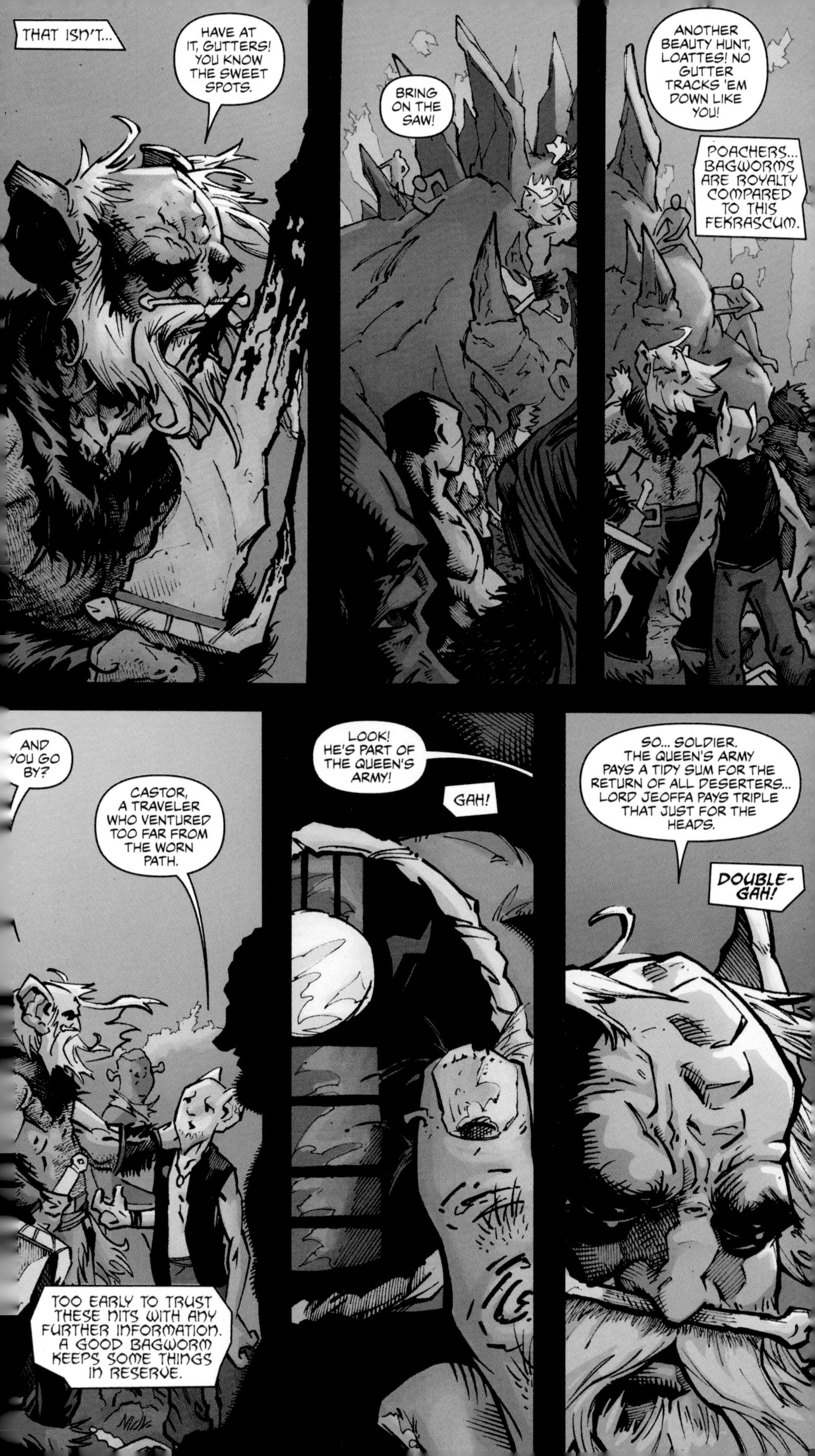
THAT ISN'T...
HAVE AT IT, GUTTERS! YOU KNOW THE SWEET SPOTS.
BRING ON THE SAW!
ANOTHER BEAUTY HUNT, LOATTES! NO GUTTER TRACKS 'EM DOWN LIKE YOU!
POACHERS... BAGWORMS ARE ROYALTY COMPARED TO THIS FEKRASCUM.
AND YOU GO BY?
CASTOR, A TRAVELER WHO VENTURED TOO FAR FROM THE WORN PATH.
TOO EARLY TO TRUST THESE NITS WITH ANY FURTHER INFORMATION. A GOOD BAGWORM KEEPS SOME THINGS IN RESERVE.
LOOK! HE'S PART OF THE QUEEN'S ARMY!
GAH!
SO... SOLDIER. THE QUEEN'S ARMY PAYS A TIDY SUM FOR THE RETURN OF ALL DESERTERS... LORD JEOFFA PAYS TRIPLE THAT JUST FOR THE HEADS.
DOUBLE-GAH!

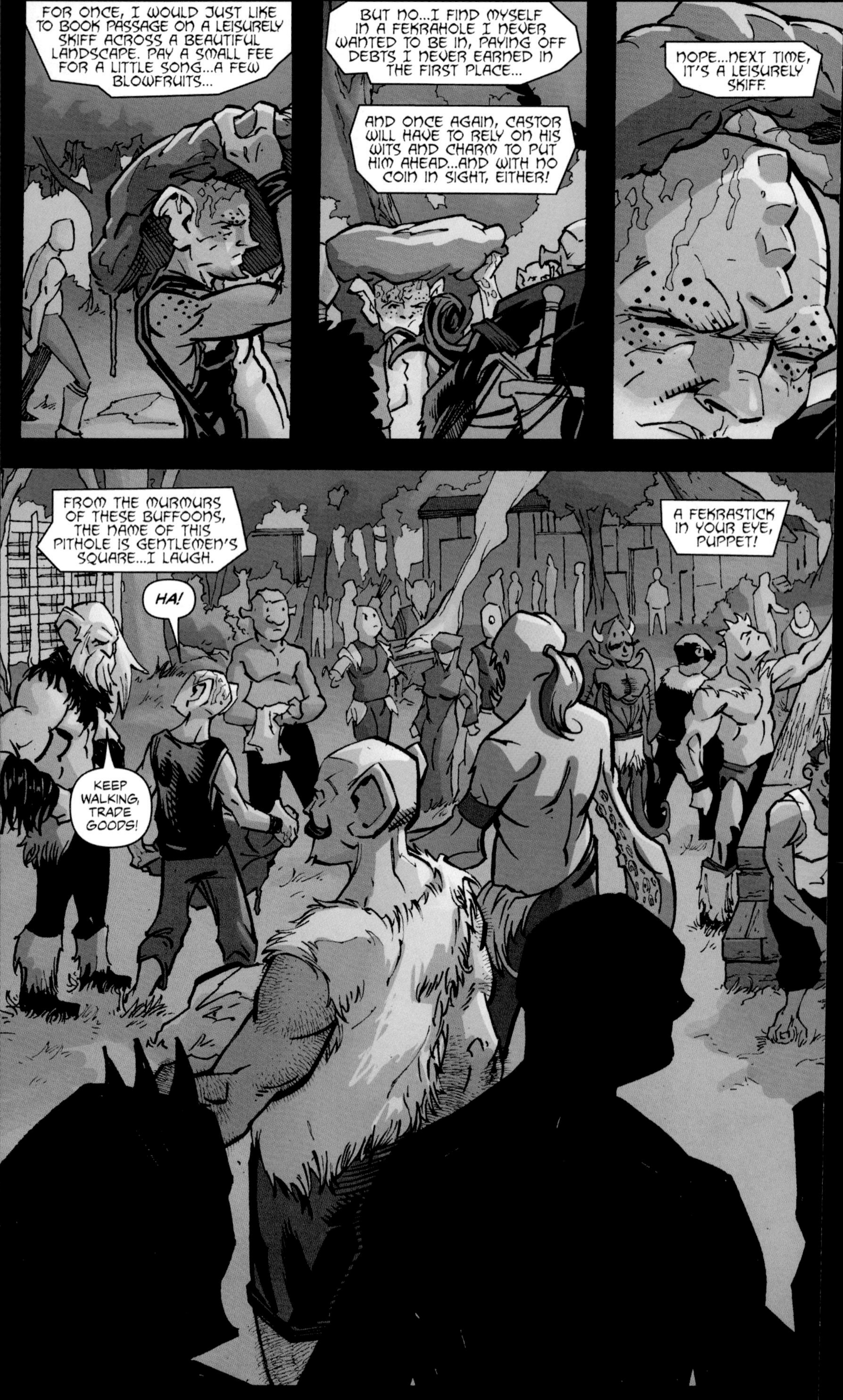
FOR ONCE, I WOULD JUST LIKE TO BOOK PASSAGE ON A LEISURELY SKIFF ACROSS A BEAUTIFUL LANDSCAPE. PAY A SMALL FEE FOR A LITTLE SONG...A FEW BLOWFRUITS...
BUT NO...I FIND MYSELF IN A FEKRAHOLE I NEVER WANTED TO BE IN, PAYING OFF DEBTS I NEVER EARNED IN THE FIRST PLACE...
AND ONCE AGAIN, CASTOR WILL HAVE TO RELY ON HIS WITS AND CHARM TO PUT HIM AHEAD...AND WITH NO COIN IN SIGHT, EITHER!
NOPE...NEXT TIME, IT'S A LEISURELY SKIFF.
FROM THE MURMURS OF THESE BUFFOONS, THE NAME OF THIS PITHOLE IS GENTLEMEN'S SQUARE...I LAUGH.
HA!
KEEP WALKING, TRADE GOODS!
A FEKRASTICK IN YOUR EYE, PUPPET!

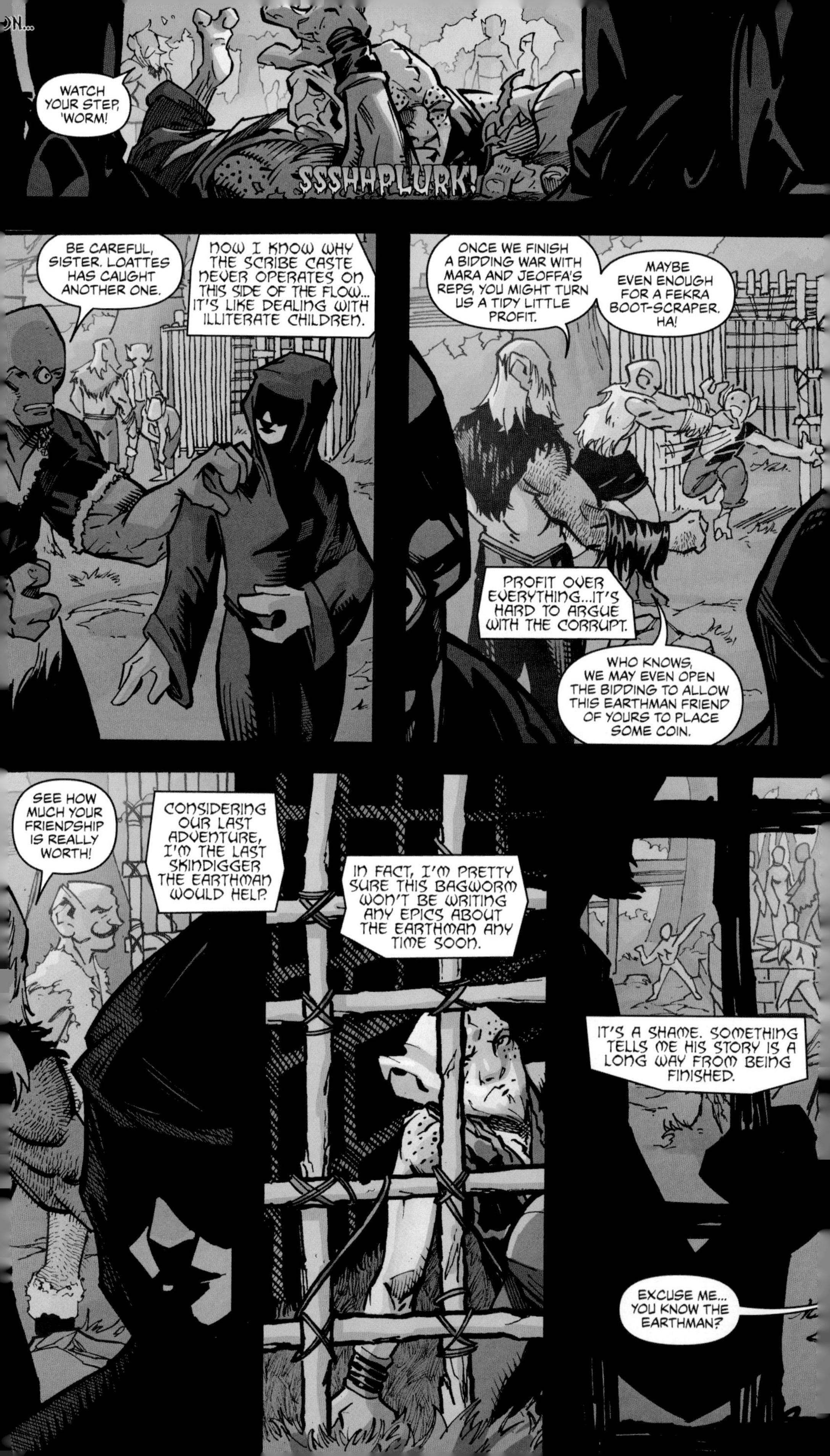

WATCH YOUR STEP, 'WORM!
SSSHHPLURK!
BE CAREFUL, SISTER. LOATTES HAS CAUGHT ANOTHER ONE.
NOW I KNOW WHY THE SCRIBE CASTE NEVER OPERATES ON THIS SIDE OF THE FLOW... IT'S LIKE DEALING WITH ILLITERATE CHILDREN.
ONCE WE FINISH A BIDDING WAR WITH MARA AND JEOFFA'S REPS, YOU MIGHT TURN US A TIDY LITTLE PROFIT.
MAYBE EVEN ENOUGH FOR A FEKRA BOOT-SCRAPER. HA!
PROFIT OVER EVERYTHING...IT'S HARD TO ARGUE WITH THE CORRUPT.
WHO KNOWS, WE MAY EVEN OPEN THE BIDDING TO ALLOW THIS EARTHMAN FRIEND OF YOURS TO PLACE SOME COIN.
SEE HOW MUCH YOUR FRIENDSHIP IS REALLY WORTH!
CONSIDERING OUR LAST ADVENTURE, I'M THE LAST SKINDIGGER THE EARTHMAN WOULD HELP.
IN FACT, I'M PRETTY SURE THIS BAGWORM WON'T BE WRITING ANY EPICS ABOUT THE EARTHMAN ANY TIME SOON.
IT'S A SHAME. SOMETHING TELLS ME HIS STORY IS A LONG WAY FROM BEING FINISHED.
EXCUSE ME... YOU KNOW THE EARTHMAN?

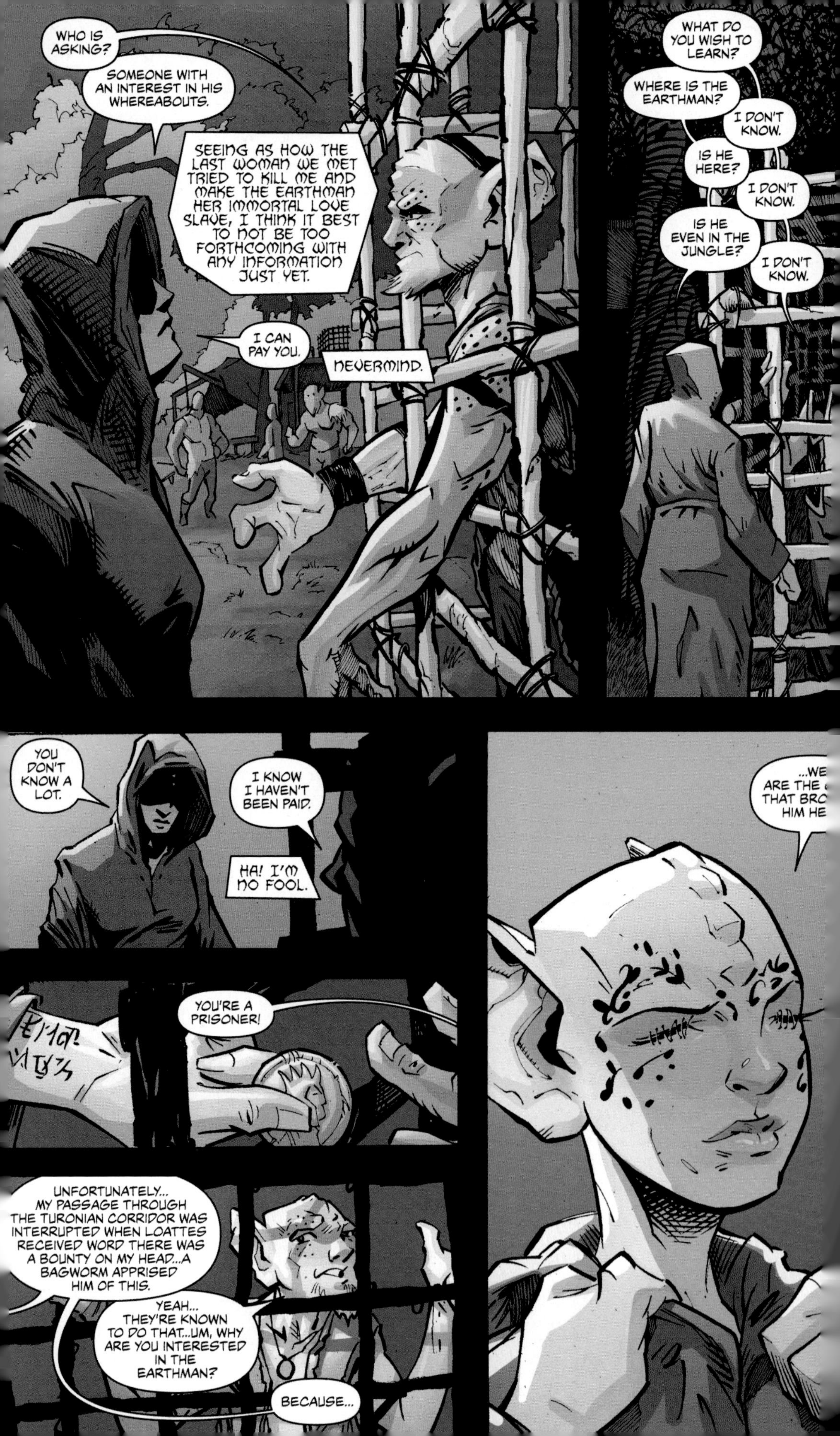
WHO IS ASKING?
SOMEONE WITH AN INTEREST IN HIS WHEREABOUTS.
SEEING AS HOW THE LAST WOMAN WE MET TRIED TO KILL ME AND MAKE THE EARTHMAN HER IMMORTAL LOVE SLAVE, I THINK IT BEST TO NOT BE TOO FORTHCOMING WITH ANY INFORMATION JUST YET.
I CAN PAY YOU.
NEVERMIND.
WHAT DO YOU WISH TO LEARN?
WHERE IS THE EARTHMAN?
I DON'T KNOW.
IS HE HERE?
I DON'T KNOW.
IS HE EVEN IN THE JUNGLE?
I DON'T KNOW.
YOU DON'T KNOW A LOT.
I KNOW I HAVEN'T BEEN PAID.
HA! I'M NO FOOL.
YOU'RE A PRISONER!
UNFORTUNATELY... MY PASSAGE THROUGH THE TURONIAN CORRIDOR WAS INTERRUPTED WHEN LOATTES RECEIVED WORD THERE WAS A BOUNTY ON MY HEAD...A BAGWORM APPRISED HIM OF THIS.
YEAH... THEY'RE KNOWN TO DO THAT...UM, WHY ARE YOU INTERESTED IN THE EARTHMAN?
BECAUSE...
...WE ARE THE THAT BRO HIM HE

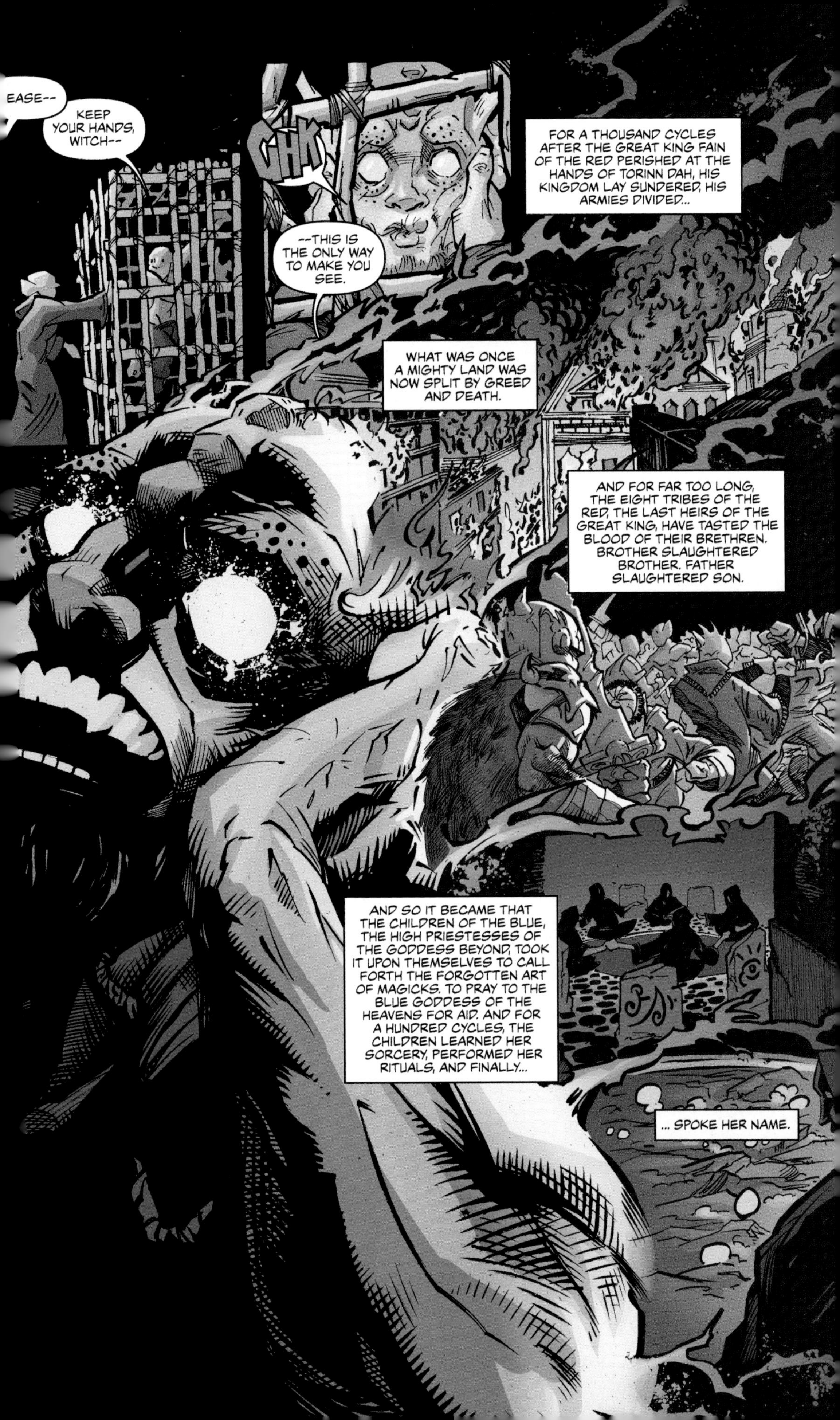
EASE--
KEEP YOUR HANDS, WITCH--
GHK
--THIS IS THE ONLY WAY TO MAKE YOU SEE.
FOR A THOUSAND CYCLES AFTER THE GREAT KING FAIN OF THE RED PERISHED AT THE HANDS OF TORINN DAH, HIS KINGDOM LAY SUNDERED, HIS ARMIES DIVIDED...
WHAT WAS ONCE A MIGHTY LAND WAS NOW SPLIT BY GREED AND DEATH.
AND FOR FAR TOO LONG, THE EIGHT TRIBES OF THE RED, THE LAST HEIRS OF THE GREAT KING, HAVE TASTED THE BLOOD OF THEIR BRETHREN. BROTHER SLAUGHTERED BROTHER. FATHER SLAUGHTERED SON.
AND SO IT BECAME THAT THE CHILDREN OF THE BLUE, THE HIGH PRIESTESSES OF THE GODDESS BEYOND, TOOK IT UPON THEMSELVES TO CALL FORTH THE FORGOTTEN ART OF MAGICKS. TO PRAY TO THE BLUE GODDESS OF THE HEAVENS FOR AID. AND FOR A HUNDRED CYCLES, THE CHILDREN LEARNED HER SORCERY, PERFORMED HER RITUALS, AND FINALLY...
... SPOKE HER NAME.

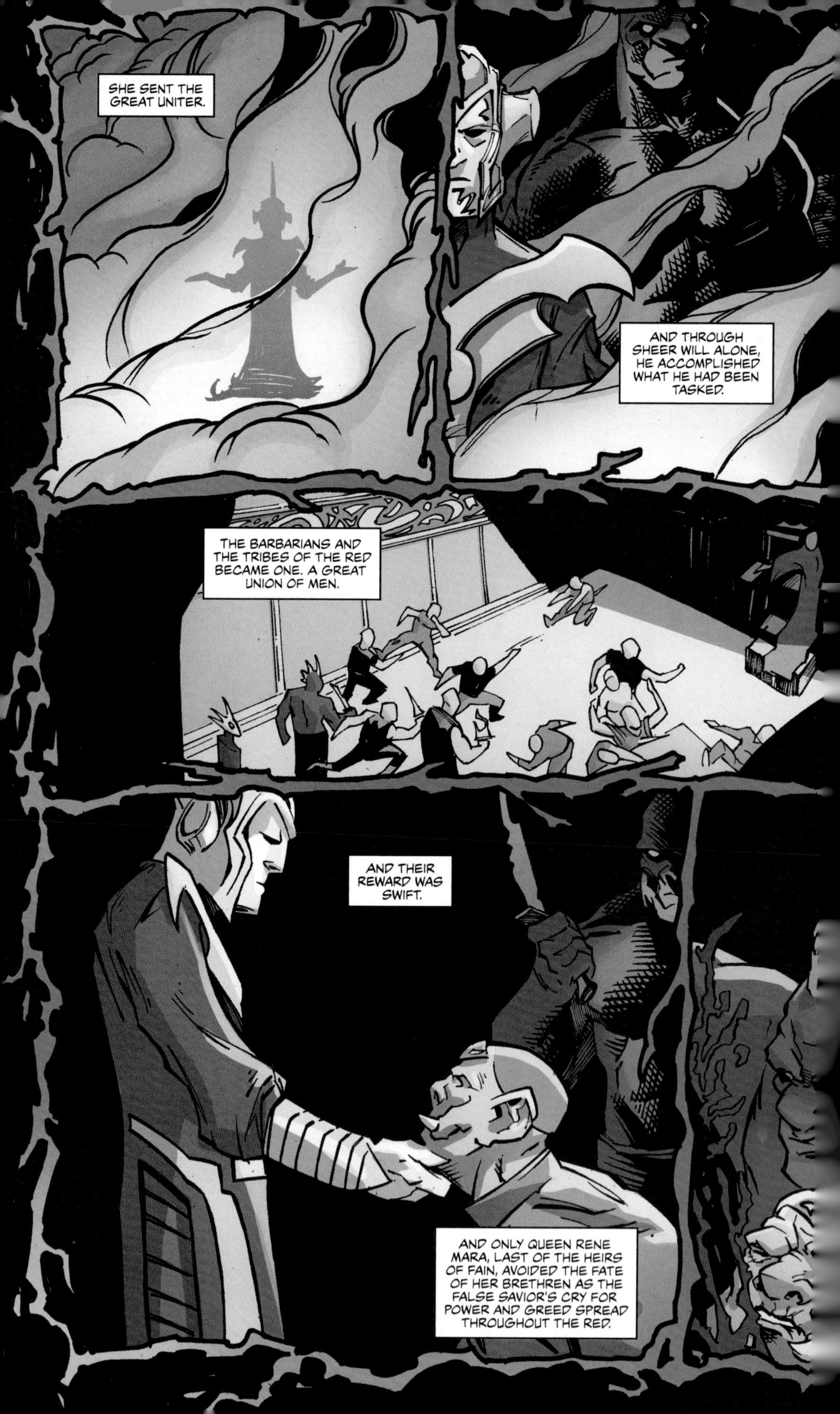
SHE SENT THE GREAT UNITER.
AND THROUGH SHEER WILL ALONE, HE ACCOMPLISHED WHAT HE HAD BEEN TASKED.
THE BARBARIANS AND THE TRIBES OF THE RED BECAME ONE. A GREAT UNION OF MEN.
AND THEIR REWARD WAS SWIFT.
AND ONLY QUEEN RENE MARA, LAST OF THE HEIRS OF FAIN, AVOIDED THE FATE OF HER BRETHREN AS THE FALSE SAVIOR'S CRY FOR POWER AND GREED SPREAD THROUGHOUT THE RED.

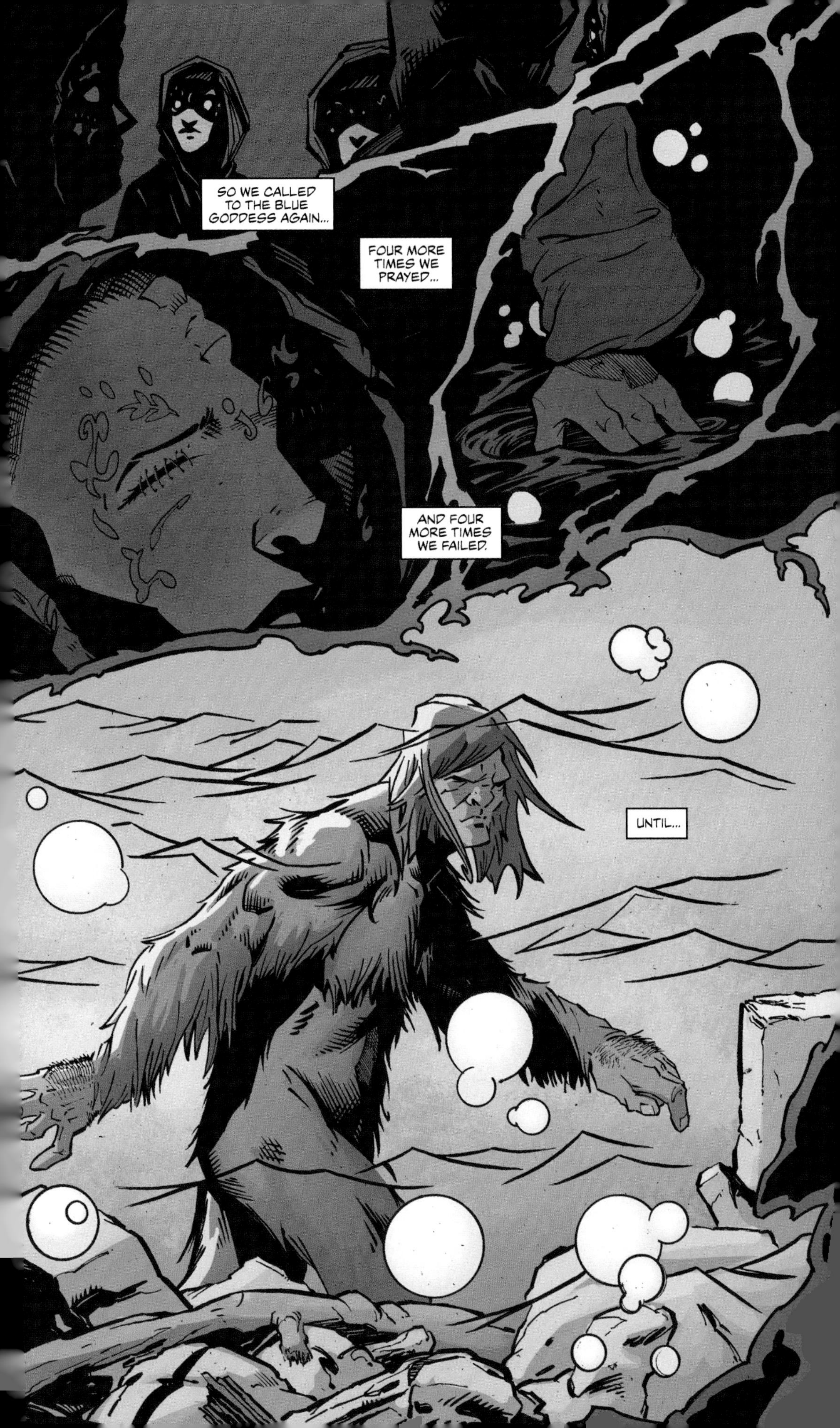
SO WE CALLED TO THE BLUE GODDESS AGAIN...
FOUR MORE TIMES WE PRAYED...
AND FOUR MORE TIMES WE FAILED.
UNTIL...

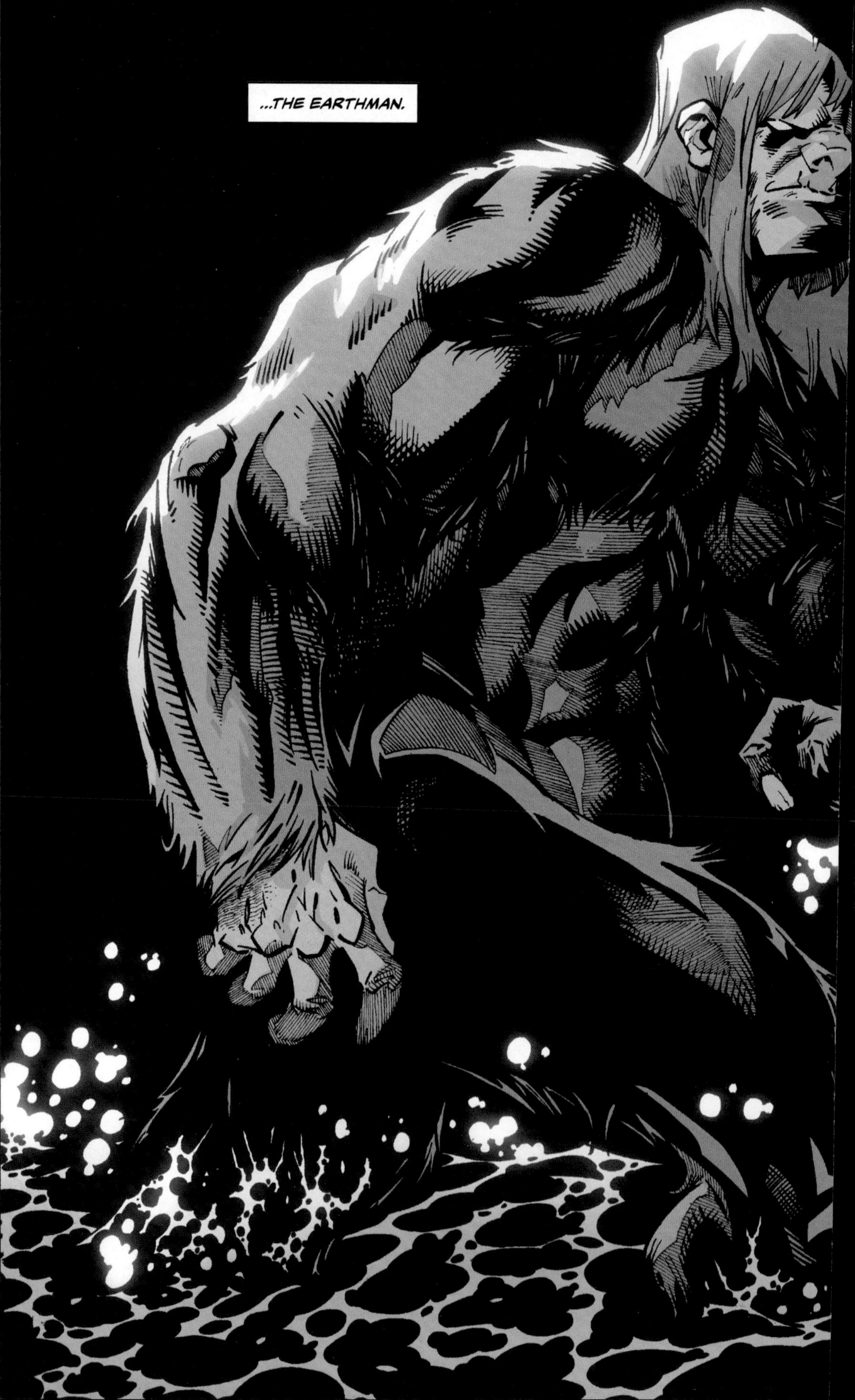
...THE EARTHMAN.

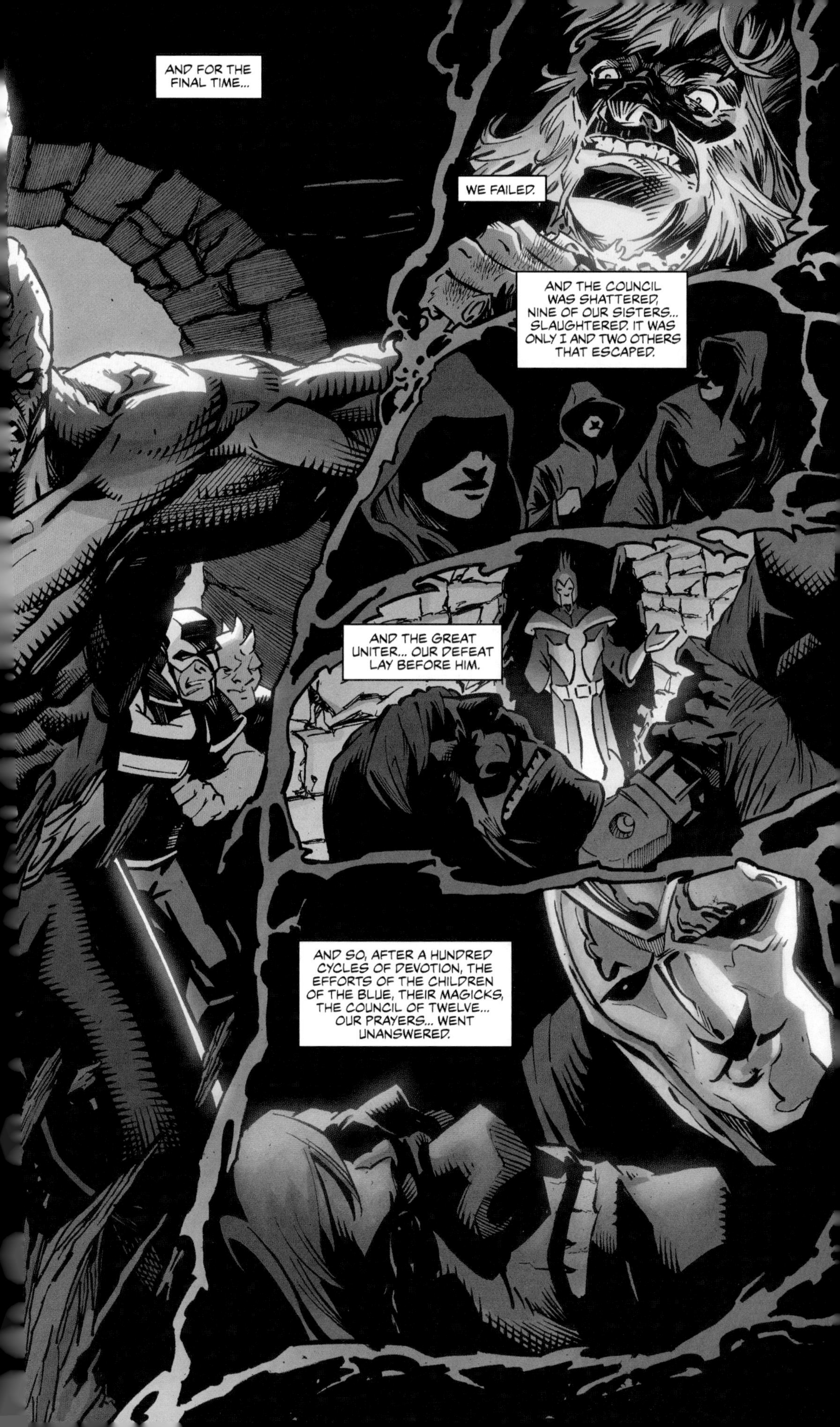
AND FOR THE FINAL TIME...
WE FAILED.
AND THE COUNCIL WAS SHATTERED, NINE OF OUR SISTERS... SLAUGHTERED. IT WAS ONLY I AND TWO OTHERS THAT ESCAPED.
AND THE GREAT UNITER... OUR DEFEAT LAY BEFORE HIM.
AND SO, AFTER A HUNDRED CYCLES OF DEVOTION, THE EFFORTS OF THE CHILDREN OF THE BLUE, THEIR MAGICKS, THE COUNCIL OF TWELVE... OUR PRAYERS... WENT UNANSWERED.

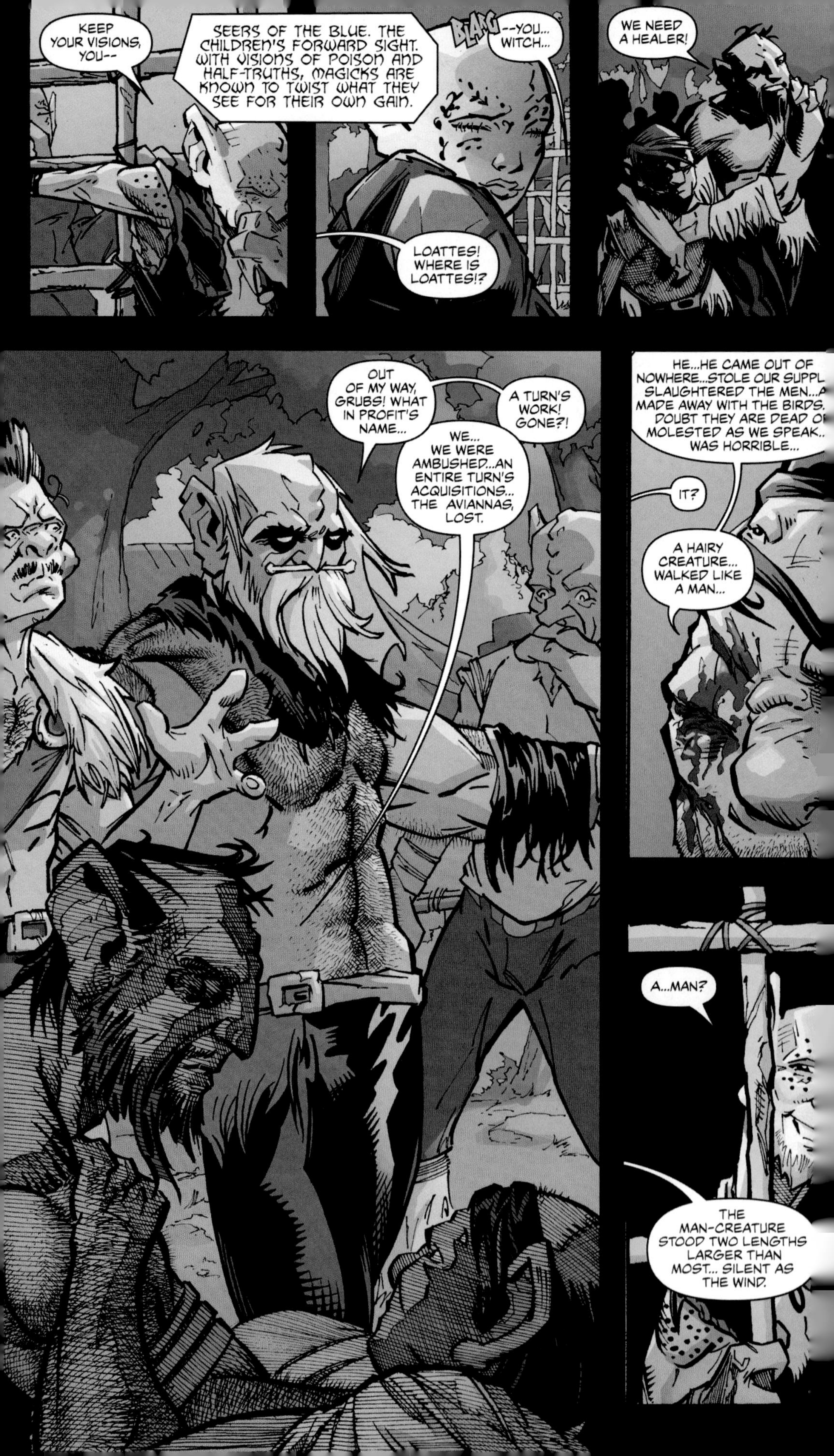
KEEP YOUR VISIONS, YOU--
SEERS OF THE BLUE. THE CHILDREN'S FORWARD SIGHT. WITH VISIONS OF POISON AND HALF-TRUTHS, MAGICKS ARE KNOWN TO TWIST WHAT THEY SEE FOR THEIR OWN GAIN.
BLAG
--YOU... WITCH...
LOATTES! WHERE IS LOATTES!?
WE NEED A HEALER!
OUT OF MY WAY, GRUBS! WHAT IN PROFIT'S NAME...
A TURN'S WORK! GONE?!
WE... WE WERE AMBUSHED...AN ENTIRE TURN'S ACQUISITIONS... THE AVIANNAS, LOST.
HE...HE CAME OUT OF NOWHERE...STOLE OUR SUPPL SLAUGHTERED THE MEN...A MADE AWAY WITH THE BIRDS. DOUBT THEY ARE DEAD O MOLESTED AS WE SPEAK.. WAS HORRIBLE...
IT?
A HAIRY CREATURE... WALKED LIKE A MAN...
A...MAN?
THE MAN-CREATURE STOOD TWO LENGTHS LARGER THAN MOST... SILENT AS THE WIND.

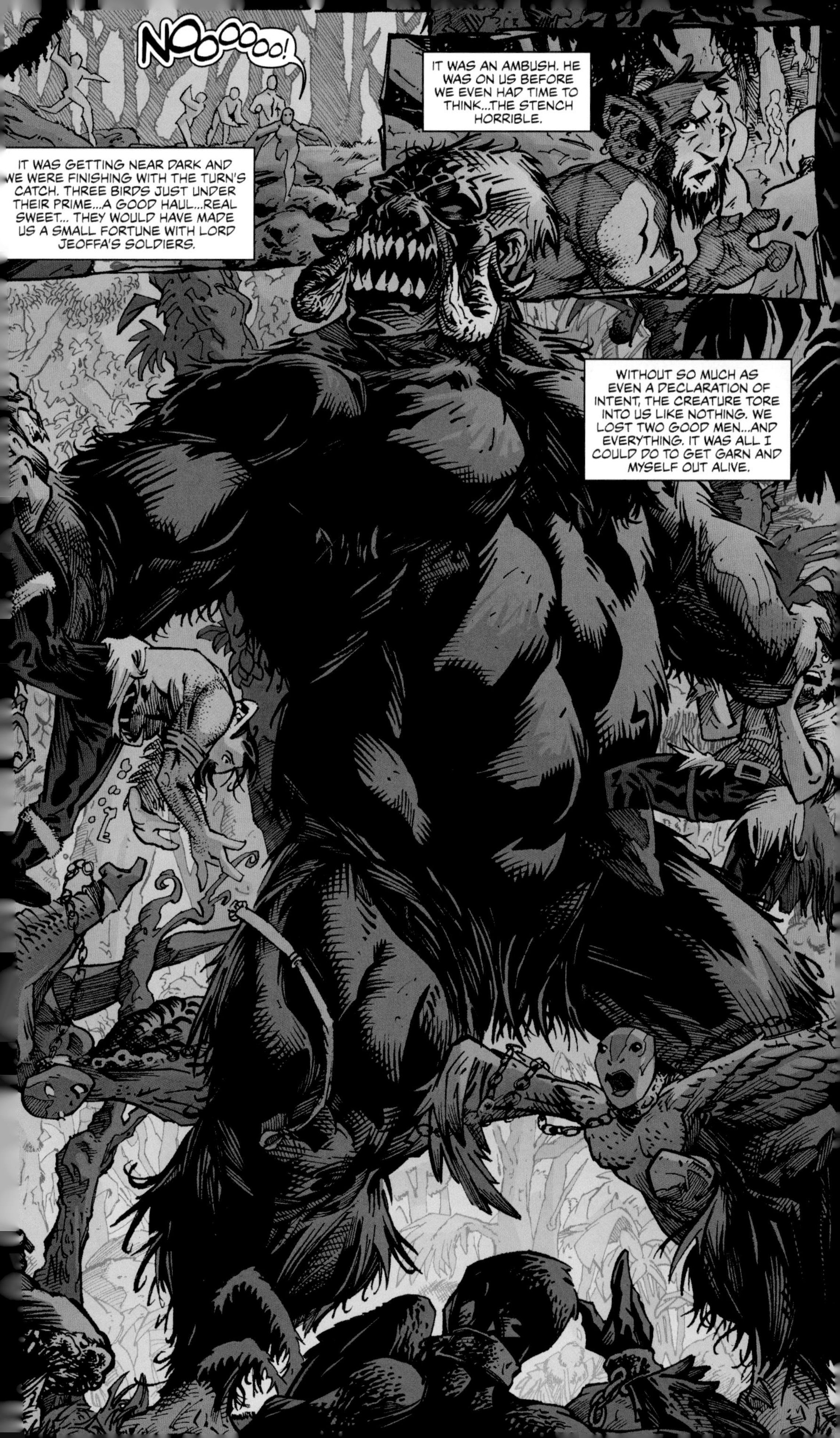
NOOOOOO!
IT WAS GETTING NEAR DARK AND WE WERE FINISHING WITH THE TURN'S CATCH. THREE BIRDS JUST UNDER THEIR PRIME...A GOOD HAUL...REAL SWEET... THEY WOULD HAVE MADE US A SMALL FORTUNE WITH LORD JEOFFA'S SOLDIERS.
IT WAS AN AMBUSH. HE WAS ON US BEFORE WE EVEN HAD TIME TO THINK...THE STENCH HORRIBLE.
WITHOUT SO MUCH AS EVEN A DECLARATION OF INTENT, THE CREATURE TORE INTO US LIKE NOTHING. WE LOST TWO GOOD MEN...AND EVERYTHING. IT WAS ALL I COULD DO TO GET GARN AND MYSELF OUT ALIVE.

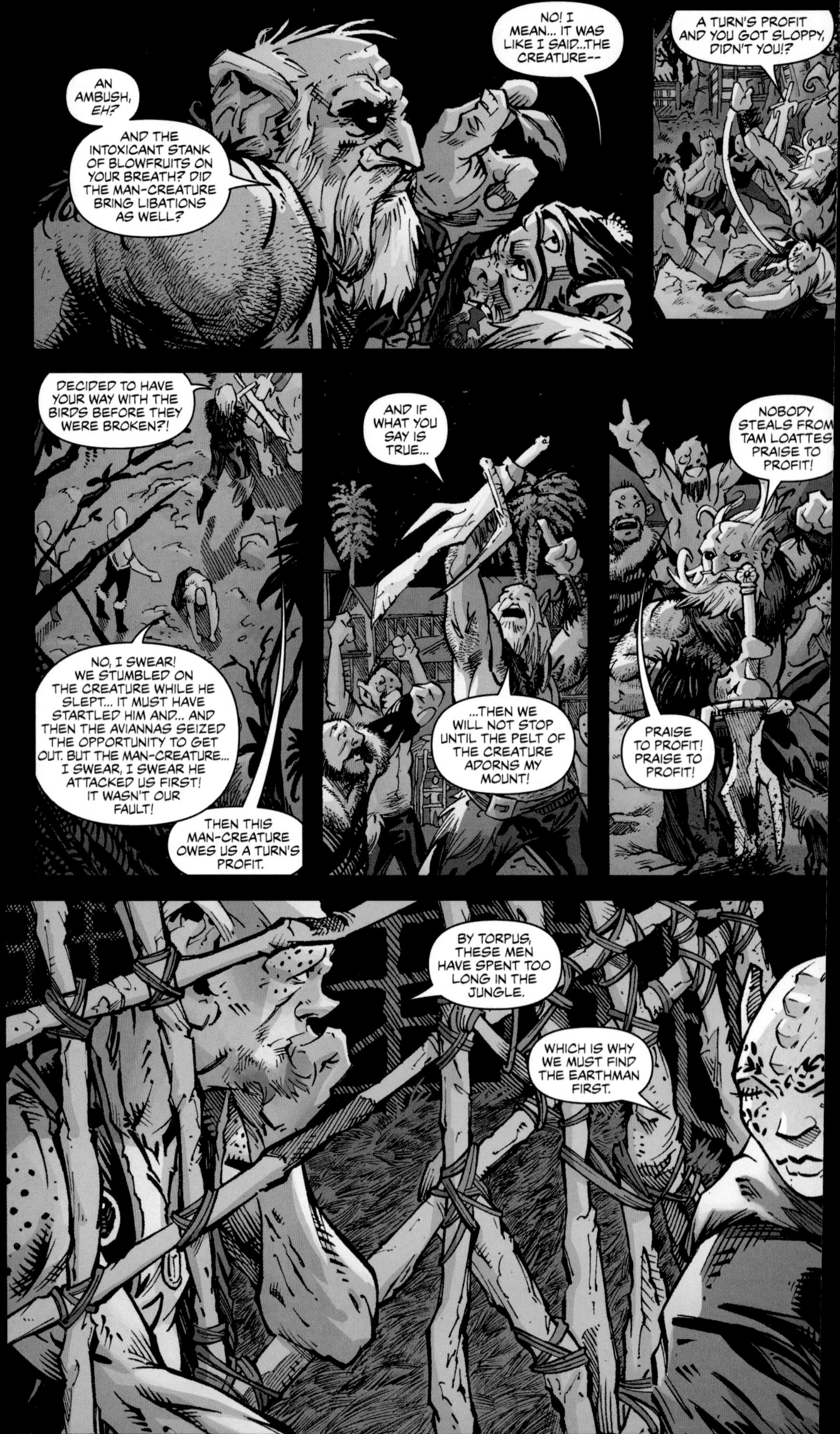
AN AMBUSH, EH?
AND THE INTOXICANT STANK OF BLOWFRUITS ON YOUR BREATH? DID THE MAN-CREATURE BRING LIBATIONS AS WELL?
NO! I MEAN... IT WAS LIKE I SAID...THE CREATURE--
A TURN'S PROFIT AND YOU GOT SLOPPY, DIDN'T YOU!?
DECIDED TO HAVE YOUR WAY WITH THE BIRDS BEFORE THEY WERE BROKEN?!
NO, I SWEAR! WE STUMBLED ON THE CREATURE WHILE HE SLEPT... IT MUST HAVE STARTLED HIM AND... AND THEN THE AVIANNAS SEIZED THE OPPORTUNITY TO GET OUT. BUT THE MAN-CREATURE... I SWEAR, I SWEAR HE ATTACKED US FIRST! IT WASN'T OUR FAULT!
THEN THIS MAN-CREATURE OWES US A TURN'S PROFIT.
AND IF WHAT YOU SAY IS TRUE...
...THEN WE WILL NOT STOP UNTIL THE PELT OF THE CREATURE ADORNS MY MOUNT!
NOBODY STEALS FROM TAM LOATTES PRAISE TO PROFIT!
PRAISE TO PROFIT! PRAISE TO PROFIT!
BY TORPUS, THESE MEN HAVE SPENT TOO LONG IN THE JUNGLE.
WHICH IS WHY WE MUST FIND THE EARTHMAN FIRST.

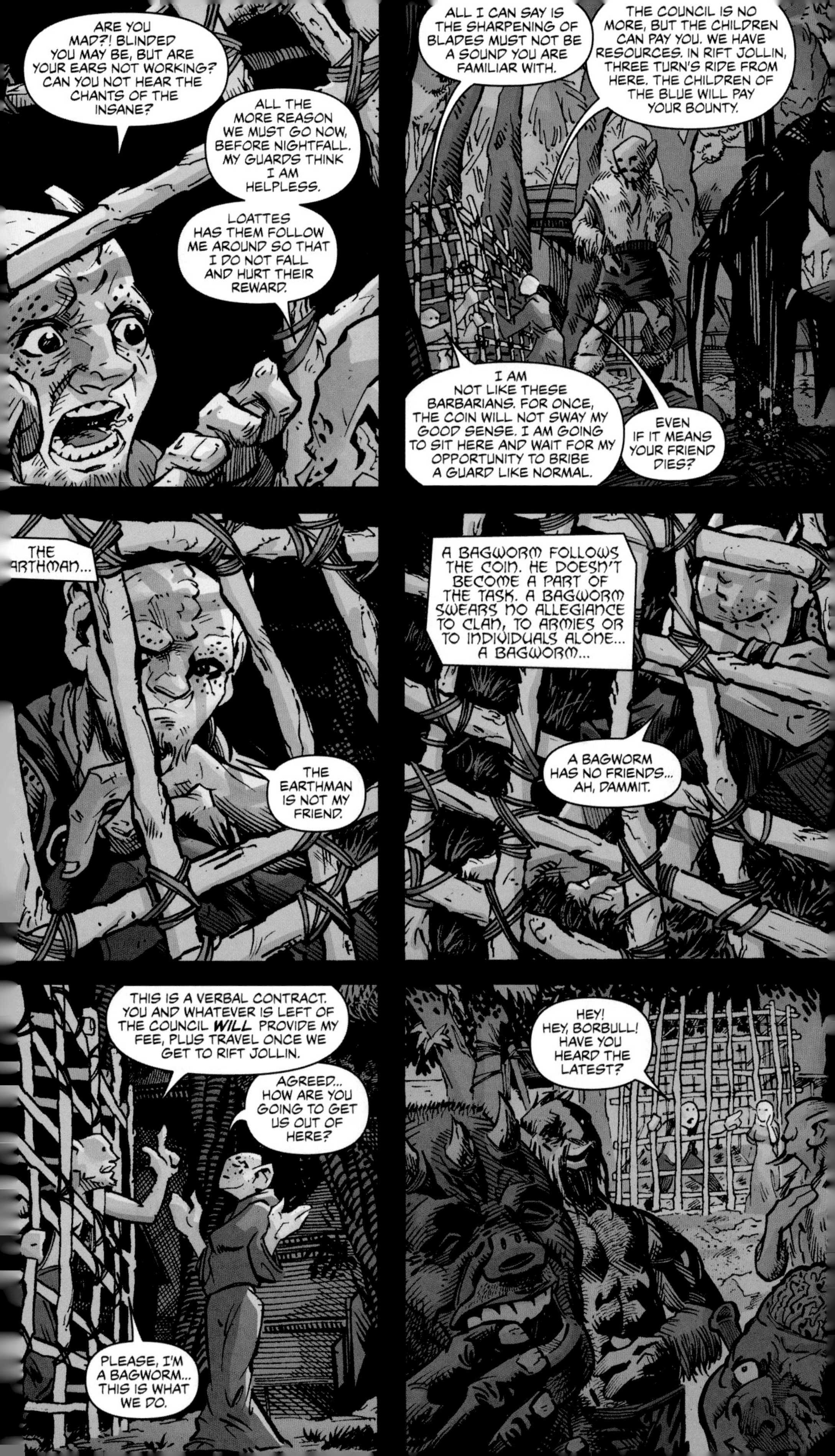

ARE YOU MAD?! BLINDED YOU MAY BE, BUT ARE YOUR EARS NOT WORKING? CAN YOU NOT HEAR THE CHANTS OF THE INSANE?
ALL THE MORE REASON WE MUST GO NOW, BEFORE NIGHTFALL. MY GUARDS THINK I AM HELPLESS.
LOATTES HAS THEM FOLLOW ME AROUND SO THAT I DO NOT FALL AND HURT THEIR REWARD.
ALL I CAN SAY IS THE SHARPENING OF BLADES MUST NOT BE A SOUND YOU ARE FAMILIAR WITH.
THE COUNCIL IS NO MORE, BUT THE CHILDREN CAN PAY YOU. WE HAVE RESOURCES. IN RIFT JOLLIN, THREE TURN'S RIDE FROM HERE. THE CHILDREN OF THE BLUE WILL PAY YOUR BOUNTY.
I AM NOT LIKE THESE BARBARIANS. FOR ONCE, THE COIN WILL NOT SWAY MY GOOD SENSE. I AM GOING TO SIT HERE AND WAIT FOR MY OPPORTUNITY TO BRIBE A GUARD LIKE NORMAL.
EVEN IF IT MEANS YOUR FRIEND DIES?
THE EARTHMAN...
THE EARTHMAN IS NOT MY FRIEND.
A BAGWORM FOLLOWS THE COIN. HE DOESN'T BECOME A PART OF THE TASK. A BAGWORM SWEARS NO ALLEGIANCE TO CLAN, TO ARMIES OR TO INDIVIDUALS ALONE... A BAGWORM...
A BAGWORM HAS NO FRIENDS... AH, DAMMIT.
THIS IS A VERBAL CONTRACT. YOU AND WHATEVER IS LEFT OF THE COUNCIL **WILL** PROVIDE MY FEE, PLUS TRAVEL ONCE WE GET TO RIFT JOLLIN.
AGREED... HOW ARE YOU GOING TO GET US OUT OF HERE?
PLEASE, I'M A BAGWORM... THIS IS WHAT WE DO.
HEY! HEY, BORBULL! HAVE YOU HEARD THE LATEST?

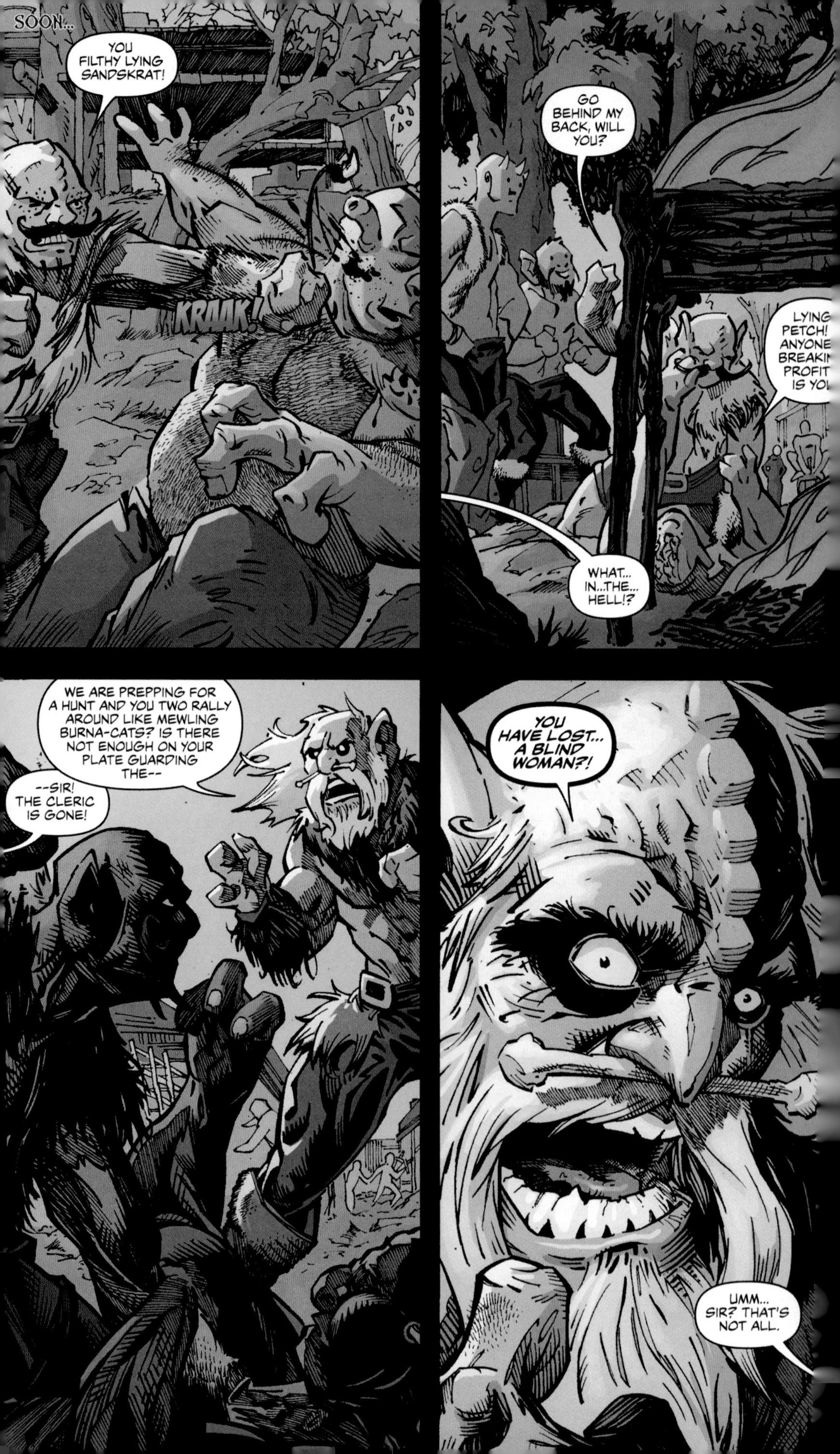
SOON...
YOU FILTHY LYING SANDSKRAT!
KRAAK!
GO BEHIND MY BACK, WILL YOU?
LYING PETCH! ANYONE BREAKIN PROFIT IS YO
WHAT... IN...THE... HELL!?
WE ARE PREPPING FOR A HUNT AND YOU TWO RALLY AROUND LIKE MEWLING BURNA-CATS? IS THERE NOT ENOUGH ON YOUR PLATE GUARDING THE--
--SIR! THE CLERIC IS GONE!
YOU HAVE LOST... A BLIND WOMAN?!
UMM... SIR? THAT'S NOT ALL.

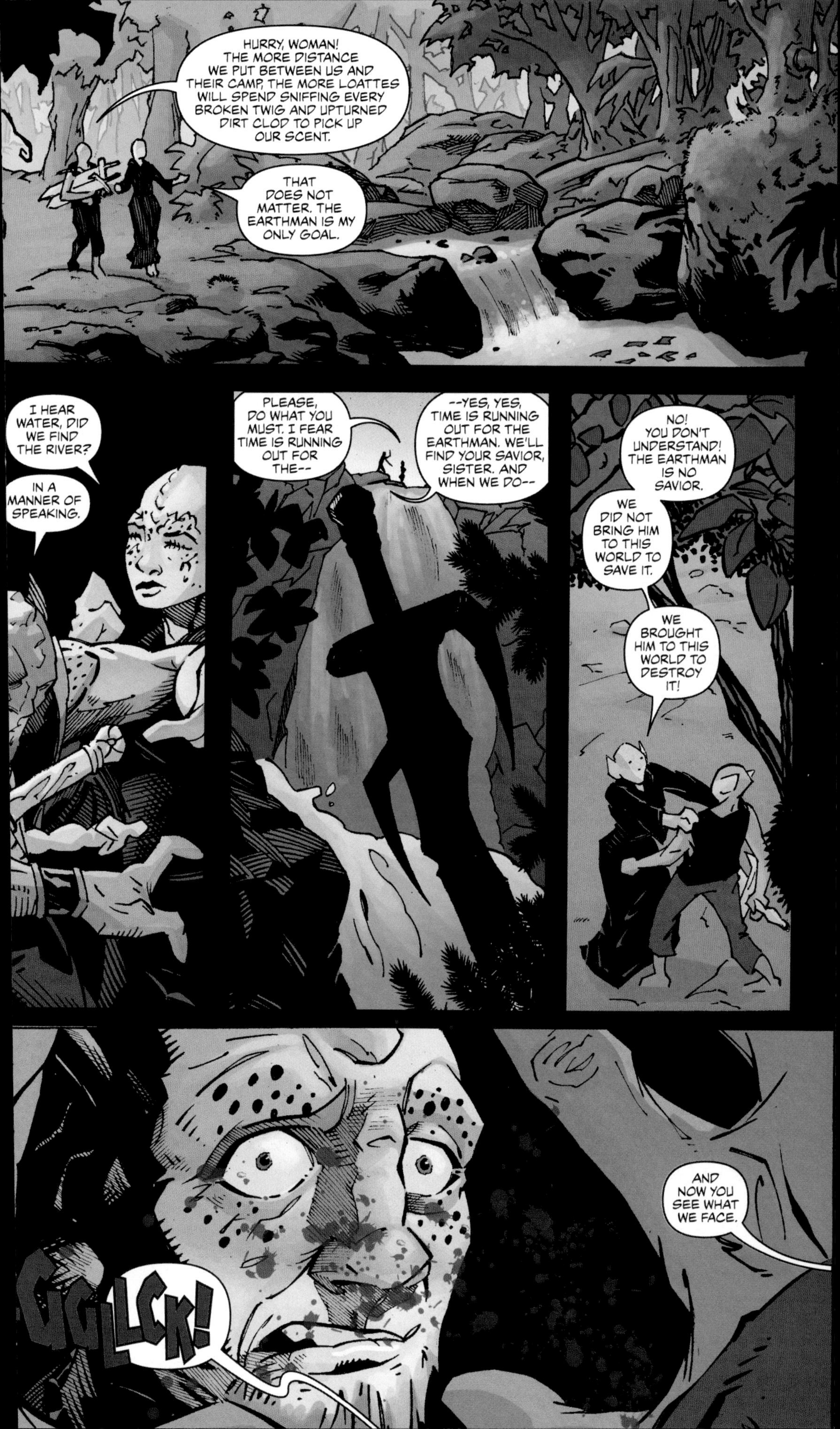
HURRY, WOMAN! THE MORE DISTANCE WE PUT BETWEEN US AND THEIR CAMP, THE MORE LOATTES WILL SPEND SNIFFING EVERY BROKEN TWIG AND UPTURNED DIRT CLOD TO PICK UP OUR SCENT.
THAT DOES NOT MATTER. THE EARTHMAN IS MY ONLY GOAL.
I HEAR WATER, DID WE FIND THE RIVER?
IN A MANNER OF SPEAKING.
PLEASE, DO WHAT YOU MUST. I FEAR TIME IS RUNNING OUT FOR THE--
--YES, YES, TIME IS RUNNING OUT FOR THE EARTHMAN. WE'LL FIND YOUR SAVIOR, SISTER. AND WHEN WE DO--
NO! YOU DON'T UNDERSTAND! THE EARTHMAN IS NO SAVIOR.
WE DID NOT BRING HIM TO THIS WORLD TO SAVE IT.
WE BROUGHT HIM TO THIS WORLD TO DESTROY IT!
AND NOW YOU SEE WHAT WE FACE.
GGLLCK!

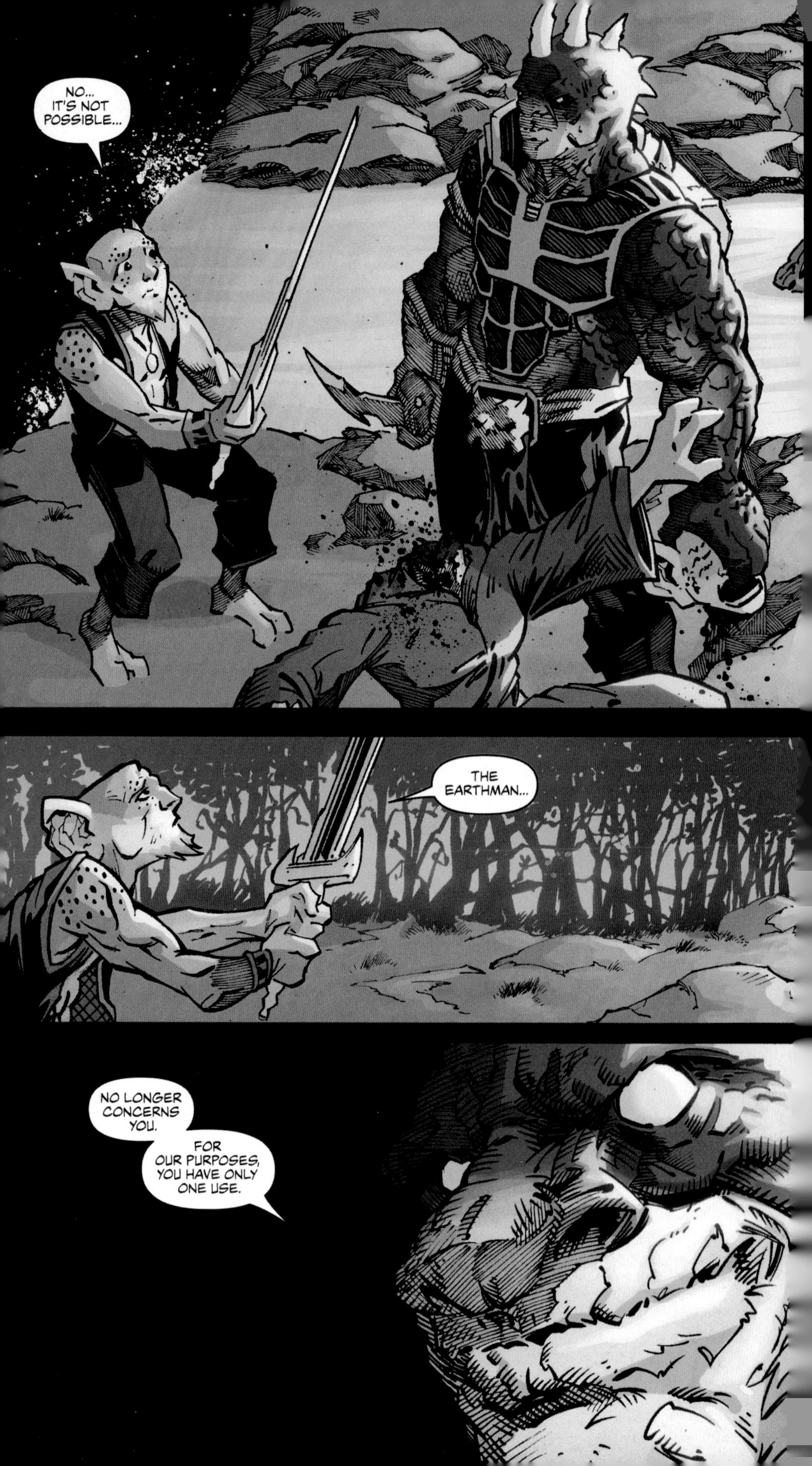
NO... IT'S NOT POSSIBLE...
THE EARTHMAN...
NO LONGER CONCERNS YOU.
FOR OUR PURPOSES, YOU HAVE ONLY ONE USE.

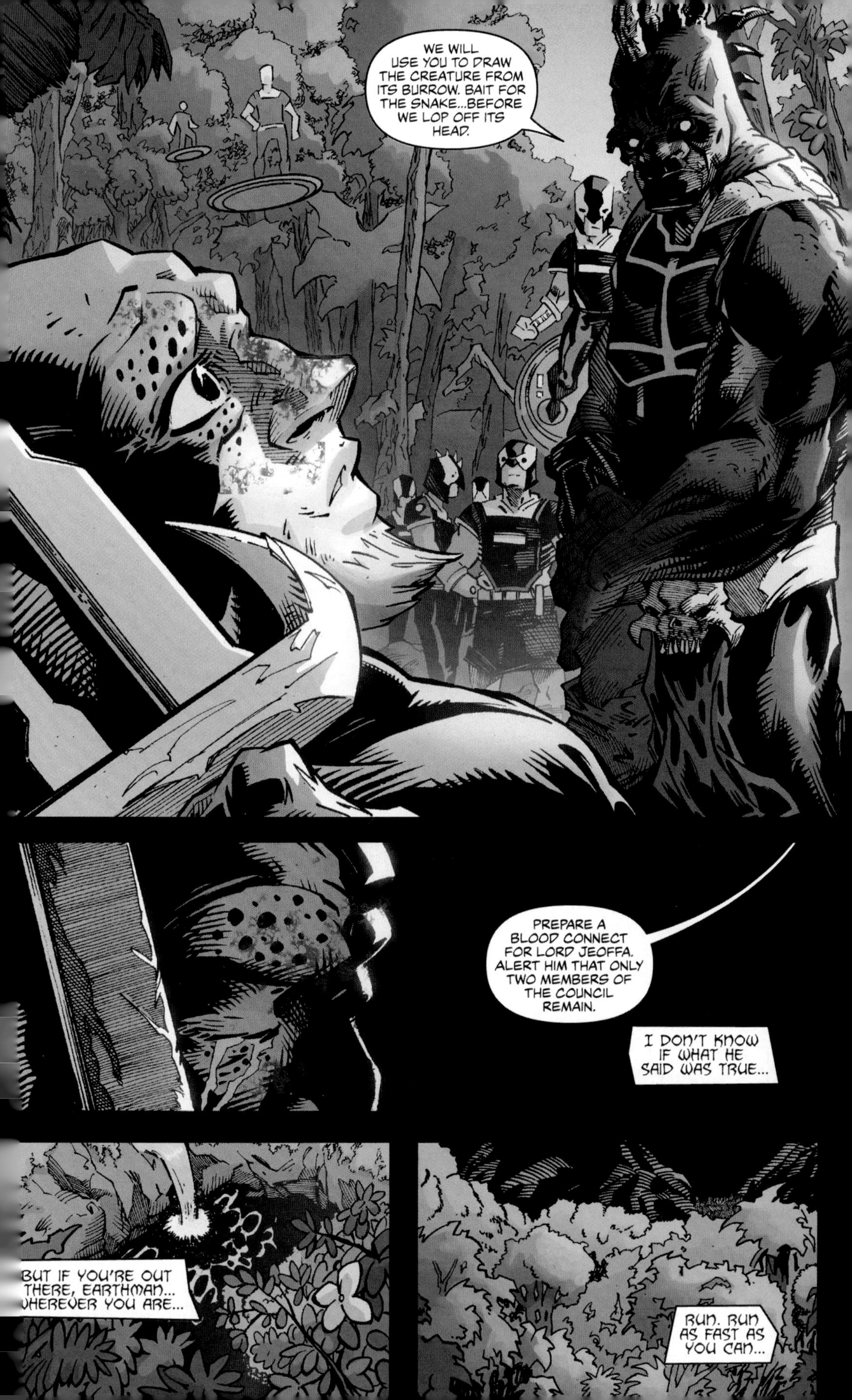
WE WILL USE YOU TO DRAW THE CREATURE FROM ITS BURROW. BAIT FOR THE SNAKE...BEFORE WE LOP OFF ITS HEAD.
PREPARE A BLOOD CONNECT FOR LORD JEOFFA. ALERT HIM THAT ONLY TWO MEMBERS OF THE COUNCIL REMAIN.
I DON'T KNOW IF WHAT HE SAID WAS TRUE...
BUT IF YOU'RE OUT THERE, EARTHMAN... WHEREVER YOU ARE...
RUN. RUN AS FAST AS YOU CAN...

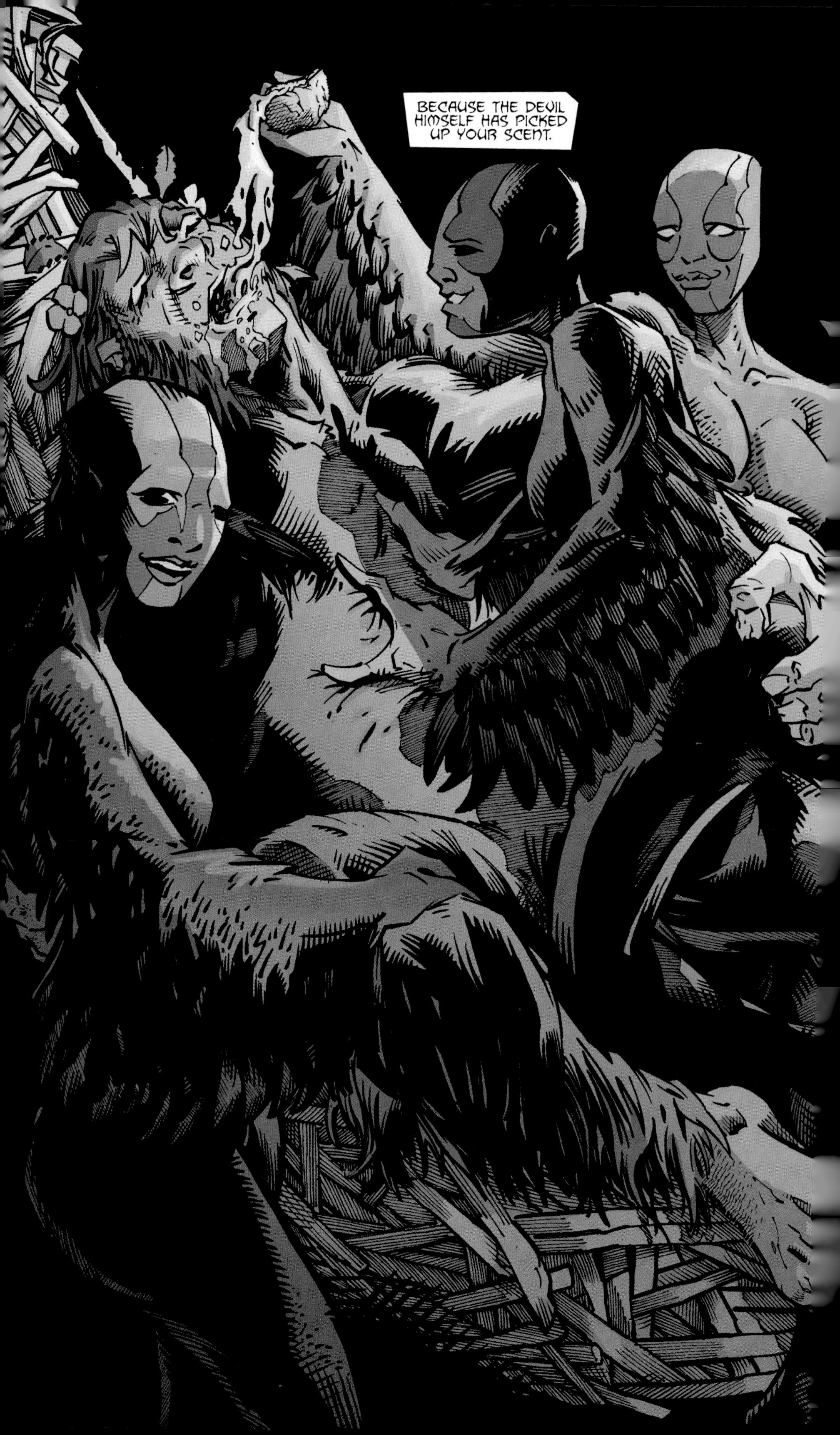
BECAUSE THE DEVIL HIMSELF HAS PICKED UP YOUR SCENT.

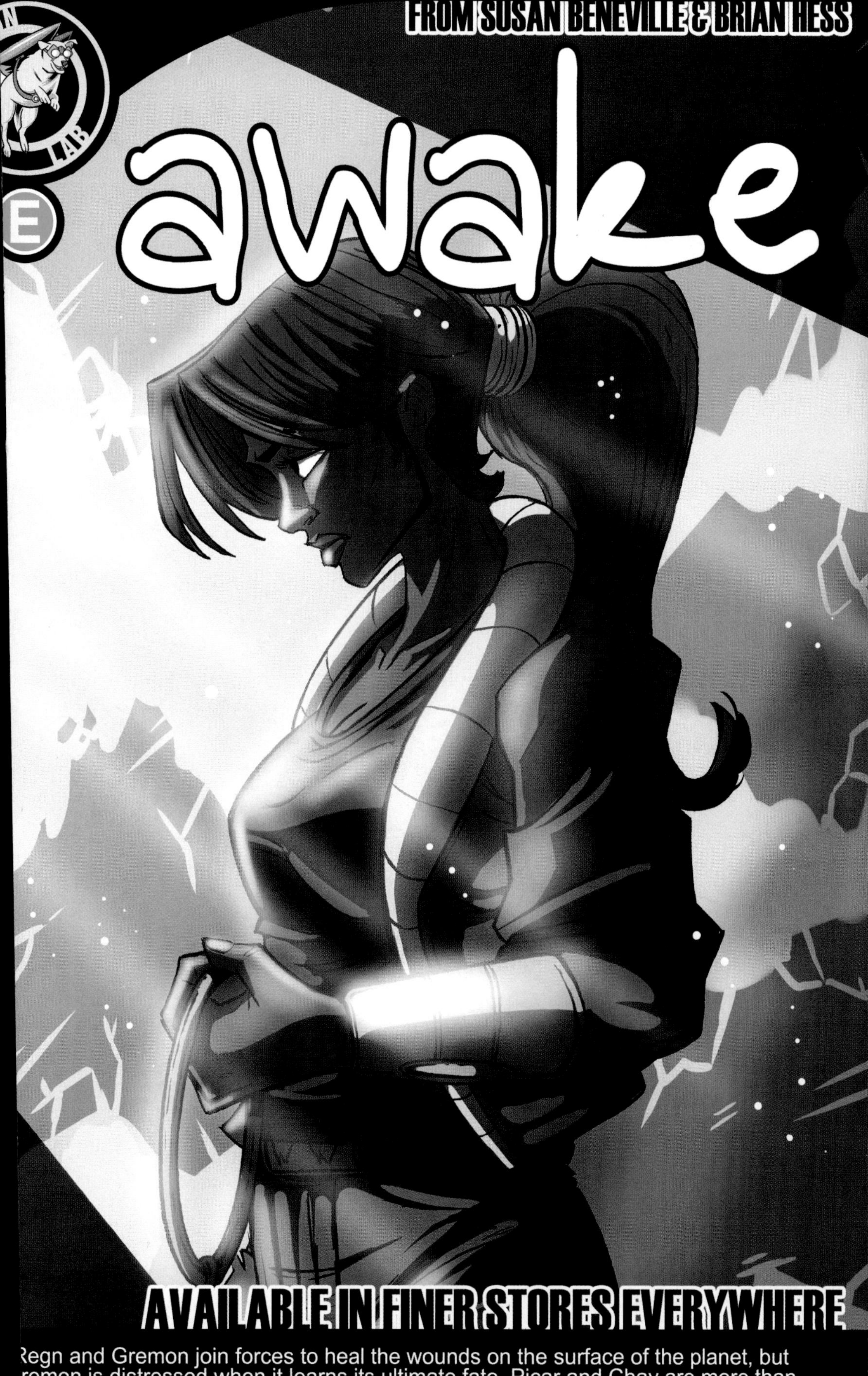
FROM SUSAN BENEVILLE & BRIAN HESS
awake
AVAILABLE IN FINER STORES EVERYWHERE

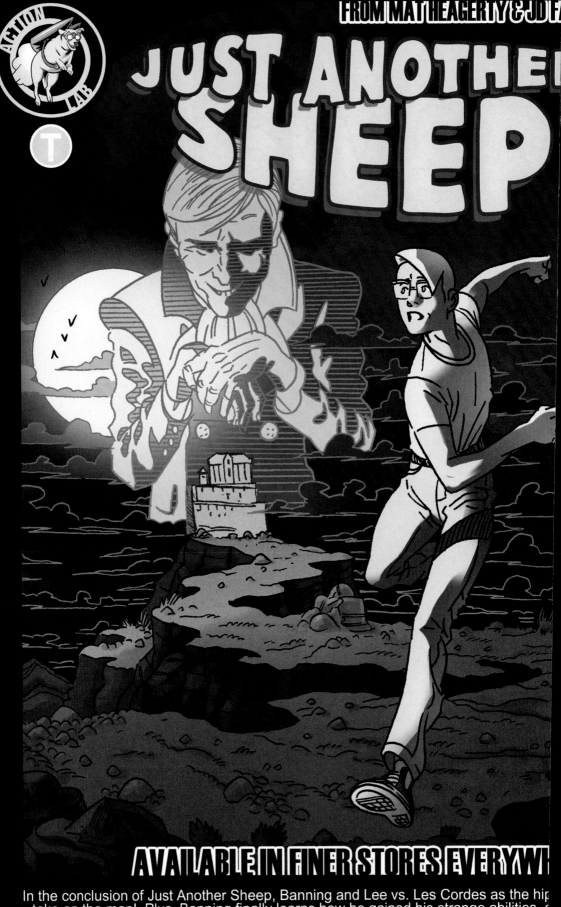

In the conclusion of Just Another Sheep, Banning and Lee vs. Les Cordes as the hip
take on the man! Plus, Banning finally learns how he gained his strange abilities, a
sets off to atone for his mistakes.

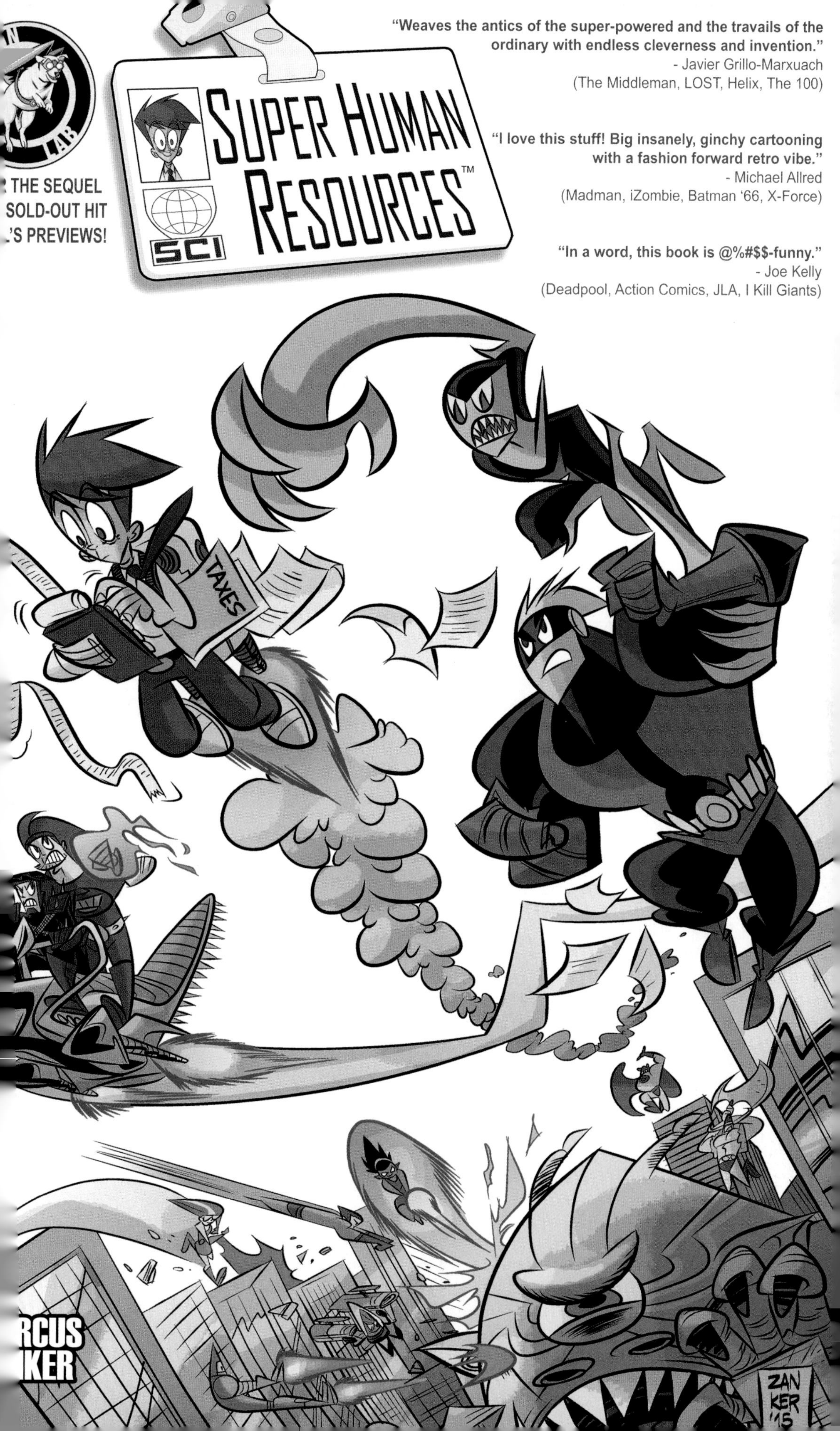
SUPER HUMAN RESOURCES™
SCI
THE SEQUEL
SOLD-OUT HIT
'S PREVIEWS!
"Weaves the antics of the super-powered and the travails of the ordinary with endless cleverness and invention."
- Javier Grillo-Marxuach
(The Middleman, LOST, Helix, The 100)
"I love this stuff! Big insanely, ginchy cartooning with a fashion forward retro vibe."
- Michael Allred
(Madman, iZombie, Batman '66, X-Force)
"In a word, this book is @%#$$-funny."
- Joe Kelly
(Deadpool, Action Comics, JLA, I Kill Giants)
TAXES
RCUS
KER
ZANKER '15

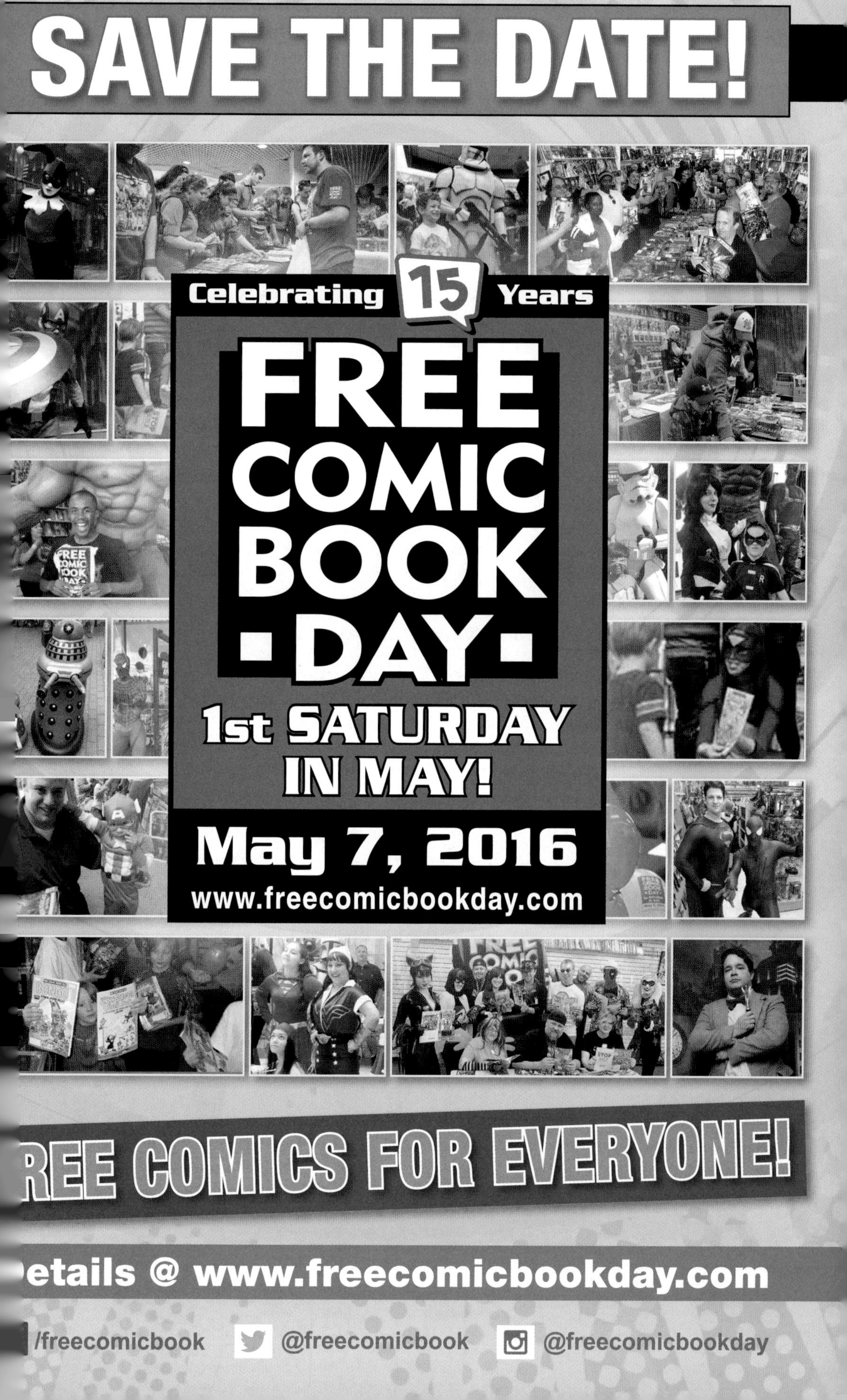
SAVE THE DATE!
Celebrating 15 Years
FREE COMIC BOOK DAY
1st SATURDAY IN MAY!
May 7, 2016
www.freecomicbookday.com
REE COMICS FOR EVERYONE!
etails @ www.freecomicbookday.com
/freecomicbook
@freecomicbook
@freecomicbookday

READ MORE NOW

ACTIONLABCOMICS.COM

BIGFOOT
SWORD OF THE EARTHMAN

#5
3.99

T

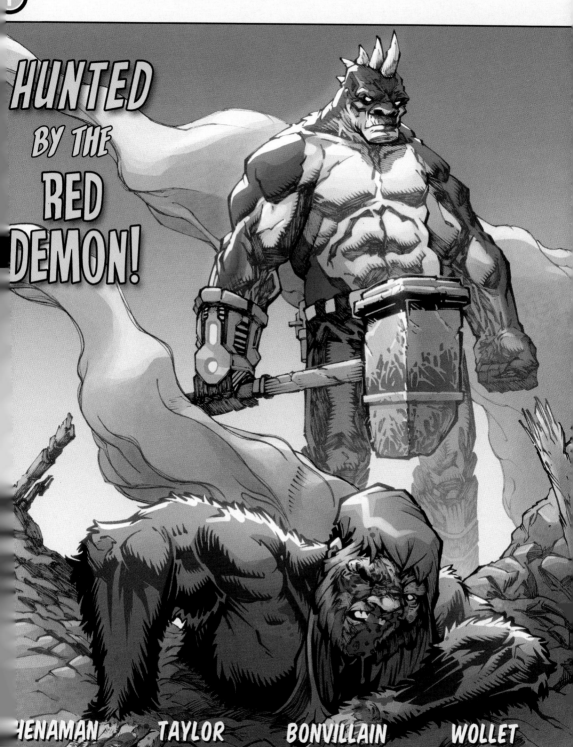

HUNTED
BY THE
RED
DEMON!

HENAMAN   TAYLOR   BONVILLAIN   WOLLET

HIS NAME IS KNOWN THROUGHOUT
THE HALLOWED HALLS OF
THE GREATEST UNIVERSITIES.

SPOKEN ONLY IN WHISPER.

MENTIONED ONLY WITH RESPECT.

THE ACHIEVEMENTS HE HAS MADE WILL BE STUDIED
FOR A THOUSAND CYCLES. THE BARREN DESERT ESCAPE.
THE RETURN OF THE DELUGE. AND THE GREAT
AGRI-REVOLUTION. HIS PIVOTAL ROLE IN HISTORY
IS UNQUESTIONED. HIS NAME... CHISELED IN THE
FOUNDATIONAL STONE OF ANTIQUITY ITSELF.

AFTER THE DRUMS OF WAR FALL SILENT AND THE
TRUMPETS OF VICTORY SOUND, WHEN THE PARADES
AND FESTIVITIES OF CELEBRATION SWELL AND
WHEN THE ORGIES OF DELIGHT BECKON...
SONGS WILL BE SUNG ABOUT HIM.

HE IS LEGEND.

HE IS THE EXTRAORDINARILY PROLIFIC,
GREATEST SCRIBE THIS SIDE OF THE FLOW.

AND HE... PROBABLY GLOSSED OVER A FEW THINGS.

HE IS...

BAGWORM

~~BIGFOOT~~

SWORD OF THE EARTHMAN

Bryan Seaton: Publisher • Dave Dwonch: President • Shawn Gabborin: Editor In Chief
Jamal Igle: Vice-President of Marketing • Vito Delsante: Director of Marketing • Jim Dietz: Social Media Direct(
Nicole DAndria: Script Editor • Chad Cicconi: Little Foot • Colleen Boyd: Submissions Editor

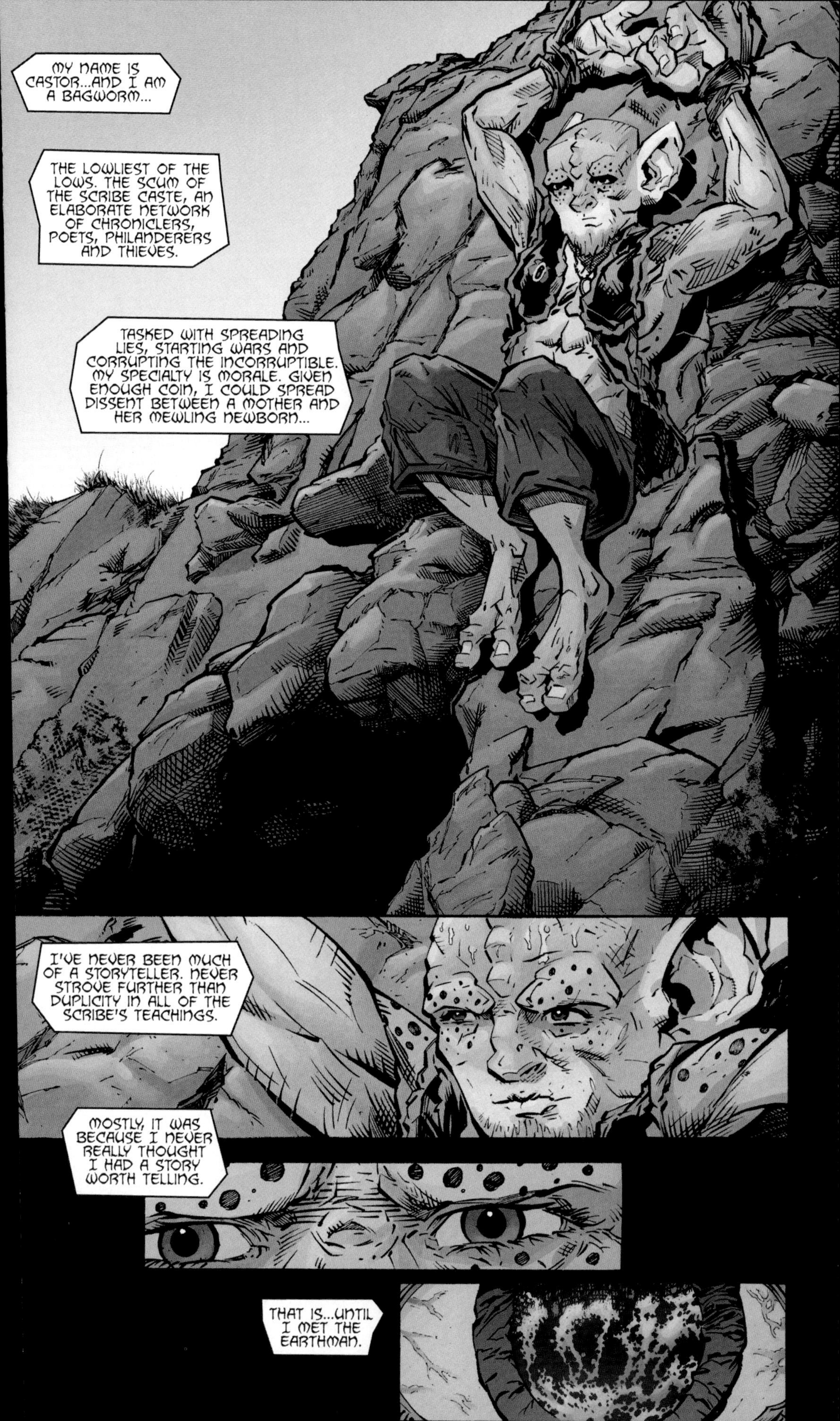

MY NAME IS CASTOR...AND I AM A BAGWORM...
THE LOWLIEST OF THE LOWS. THE SCUM OF THE SCRIBE CASTE, AN ELABORATE NETWORK OF CHRONICLERS, POETS, PHILANDERERS AND THIEVES.
TASKED WITH SPREADING LIES, STARTING WARS AND CORRUPTING THE INCORRUPTIBLE. MY SPECIALTY IS MORALE. GIVEN ENOUGH COIN, I COULD SPREAD DISSENT BETWEEN A MOTHER AND HER MEWLING NEWBORN...
I'VE NEVER BEEN MUCH OF A STORYTELLER. NEVER STROVE FURTHER THAN DUPLICITY IN ALL OF THE SCRIBE'S TEACHINGS.
MOSTLY, IT WAS BECAUSE I NEVER REALLY THOUGHT I HAD A STORY WORTH TELLING.
THAT IS...UNTIL I MET THE EARTHMAN.

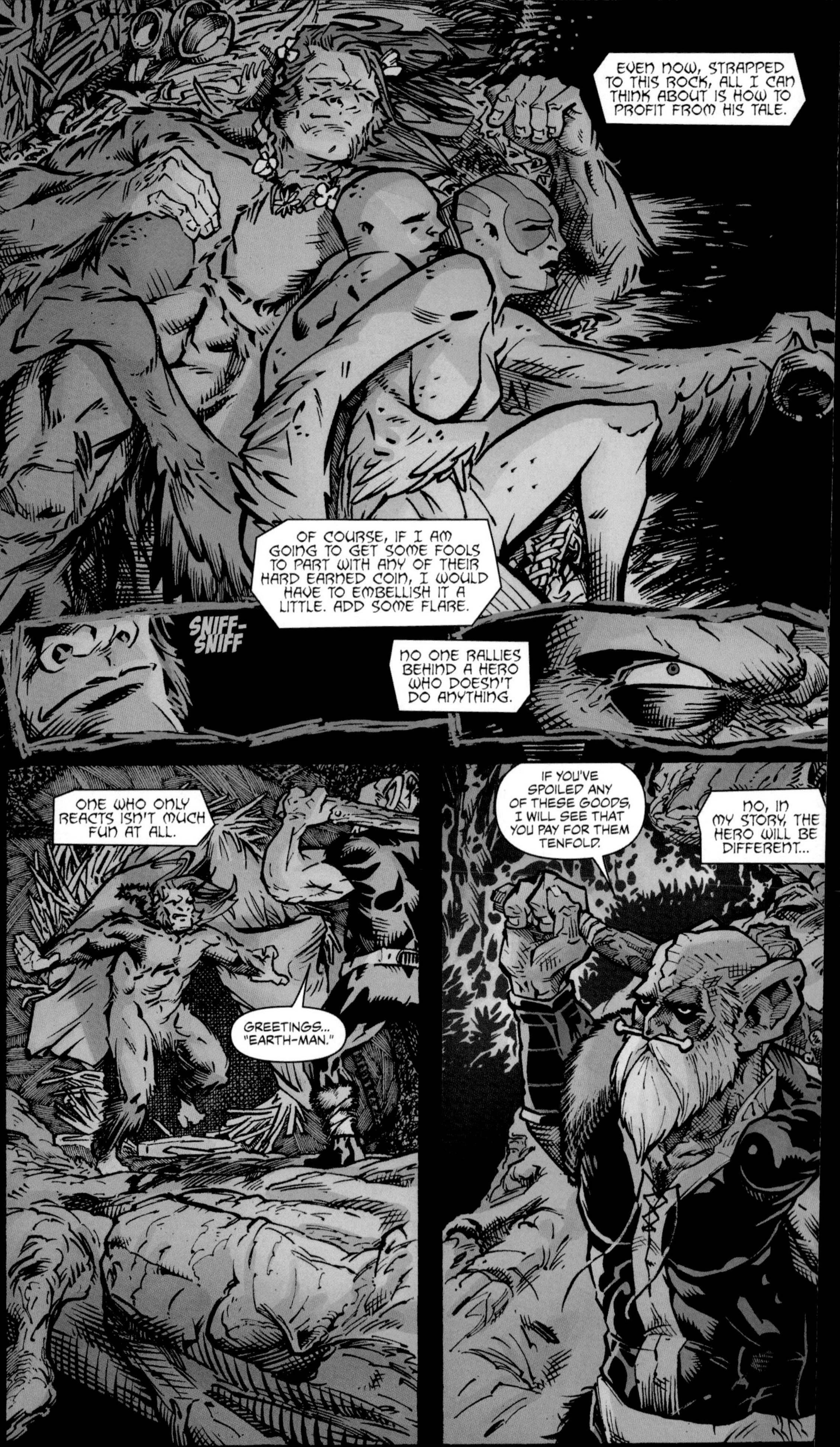
EVEN NOW, STRAPPED TO THIS ROCK, ALL I CAN THINK ABOUT IS HOW TO PROFIT FROM HIS TALE.
OF COURSE, IF I AM GOING TO GET SOME FOOLS TO PART WITH ANY OF THEIR HARD EARNED COIN, I WOULD HAVE TO EMBELLISH IT A LITTLE. ADD SOME FLARE.
SNIFF-SNIFF
NO ONE RALLIES BEHIND A HERO WHO DOESN'T DO ANYTHING.
ONE WHO ONLY REACTS ISN'T MUCH FUN AT ALL.
GREETINGS... "EARTH-MAN."
IF YOU'VE SPOILED ANY OF THESE GOODS, I WILL SEE THAT YOU PAY FOR THEM TENFOLD.
NO, IN MY STORY, THE HERO WILL BE DIFFERENT...

ONE OF ACTION!

ONE OF CHARISMA!

ONE OF CHARACTER!

ONE THAT ISN'T AFRAID TO STAND AGAINST EVIL AND LOOK IT IN THE EYE!

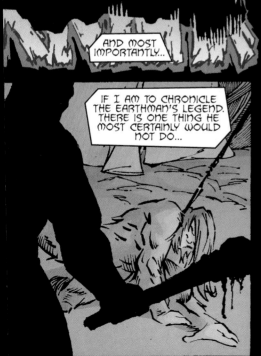

AND MOST IMPORTANTLY...

IF I AM TO CHRONICLE THE EARTHMAN'S LEGEND, THERE IS ONE THING HE MOST CERTAINLY WOULD NOT DO...

I HAVE SECURED YOUR PRIZE, SOLDIER. ALIVE. MY FEE WILL BE DOUBLE WHAT WE DISCUSSED.

IT IS DONE, LOATTES. PREPARE THE CREATURE FOR THE JOURNEY...AND BRING ME THE BAGWORM.

HE WOULD NOT ABANDON ME IN THE JUNGLE TIED TO THIS FEKRA-STAINED ROCK!

SOON...

SO, WE'RE NOT DEAD YET...I THINK THIS IS BECOMING A THEME TO OUR EXISTENCE.

CAPTIVE TO AN ARMY WE WANT NO PART OF.

PAWNS IN A MUCH GRANDER SCHEME.

A SCHEME THAT INVOLVES WHATEVER PLOT LORD JEOFFA, THE SO-CALLED GREAT UNITER OF THE BARBARIAN HORDES, HAS IN MIND AGAINST HIS LAST ENEMY OF HIS THUG STATE. QUEEN MARA OF THE NORTHLANDS.

AND THE CHILDREN OF THE BLUE? THE COUNCIL OF TWELVE? THEY'RE RESPONSIBLE FOR BOTH THE EARTHMAN AND LORD JEOFFA? WHOSE SIDE ARE THEY ON?

AND IF THE EARTHMAN REALLY WAS THEIR CHAMPION... THEN THEY CERTAINLY HAVE A LOT TO BE WORRIED ABOUT.

TORPUS BOIL ME ALIVE, I HA THE DESERT.

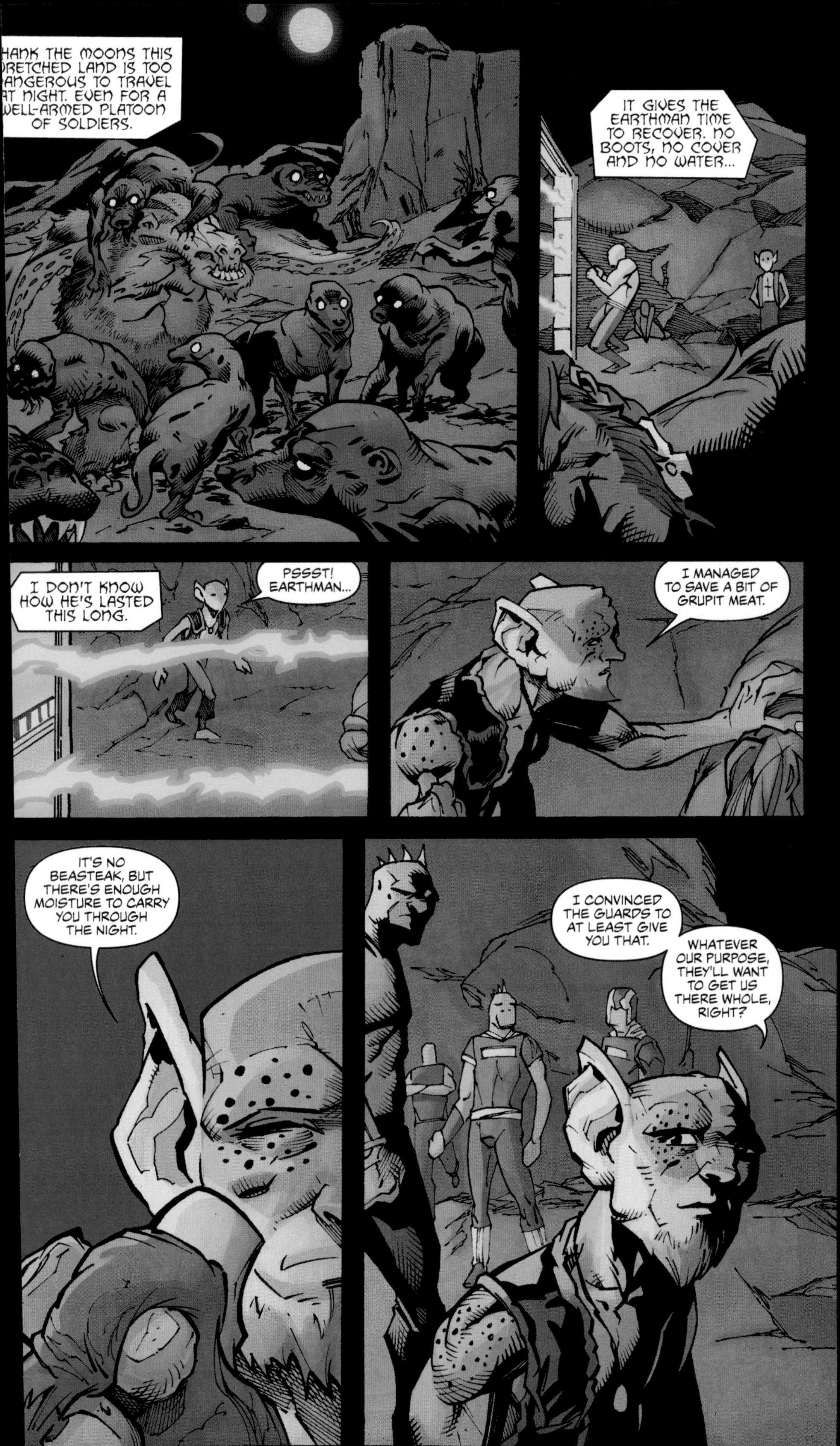
HANK THE MOONS THIS RETCHED LAND IS TOO ANGEROUS TO TRAVEL AT NIGHT. EVEN FOR A WELL-ARMED PLATOON OF SOLDIERS.
IT GIVES THE EARTHMAN TIME TO RECOVER. NO BOOTS, NO COVER AND NO WATER...
I DON'T KNOW HOW HE'S LASTED THIS LONG.
PSSST! EARTHMAN...
I MANAGED TO SAVE A BIT OF GRUPIT MEAT.
IT'S NO BEASTEAK, BUT THERE'S ENOUGH MOISTURE TO CARRY YOU THROUGH THE NIGHT.
I CONVINCED THE GUARDS TO AT LEAST GIVE YOU THAT.
WHATEVER OUR PURPOSE, THEY'LL WANT TO GET US THERE WHOLE, RIGHT?

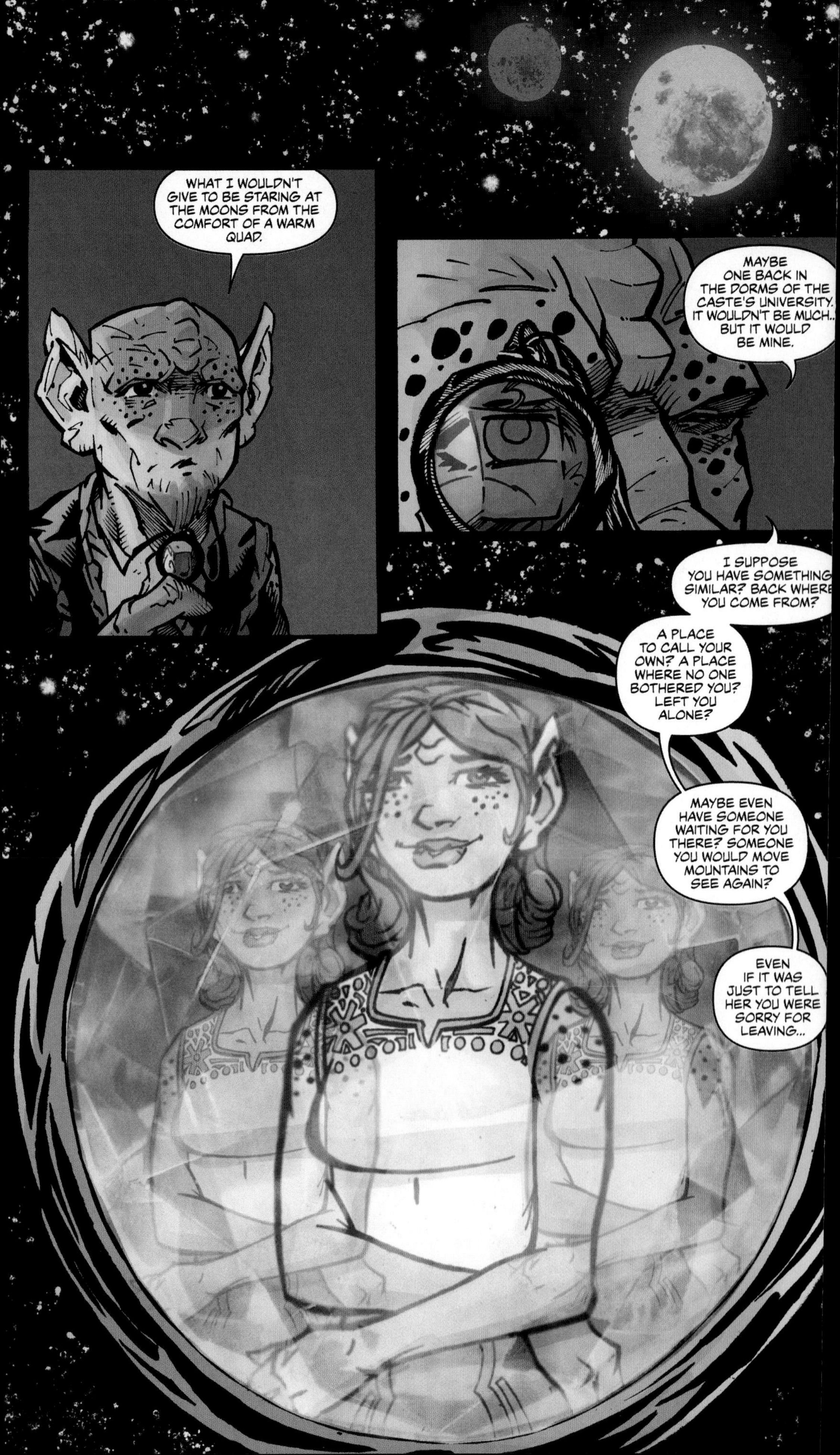
WHAT I WOULDN'T GIVE TO BE STARING AT THE MOONS FROM THE COMFORT OF A WARM QUAD.
MAYBE ONE BACK IN THE DORMS OF THE CASTE'S UNIVERSITY. IT WOULDN'T BE MUCH.. BUT IT WOULD BE MINE.
I SUPPOSE YOU HAVE SOMETHING SIMILAR? BACK WHERE YOU COME FROM?
A PLACE TO CALL YOUR OWN? A PLACE WHERE NO ONE BOTHERED YOU? LEFT YOU ALONE?
MAYBE EVEN HAVE SOMEONE WAITING FOR YOU THERE? SOMEONE YOU WOULD MOVE MOUNTAINS TO SEE AGAIN?
EVEN IF IT WAS JUST TO TELL HER YOU WERE SORRY FOR LEAVING...

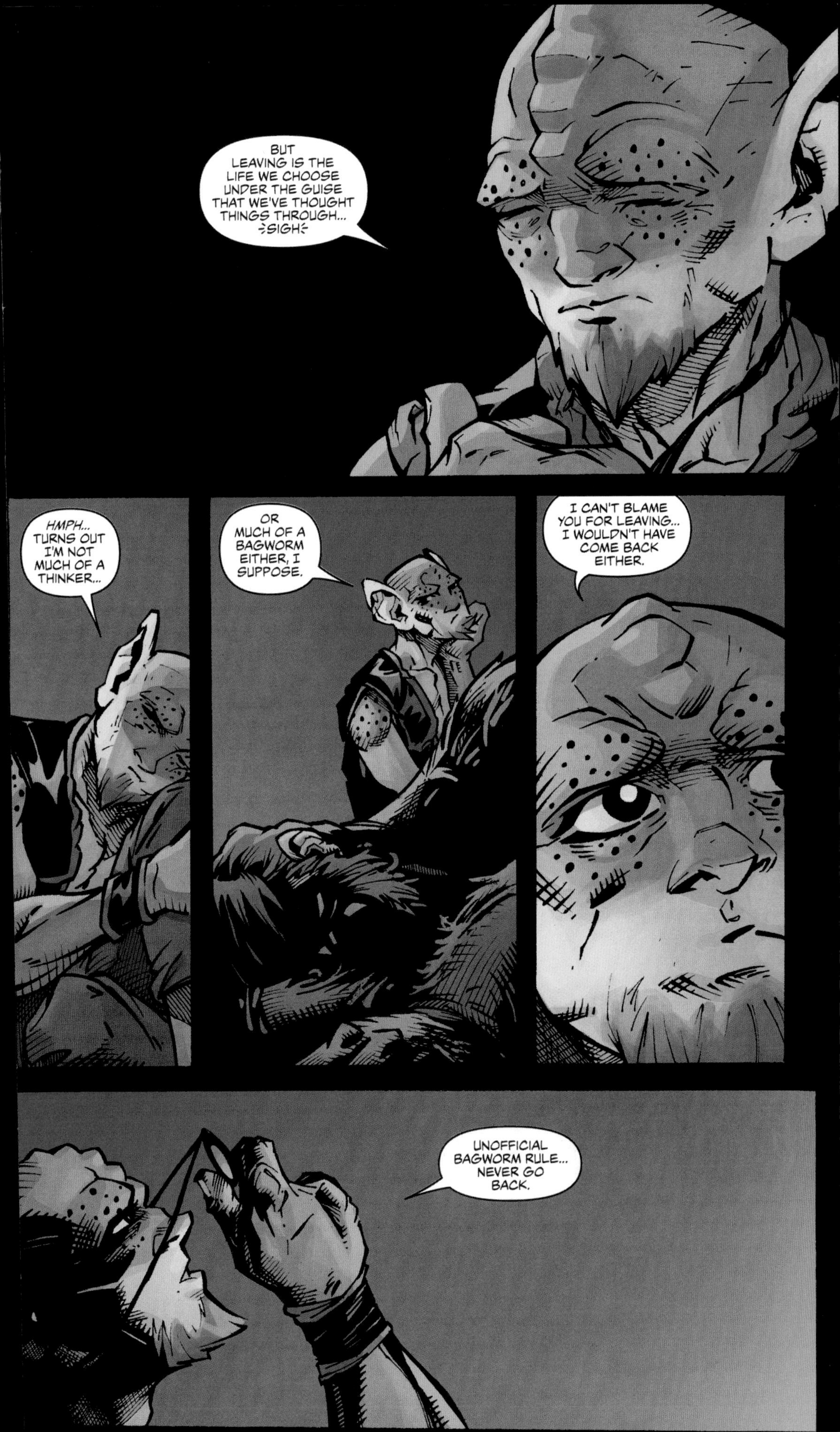
BUT LEAVING IS THE LIFE WE CHOOSE UNDER THE GUISE THAT WE'VE THOUGHT THINGS THROUGH... -SIGH-
HMPH... TURNS OUT I'M NOT MUCH OF A THINKER...
OR MUCH OF A BAGWORM EITHER, I SUPPOSE.
I CAN'T BLAME YOU FOR LEAVING... I WOULDN'T HAVE COME BACK EITHER.
UNOFFICIAL BAGWORM RULE... NEVER GO BACK.

FIRST LIGHT AND THEY COULDN'T LET US EASE INTO THE DAY?

FOR THE BETTER PART OF AN ARC THEY HAVE HAD US TROMPING SAND.

BUT NOW THE BORBULLS HAVE FALLEN SILENT. SAVING THEIR WITS BY KEEPING ALL EYES ON US NOW.

AND WITH NO BREAKS FOR WATER AND NO REST, NOT EVEN FOR THEMSELVES, THAT CAN ONLY MEAN ONE THING.

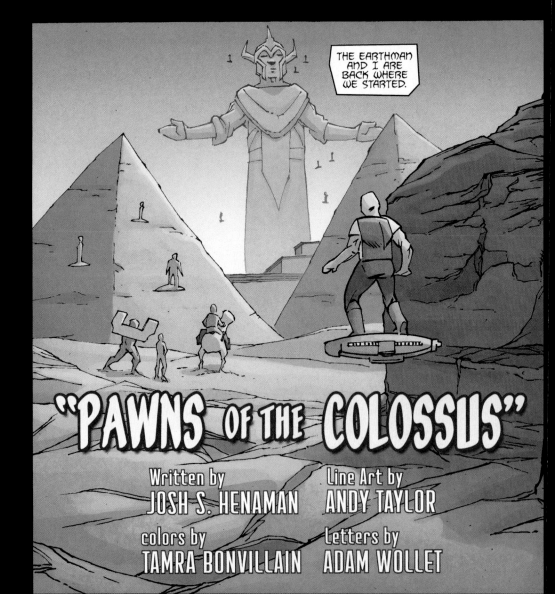

THE EARTHMAN AND I ARE BACK WHERE WE STARTED.

"PAWNS OF THE COLOSSUS"

Written by
JOSH S. HENAMAN

Line Art by
ANDY TAYLOR

colors by
TAMRA BONVILLAIN

Letters by
ADAM WOLLET

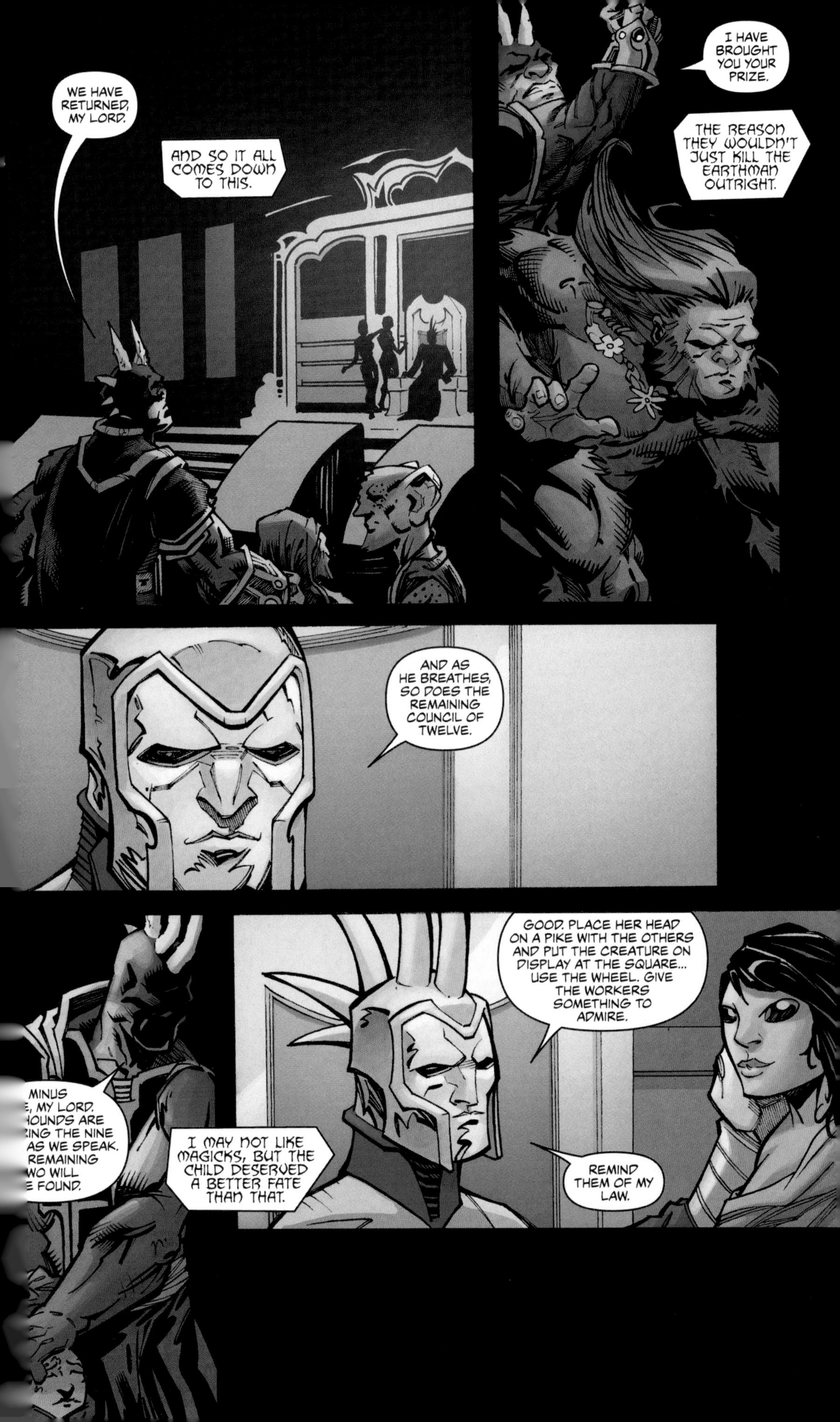
WE HAVE RETURNED, MY LORD.
AND SO IT ALL COMES DOWN TO THIS.
I HAVE BROUGHT YOU YOUR PRIZE.
THE REASON THEY WOULDN'T JUST KILL THE EARTHMAN OUTRIGHT.
AND AS HE BREATHES, SO DOES THE REMAINING COUNCIL OF TWELVE.
MINUS
E, MY LORD.
HOUNDS ARE
RING THE NINE
AS WE SPEAK.
REMAINING
WO WILL
E FOUND.
GOOD. PLACE HER HEAD ON A PIKE WITH THE OTHERS AND PUT THE CREATURE ON DISPLAY AT THE SQUARE... USE THE WHEEL. GIVE THE WORKERS SOMETHING TO ADMIRE.
I MAY NOT LIKE MAGICKS, BUT THE CHILD DESERVED A BETTER FATE THAN THAT.
REMIND THEM OF MY LAW.

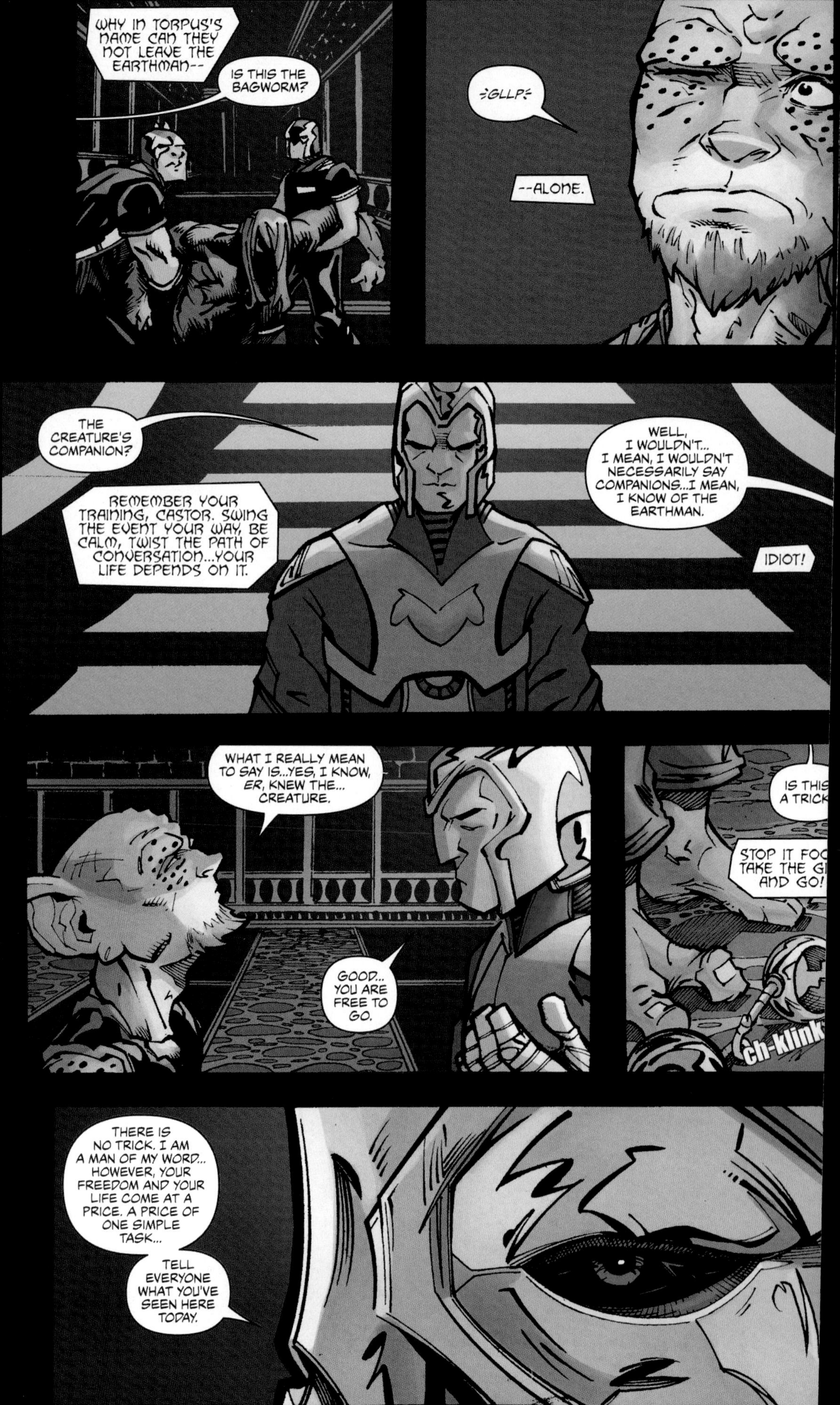
WHY IN TORPUS'S NAME CAN THEY NOT LEAVE THE EARTHMAN--
IS THIS THE BAGWORM?
GLLP
--ALONE.
THE CREATURE'S COMPANION?
REMEMBER YOUR TRAINING, CASTOR. SWING THE EVENT YOUR WAY, BE CALM, TWIST THE PATH OF CONVERSATION...YOUR LIFE DEPENDS ON IT.
WELL, I WOULDN'T... I MEAN, I WOULDN'T NECESSARILY SAY COMPANIONS...I MEAN, I KNOW OF THE EARTHMAN.
IDIOT!
WHAT I REALLY MEAN TO SAY IS...YES, I KNOW, ER, KNEW THE... CREATURE.
GOOD... YOU ARE FREE TO GO.
IS THIS A TRICK
STOP IT FOO TAKE THE GI AND GO!
ch-klink
THERE IS NO TRICK. I AM A MAN OF MY WORD... HOWEVER, YOUR FREEDOM AND YOUR LIFE COME AT A PRICE. A PRICE OF ONE SIMPLE TASK...
TELL EVERYONE WHAT YOU'VE SEEN HERE TODAY.

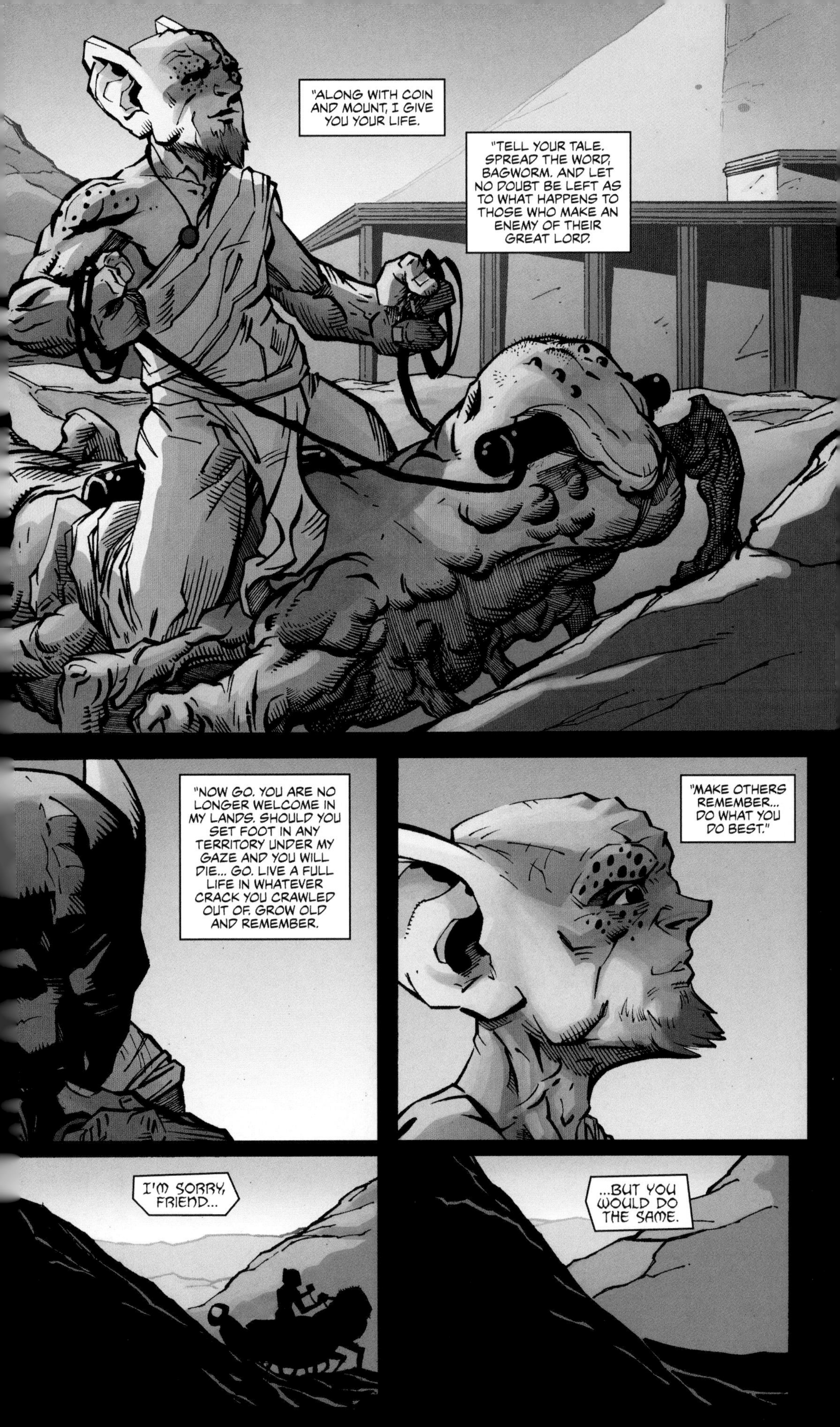
"ALONG WITH COIN AND MOUNT, I GIVE YOU YOUR LIFE.
"TELL YOUR TALE. SPREAD THE WORD, BAGWORM. AND LET NO DOUBT BE LEFT AS TO WHAT HAPPENS TO THOSE WHO MAKE AN ENEMY OF THEIR GREAT LORD.
"NOW GO. YOU ARE NO LONGER WELCOME IN MY LANDS. SHOULD YOU SET FOOT IN ANY TERRITORY UNDER MY GAZE AND YOU WILL DIE... GO. LIVE A FULL LIFE IN WHATEVER CRACK YOU CRAWLED OUT OF. GROW OLD AND REMEMBER.
"MAKE OTHERS REMEMBER... DO WHAT YOU DO BEST."
I'M SORRY, FRIEND...
...BUT YOU WOULD DO THE SAME.

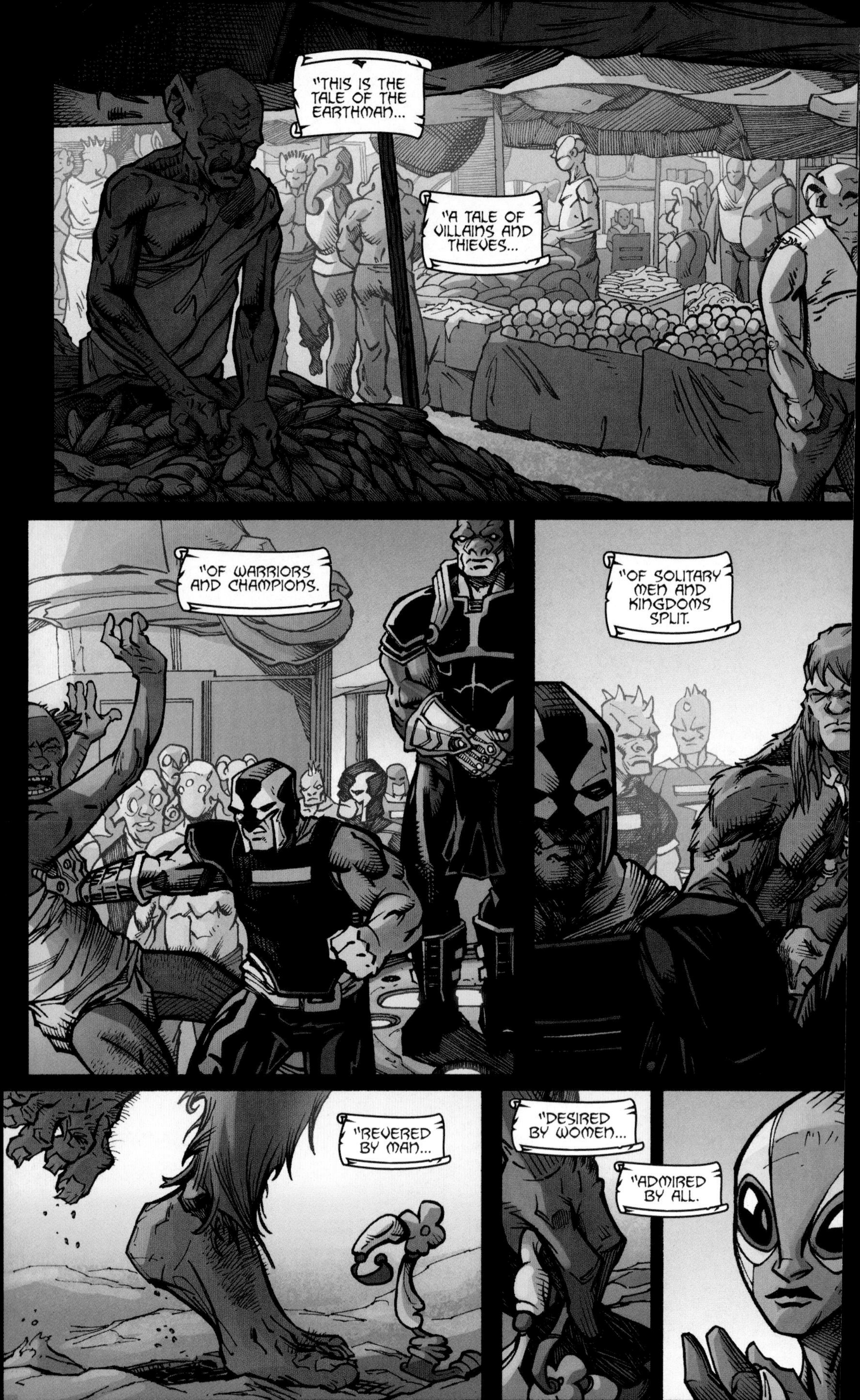
"THIS IS THE TALE OF THE EARTHMAN...
"A TALE OF VILLAINS AND THIEVES...
"OF WARRIORS AND CHAMPIONS.
"OF SOLITARY MEN AND KINGDOMS SPLIT.
"REVERED BY MAN...
"DESIRED BY WOMEN...
"ADMIRED BY ALL.

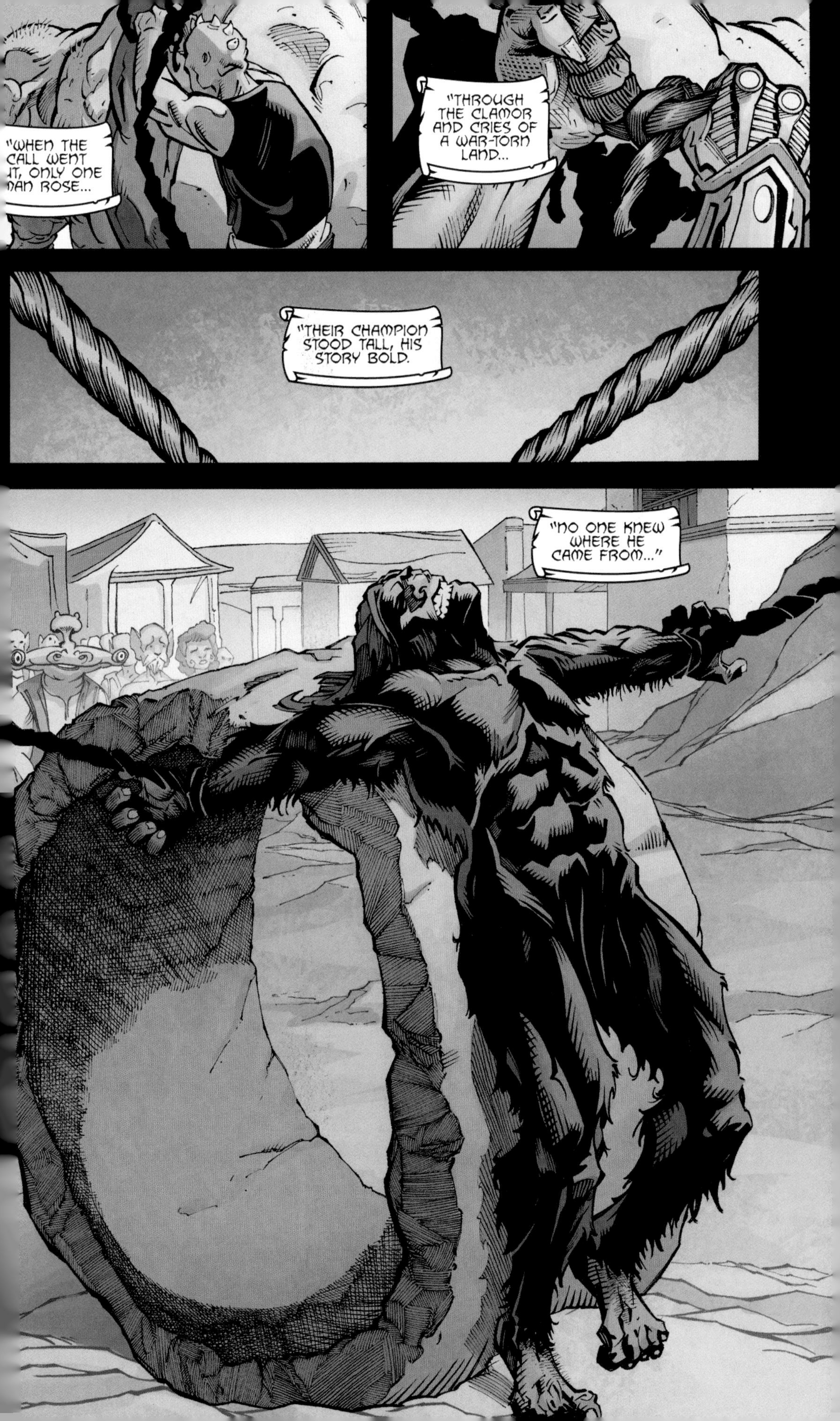
"WHEN THE CALL WENT T, ONLY ONE AN ROSE...
"THROUGH THE CLAMOR AND CRIES OF A WAR-TORN LAND...
"THEIR CHAMPION STOOD TALL, HIS STORY BOLD.
"NO ONE KNEW WHERE HE CAME FROM..."

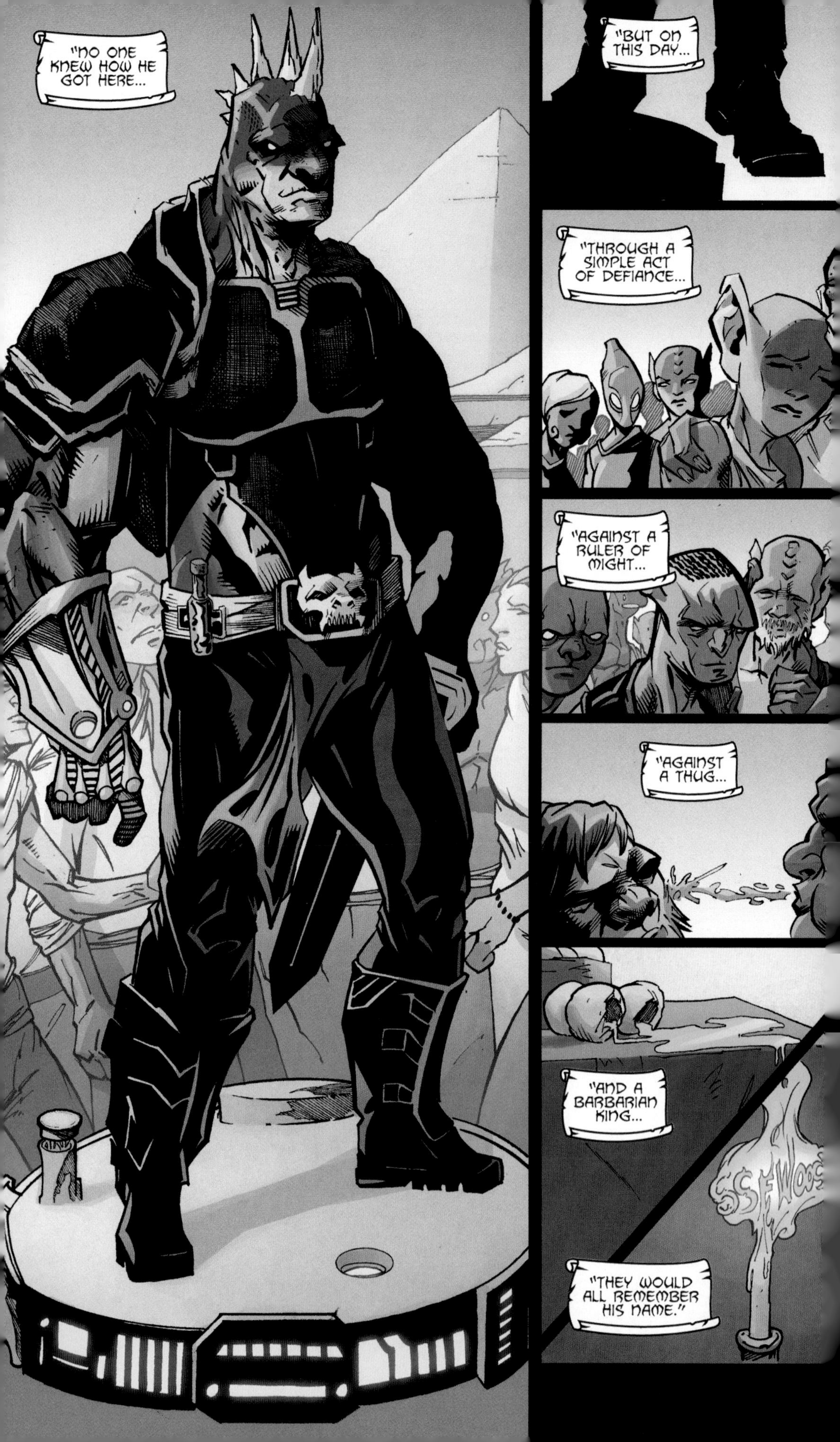
"NO ONE KNEW HOW HE GOT HERE...
"BUT ON THIS DAY...
"THROUGH A SIMPLE ACT OF DEFIANCE...
"AGAINST A RULER OF MIGHT...
"AGAINST A THUG...
"AND A BARBARIAN KING...
"THEY WOULD ALL REMEMBER HIS NAME."

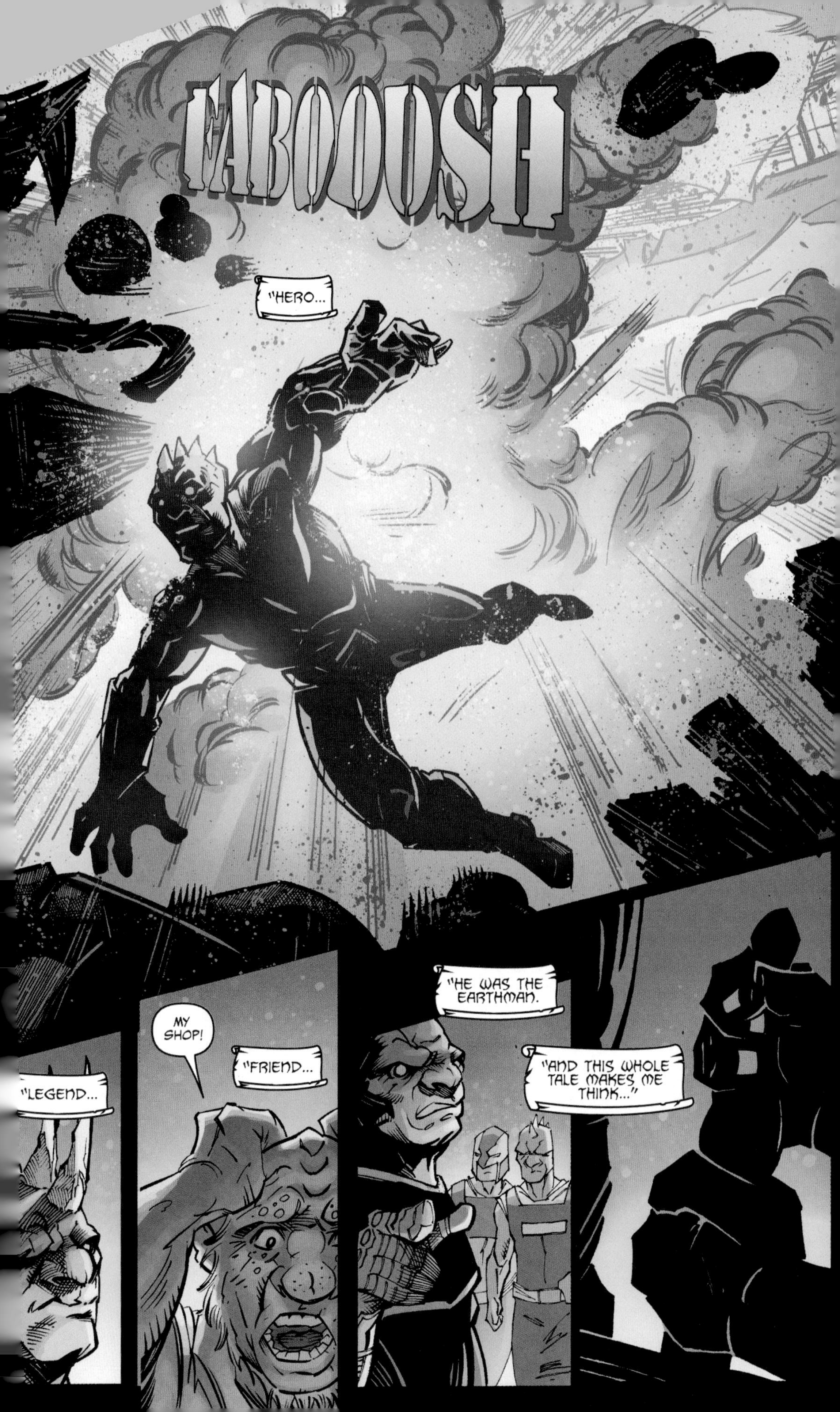
FABOOOSH
"HERO...
"LEGEND...
MY SHOP!
"FRIEND...
"HE WAS THE EARTHMAN.
"AND THIS WHOLE TALE MAKES ME THINK..."

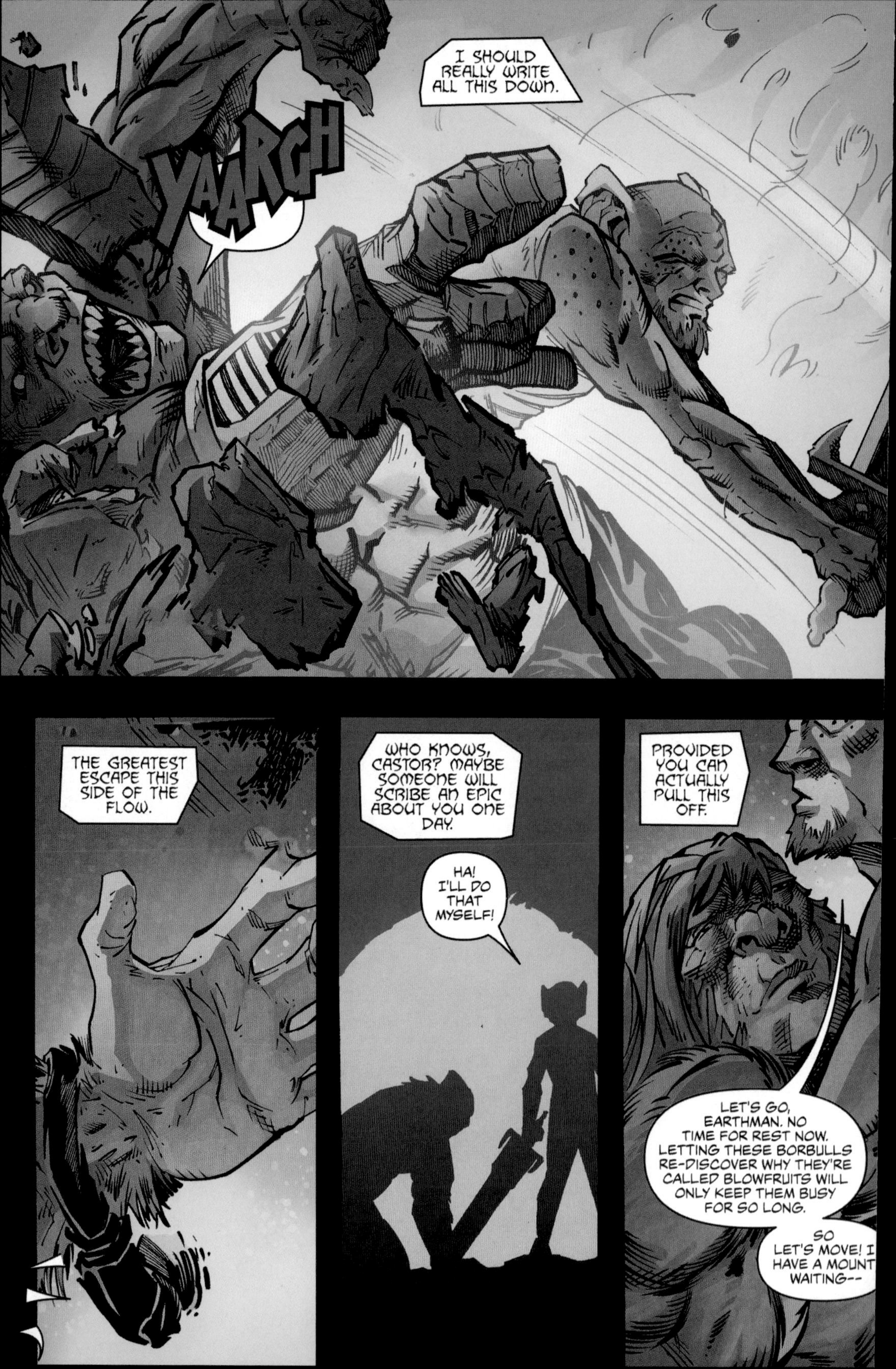
I SHOULD REALLY WRITE ALL THIS DOWN.
YAARGH
THE GREATEST ESCAPE THIS SIDE OF THE FLOW.
WHO KNOWS, CASTOR? MAYBE SOMEONE WILL SCRIBE AN EPIC ABOUT YOU ONE DAY.
HA! I'LL DO THAT MYSELF!
PROVIDED YOU CAN ACTUALLY PULL THIS OFF.
LET'S GO, EARTHMAN. NO TIME FOR REST NOW. LETTING THESE BORBULLS RE-DISCOVER WHY THEY'RE CALLED BLOWFRUITS WILL ONLY KEEP THEM BUSY FOR SO LONG.
SO LET'S MOVE! I HAVE A MOUNT WAITING--

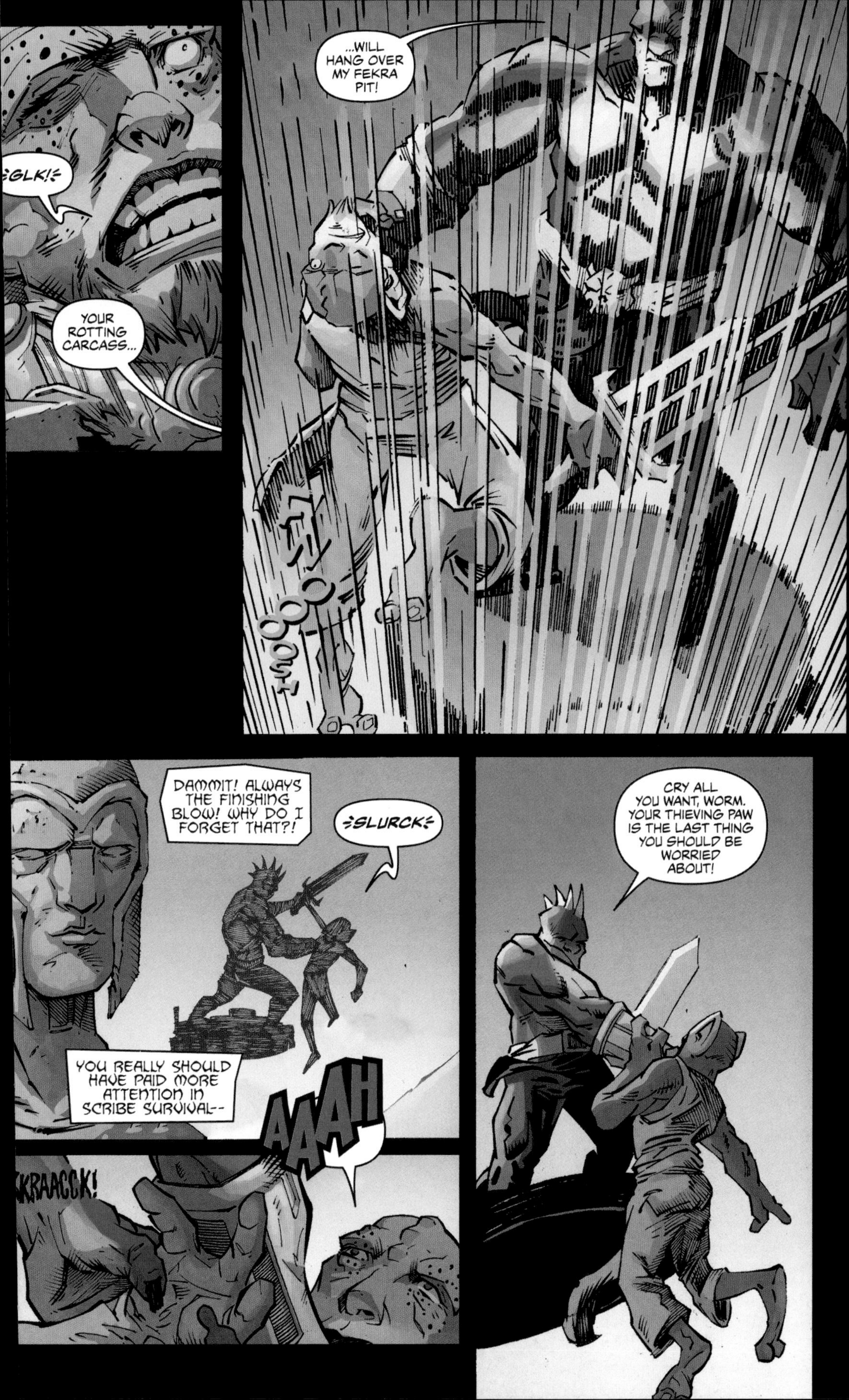

GLK!
YOUR ROTTING CARCASS...
...WILL HANG OVER MY FEKRA PIT!
DAMMIT! ALWAYS THE FINISHING BLOW! WHY DO I FORGET THAT?!
SLURCK
YOU REALLY SHOULD HAVE PAID MORE ATTENTION IN SCRIBE SURVIVAL--
AAAH
KRAACCK!
CRY ALL YOU WANT, WORM. YOUR THIEVING PAW IS THE LAST THING YOU SHOULD BE WORRIED ABOUT!

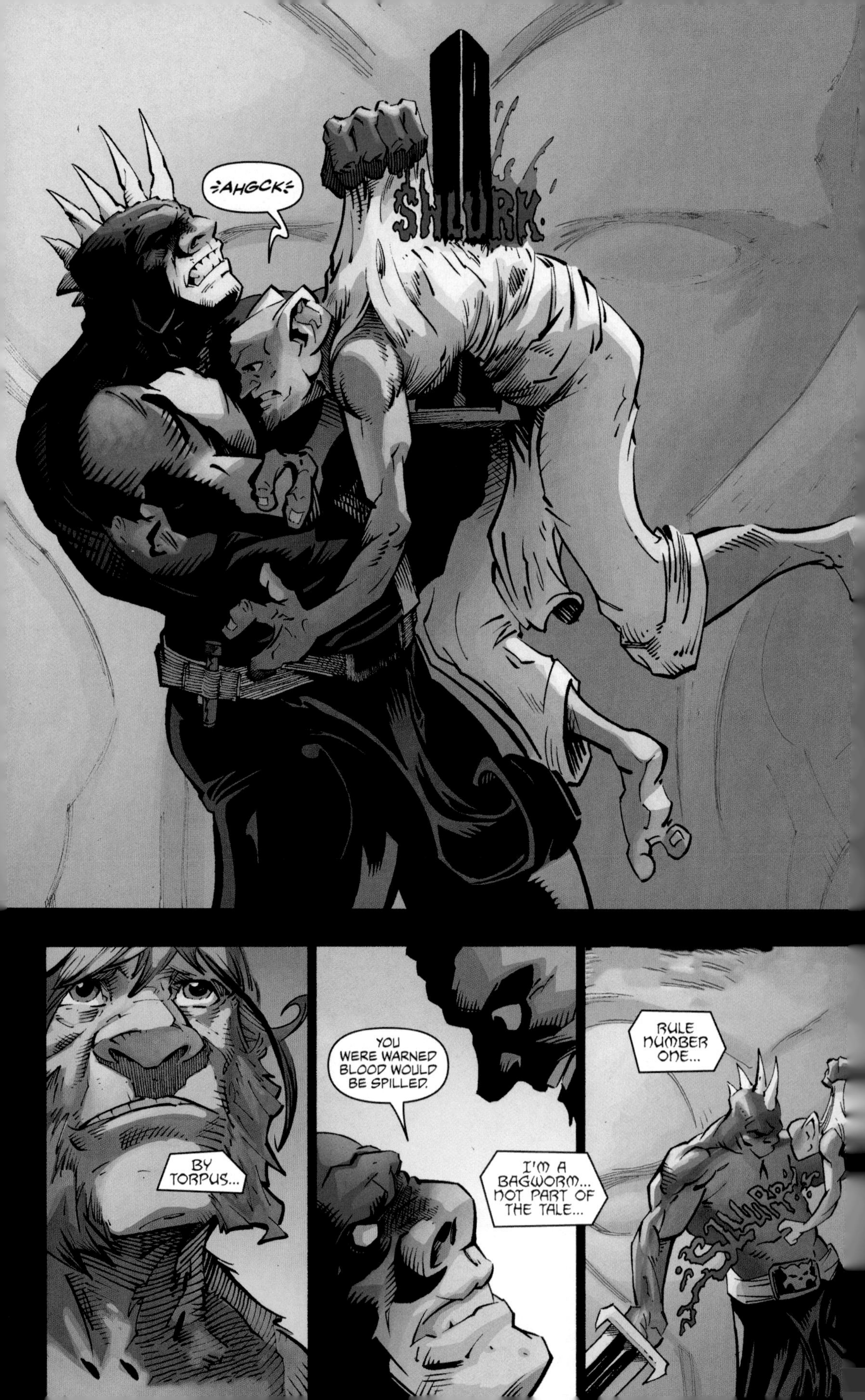
AHGCK
SHLURK
BY TORPUS...
YOU WERE WARNED BLOOD WOULD BE SPILLED.
I'M A BAGWORM... NOT PART OF THE TALE...
RULE NUMBER ONE...

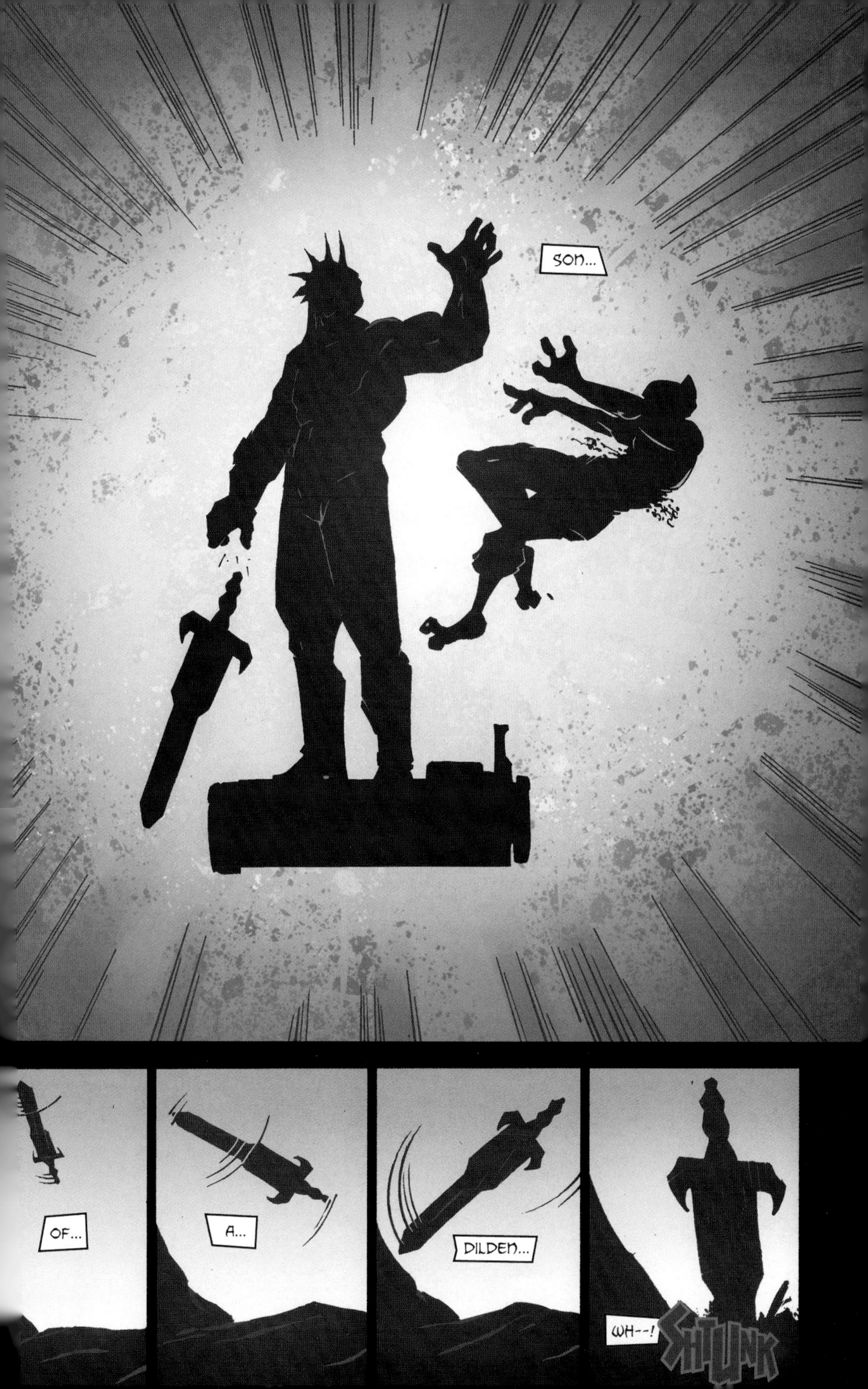
SON...
OF...
A...
DILDEN...
WH--!
SHTUNK

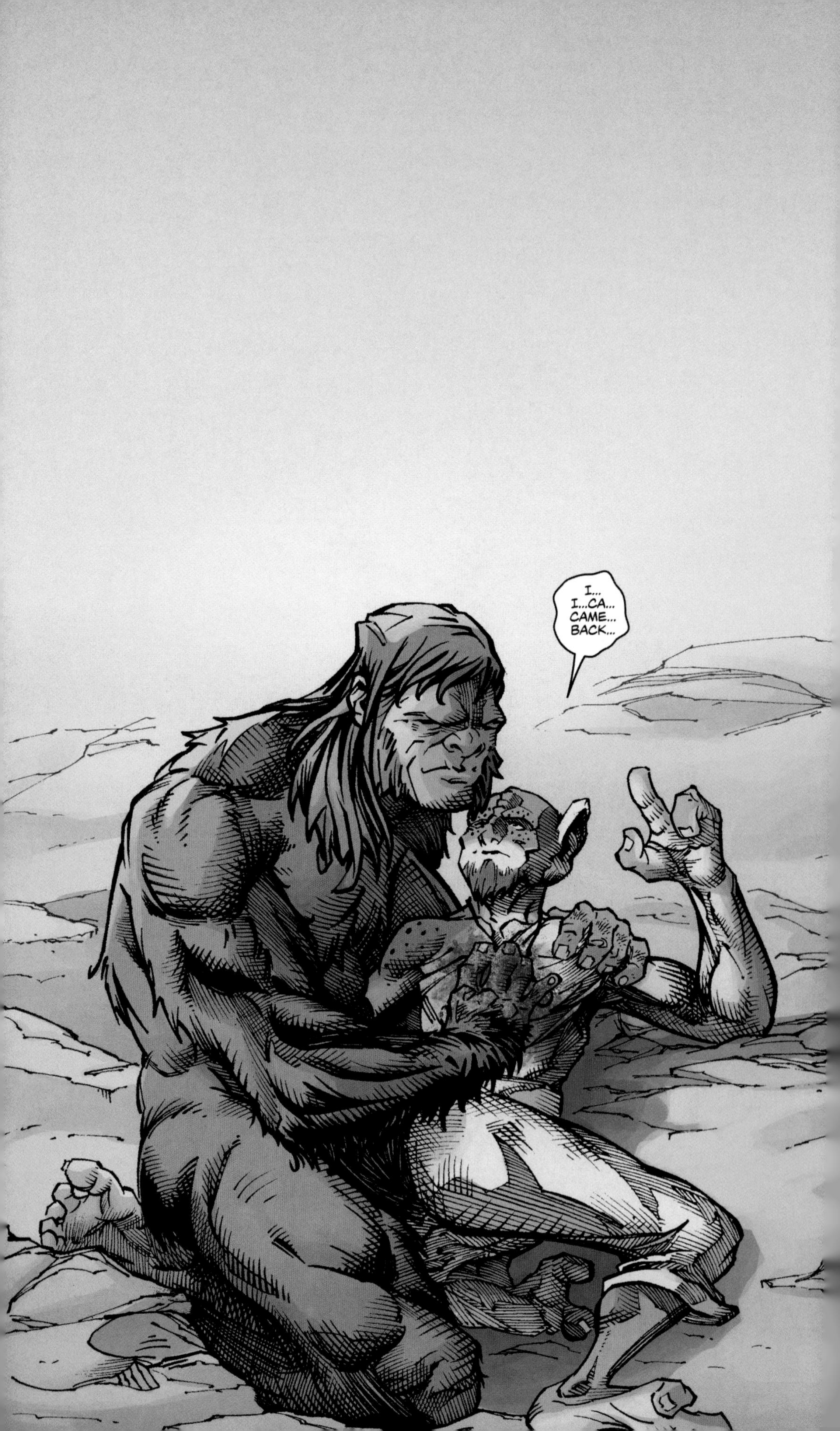
I... I...CA... CAME... BACK...

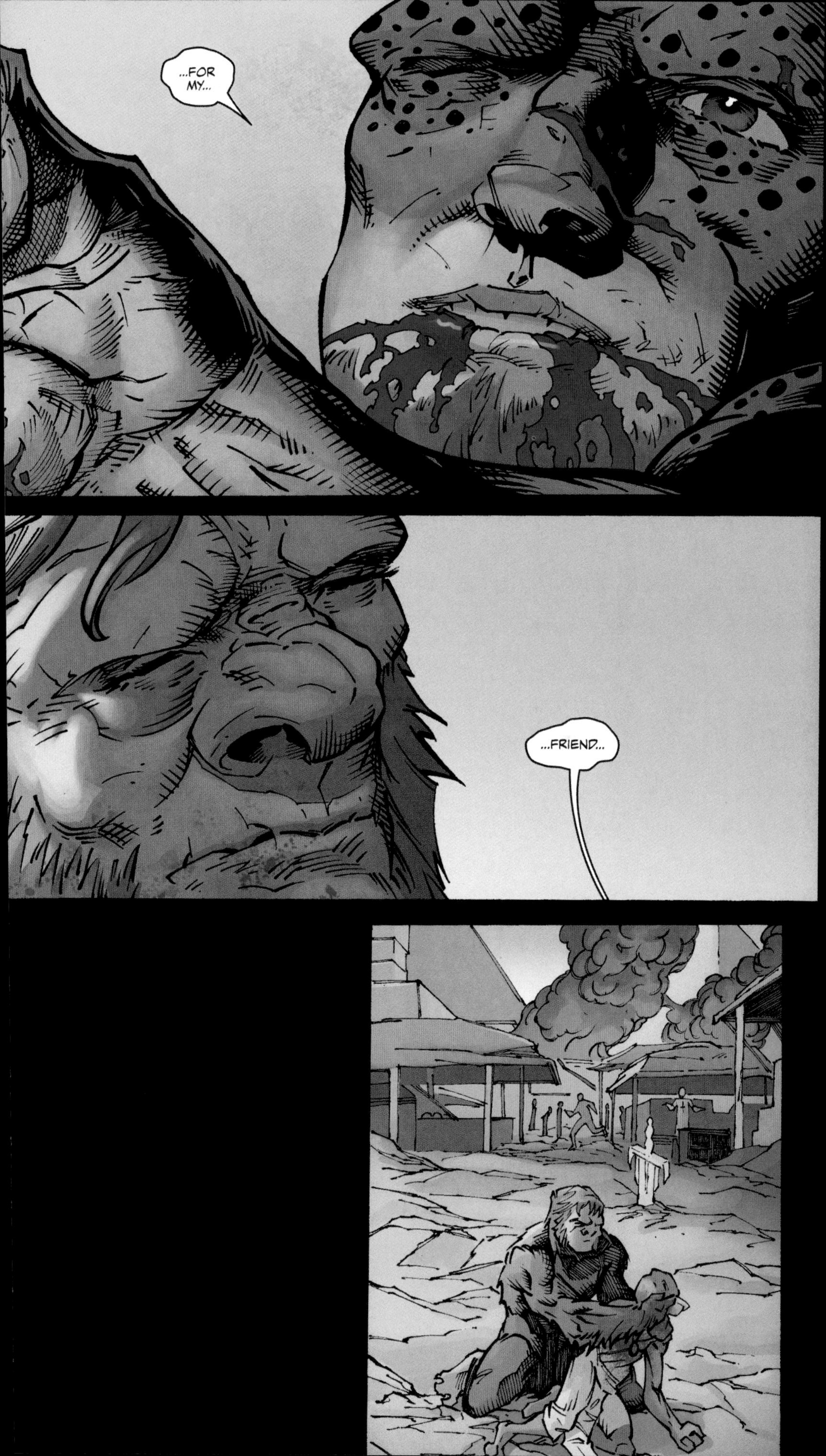

...FOR MY...
...FRIEND...

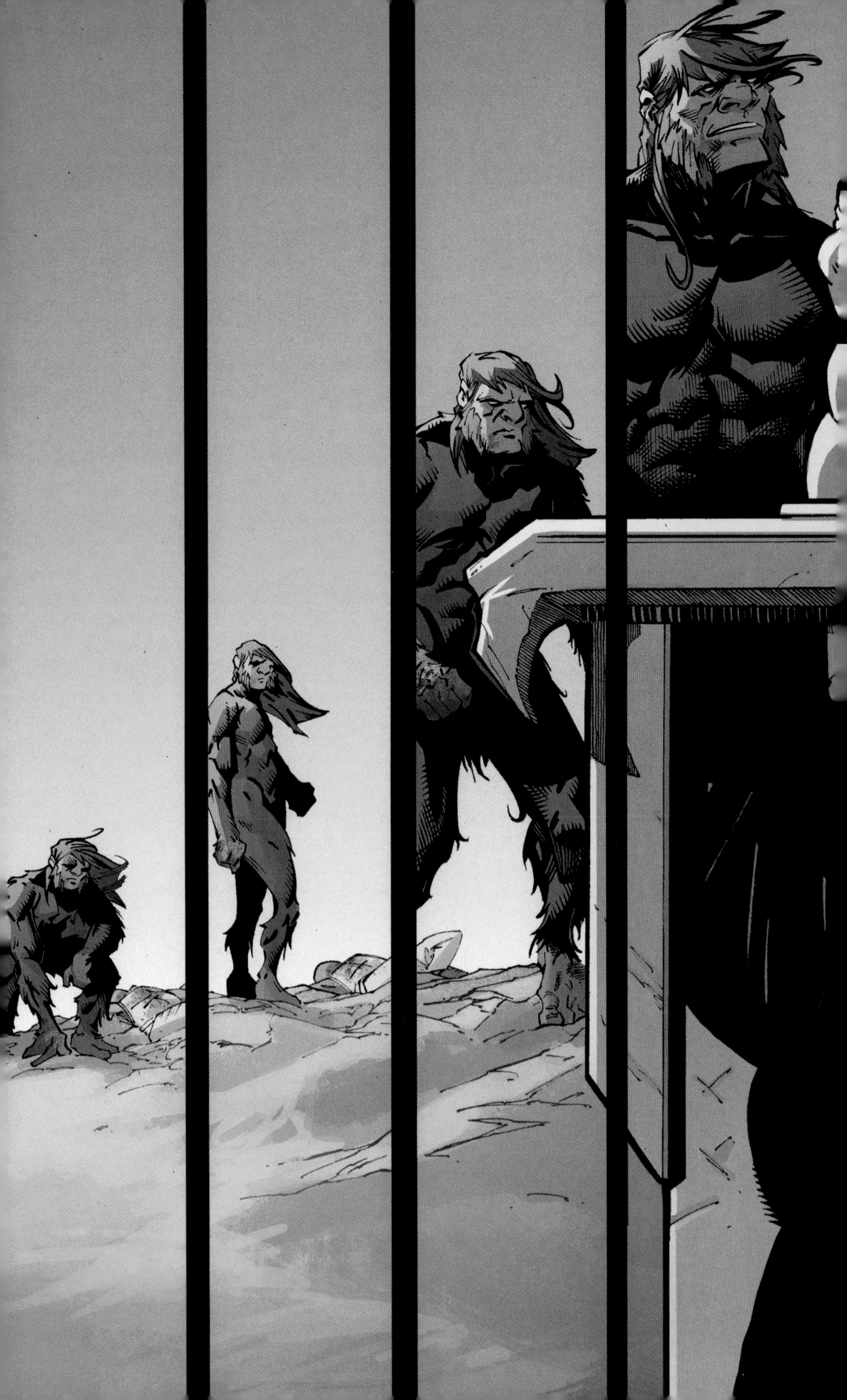

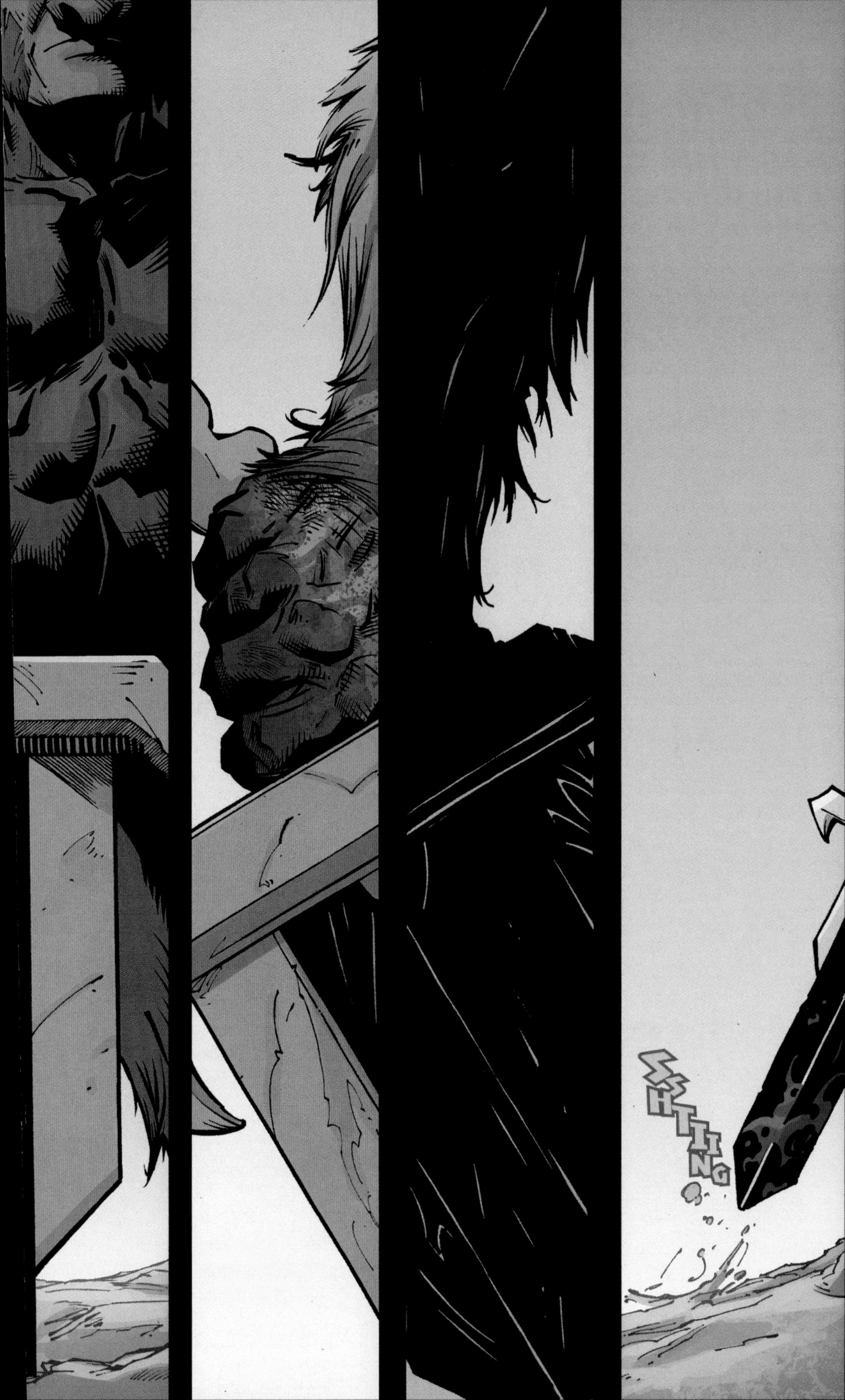
SSHTIING

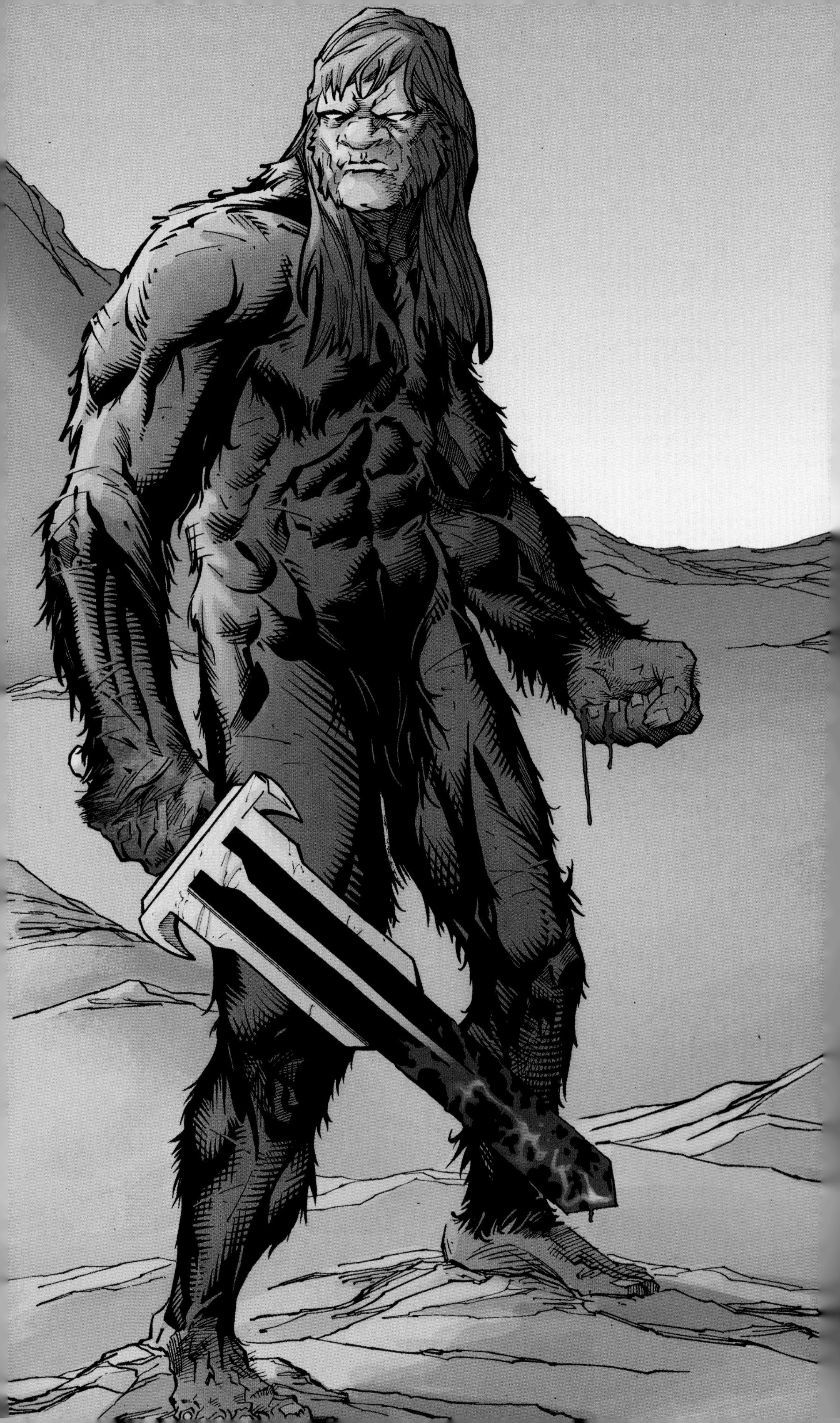

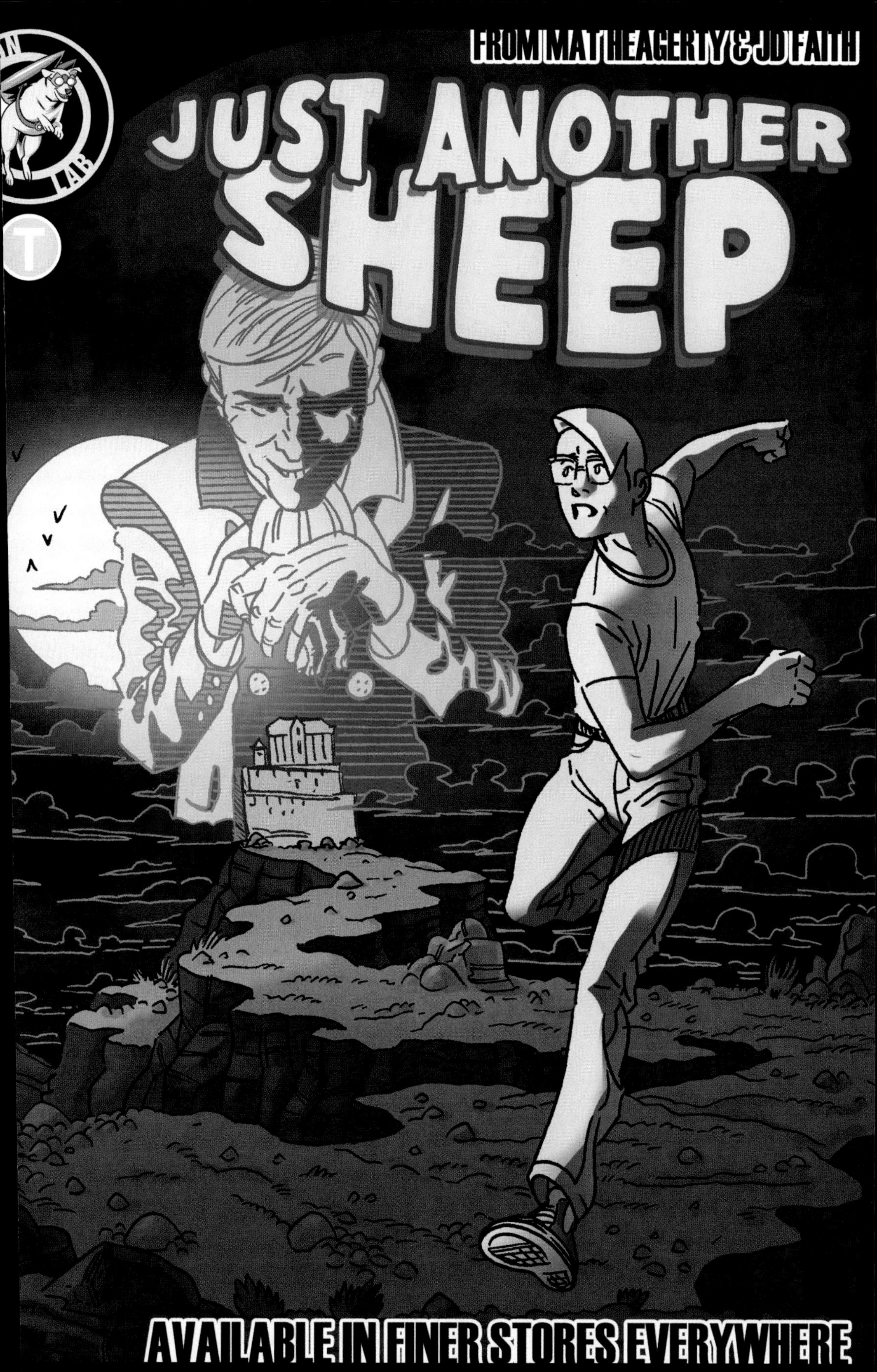
FROM MAT HEAGERTY & JD FAITH
JUST ANOTHER SHEEP
AVAILABLE IN FINER STORES EVERYWHERE

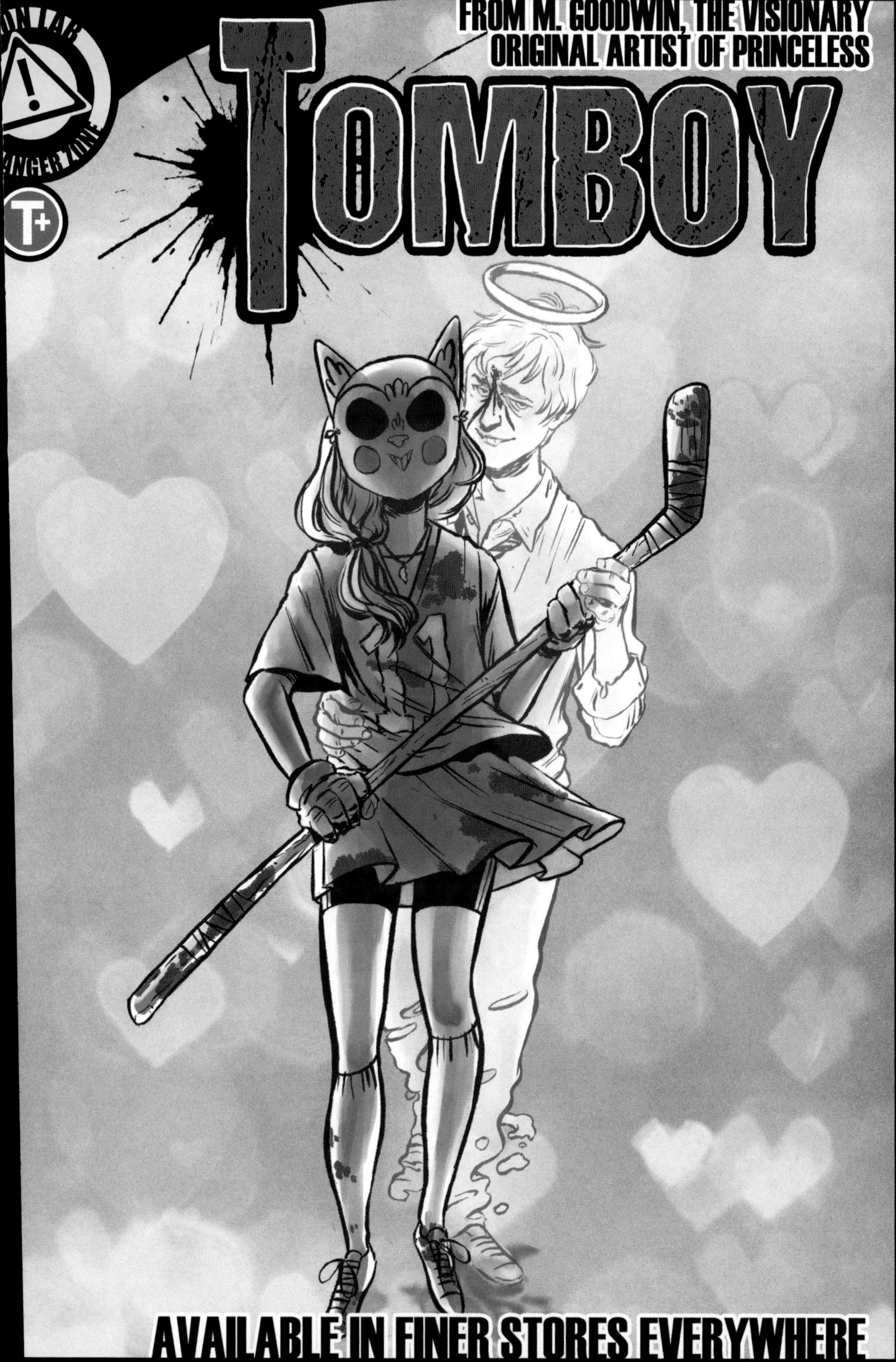
FROM M. GOODWIN, THE VISIONARY ORIGINAL ARTIST OF PRINCELESS
TOMBOY
T+
AVAILABLE IN FINER STORES EVERYWHERE

ıerever she goes, death is sure to follow. Four months after the funeral of her best ıd, Addison has embraced her new life as a vigilante, but trouble is on the horizon Detective Tico closes in on his suspect and the notorious Irene Trent finally steps out of the shadows.

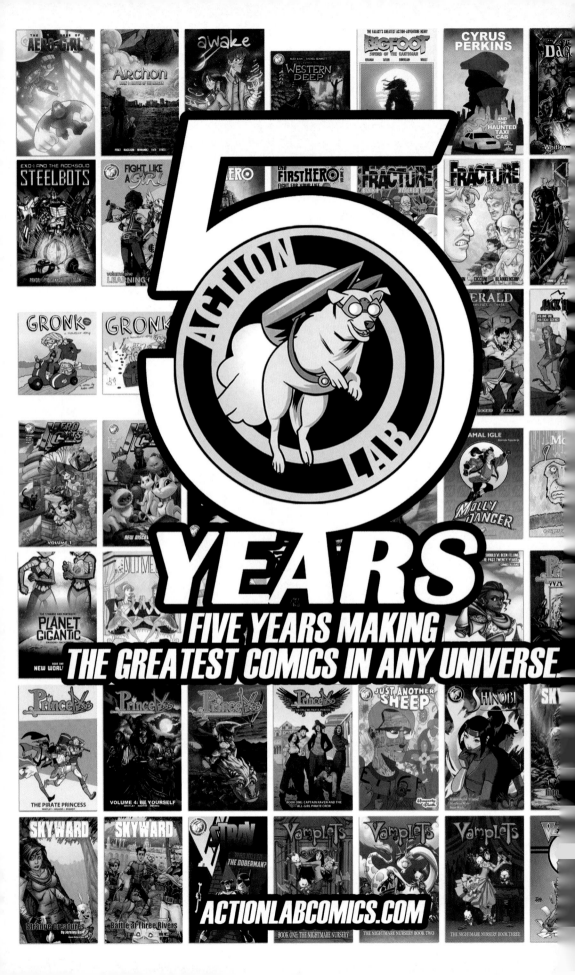

ACTION LAB

5 YEARS

FIVE YEARS MAKING
THE GREATEST COMICS IN ANY UNIVERSE.

ACTIONLABCOMICS.COM

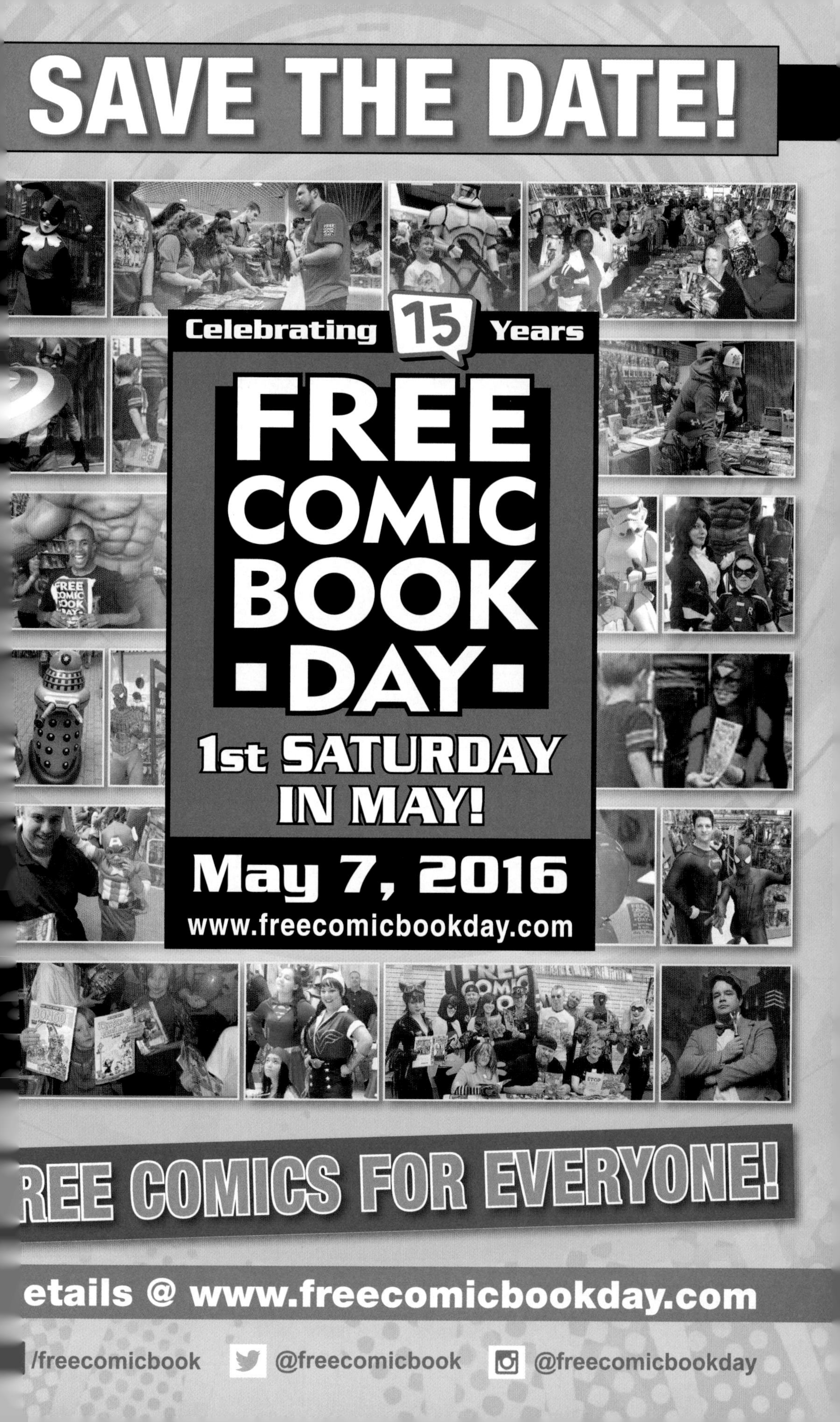
SAVE THE DATE!
Celebrating 15 Years
FREE COMIC BOOK DAY
1st SATURDAY IN MAY!
May 7, 2016
www.freecomicbookday.com
REE COMICS FOR EVERYONE!
etails @ www.freecomicbookday.com
/freecomicbook
@freecomicbook
@freecomicbookday

ACTION LAB

READ MORE NOW

Bigfoot: Sword Of The Earthman - Action Lab
www.actionlabcomics.com
00511
7 02382 69116 5

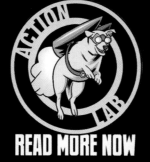

ACTIONLABCOMICS.COM

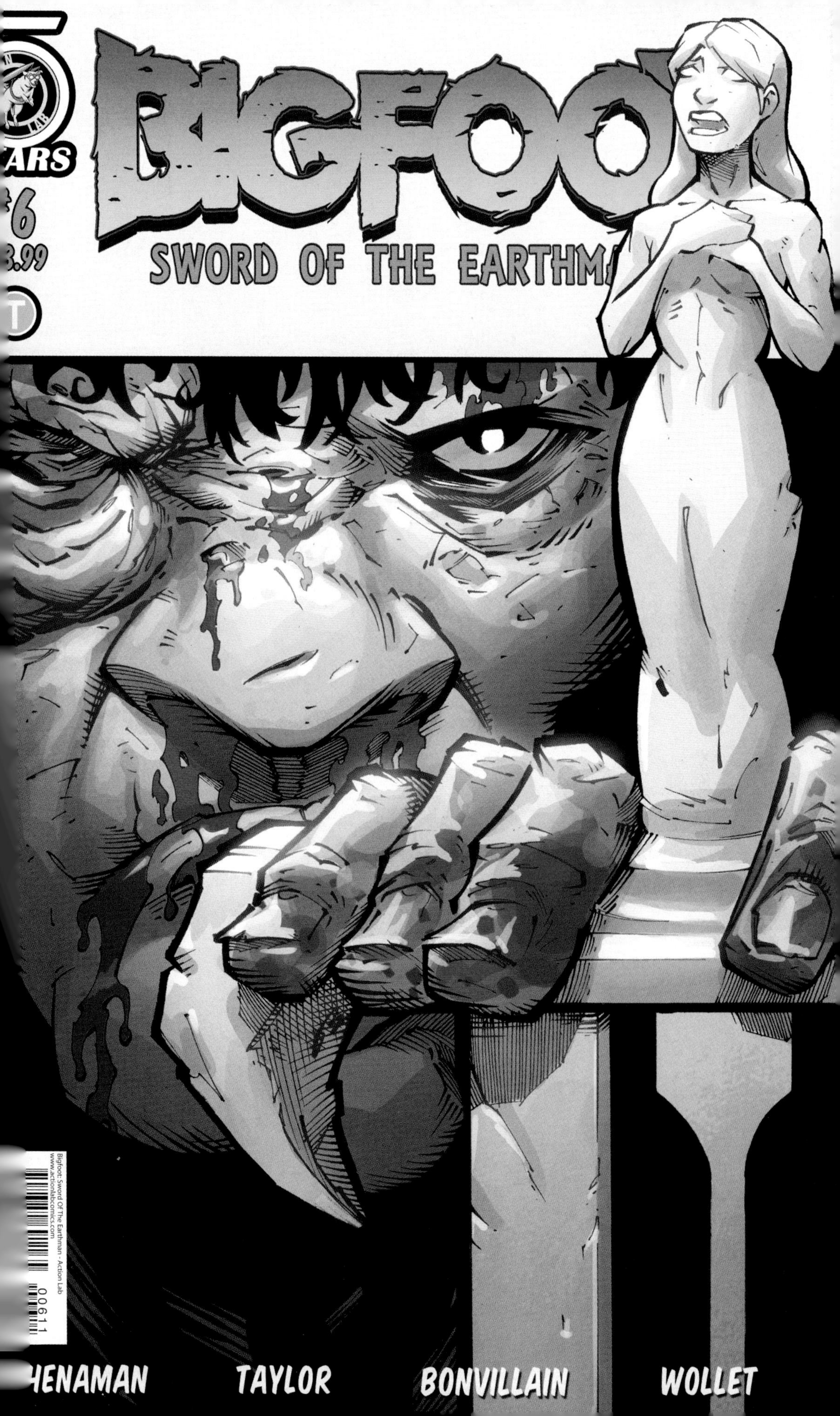
BIGFOO
SWORD OF THE EARTHMA
ARS
6
3.99
Bigfoot: Sword Of The Earthman - Action Lab
www.actionlabcomics.com
00611
HENAMAN
TAYLOR
BONVILLAIN
WOLLET

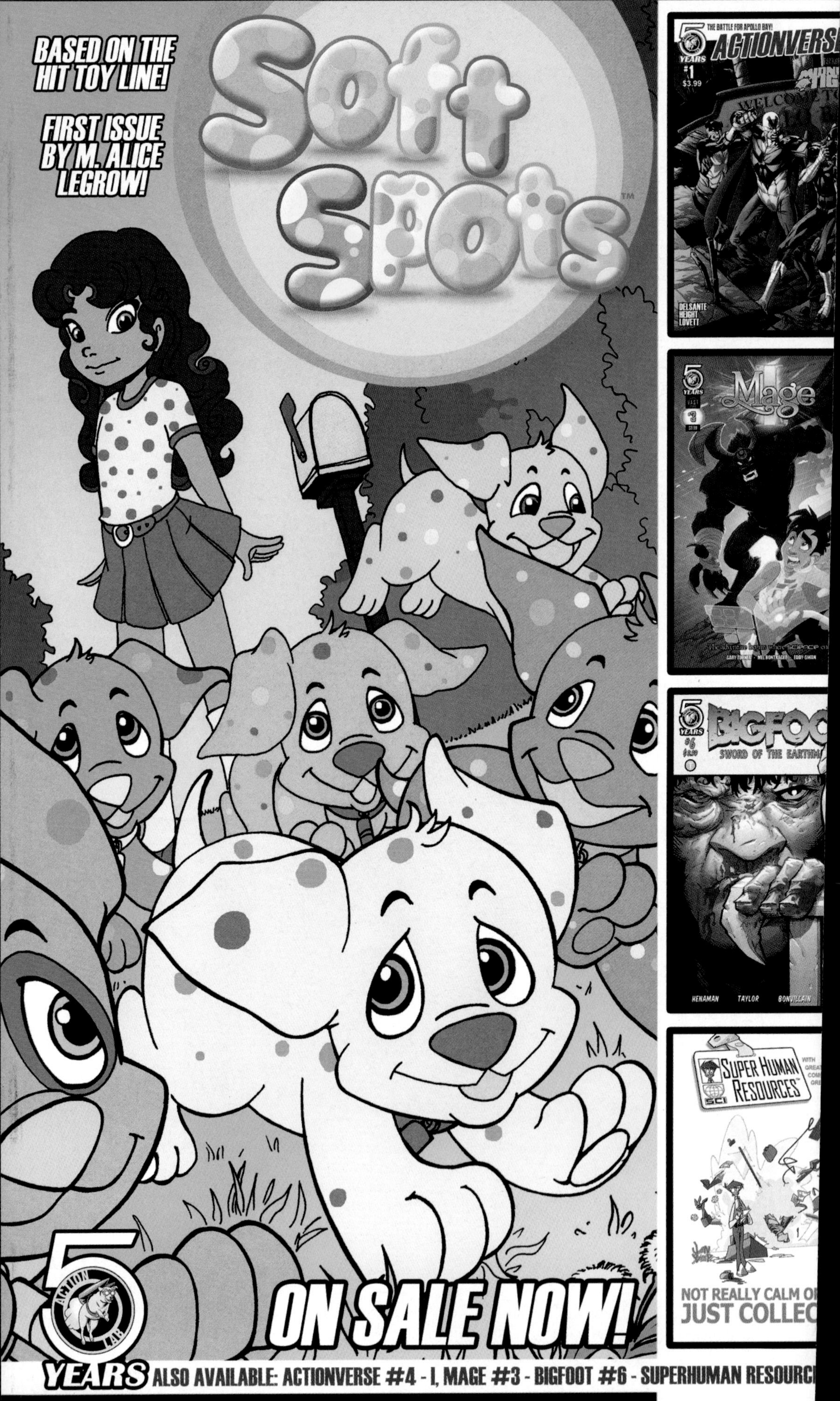

BASED ON THE HIT TOY LINE!
FIRST ISSUE BY M. ALICE LEGROW!
Soft Spots™
THE BATTLE FOR APOLLO BAY!
#1
$3.99
DELSANTE
HEIGHT
LOVETT
Mage
#3
HENAMAN TAYLOR BONVILLAIN
SUPER HUMAN RESOURCES™
ON SALE NOW!
YEARS ALSO AVAILABLE: ACTIONVERSE #4 - I, MAGE #3 - BIGFOOT #6 - SUPERHUMAN RESOURC

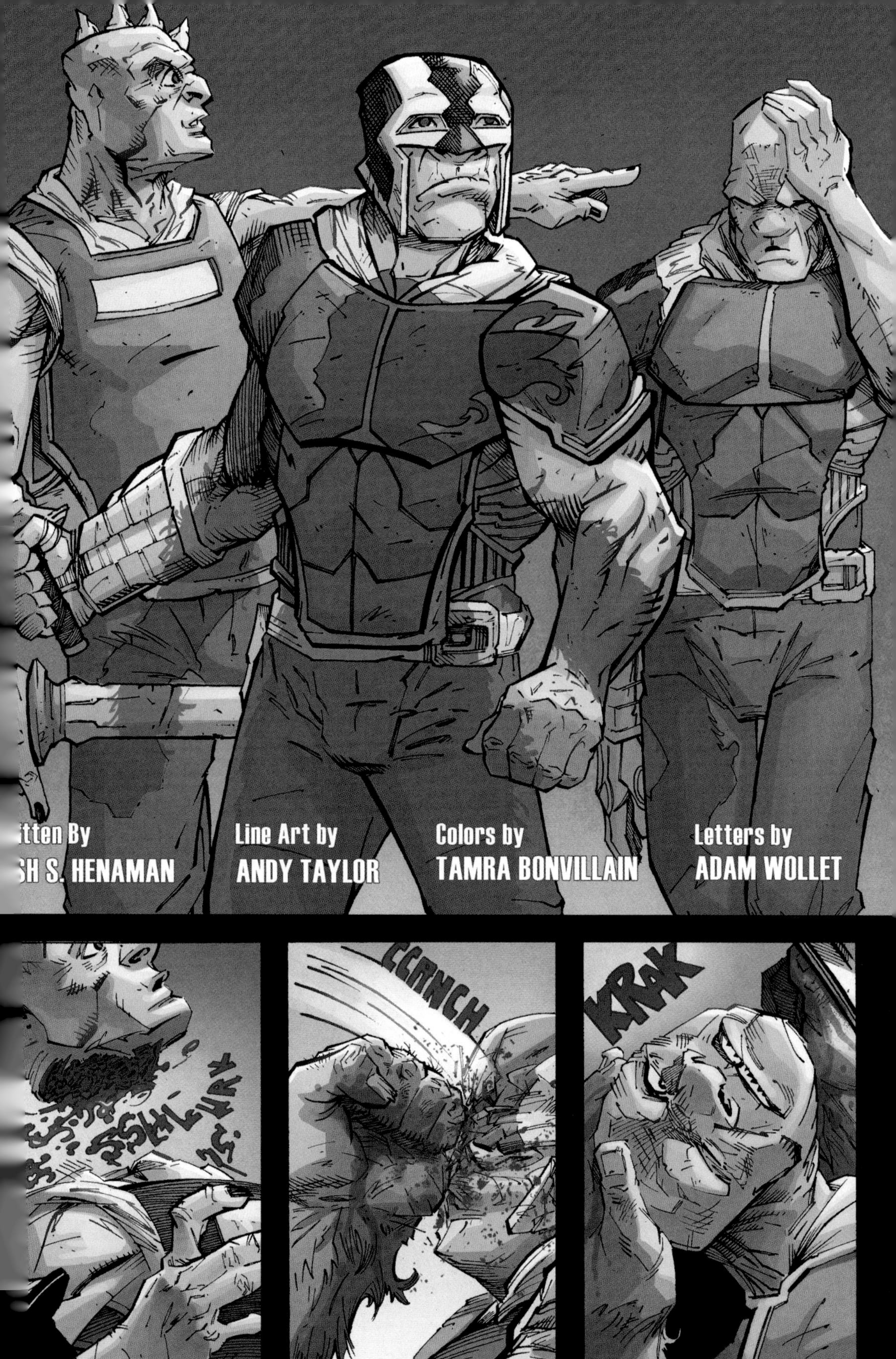
itten By
SH S. HENAMAN
Line Art by
ANDY TAYLOR
Colors by
TAMRA BONVILLAIN
Letters by
ADAM WOLLET
CCRNCH
KRAK

Bryan Seaton: Publisher • Dave Dwonch: President • Shawn Gabborin: Editor In Chief
mal Igle: Vice-President of Marketing • Vito Delsante: Director of Marketing • Jim Dietz: Social Media Director
Nicole DAndria: Script Editor • Chad Cicconi: Little Foot • Colleen Boyd: Submissions Editor

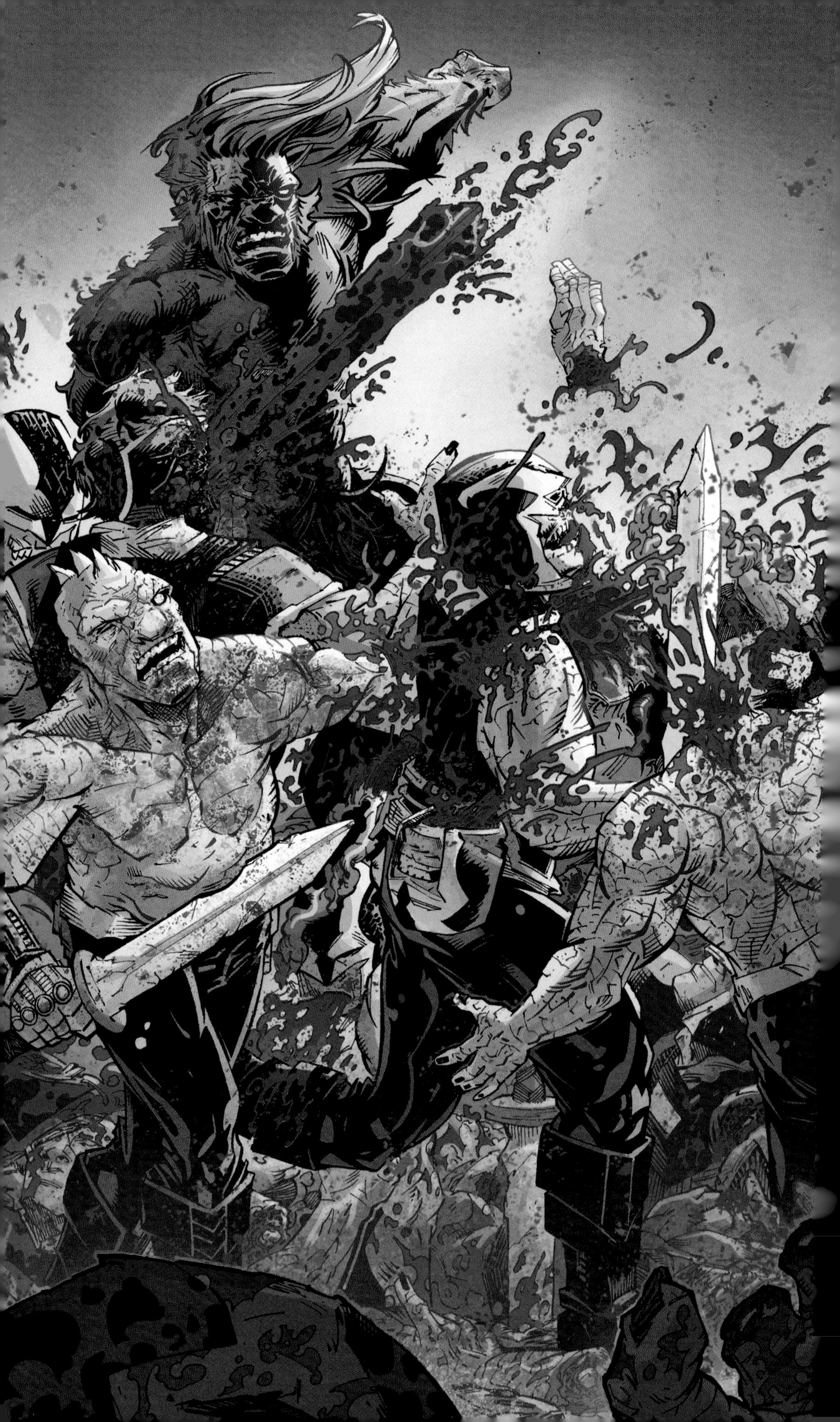

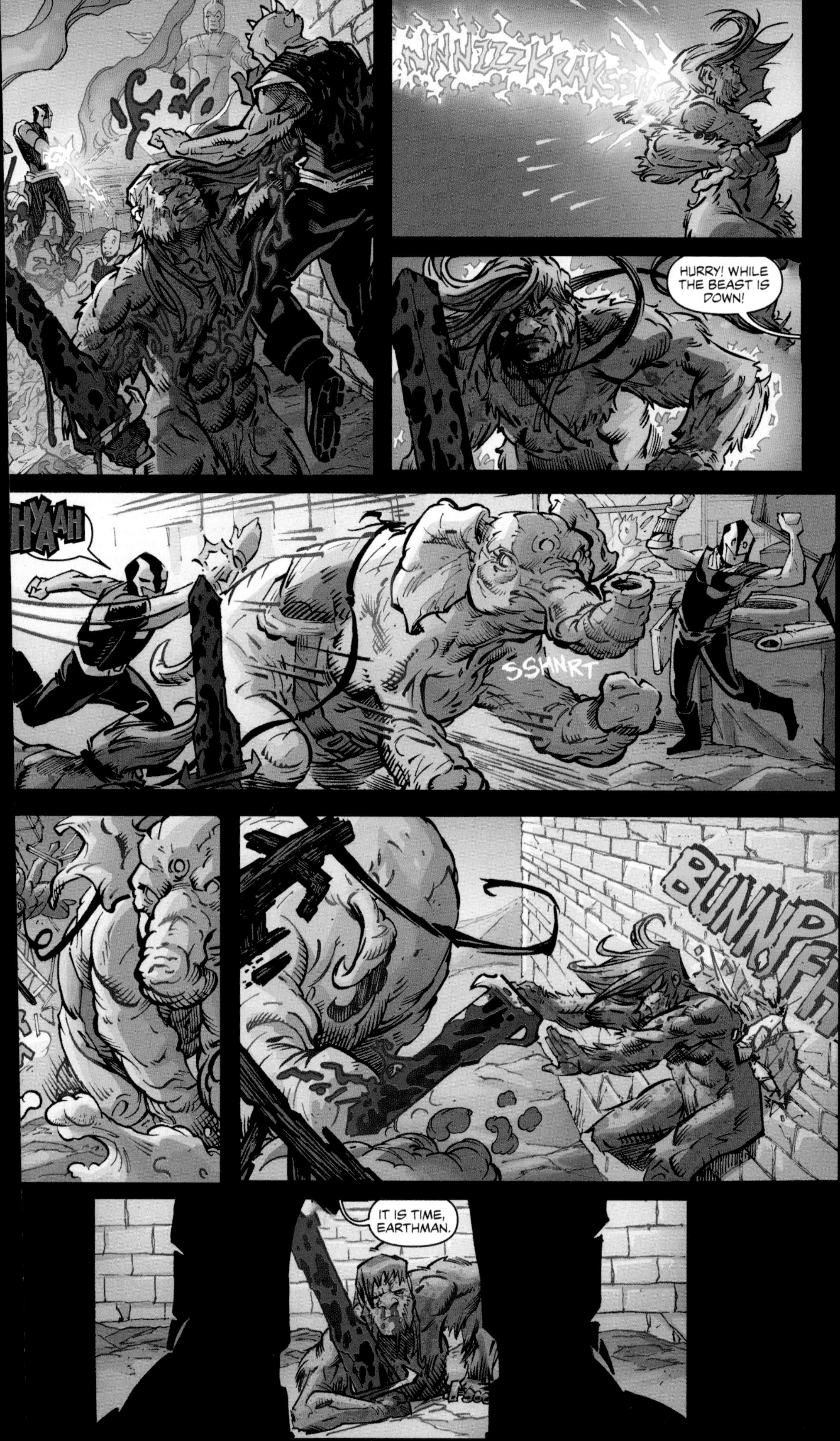

NNNIZZKRAKSSHH
HURRY! WHILE THE BEAST IS DOWN!
HYAAH
SSHNRT
BUNNPFH
IT IS TIME, EARTHMAN.

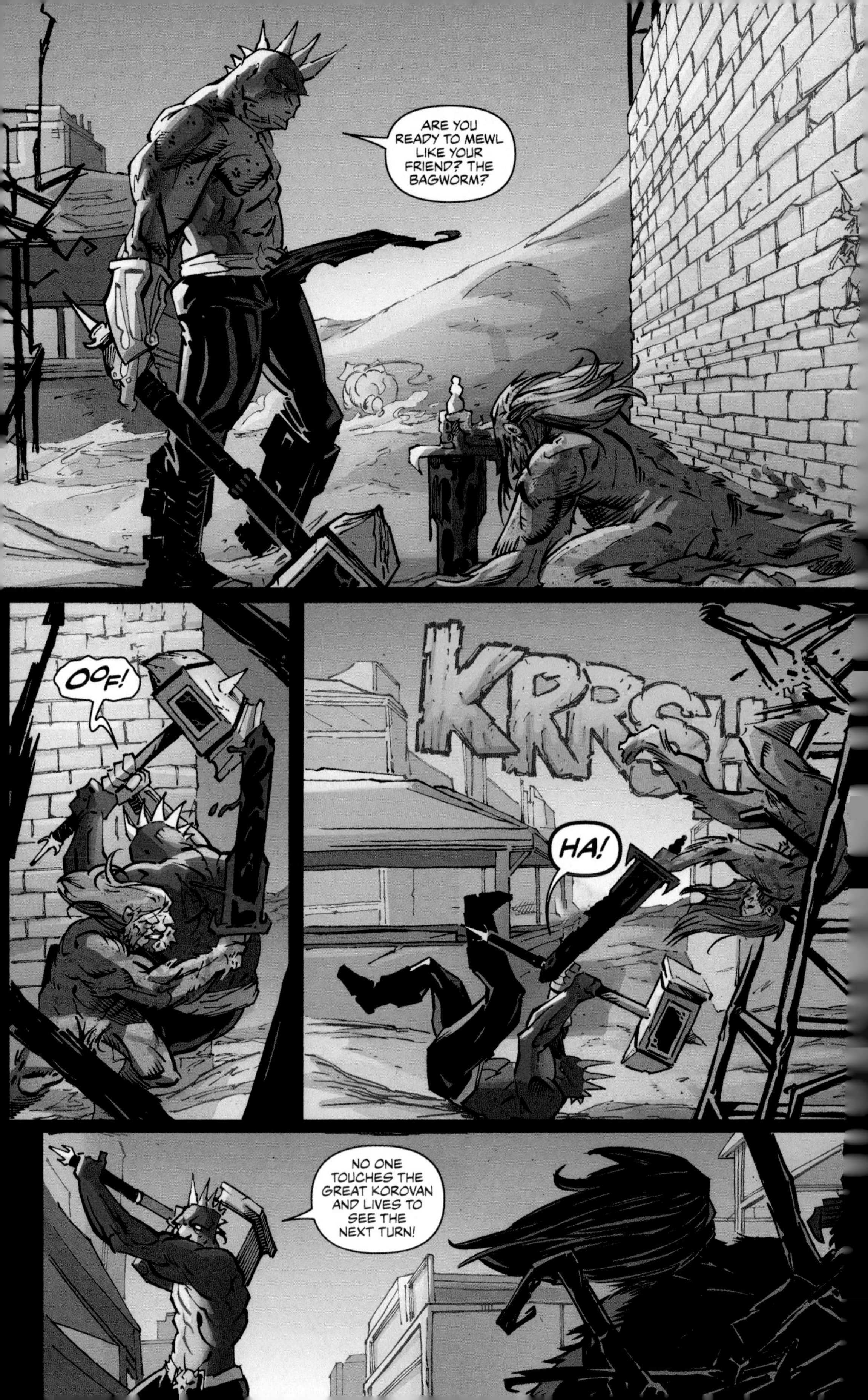
ARE YOU READY TO MEWL LIKE YOUR FRIEND? THE BAGWORM?
OOF!
KRRSH
HA!
NO ONE TOUCHES THE GREAT KOROVAN AND LIVES TO SEE THE NEXT TURN!

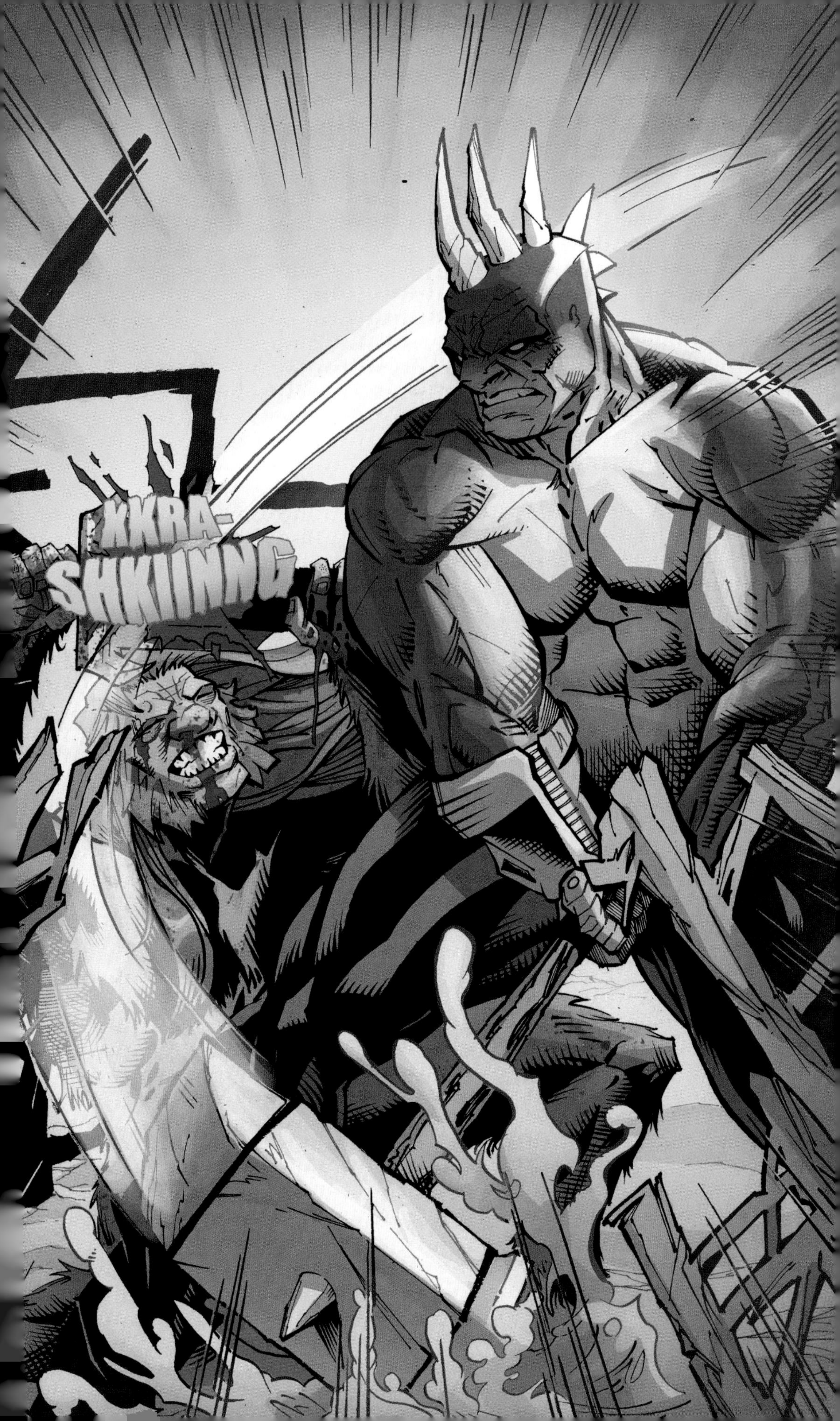
KKRA-SHKIINNG

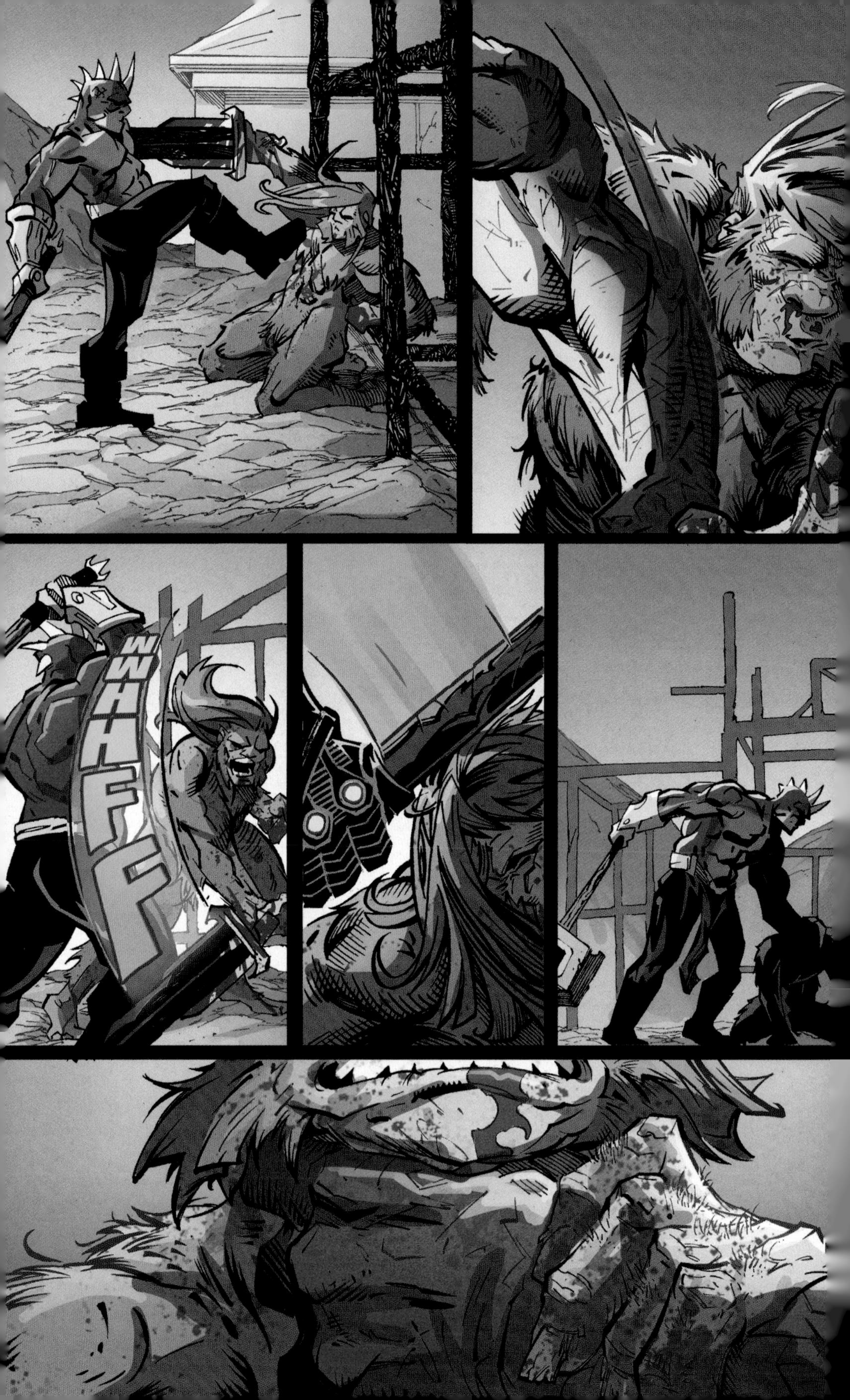
WWHHFF

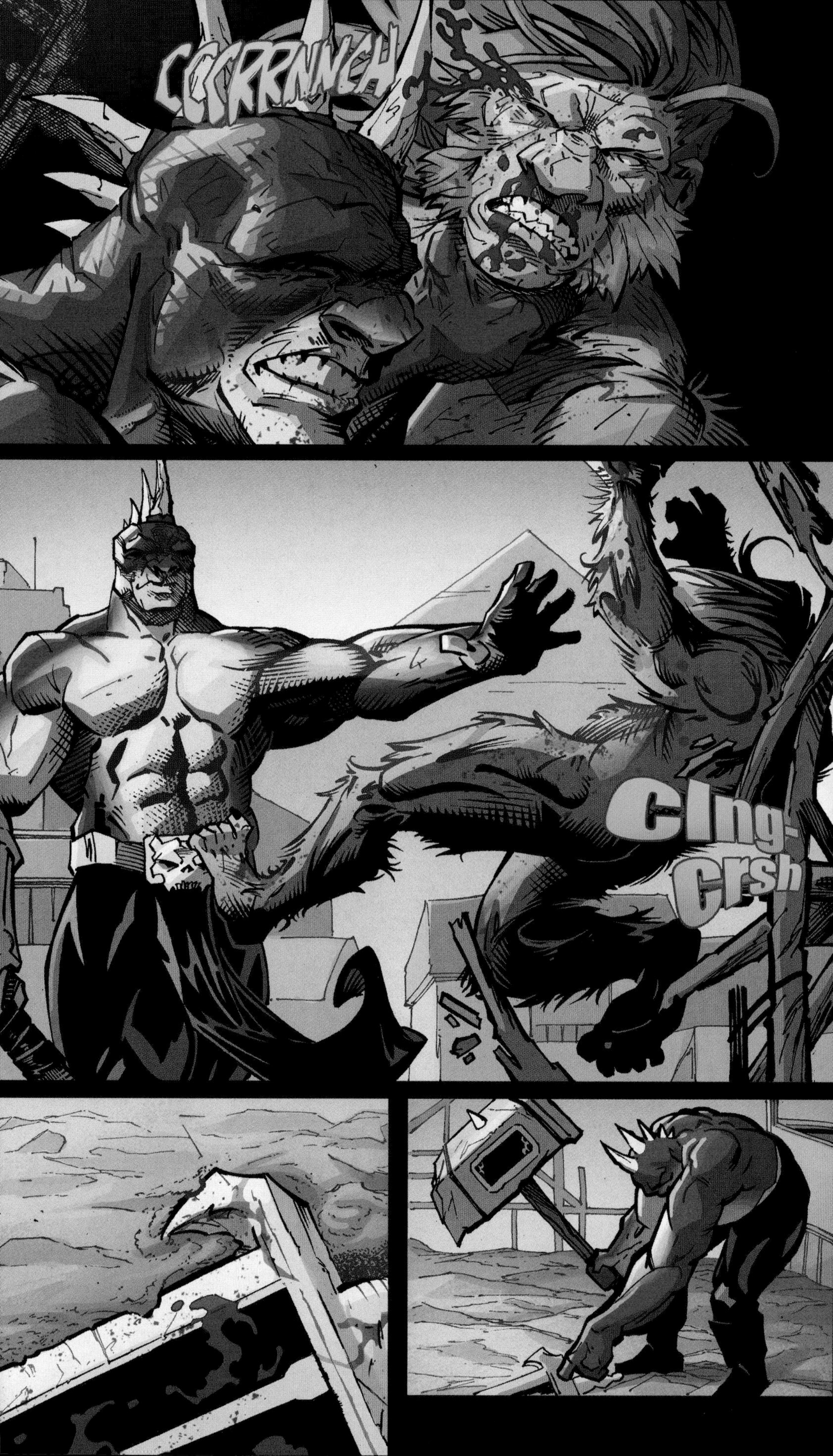
CCCRRNNCH
Clng-
Crsh

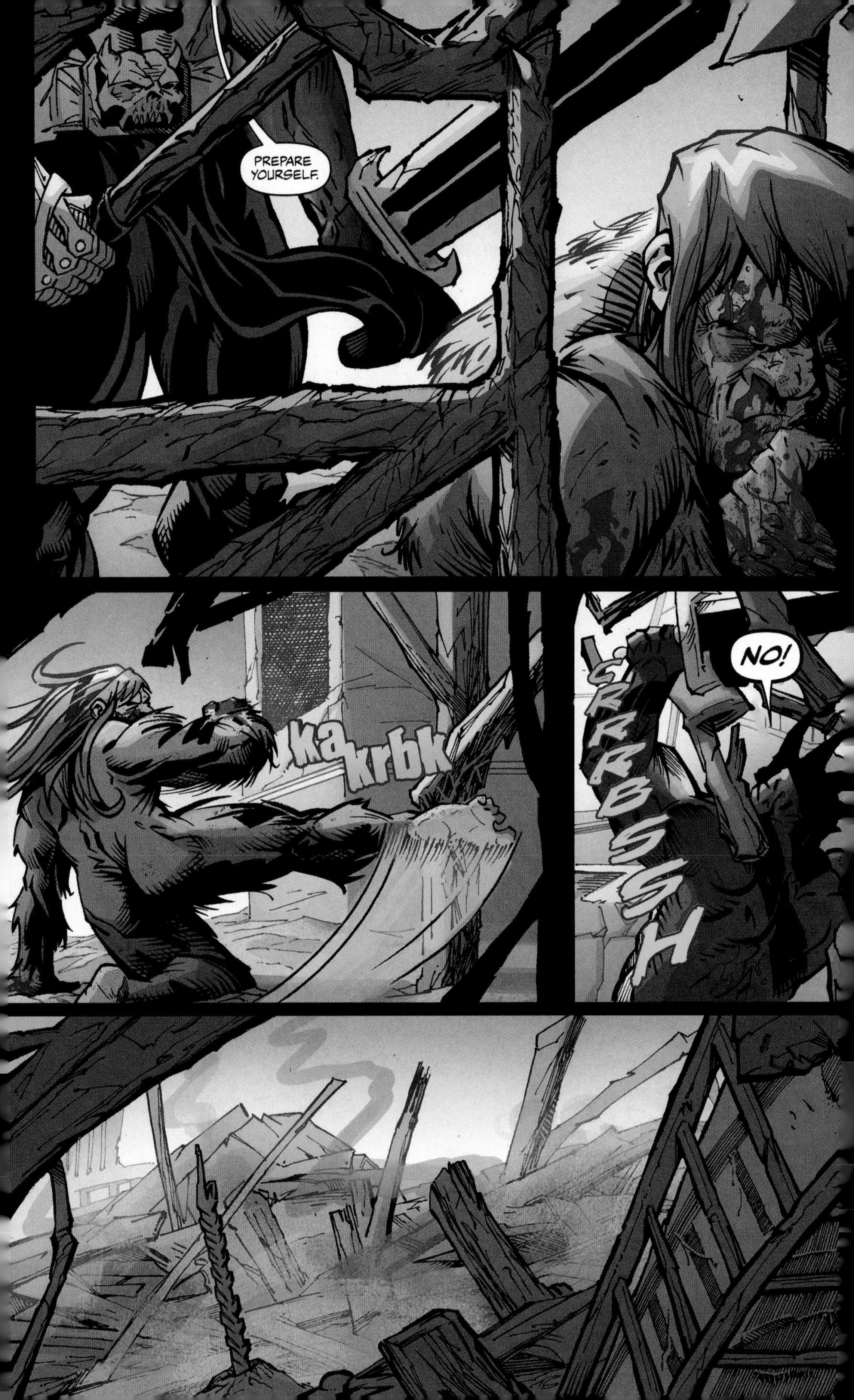
PREPARE YOURSELF.
KA KRBK
NO!
SKRRBSSH

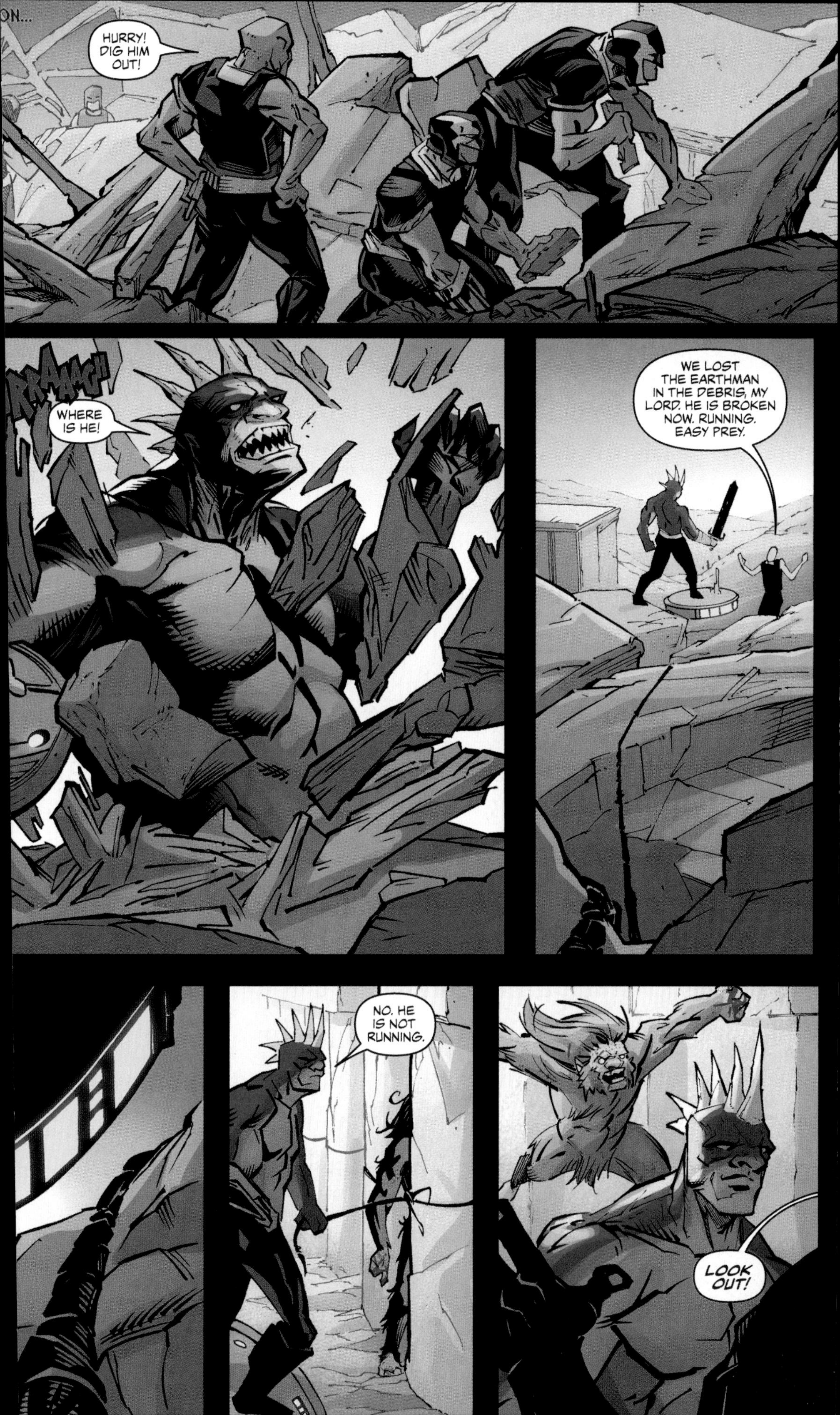
HURRY! DIG HIM OUT!
WHERE IS HE!
WE LOST THE EARTHMAN IN THE DEBRIS, MY LORD. HE IS BROKEN NOW. RUNNING. EASY PREY.
NO. HE IS NOT RUNNING.
LOOK OUT!

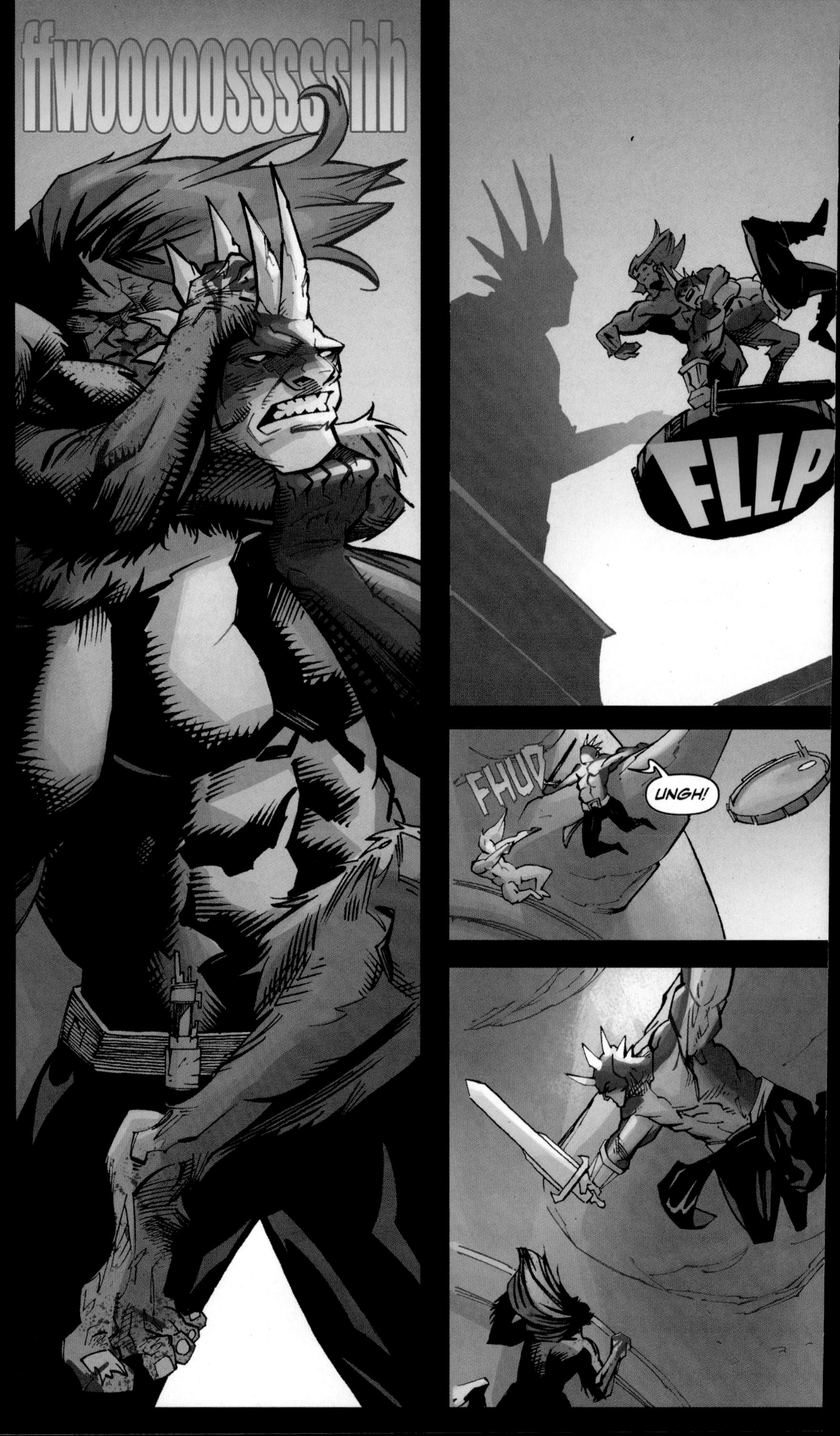
ffwoooooossssshh
FLLP
FHUD
UNGH!

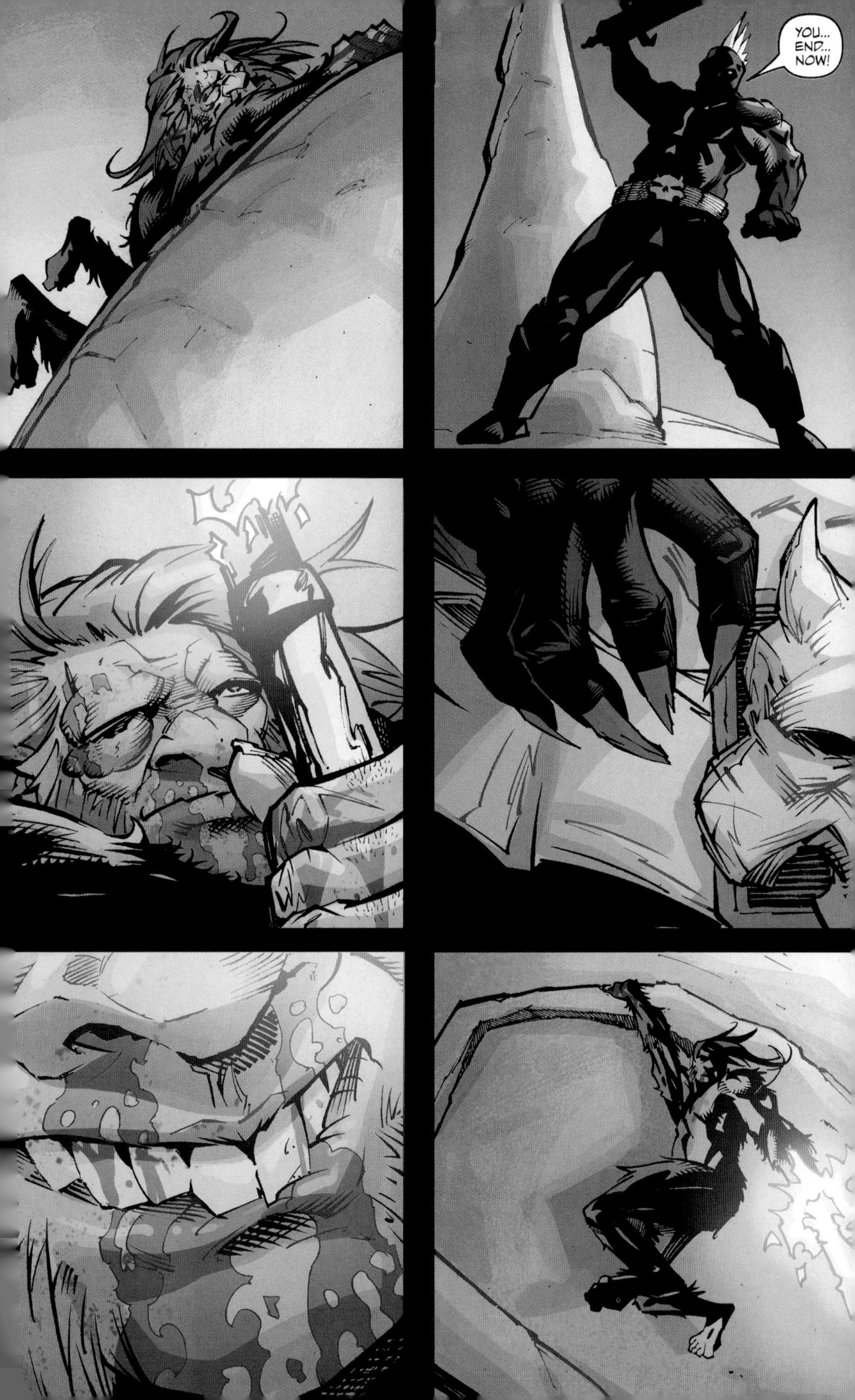
YOU... END... NOW!

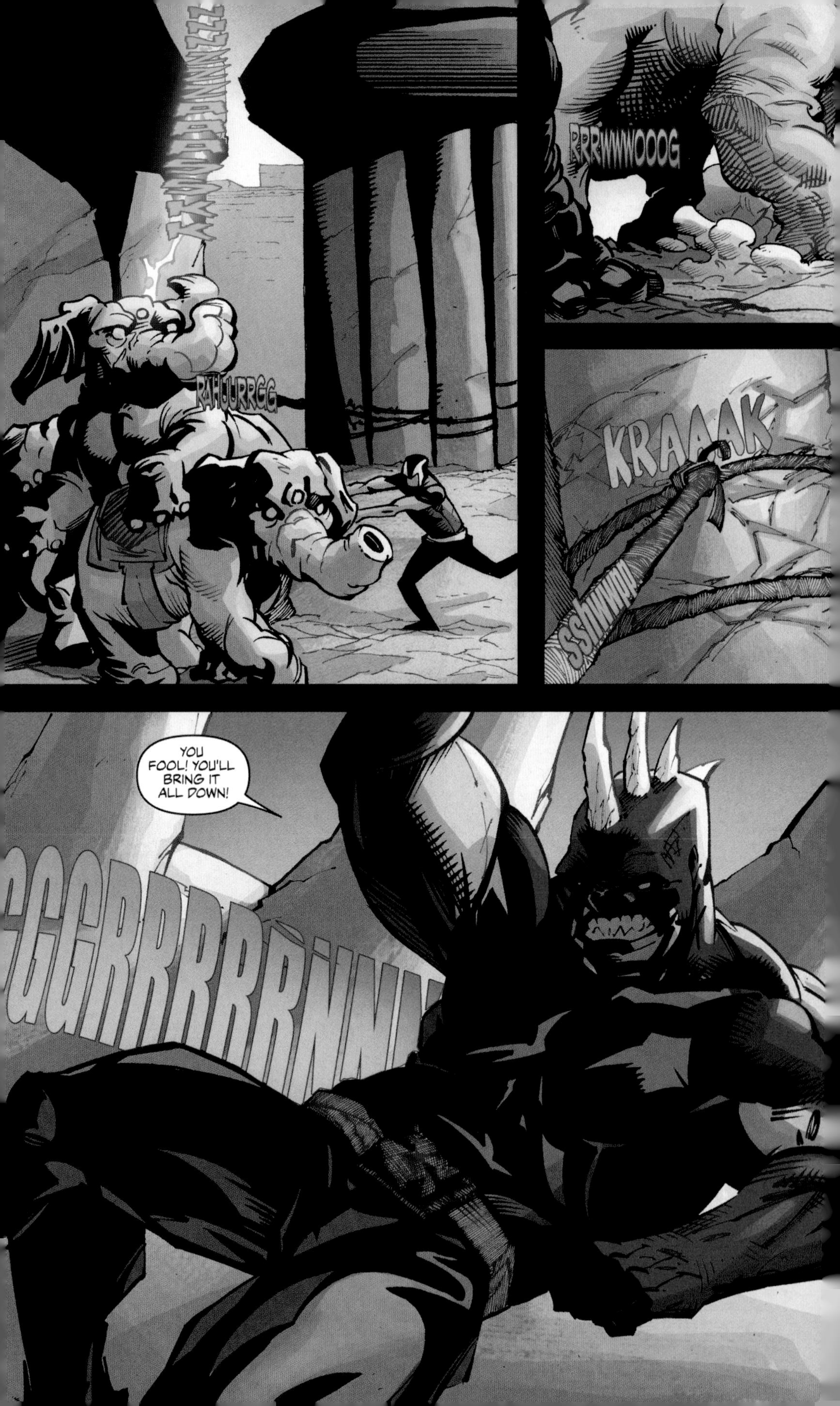
RAHUURRGG
RRRWWWOOOG
KRAAAK
sshwww
YOU FOOL! YOU'LL BRING IT ALL DOWN!
GGRRRRRNNN

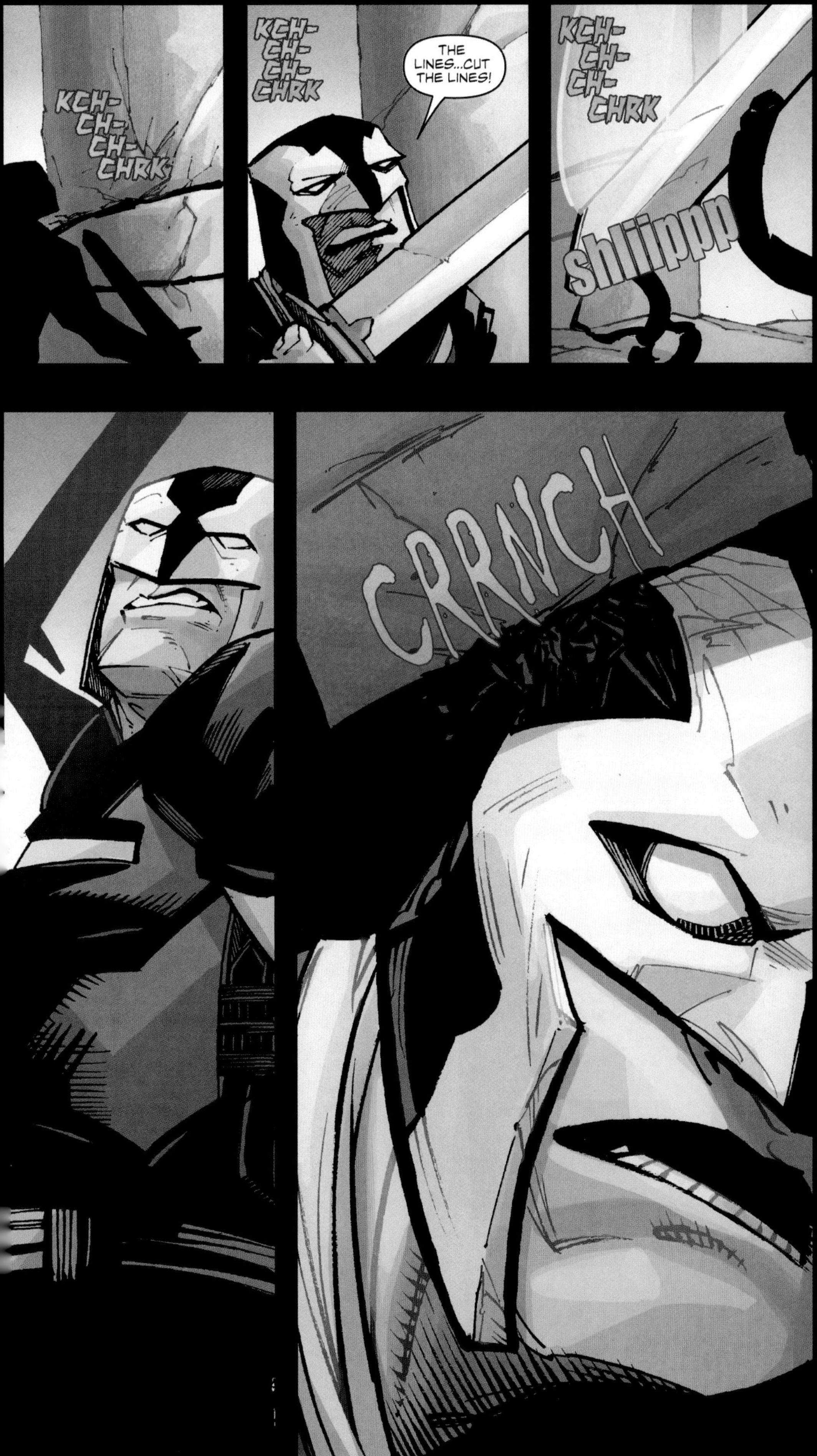
KCH-
CH-
CH-
CHRK
KCH-
CH-
CH-
CHRK
THE LINES...CUT THE LINES!
KCH-
CH-
CH-
CHRK
shliippp
CRRNCH

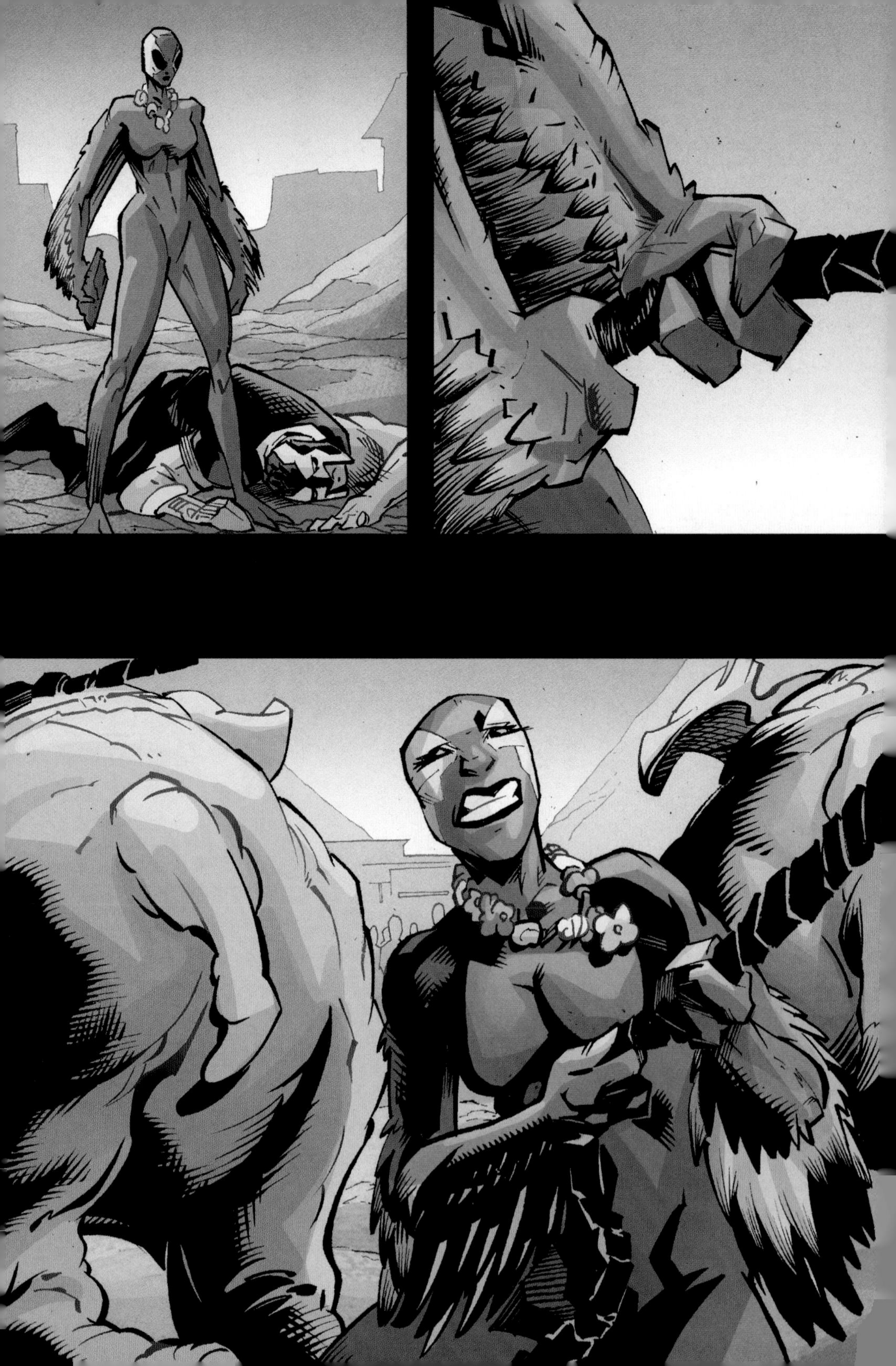

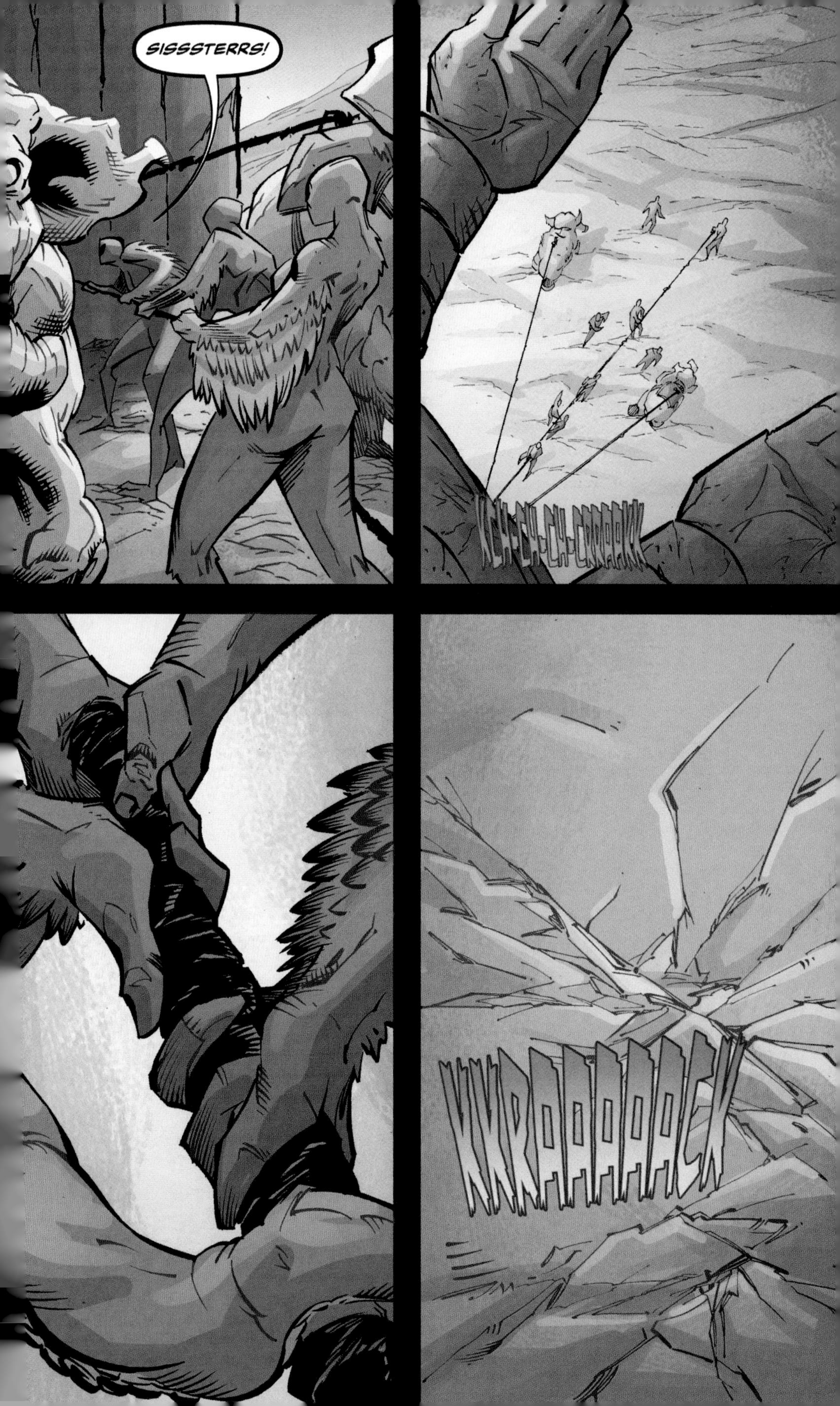
SISSSTERRS!
KCH-CH-CRRAAKK
KKRAAAAACK

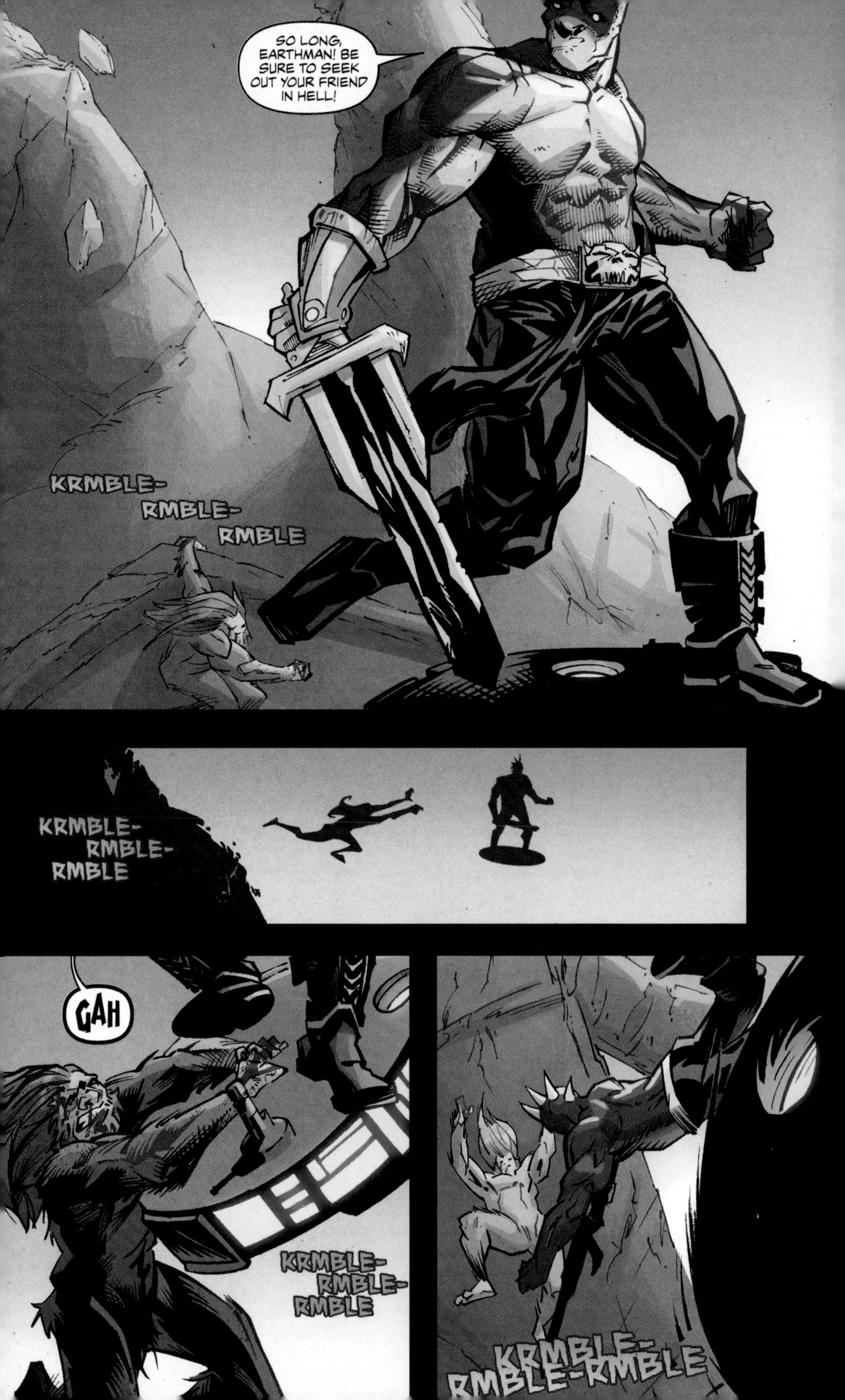
SO LONG, EARTHMAN! BE SURE TO SEEK OUT YOUR FRIEND IN HELL!
KRMBLE-RMBLE-RMBLE
KRMBLE-RMBLE-RMBLE
GAH
KRMBLE-RMBLE-RMBLE
KRMBLE-RMBLE-RMBLE

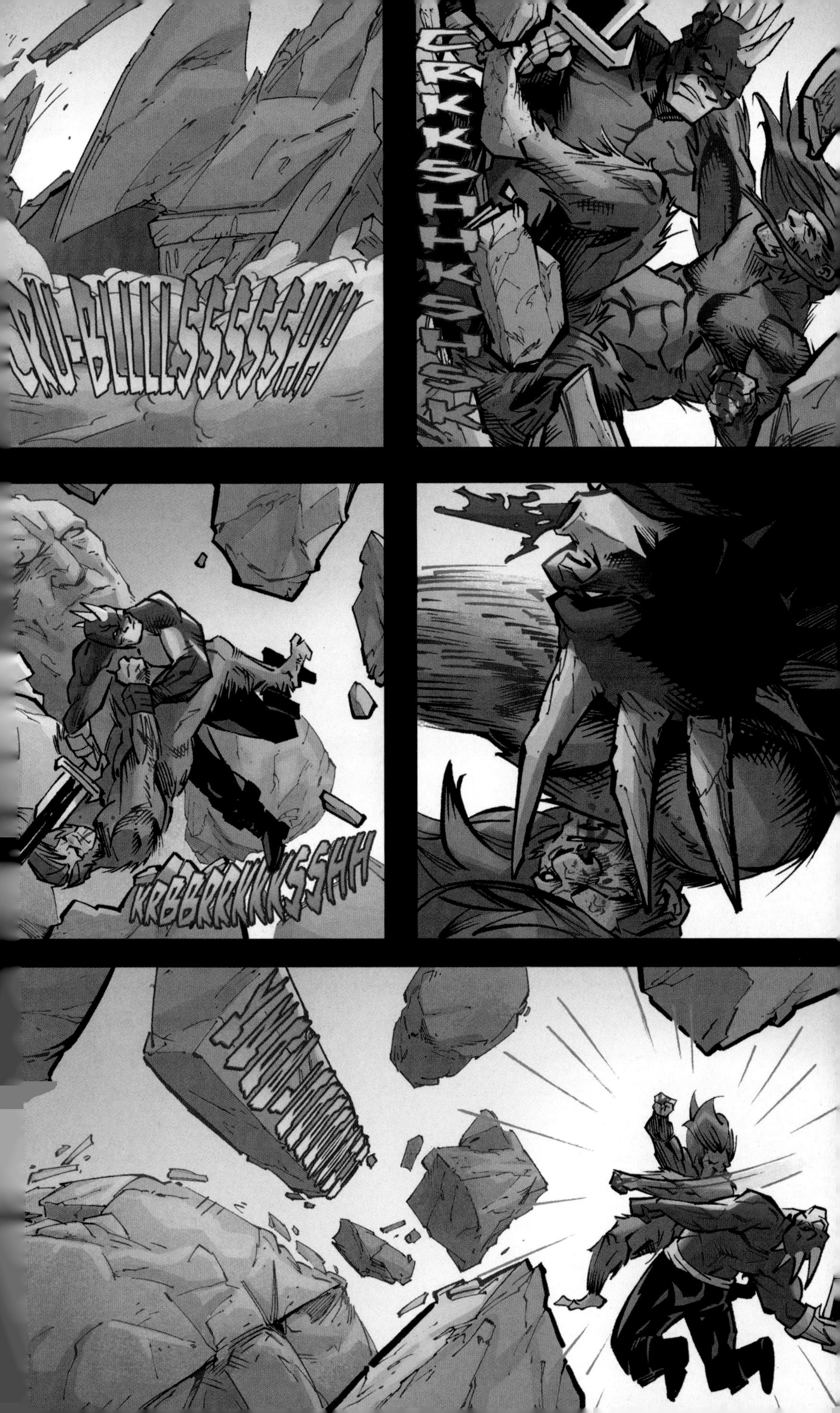

RU-BLLLLSSSSSH!!
CRKKSHKSHSK
KRBBRRKKSSHH

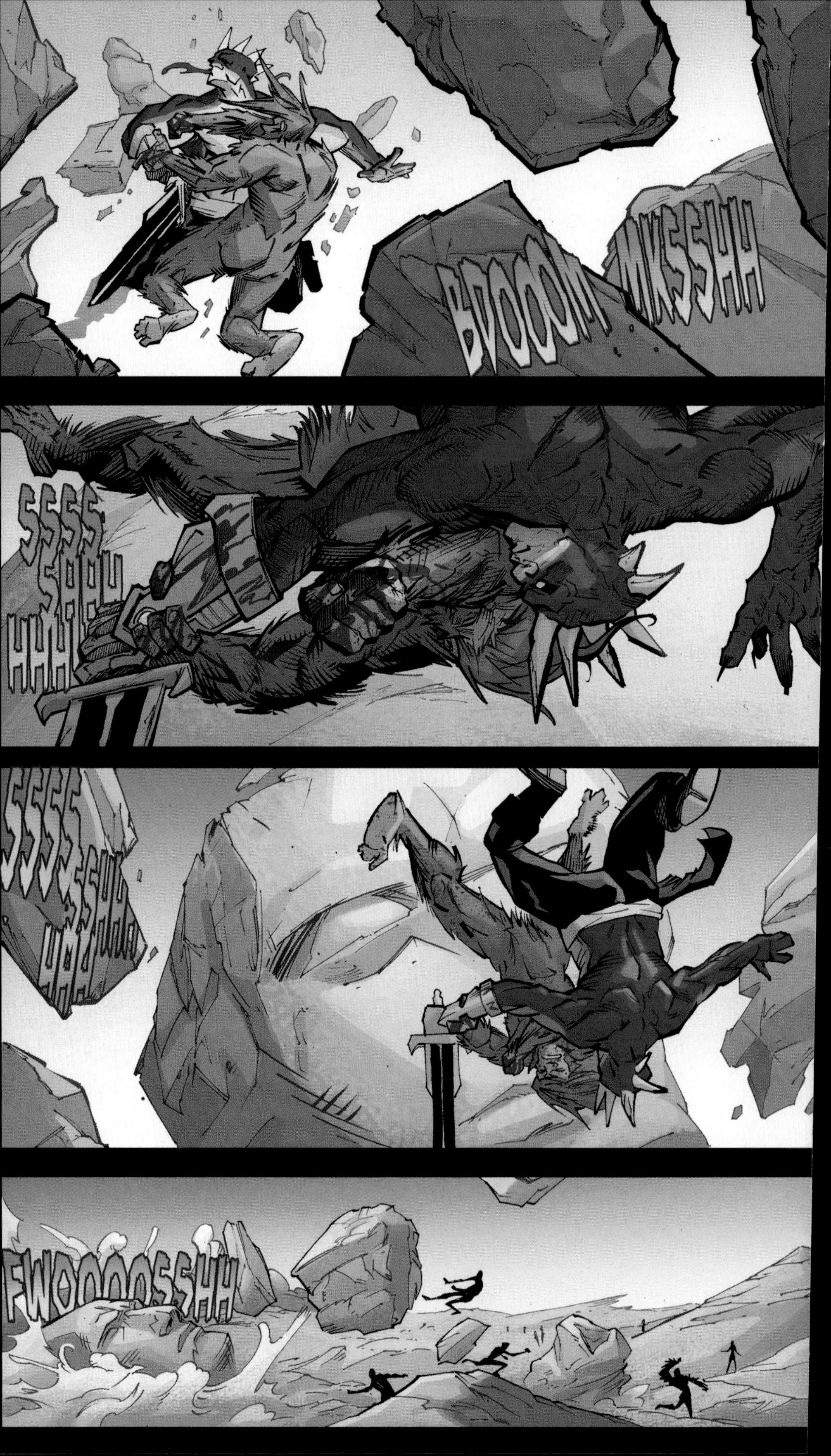
BOOOOM
MKSSHH
FWOOOOSSHH

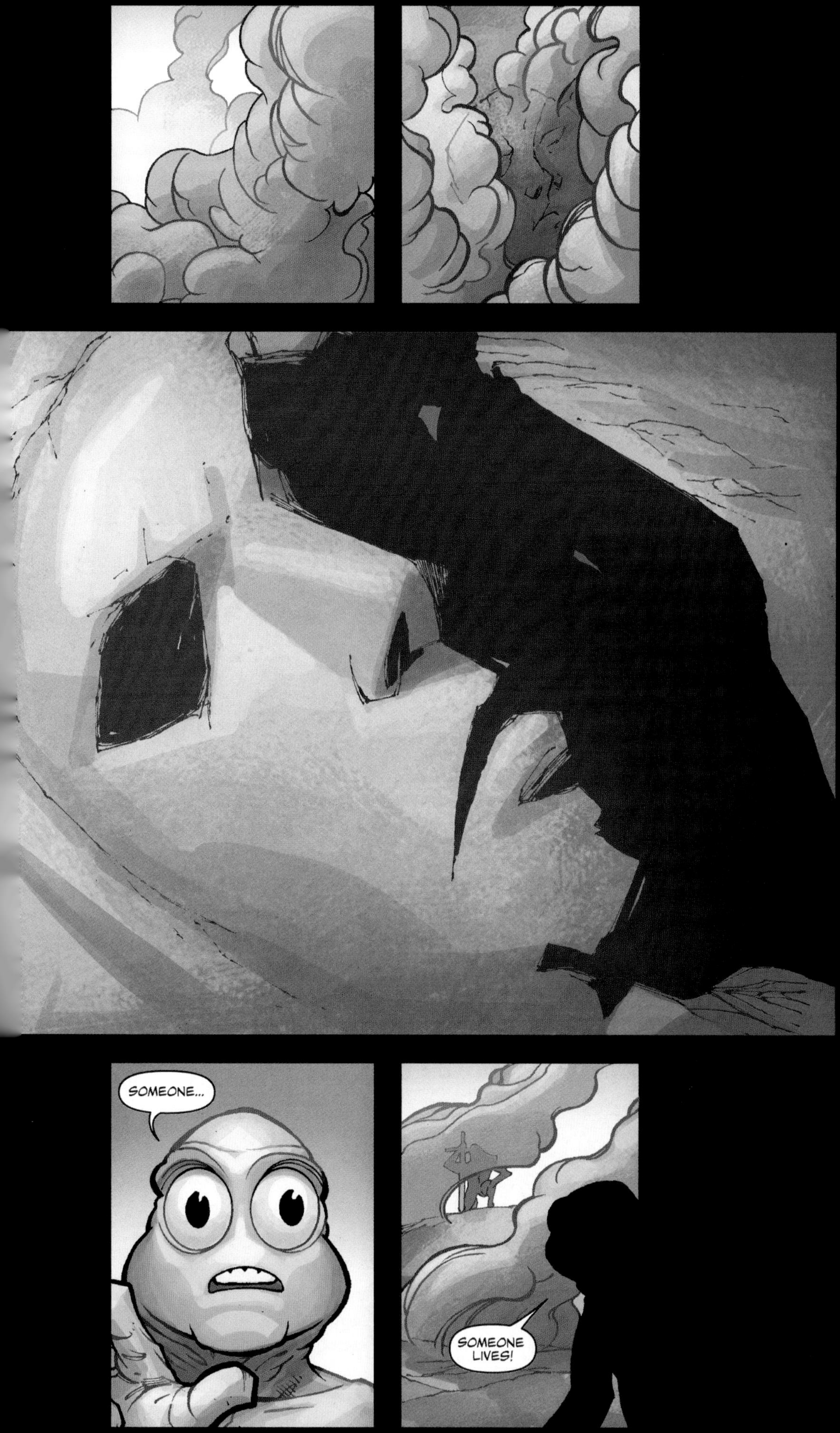
SOMEONE...
SOMEONE LIVES!

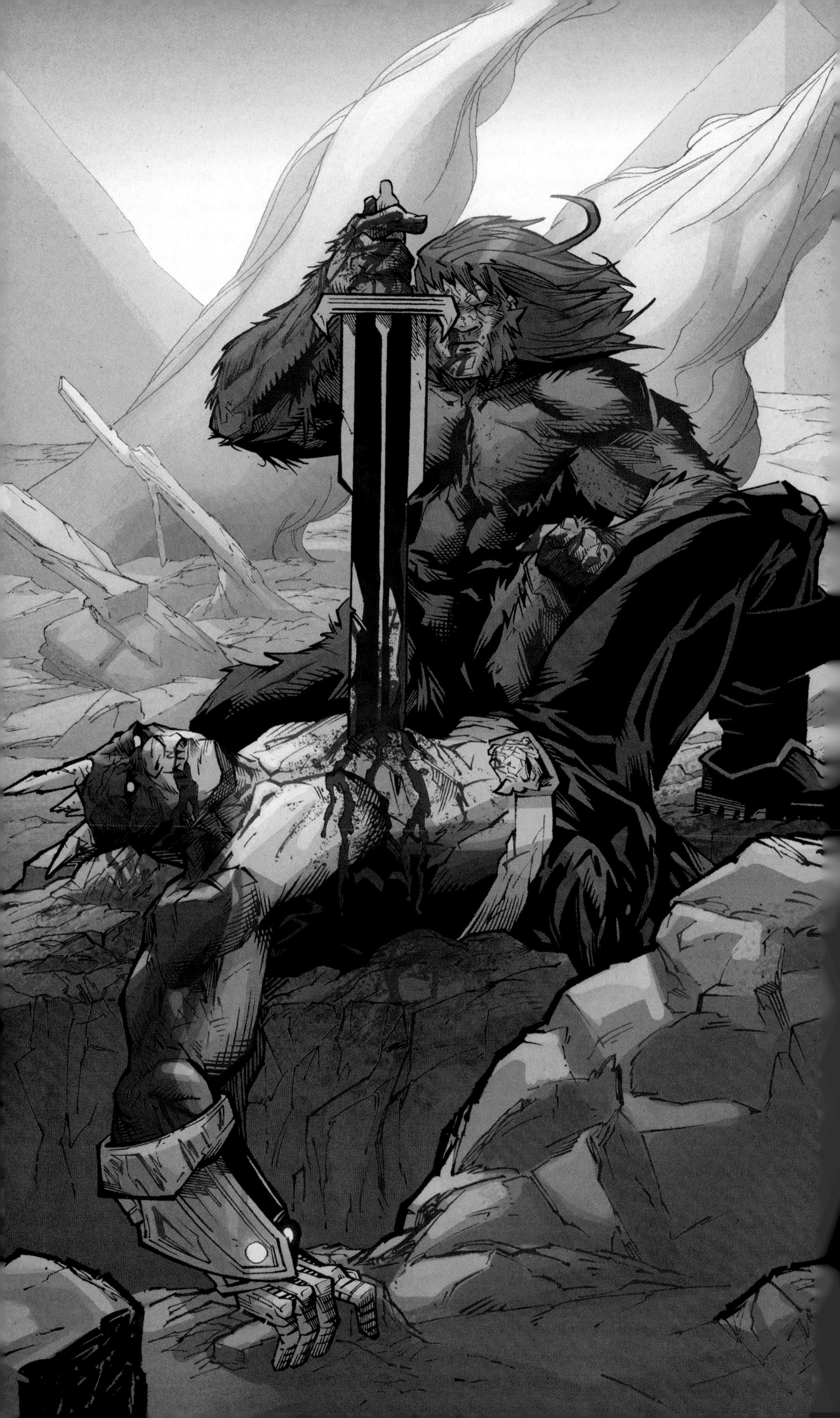

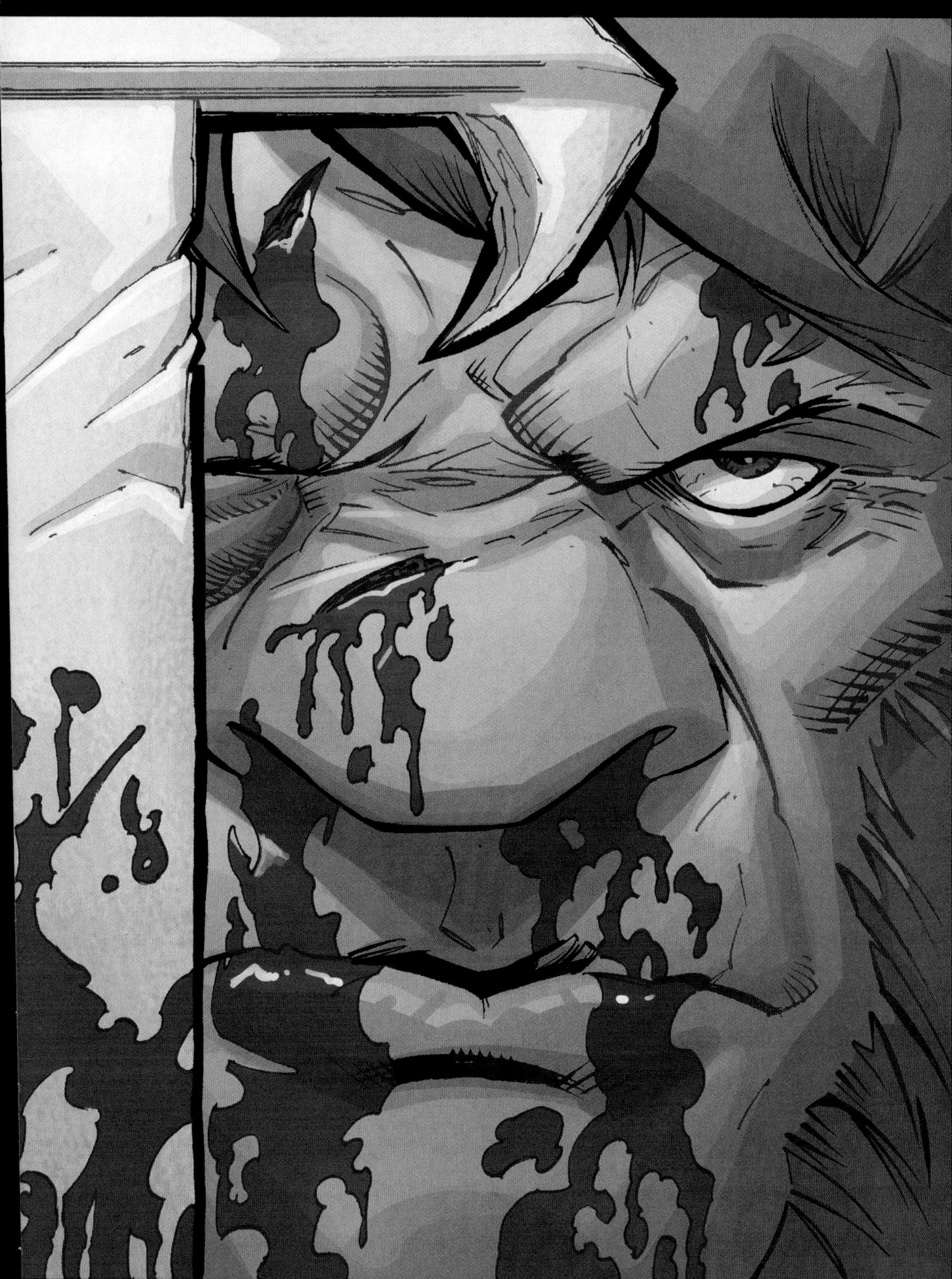

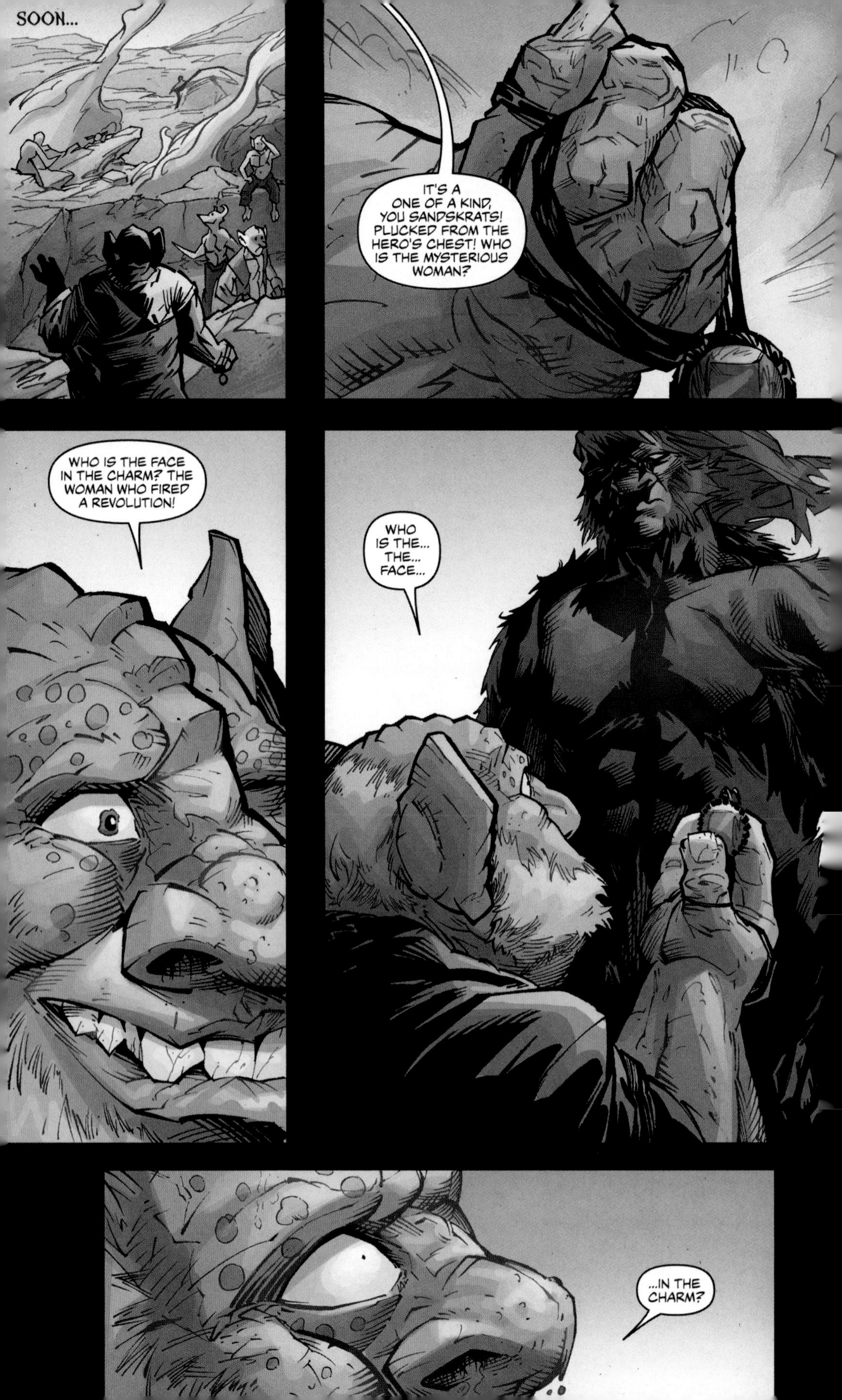
SOON...
IT'S A ONE OF A KIND, YOU SANDSKRATS! PLUCKED FROM THE HERO'S CHEST! WHO IS THE MYSTERIOUS WOMAN?
WHO IS THE FACE IN THE CHARM? THE WOMAN WHO FIRED A REVOLUTION!
WHO IS THE... THE... FACE...
...IN THE CHARM?

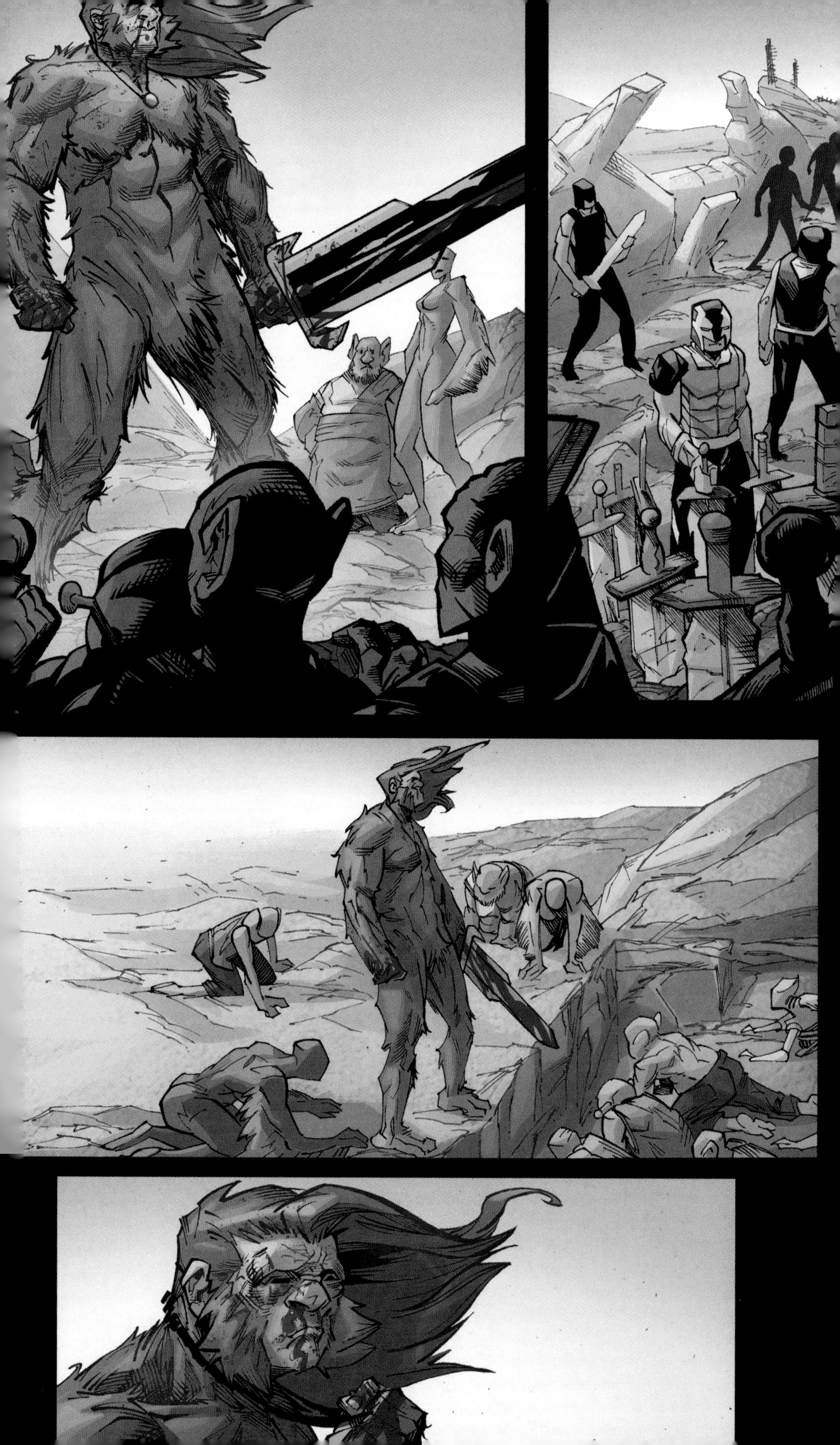

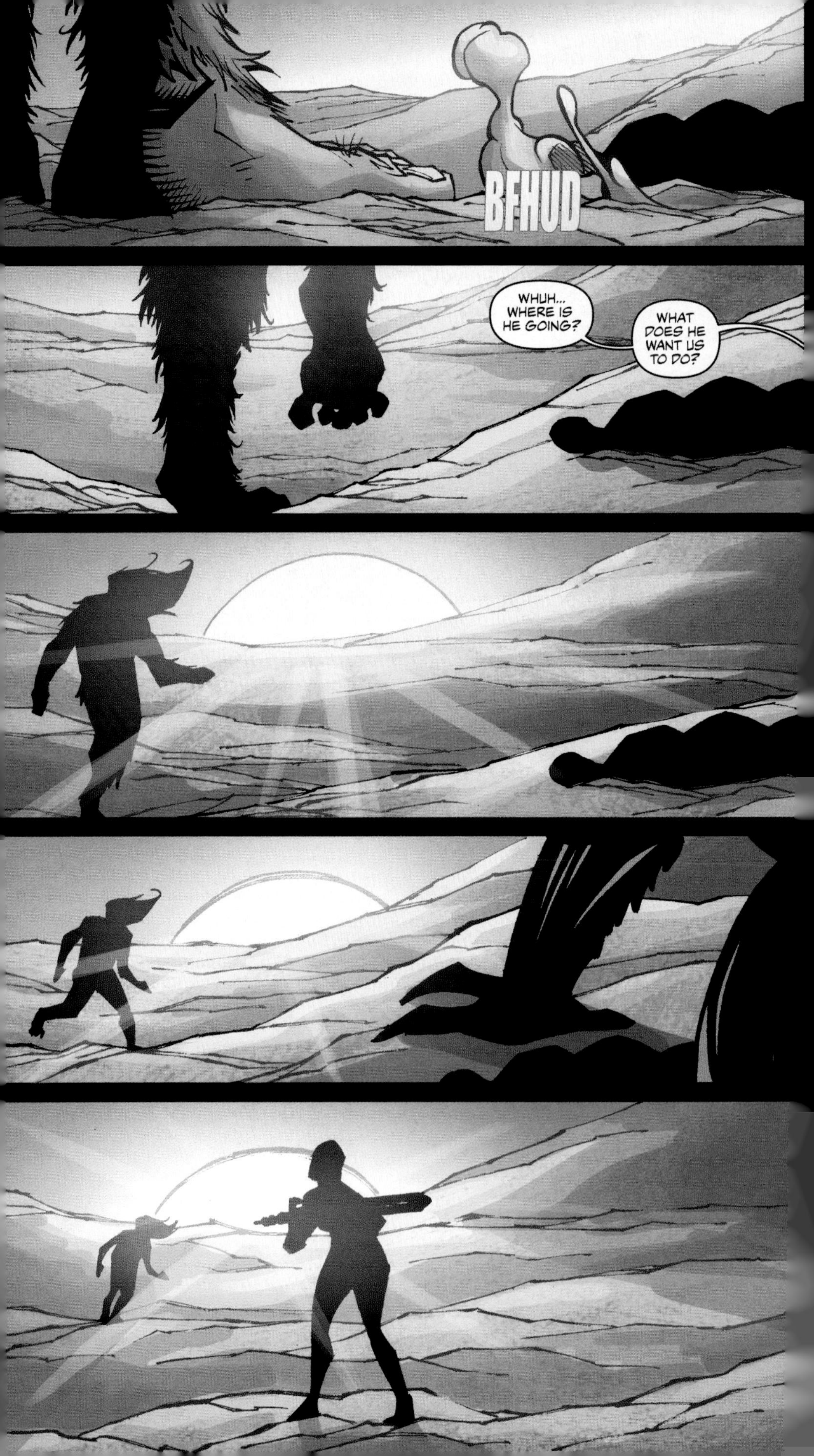
BFHUD
WHUH... WHERE IS HE GOING?
WHAT DOES HE WANT US TO DO?

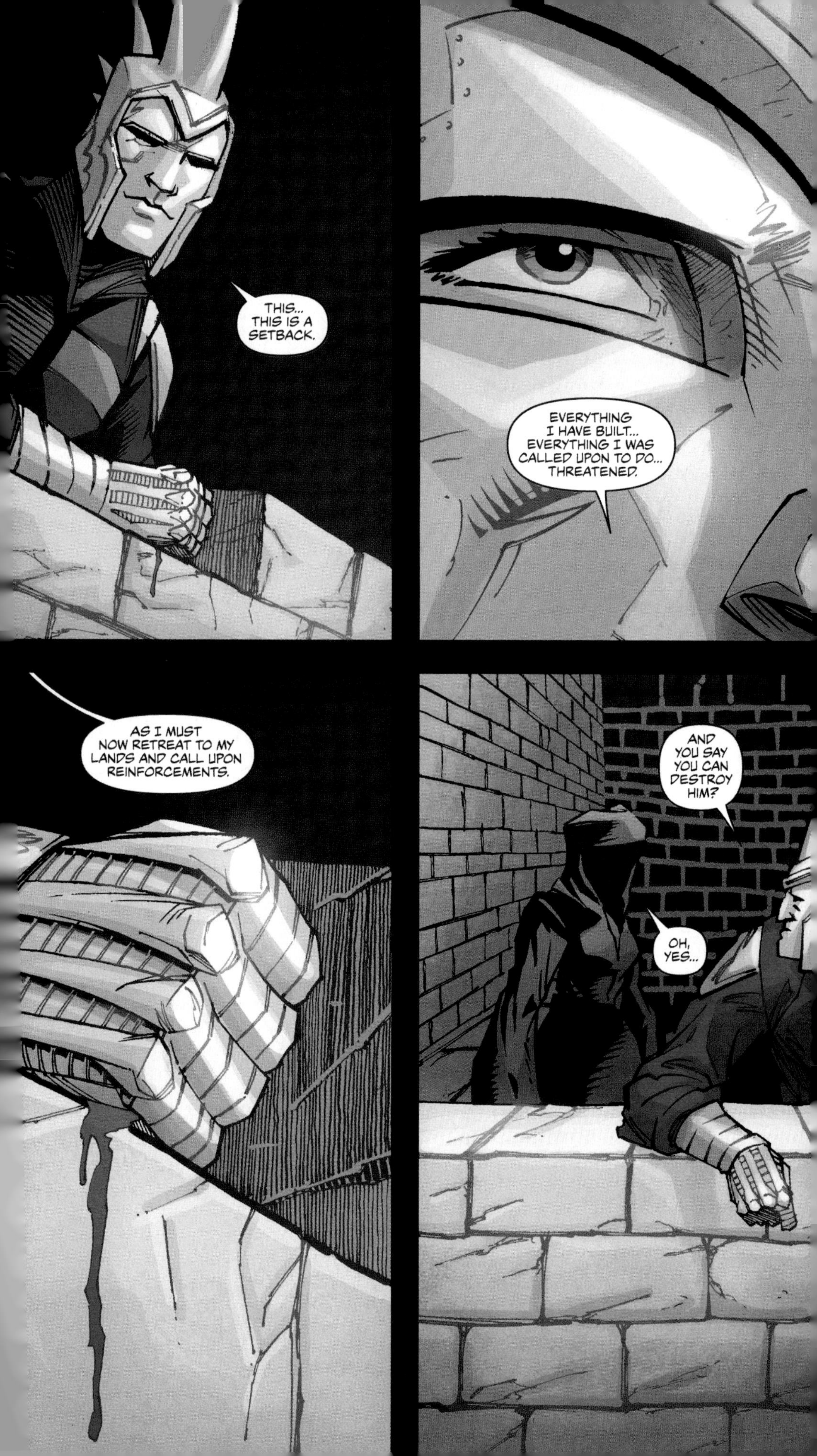
THIS... THIS IS A SETBACK.
EVERYTHING I HAVE BUILT... EVERYTHING I WAS CALLED UPON TO DO... THREATENED.
AS I MUST NOW RETREAT TO MY LANDS AND CALL UPON REINFORCEMENTS.
AND YOU SAY YOU CAN DESTROY HIM?
OH, YES...

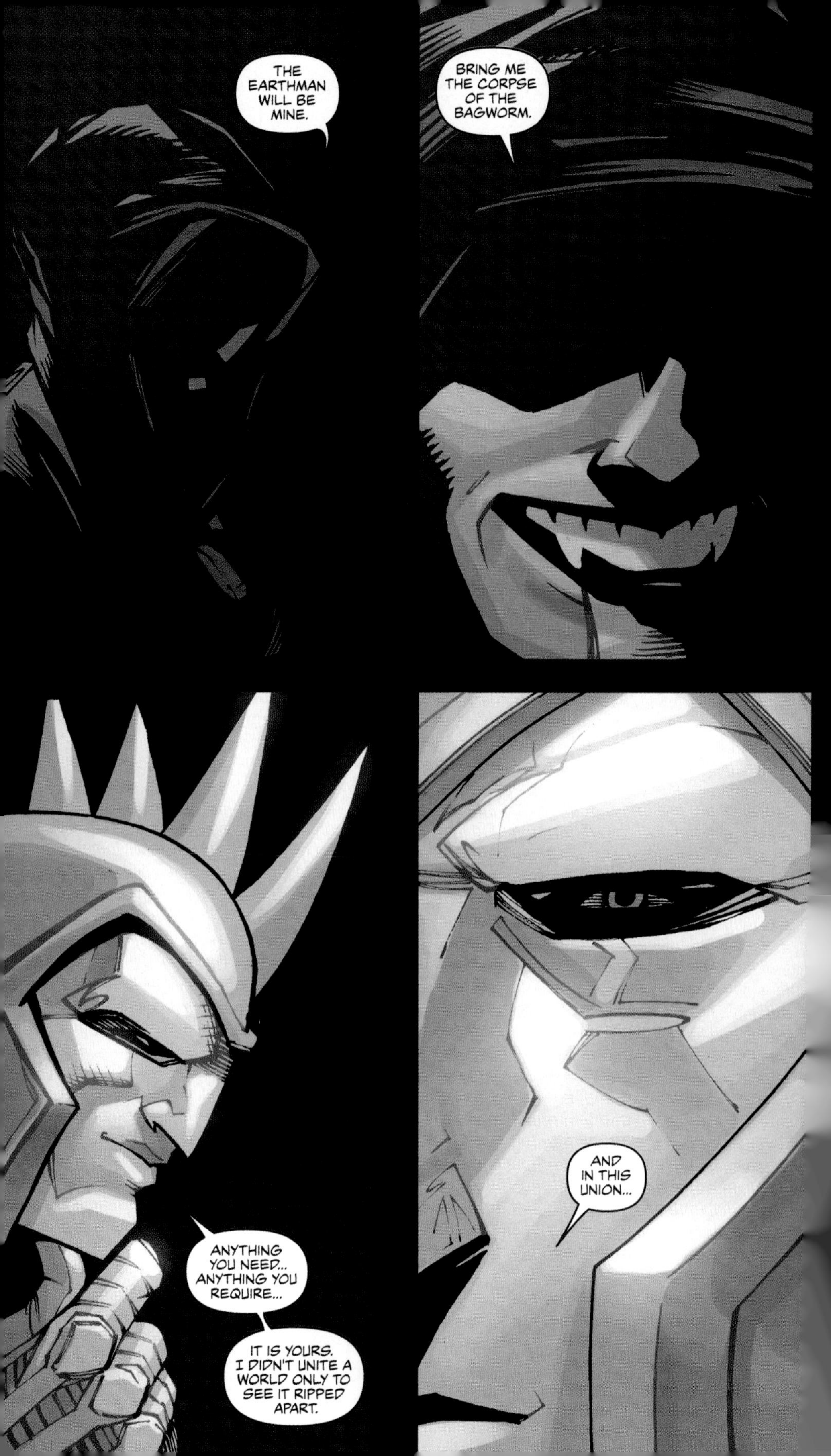
THE EARTHMAN WILL BE MINE.
BRING ME THE CORPSE OF THE BAGWORM.
ANYTHING YOU NEED... ANYTHING YOU REQUIRE...
IT IS YOURS. I DIDN'T UNITE A WORLD ONLY TO SEE IT RIPPED APART.
AND IN THIS UNION...

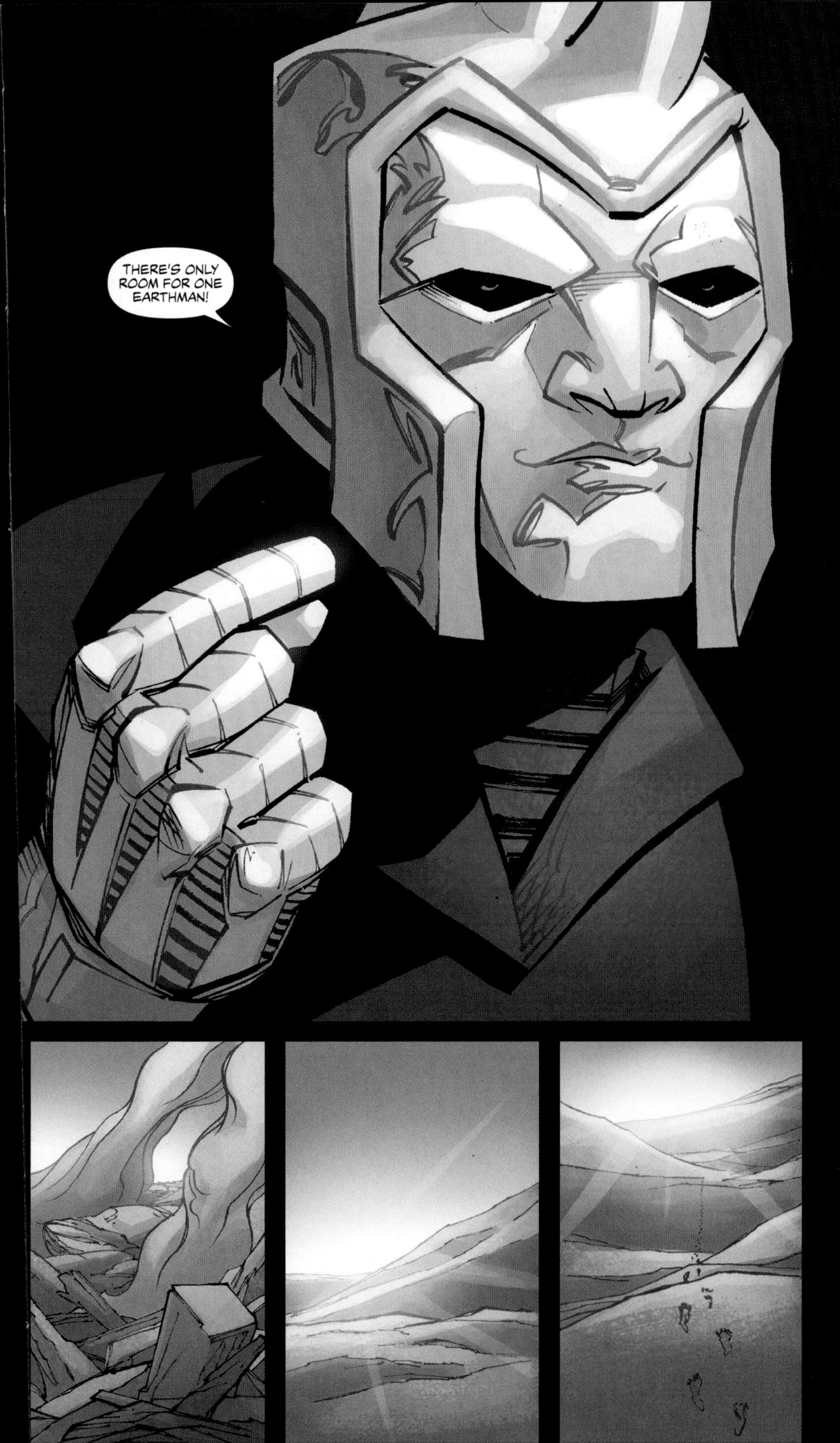
THERE'S ONLY ROOM FOR ONE EARTHMAN!

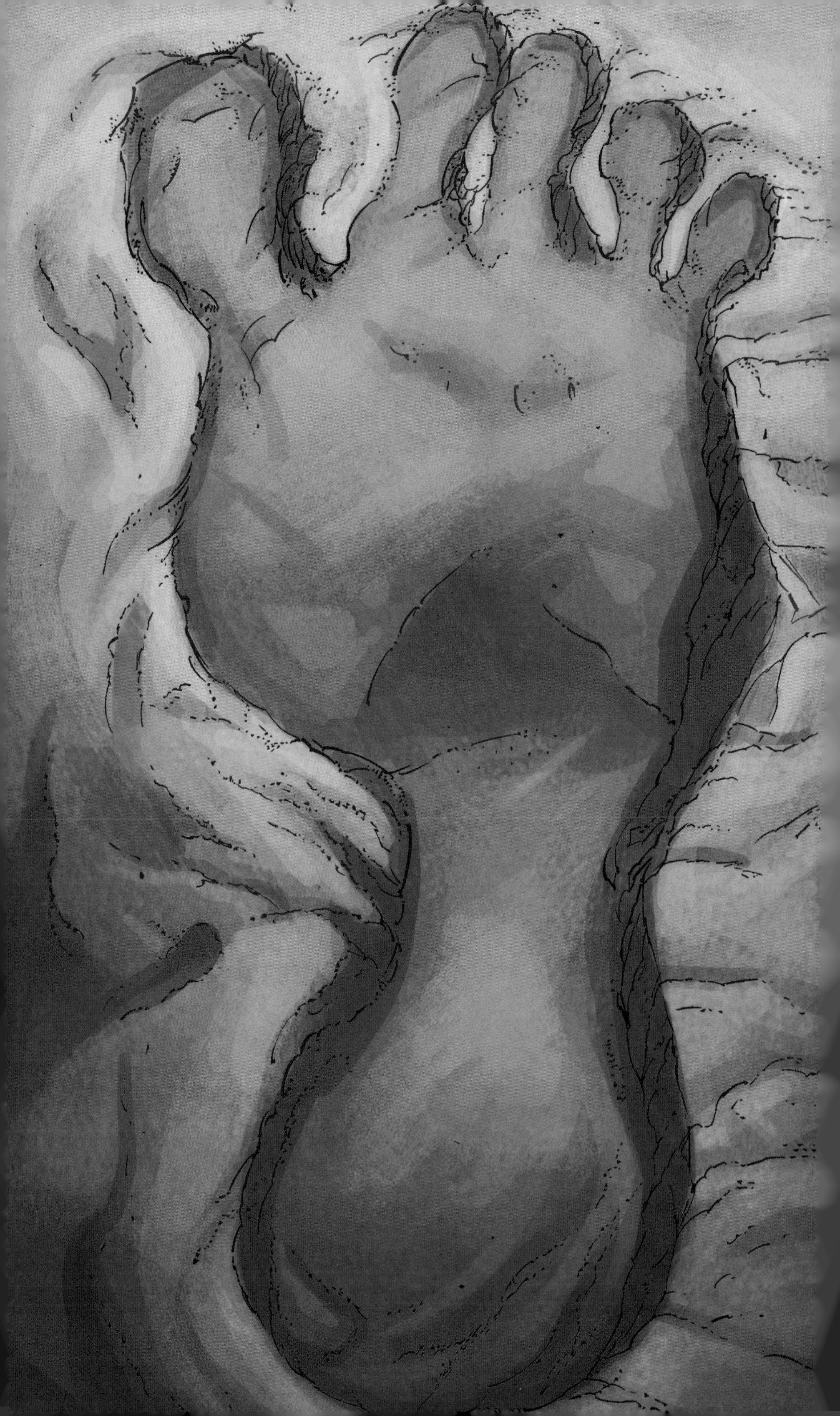

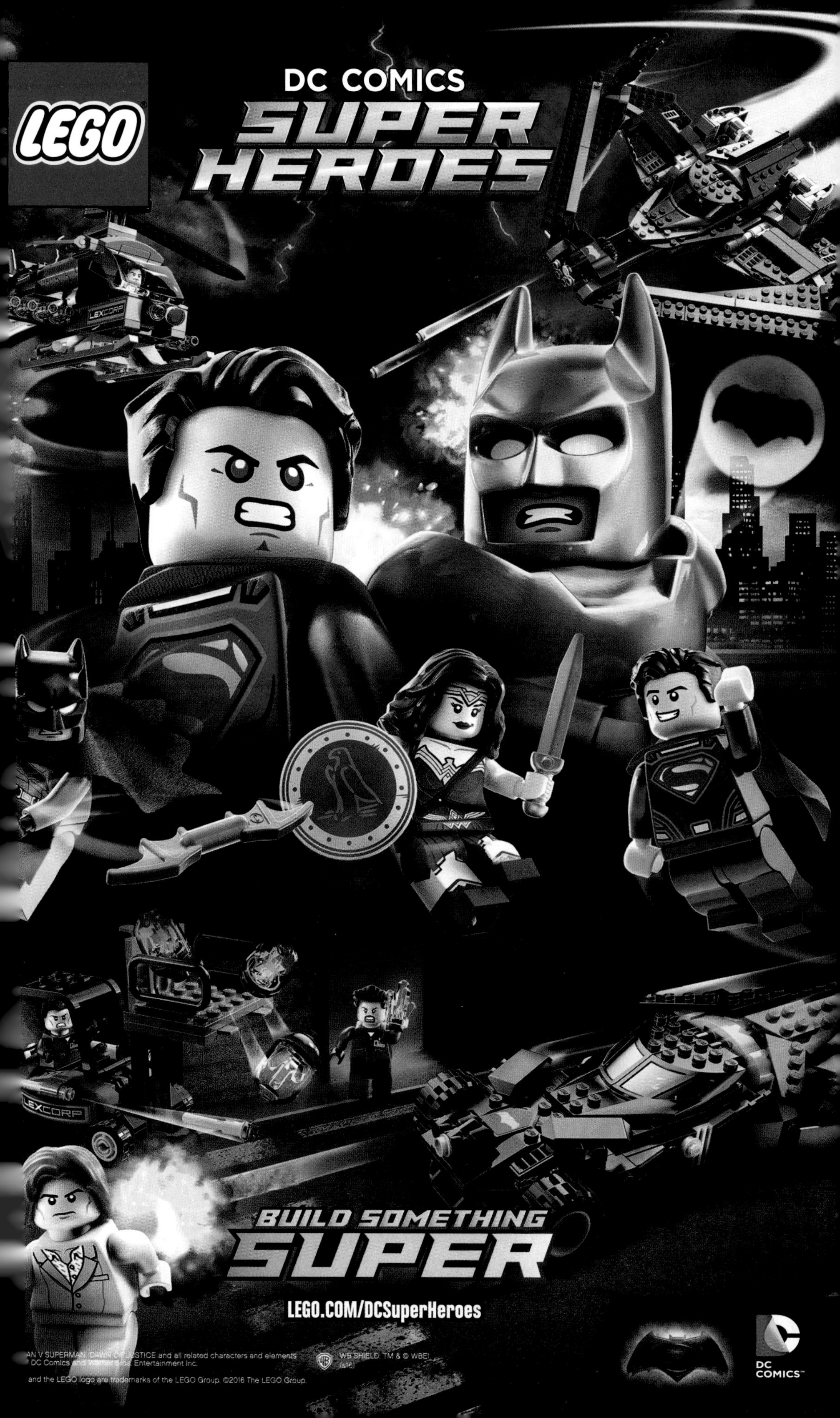

LEGO
DC COMICS
SUPER HEROES
LEXCORP
LEXCORP
BUILD SOMETHING
SUPER
LEGO.COM/DCSuperHeroes
AN V SUPERMAN: DAWN OF JUSTICE and all related characters and elements
DC Comics and Warner Bros. Entertainment Inc.
WB SHIELD: TM & © WBEI
(s16)
and the LEGO logo are trademarks of the LEGO Group. ©2016 The LEGO Group.
DC COMICS™

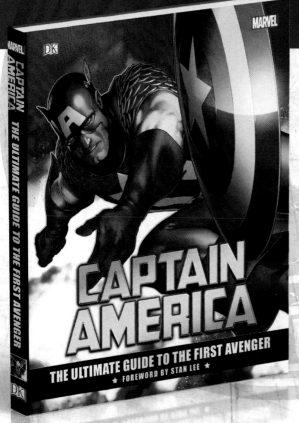